The Aeneid of Virgil

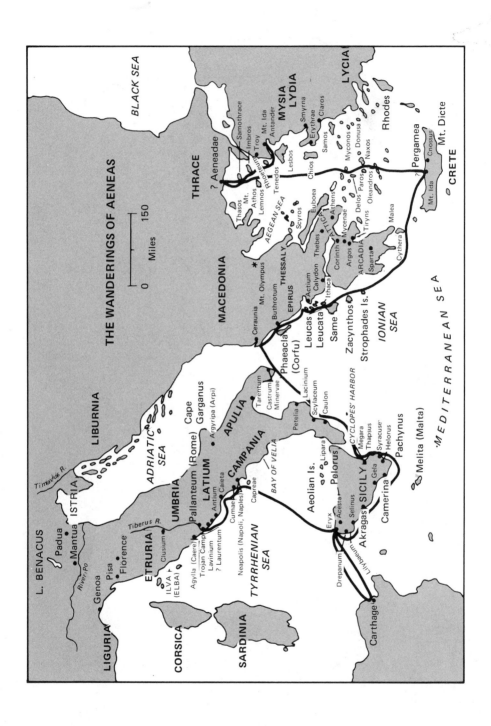

THE WANDERINGS OF AENEAS

BLACK SEA

THRACE

MACEDONIA

THESSALY

EPIRUS

LIBURNIA

ISTRIA

ADRIATIC SEA

UMBRIA

ETRURIA

LATIN

CAMPANIA

APULIA

TYRRHENIAN SEA

CORSICA

SARDINIA

LIGURIA

L. BENACUS

Padua

Mantua

Genoa

Pisa

Florence

Clusium

River Po

Tiberus R.

Agylla (Caere)

Trojan Camp

Lavinium

? Laurentum

Antium

Caieta

Cumae

Neapolis (Napoli, Naples)

Capreae

BAY OF VELIA

Pallanteum (Rome)

Cape Garganus

Argyripa (Arpi)

Tarentum

Castrum Minervae

Lacinium

Petelia

Scylaceum

Caulon

CYCLOPES' HARBOR

Megara

Thapsus

Syracuse

Helorus

Pachynus

Camerina

Gela

Akragas

Selinus

Acesta

Eryx

Drepanum

Lilybaeum

Aeolian Is.

Lipara

Pelorus

SICILY

Melita (Malta)

Carthage

Timavius R.

ILVA (ELBA)

Caeraunia

Mt. Olympus

Buthrotum

Actium

Calydon

Ithaca

Leucas

Leucata

Same

Zacynthos

Strophades Is.

Phaeacla (Corfu)

IONIAN SEA

MEDITERRANEAN SEA

AEGEAN SEA

Mt. Athos

Thasos

Samothrace

Imbros

Lemnos

Troy

Antander

Mt. Ida

Aeneadae

? Aeneadae

Rhoeteum

Tenedos

Lesbos

Chios

Scyros

Euboea

ATTICA

Athens

Thebes

Corinth

Mycenae

Argos

Tiryns

ARCADIA

Sparta

Malea

Cythera

Delos

Paros

Oleandros

Naxos

Donusa

Myconos

Samos

Smyrna

Erythrae

Claros

MYSIA

LYDIA

LYCIA

Rhodes

Pergamea

? Mt. Ida

CRETE

Cnossus

Mt. Dicte

0   Miles   150

THE

AENEID

OF

VIRGIL

A VERSE TRANSLATION BY

Rolfe Humphries

EDITED, AND WITH NOTES, BY

BRIAN WILKIE
University of Arkansas, Fayetteville

A Scribner/Macmillan Book

MACMILLAN PUBLISHING COMPANY
NEW YORK
COLLIER MACMILLAN PUBLISHERS
LONDON

This translation was originally published in 1951 by Charles
Scribner's Sons.

Macmillan Publishing Company
866 Third Avenue, New York, New York 10022

Collier Macmillan Canada, Inc.

Library of Congress Cataloging-in-Publication Data

Virgil.
  The Aeneid of Virgil.

  "A Scribner/Macmillan Book."
  I. Humphries, Rolfe.   II. Wilkie, Brian,
III. Title.
PA6807.A5H8   1987   873'.01   86–12480
ISBN 0–02–427780–0

Printing: 3 4 5 6 7   Year: 8 9 0 1 2 3

ISBN   0-02-427780-0

PREFACE

◻

Virgil's *Aeneid* has never lacked either for readers or for people professionally interested in clarifying and disseminating it. The last few decades, however, have been especially noteworthy: the poem's two-thousandth anniversary was recorded a few years back, a number of excellent books and commentaries have appeared, and gifted translators have devoted their talents to the poem. Among them is the late Rolfe Humphries, whose fresh and spirited version retains its wide popularity among general readers and students. In the Introduction to this volume, I advance some reasons for Humphries' perennial appeal.

What has been missing in most of the good translations is explanatory notes. It is characteristic of skillful and imaginative translators, including Humphries, that they minimize the need for such notes. But translation in itself can go only so far toward making intelligible a work of ancient literature, especially one that is so rich in names, places, and mythological allusions as *The Aeneid.* The addition of footnotes is the principal innovation in the present revised edition.

In these notes, one cardinal aim has been to eliminate, as far as possible, the need for readers to flip through pages. The result has been a certain amount of repetitiousness; I recognize the limitations of human memory and do not assume that information absorbed from an early footnote has been totally and forever absorbed. Another reason for the repetitions is my awareness that *The Aeneid,* when it is assigned in course work, is not always assigned *in toto* and that many general readers also prefer to dip into the poem—*in medias res,* as it were—rather than read it through consecutively. Except for a few, which are essentially extensions of the translation text, the notes are factual and explanatory, not interpretive.

The earlier edition of the Humphries translation included two Introductions by him, one (at the beginning of the book) on *The Aeneid* and one (at the back of the book) on Virgil's life and times. These have been replaced by the single, expanded Introduction that appears in the present book. In this new Introduction, I draw to some extent on the superseded ones by Humphries, and also on the Introduction to Virgil in *Literature of the Western World,* edited by Brian Wilkie and James Hurt (Macmillan, 1984), but of course any errors that may appear are my sole responsibility. The Cast of Characters that Humphries appended to the original edition has been retained as he wrote it.

Other new features of this revised edition include a map tracing the journey of Aeneas and the Trojans through the Mediterranean and locating the principal sites of the action in Italy, and a list of well-known quotations from *The Aeneid,* in both Virgil's Latin and Humphries' English renderings. The lines have been numbered and the type reset, a few obvious errors being corrected in the process.

Several people have read parts of the manuscript of this new edition and given valuable expert advice on it: Martin Irvine, Wayne State University; Alice Wilson, State University of New York at Stony Brook; James Hurt, University of Illinois; and Daniel Levine, University of Arkansas. Joan E. Carr, University of Arkansas, did not see the manuscript but gave me some useful pointers. Jennifer Crewe, my editor, provided helpful, supportive, and invariably intelligent advice. Patricia Cabeza and her crew, including Joyce Rappaport, solved myriad problems of production and, better still, anticipated what might, without them, have become problems. My wife, Ann Wilkie, helped in innumerable ways, as she has done with almost everything I have written.

B.W.

CONTENTS

◻

Introduction

□

Virgil's Life and Times

One of the marks of human presumptuousness is the tendency people have to believe that their own age, whichever it may be, is a critical turning point in history or human culture. Publius Vergilius Maro, the man we call Virgil, may not have believed that about his age (he took a long view of time, and his mind had a modest bent), but he fervently hoped that it would be true. At any rate, it was true. Virgil could not have been aware of the drama that would unfold in Palestine not long after he died (though in fact many Christians later came to believe that he had predicted the coming of Messiah). But in sensing that current events in Rome might have a lasting impact on the world, he was right. He witnessed the birth of the Roman empire, a political entity the impress of which is still evident in modern Europe and a number of its languages, not to mention religion in Europe and elsewhere and the legal systems of many modern countries.

His own achievement created an equally lasting inheritance. Anchises, the father of the hero Aeneas for whom Virgil named his *magnum opus,* tells his son in Book VI (lines 888–96 of the present translation) that government, not the fine arts, will be the Romans' special contribution, but as regards poetry this disclaimer by Anchises (and Virgil) was ironically over-modest. The century that ended a little after the birth of Christ produced a gallery of Latin poets who rank among the world's greatest: Lucretius, Catullus, Horace, Ovid, and above even them, Virgil himself.

Like a number of these poets, Virgil came to Rome from the provinces, in his case from Cisalpine Gaul (the "near" side of Gaul, south of the Alps), where he was born in 70 B.C. His father had a farm near the city of Mantua, and Virgil's devotion to the countryside and practical knowledge of farm-

ing are apparent in all his works. The family could afford
to give him a good education. He was fortunate enough to
study under excellent masters in Cremona and then Milan,
where the emphasis was on humanistic studies such as literature and philosophy. At seventeen, Virgil moved on to Rome
to train for the law—a profession, as it turned out, that proved
uncongenial, apparently because he lacked the necessary ag-
gressiveness and hardihood. (He is said to have pleaded only
one case, which he lost.)

Though in appearance a tall, rather rawboned and gangly
country boy, he was not robust, and his manner was a little
shy (he was never, for example, to marry). In his early twenties, he seems to have been pressed into military service under
Julius Caesar but later discharged because of his health. He
then resumed his education in the south-Italian city of Naples,
studying Greek and Eastern philosophy with some well-
known teachers (especially the philosophy of the Epicureans,
which influenced his early poetry before the Stoics superseded them in Virgil's world-view). In Naples he also made
the acquaintance of a number of prominent men who became
his lifelong friends. Indeed, though Virgil later was awarded
an official residence in Rome and did a fair amount of travel-
ing, Naples was essentially his home for the rest of his life.
By his late twenties, he had become a full-time poet, and
this remained his sole profession.

Virgil's three principal works were the *Eclogues* (written
between 43 and 37 B.C.), the *Georgics* (36–29), and *The Aeneid*
(29–19). The *Eclogues* are ten pastoral poems modeled on
those of the Greek poet Theocritus, depicting the idyllic life
of shepherds. The poems are by no means mere escapist
fantasy, however; in their references to recent topical events,
including the expropriation of farmlands to reward veterans
of the civil wars, they display keen political awareness and
compassion for the distressed and dispossessed—a typical
Virgilian theme. (Virgil's own family farm seems to have been
among those taken over, though it was later restored.) The
famous Fourth ("Messianic") Eclogue, with its prophecy of
a wondrous child who would restore the Golden Age, is the
one Christians later took as a heralding of Jesus. Octavian,
at that time co-ruler of Rome, was far-sighted enough to

want the support of the poets; accordingly, Maecenas, one of his counsellors and a patron of the arts, presented Virgil with a villa. (Horace was also honored, despite his earlier opposition to Octavian.) Henceforth Virgil was to have freedom, security, and recognition.

The *Georgics,* dedicated to Maecenas and often acclaimed as the most perfect of all Latin poems, again has a rural setting; in fact, it is largely a detailed and practical handbook of farming, for the benefit of war veterans unacquainted with such work. It also had a larger patriotic goal, however: the restoration of Italian agriculture was to accompany the revival of the traditional moral values that, then as now, tended to be associated with it. All this was part of Octavian's program to restore conservative values among Roman citizens. The poem was perhaps a little too realistic to be good propaganda, however; Virgil's account of the tribulations of the farmer's lot is far from idealized. In any case, the poem's vision transcends the literally agricultural theme, by blending dream with reality, pessimism with optimism, and comic with tragic visions of life.

The last decade of Virgil's life was occupied with the composition of *The Aeneid.* This poem was the culmination of what seems to have been a lifelong yearning to write a national epic that would be for Romans and their values what Homer's *Iliad* and *Odyssey* were for the Greeks. Virgil never quite finished it. Allotting himself three more years to put the poem in its final form, he left on a trip to the eastern Mediterranean in order to familiarize himself better with the settings of the poem's early books. On this journey he took sick and was brought back to Brundisium, in southeastern Italy, where he died in 19 B.C. *The Aeneid* already had some fame, from Virgil's public readings of the work in progress, but he nevertheless left death-bed instructions that the poem should be burned. Fortunately, Octavian, now known as Caesar Augustus, countermanded the order.

Virgil never took an active part in public affairs, and his temperament was retiring, but it was impossible for anyone to remain aloof from the turbulent politics of his era. By the time of Virgil's youth, the old republican forms under which Rome had lived for more than four hundred years

were being strained to the breaking-point. The farm economy
of the past was yielding to a commercial, almost an industrial
economy, and this development coincided with civil conflict
that had already become widespread when Virgil was born
in 70 B.C. In that year, the first of a series of particularly
ambitious and powerful men, Pompey the Great, assumed
one of the two consulships, though he was legally too young
for the post. His meteoric career as general and legislator
brought him in the year 52 (when Virgil was eighteen) to
the post—illegal under republican law—of sole consul (in
effect, dictator), charged with putting a stop to gang warfare
in the streets. The hope for civil peace and political order
seemed to some Romans—including Cicero, the great states-
man and author—to depend on the establishment of a cen-
tralized autocracy.

Pompey was challenged, however, by an even more ambitious man: an impoverished nobleman, skillful politician, and
brilliant military leader named Julius Caesar (thirty years
older than Virgil). Caesar had been leading conquering armies in Gaul (roughly, modern France and Belgium) and
had even made incursions into Britain. After being declared
a public enemy by the Roman senate, he committed what
was technically treason by crossing, in 49, the north-Italian
brook named the Rubicon, the limit of the province assigned
him, and embarked on war against Pompey. Final victory
in this stage of the civil wars arrived in 48, when, in the
battle of Pharsalus, Caesar defeated Pompey, who soon thereafter was assassinated in Egypt.

Over the next four years, Julius Caesar remodeled the Roman state as a monarchy on the model of the Greek conqueror Alexander the Great. In reaction, a number of idealis-
tic republicans and other conspirators, including Cassius and
two men named Brutus, joined to assassinate Caesar on the
Ides (the 15th) of March in the year 44. (Virgil was then
twenty-six.) The conspirators' party had no effective organi-
zation, however, or program of action. They were opposed
and soon defeated by a force led by Mark Antony, co-consul
with Caesar, and Octavian, Caesar's eighteen-year-old great-
nephew and adopted son. Over the succeeding years, Octavian, one of the most masterful politicians in world history,

made his way through a labyrinth of political confusion and bloodshed until he had the general support of the Romans. Antony, by now his rival for power, had meanwhile become infatuated with the Egyptian queen, Cleopatra, to whom he even planned to yield part of the Roman domain. The rivalry was settled climactically in 31 B.C., at the naval battle of Actium, west of Greece, where the forces of the two men opposed each other. (Virgil was thirty-nine, and had almost finished writing the *Georgics.*) The fleets led by Antony and Cleopatra returned to Egypt, humiliated, and both he and she committed suicide shortly thereafter. Octavian was thus left in supreme command. In 27 he was given the title Caesar Augustus.

Under Octavian/Augustus, Rome enjoyed peace for the first time in many decades. It was natural that Virgil, with his pacific temperament, should welcome this new era, especially since the civic program sponsored by Octavian was congenial to him, with its aims to restore Rome architecturally and to renew it spiritually by fostering religion and patriotic fervor. Virgil formulated his vision of this new golden age in the words of Jupiter to Venus in *The Aeneid:*

> wars will cease, and a rough age grow gentler,
> White Faith and Vesta, Romulus and Remus,
> Give law to nations. War's grim gates will close,
> Tight-shut with bars of iron, and inside them
> The wickedness of war sit bound and silent,
> The red mouth straining and the hands held tight
> In fastenings of bronze, a hundred hundred. (I.305–11)

The ideal is formulated again in the speech by Anchises mentioned earlier, where the vision of peace is broadened to include a vision of world order:

> Others, no doubt, will better mould the bronze
> To the semblance of soft breathing, draw, from marble,
> The living countenance; and others plead
> With greater eloquence, or learn to measure,
> Better than we [Romans], the pathways of the heaven,
> The risings of the stars: remember, Roman,
> To rule the people under law, to establish
> The way of peace, to battle down the haughty,

To spare the meek. Our fine arts, these, forever.
(VI.888–96)

In fact, however, Anchises' disclaimer about the arts notwithstanding, Octavian wanted the support of Virgil and other artists. Virgil created in *The Aeneid* a work that far transcends in its vision the goals of any political party or regime, but the poem does express a sense of Roman aspiration and hope that were in keeping with the imperial program.

The Aeneid

More than any other poem, *The Aeneid* has been continuously revered in the Western literary tradition. (Most of the works of Greek antiquity that rival it in greatness virtually disappeared from European consciousness during the thousand years preceding the Renaissance.) As a result, it is very difficult and perhaps impossible to come to *The Aeneid* "fresh," to determine what it "really" means or to read it for what it is "in itself." Almost every period of history has canonized this immensely rich and complex poem for its own special reasons, in the process developing also certain interpretive blind spots that get in the way of comprehensive and accurate understanding. Moreover, the various forms of canonization have, inevitably, stimulated iconoclasts, often in the next following era, who have reacted with vehemence against certain real or imaginary qualities in the poem. The introductory remarks that follow must therefore be concerned not only with objective facts about *The Aeneid* but also with certain of the interpretive encrustations that, almost as much as its verbal text itself, have constituted the lifeline of the poem for two thousand years. The purpose of this introduction is largely to present the reader with a set of options in reading and interpreting the poem.

Admirers (and backlash detractors) of Virgil have too often tended to focus either on his style and artistry (often understood narrowly, as a concern with rhetoric and sound effects almost for their own sake) or on his message (often understood simplistically, as propaganda or preaching). Virgil was honored by his contemporary Romans both for the content of *The Aeneid*—particularly its vision of Roman history and its ideal of the Roman character—and for his artistry, especially his mastery of style, rhetoric, and versification. Some later devotees have been able to maintain this balanced, if sometimes limited, view of Virgil's accomplishment; for example, in the *Divine Comedy* (fourteenth century), Dante credits Virgil with having formed his own poetic style and also makes Virgil the supreme sage, commissioned by Heaven to explain to Dante all those mysteries of life and the afterlife that can be understood without the help of Christian revelation. The view of Virgil as sage, however, even as wizard or sorcerer, was the more dominant image of him in the Middle Ages. The neoclassical period, in the late-seventeenth and eighteenth centuries, admired Virgil's style but found him even more valuable as (supposedly) the spokesman for the civilized virtues of political order and emotional self-control (does not Aeneas renounce his love for Dido for a "higher" destiny?). Adopting this same half-truth but reversing the ensuing judgment, the nineteenth-century Romantics came to view Virgil (and Aeneas) as cold, especially in contrast with Homer, who was more "spontaneous," "primitive," "natural." (Samuel Taylor Coleridge, the Romantic poet and literary theorist, wondered what would be left of Virgil if you took away his sound and rhythm.) This somewhat overcivilized Virgil was a little more appealing to the Victorians, who better recognized, for example, the distinctive Virgilian sympathy with nature and with human suffering—though in the process they turned Virgil into a much more sentimental poet than he was.[1]

Certain of these approaches, and others, survive in the twentieth century, at least vestigially, but new approaches have emerged also. In recent decades, critics have tended to approach literary works, including *The Aeneid*, as integrated works of art, despite some dissent from this approach in

[1] These stages in Virgil's reputation, among others, are discussed by R. D. Williams, "Changing Attitudes to Virgil: A Study in the History of Taste from Dryden to Tennyson," in *Virgil*, ed. D. R. Dudley (New York, 1969), pp. 119–38.

very recent years. As a result, Virgil's message (construed as something more complex than mere praise of Augustus Caesar or the direct inculcation of personal or political morality) has been viewed as more organically related to his artistry (construed not merely as the stylistic virtuosity that all ages have recognized in Virgil but also as including functional patterns of structure, imagery, and symbolism). In short, there has arisen a new kind of concern with literary form, considered not simply in terms of mechanical rules governing a genre but as a functional fusion of the content and shape of the work.

Such concerns affect, in the first place, our understanding of what *The Aeneid* is. All ages have agreed to consider it an epic, but what *is* an epic? Neoclassic theorists three centuries ago labored long and often to define it on formal grounds, with no very impressive success, agreeing with one another on only two points: an epic had to be long and had to tell a story. (Are all novels, then, epics?) They also came close to agreement on certain aspects of content: an epic poem tended to celebrate the values of a people or nation, and it promulgated an ideal of heroism, or at least admirable conduct. But such vague or general traits seem only distantly pertinent to the reader's experience of epics, especially to one's sense that epics are eerily similar to one another in their texture—sieges, journeys, visits to the Underworld, prophecies of the future, nocturnal scouting missions, animal similes, flashback narratives, deities who half-direct the action, omens, and so on and on. And yet the absence of any one of these things does not disqualify a work for the epic pantheon. It is perhaps best to define an epic simply as a poem that puts itself in the line of earlier epics, by imitating them. According to this view, epic is not a genre but a tradition.

Moreover, these imitative aspects of texture and technique, along with the use of a standard meter (for the ancients, dactylic hexameter) capable both of sustaining dignity and of narrating events, can be integrated with the larger thematic purpose of an epic: it imitates earlier ones so closely and compulsively exactly because it purports to show the supersession of older heroic codes or ideals of conduct by newer ones. The new values are to be understood as occupying in the epic poet's own age the same preeminent place that older values occupied in the past.[2]

This strategy seems to have been Virgil's; at any rate, it was he who, for the purposes of later literary history, established the pattern of using old epic forms and precedents in order to delineate clearly and emphatically how the present (and presumably the future also) differed from the past. Virgil was a learned man, who drew for content, wording, and strategy on the works of many earlier poets (some of which have survived, some not), but in the form of epic his dominant literary precursor was obvious to him and to his audience. It was Homer. Rome needed a bible, so to speak, that would serve its purposes—political, ethical, and literary—as Homer's *Iliad* and *Odyssey* had served the purposes of Greece for centuries. Virgil's task, then, was not simply to write a poem as great as these, or to write a rough equivalent of them. He also had to delineate exactly how the ideal of heroism had changed since Homer's day, by taking a Trojan hero, Aeneas, from among those whom Greece had defeated in Homer's two great stories of the Trojan war and its aftermath, and then turning this saga of defeat into a saga of hard-won victory by Aeneas in his role as the prototype of the Romans. No longer was it adequate for a hero to be obsessed with his own personal glory and gratification, like Homer's Achilles and Odysseus; the new Roman world of civilized order required an ethic of self-renunciation, such as Aeneas illustrates when he dutifully chokes off his love affair with Dido. Moreover, a hero such as Aeneas did not always have to be masterful; he could be shown as weak, self-doubting, perhaps a little contemptible once or twice. He could be shown also as outgrowing, rather awkwardly as in Books I to VI, the older code of derring-do, however attractive that simpler and forever vanished code might be in nostalgic retrospect.

One can recognize, then, as readers have done from the beginning, that Virgil meticulously copied Homer's tale of

---

[2] For this view of epic, see Brian Wilkie, *Romantic Poets and Epic Tradition* (Madison, Wisconsin, 1965), pp. 3–29.

wandering—*The Odyssey*—in Books I to VI of *The Aeneid* and Homer's tale of siege and war—*The Iliad*—in Books VII to XII,[3] without regarding Virgil as a mere mockingbird. The pattern of creative imitation is, in fact, much more intricate than that; for example, the second Book of Virgil's *"Iliad"* (Book VIII of *The Aeneid*) provides the first view of what will be Rome (Pallanteum), just as the second Book of his *"Odyssey"* (Book II of *The Aeneid*) provides the last view of Troy[4]—a symmetrical arrangement that shows how far the Trojans, and by implication the Romans, have come from the values of the old Homeric world. (At the same time, the primitive culture of Pallanteum in Book VIII implies that certain of its rude and simple virtues ought to be preserved, even in sophisticated Rome.) In the last half of *The Aeneid,* we see two besieged towns reminiscent of once-beleaguered Troy as it was depicted in *The Iliad* and in Book II of *The Aeneid;* the first of these sieges (of the Trojan camp, by the Italians) shows the Trojans in their old, humiliating posture of defense, while the second (of the city of Latinus, by the Trojans) shows the ultimate reversal of their role as defeated victims. Such patterns show that Virgil transformed Homer rather than copied him.

Perhaps the most awesome way in which Virgil transformed the Homeric epic was in his vision of history, indeed his vision of time. Homer's age believed that the Trojan war was indeed historical, that it had happened to certain real people at a certain time. But time and history have no particular pattern or shape in Homer; there is no sense of movement according to a grand and purposeful providential plan. Such a cosmic design is at the very heart of *The Aeneid.* As certain of the philosophic passages in Book VI indicate, Virgil believed in some important ways in a cyclical pattern of time that included, for example, a version of human reincarnation. But the narrative design of the poem suggests even more emphatically a providential, linear, progressive movement

---

[3] On this aspect of the structural relationship of *The Aeneid* to Homer's *Iliad* and *Odyssey,* see Brooks Otis, "The Originality of the Aeneid," in Dudley, pp. 27–66.

[4] This observation is made by R. D. Williams, *The Aeneid of Virgil, Books 7–12* (London, 1973), p. xx.

that is much closer to the Exodus story, indeed to the Jewish and Christian Bible as a whole, than it is to Homer. Virgil is depicting events that are to be understood as happening hundreds of years in the past but that nevertheless have the most detailed, intimate, causal connection with the world of contemporary Rome. This view of history, no doubt, is another reason why *The Aeneid* has appealed so strongly to readers in the Judaeo-Christian tradition.

There are myriad patterns in *The Aeneid,* however, besides those that take their pointedness from Virgil's relationship to Homer. To cite a relatively minor one, there is the flame imagery in Book IV, beginning with the wedding torch symbolic of Dido's old and new loves and culminating in her funeral pyre. There is also the contrast between the beginning of Book V, where Aeneas, demoralized in the wake of the Dido episode, passively follows the advice of his helmsman Palinurus, and the end of the same book, where (at the climax of one of the eeriest and loveliest passages in the poem) Aeneas takes over after Palinurus has been cast into the sea by the god of sleep. The quiet fifth book, it seems, has after all an important function, helping to prepare us for the spiritual transformation of Aeneas through the visions of Book VI.[5] Such patterns raise questions about interpretative method, since they may or may not have been consciously in Virgil's mind. On this matter the advice of W. A. Camps seems sound: "for a commentator at least it is often necessary to make a distinction between what Virgil says and what he seems to a given reader to imply; about the former there can be agreement, but the latter depends to a great extent on the subjective response of the individual reader. For the individual reader, as opposed to the commentator, it may be right to yield himself to this subjective response, however personal, because the power to evoke such response, often highly personal, is a peculiar virtue of Virgil's poetry."[6]

Two further examples of pattern in *The Aeneid* will illustrate

---

[5] See Kenneth Quinn, *Virgil's "Aeneid": A Critical Description* (London, 1968), pp. 156, 158–59.

[6] W. A. Camps, *An Introduction to Virgil's Aeneid* (London, 1969), p. 7.

this seeming paradox, by which Virgil tends to evoke for all (or most) readers responses that each of them may consider merely private and subjective; the examples will also suggest that the poem has other patterns beside those of epic—tragedy, for one. That Virgil consciously intended tragic effects seems clear at times, as when he introduces one of the Furies, tragic agents of doom, during the fight between Aeneas and Turnus in Book XII, or when he describes Dido's death. But indeed a tragic pattern, sometimes largely implicit, underlies the whole of both the Turnus and the Dido stories, which convey a painful sense of waste and of terrible irony.

The touchingly young Pallas has been entrusted by his father, Evander, to the protection and military tutelage of Aeneas, a veteran warrior and a renowned one. But in his very first battle, Pallas has the misfortune of encountering Turnus, the greatest of the enemy soldiers, who kills the youngster and then callously strips him of his armor, while sneering at his father Evander's anticipated grief. Virgil tells us explicitly here that Turnus' deed will come back to haunt him, as indeed it does, when Turnus later encounters Aeneas. Reduced to helplessness in this encounter, Turnus (himself a young man) appeals for clemency, in the name of his own father and of Aeneas' father, Anchises. Now, this is exactly the kind of appeal that would normally be best calculated to soften Aeneas, whose filial devotion to Anchises and paternal devotion to his son Ascanius constitute, very nearly, the core of his personality. But Aeneas is suddenly enraged at the sight of the dead Pallas' spoils, and this sight, along with the bitter remorse we can imagine Aeneas to feel at having failed Evander as his son's protector, leads Aeneas to kill Turnus, furiously and savagely. This lack of self-control, ironically, is what we have come to expect of Turnus but not of the peaceable and even-tempered Aeneas. Ironically, the evocation of the father-son motif, which might have softened Aeneas, is the very thing that, at the supreme moment, hardens him.

Virgil makes this tragic pattern half-explicit. The ironic and tragic pattern in the Dido story is even more complex, and more dependent on the reader's imaginative discernment. The tragedy does not consist only in the obvious facts of pain—Dido's agony of tortured love turned largely to hate, Aeneas' need to stifle his expressions of affection. Nor does the tragedy reside only in the public realm: the grim reminders that this broken love affair will lead to three future wars between Rome and Dido's city, Carthage. The pattern consists also in the tantalizing fact that the lives and fates of Dido and Aeneas are in studied parallel but are out of synchronization.

Both Dido and Aeneas are rulers; both have led their people as refugees from a violent past in the East so as to found a new city in the West; both have lost their spouses as part of their traumatic personal histories. But after the two meet, their public and private careers are out of phase. Dido, her new city finally rising, struggles at first against any return to the "private" roles of lover and wife that had been hers before her husband's death made her, perforce, a public leader. The rhythm of Aeneas' life, on the other hand, calls at this point for an escape from public responsibilities, and when Dido's sister Anna gives her both public and personal reasons why she should allow herself to fall in love again, Dido gives in and—prompted also by the ominous machinations of Aeneas' mother, Venus—the affair begins. But when the gods sternly recall Aeneas to his neglected public responsibilities, he can and does reassume them, while Dido cannot. Perhaps we are to understand that this is because she is a woman and cannot get away scot-free from such emotional involvements; if so, there is powerful irony on Virgil's part in Mercury's contemptuous warning to Aeneas about female "inconstancy": *"varium et mutabile semper / femina,"* "A shifty, fickle object / Is woman, always" (IV. 603–04). At any rate, the tragedy of her earthly life is not only a woman's but also a queen's. The ironic pattern of the tragedy is given its final touch when Aeneas meets Dido in the Lower World and she refuses to speak to him. Aeneas has visited the realm of the dead in order to prepare himself for his ultimate crisis as a public leader, while Dido has returned to her "private" role as the beloved wife of Sychaeus, the husband whose death had first thrust her into a public role and whose memory she had once feared to betray.

The history of interpretation of *The Aeneid* is replete with half-truths and begged questions that implicitly undervalue the complexity of Virgil's vision. For example, if the poem is taken to be simply propaganda for Caesar Augustus, or even for Rome, Virgil must have "failed" by making Aeneas, the "mirror" of Augustus, less attractive than adversaries such as Turnus, or Dido, or even the wicked Mezentius. If Virgil believed that reason should govern emotions, he must have "failed" in presenting too sympathetically the pain of the frenzied Dido and presenting too unsympathetically the emotionally frigid Aeneas of the end of Book IV. If he believed that Aeneas and the Trojans were the prototypes of the virile Romans of later times, he inexplicably "failed" by allowing the Italians several cuttingly effective taunts directed at the "effeminate," "Phrygian" invaders. And so on. Many objections of this kind arise from what are in the first place simplistic assumptions about what Virgil wanted to do in *The Aeneid.* If we recognize the poem for what it is, the product of a rich and complex mind and personality, we can appreciate that the tensions, even contradictions within it—whether they are resolvable or not—are legitimate causes of the endless fascination it has exerted for readers of all eras.

The Translation

Of all the great narrative poems in the Western tradition, *The Aeneid* is arguably the most maddening to translate into English. The most general way to state the difficulty is that, while he was out to tell a story, Virgil composed almost every one of the poem's 9,896 (Latin) lines in such a way as to give them the density of meaning and nuance, and the richness of sound effect, that most poets can sustain only for much shorter stretches, in sonnets or odes or other lyric poems. As an illustration of Virgil's compression, consider the following famous passage, not quite two lines long:

> sunt hic etiam sua praemia laudi,
> sunt lacrimae rerum et mentem mortalia tangunt.

Rolfe Humphries does a creditable job with these lines by rendering them almost word-for-word:

> even here there are rewards for praise,
> There are tears for things, and what men suffer touches
> The human heart. (I.482–84)

W. F. Jackson Knight, in demonstrating Virgil's density of language, maintains that the poet meant "not much less than" this: "There is no denying that even in this far land honour gets its due, and they can weep at human tragedy; the world has tears as a constitutent part of it, and so have our own lives, hopeless and weary; and the thought how things have always their own death in them breaks our hearts and will and clouds our vision." In Virgil, words almost magically enrich one another and attract implications from innumerable other passages, in other parts of the poem or outside it.[7] Merely to discern how this enrichment works is challenge enough; the attempt to suggest it in another language is enough to make the bravest translator turn pale.

Translators of Virgil must often feel that he composed verse with one cardinal principle in mind: never say anything directly and without complication. Strictly speaking, this would be a false charge; Virgil can be businesslike, and he can sometimes—as in some of the descriptions of the lovesick Dido—resort to a simplicity that is heartstopping in its emotional power. But that is exactly the point: simplicity is a piece of rhetorical virtuosity in Virgil, a change of his usual pace that can startle readers as sudden fireworks might in other poets. In an age like our own, which at least claims to prefer nature to artifice, translating Virgil is problematical to say the least.

There is, for one thing, the challenge of Virgil's diction, which is often earnestly and unabashedly "poetic." The great poets of the early twentieth century, rebelling against such monumental poets of artifice as Tennyson (who loved Virgil, incidentally), led a militant and highly successful crusade against the use of poetic diction in serious poetry, a taboo

---

[7] For this point and the words quoted, see W. F. Jackson Knight, *Roman Vergil*, revised ed. (Harmondsworth, England, 1966), p. 240.

that has come to govern translators as much as it governs poets. But even if translators chose to defy the taboo, the defiance would do them no good, for poetic diction is not merely outlawed, it no longer exists at all, except, after a fashion, in the circumlocutions of sports journalism and in certain other facetious holdovers. Even in popular song lyrics, normally the last refuge of dying poetic diction, it has almost completely disappeared in recent decades.

To get an idea what this can mean for translators of Virgil, consider Dido's memorable words when she tells her sister Anna that she feels love coming on again after years of emotional tranquillity as a widow: *agnosco veteris vestigia flammae,* "I recognize the signs of the old flame." This is by no means one of Virgil's more extravagant or original locutions; the love-as-flame metaphor was considered only mildly "poetic." Nevertheless, Virgil's phrase was memorable enough so that Dante, meeting his former love, Beatrice, on the threshold of heaven, said the same thing, in a word-for-word Italian translation, and Dante did not have to worry about being laughed at for saying it. Poets for many centuries after Dante could similarly describe love as a flame, right up through the lyricists of Tin Pan Alley ("I hear your name, and I'm aflame"). Today, however, "old flame" is old hat, a joking epithet for someone who was once the object of an infatuation long since faded. Translators therefore have to tiptoe warily around this little booby trap and many others similar to it.

Of hundreds of other illustrations one might provide, here are three: The grain spoiled by the shipwreck in Book I and the bread-making utensils are *Cererem corruptam undis Cerealiaque arma,* "Ceres spoiled by the waves, and the tools of Ceres." (Ceres was the harvest-goddess of grain; "spoiled cereal" would be an insane translation but not utterly untrue to the Virgilian spirit of word play.) To describe 11 P.M., Virgil writes, *Necdum orbem medium Nox Horis acta subibat,* "Night, urged on by the Hours, was not yet at the midpoint of her circular course." Or, going back to the torch-carrying Dido, we have *solus hic inflexit sensus, animumque labantem / impulit,* rendered by the nineteenth-century commentator A. Sidgwick, in language no one could get away with today, as "He only swayed my sense, and o'erthrew my faltering heart." Normally, translators will try to get as close to their original as the idiom of their own languages permits. Their problem in passages like those just quoted is that the closer they come to Virgil's own literal content and his tone, the farther they get from what modern readers will accept as good sense or emotionally credible expression.

Virgil's poetic diction is not, however, simply a matter of floweriness or elaborate circumlocutions. He heightens language of all sorts, for all sorts of subjects and tones. He hated war, but his gruesome descriptions of it are perhaps even more linguistically explicit and graphically horrific than Homer's, and his warriors and other heroes are quite unlike the strong silent masters of understatement whom we have been taught to admire today. Virgil also liked to indulge here and there a heightened language of spooky gothic melodrama closer to Poe, Dickens, and Conan Doyle than to the clipped, self-controlled idiom of, say, modern science-fiction thrillers.

Curiously, however, all this can be looked at in a different way. The same twentieth-century poets who taught us not to take seriously "old flames" or to call champagne (in Tennyson's notorious periphrase) the "foaming grape of eastern France" have also taught us that poetry should (as T. S. Eliot put it) "dislocate" language into meaning. And that is, precisely, what Virgil does again and again. The poet who coined new words such as *imperterritus,* meaning something like "totallynottotallyterrified," is closer to e. e. cummings ("this busy monster,manunkind") than to Tennyson. The master of the unsettling "transferred epithet," who describes an arrow as flying through *celeres umbras,* "the swift shadows," the master of inversion who has Turnus offer to exchange his death (instead of his life) for fame, *letum pro laude pacisci,* might well have kept his equilibrium on Yeats' "dolphin-torn, . . . gong-tormented sea" and felt at ease with T. S. Eliot's ladies who "lift and drop a question on your plate." In hundreds of similarly dislocated Virgilian expressions, translators have to decide whether or not they can get away with lan-

guage as daring or futuristic as Virgil's.[8] Sticking too close
to Virgil can make them sound quaint, but it can also make
them sound a little crazed (or perhaps just slightly intoxi-
cated).

Since Rolfe Humphries' translation was first published
thirty-odd years ago, it has held up admirably. The main
reason, I think, is that Humphries knows when to pit himself
against Virgil and when not to. In describing 11 P.M., he
knows better than to repeat verbatim Virgil's elaborate circumlocution, and he knows that no really equivalent English
figure of speech exists. ("The eleventh hour" might work
in more melodramatic contexts, but not in this one.) He
therefore give us, simply, "it was not yet midnight" (III.518).
Imperterritus becomes the unflashy "unfrightened" (X.863).
The line about spoiled Ceres and the Cereal tools is rendered,
a little more concretely but straightforwardly, as "the soaked
and salty corn, / The hand-mills, stone and mortar" (I.189–
90). Competing a little more actively, he has Turnus "trade
death for renown" (XII.62), capturing some of the boldness
of Virgil's phrase but remaining faithful to good sense and
English idiom. For the love reborn in Dido, Humphries retains the incendiary metaphor but avoids the "old flame"
booby trap: "I recognize / The marks of an old fire" (IV.22–
23). Aeneas is "the only man / Who has moved my spirit,
shaken my weak will" (IV.20–21)—a concession to romantic
phrasing that nevertheless avoids the language of sentimental
or heroic melodrama. With the "swift shadows," Humphries
is ingenious to the point of cheating: "an arrow . . . cleaving
shadows / Swifter than man may know" (XII.925–28); the
trick here is an ambiguously placed modifier, leaving it to
us whether *swifter* modies *shadows* (as in Virgil) or *cleaving*
(as in sober, levelheaded fact). On a very few occasions, Humphries seems needlessly timid; he renders Virgil's marvellous
clamore incendunt caelum, "[Trojans and Latins] set the sky
on fire with their shouting," as "Trojan and Latin uproar
swelled to heaven" (X.999). But such over-cautiousness is
rare. He rises to the challenge, for example, in *pulvere caelum /*

---

[8] Knight compares Virgil to such modernist writers as James Joyce,
T. S. Eliot, and Gerard Manley Hopkins; see pp. 260, 300–01, 318.

stare vident, "They see the sky / Standing on dust" (XII.458–59).

Sometimes, when Humphries avoids such challenges, he has good reason. For example, during the climactic fight between Aeneas and Turnus at the end of the poem, Jupiter sends down one of the Furies, daughters of *Nox intempesta,* in the shape of a screech-owl, to terrify Turnus and warn off his protecting sister, Juturna. Humphries renders the Latin phrase simply as "Night" (XII.917), supplying no equivalent of the adjective *intempesta.* The fact is that Latin scholars are not entirely sure they know what this word, which Virgil borrowed from earlier writers, means. A number of them, however, propose a fascinating psychological origin of the term, namely that it suggests the uncanny quality of the period of deepest night, when time seems suspended because there are no familiar human activities to help us sense its passage. Clearly, no single adjective, or indeed any brief phrase or clause, can convey this eerie meaning. *Timeless* would come very close if that word, unfortunately for the translator's purpose here, did not already exist in English and mean something completely different. Short of inserting a whole little non-Virgilian essay into the translation, or choosing an adjective like *mysterious* that will itself remain a small mystery to the reader, there is not much a translator can do with *intempesta.* Better, with Humphries, to leave it as "Night," with a silent and frustrated bow to Virgil's justly-acclaimed power of suggestion and compression.

On the other hand, Humphries is often brilliantly successful in capturing what a filmmaker might call Virgil's special effects. Quite a few of these have to do with the sound of the verse—exactly that aspect of poetry generally recognized as least capturable in translation. For example, in one of the many animal similes that Virgil, reprocessing Homer, likes to introduce, we have a description of a lion at large in a sheepfold, expressed with the kind of symmetry and alliteration Virgil was particularly fond of: *manditque trahitque / molle pecus mutumque metu; fremit ore cruento.* Here the first two words express the lion's violence, the next four the sheep's timorousness. Humphries gets this effect forcefully:

"gnashing and dragging, raging / With bloody mouth against the fearful feeble" (IX.355–56). So also with this description of the ghastly, random litter of a battlefield (bear in mind that both *et* and *-que* in Latin mean "and"):

> tum vero et gemitus morientum, et sanguine in alto
> armaque corporaque et permixti caede virorum
> semianimes volvuntur equi;

Humphries translates this as

>   Dying men
> Groaned, and the blood was deep, and men and armor
> And wounded horses and wounded men and bodies
> Of men and horses were in it all together. (XI.724–27)

Humphries confessed to taking liberties with *The Aeneid,* and it is true that he does take more of them than some translators allow themselves. Most of these liberties are inconsequential, even by rather strict standards, and some others (as with *intempesta*) are responsible alternatives to either pedantry or mystification. Some of them are meant, sensibly, to reduce the information gap between modern readers and Romans of Virgil's day who would have understood without footnotes the meaning of proper names and allusions. Thus, for example, Humphries reduces to a few words ("a matter of three years / From victory to settlement"—I.277–78) a reference to the Rutulians (whom the reader will not meet until Book VII) and a Virgilian circumlocution about military encampment that would be a little distracting to readers unfamiliar with still-unrelated events.

Humphries also cheerfully called his translation "unscrupulous," and though he disclaimed modesty in making such a statement, he was indeed being too modest. In countless phrases his translation indicates a nice awareness not just of overtones and implications in the Latin original but also of the learned controversies about it. In rendering many passages of *The Aeneid,* translators have to commit themselves to one or another of certain alternative versions of the Latin text, where the correct version is sometimes in doubt, and it is often clear that Humphries has pondered the alternatives with some care. Most impressive of all is his ability to cut the Gordian knots that commentators have trouble untangling. When, in VIII.640, Humphries calls Vulcan "the great prophetic Lord of Fire," he achieves an unobtrusive and learned elegance, since certain other translations of the Latin *haud vatum ignarus,* "not ignorant of prophets," can raise distracting questions about whether the god had to go to human prophets in order to know the future, could gain such knowledge from other gods, or possessed foreknowledge in his own right—questions of some interest but only to specialists. The slight vagueness in Humphries' wording is exactly what good, functional translation calls for. Snares and distractions like this, large ones and small, are everywhere in Virgil. Just a few lines earlier, Virgil has referred to an ancient custom among the *Pelasgi,* regarded as earlier inhabitants of Italy. If one translates this as "Pelasgians" and somehow hopes that the reader gets the intended meaning, a small problem still remains, at least for purists, because Virgil's reference to the Pelasgians is historically dubious. Humphries cuts this knot by simply referring to "the old people" (VIII.615).

As a matter of personal temperament or conscious esthetic decision, every translator of *The Aeneid,* however versatile in changing tone or narrative rhythm, is necessarily forced to adopt some one style as a home base, to be sustained or departed from as the poem demands and the translator's skill allows. This basic style might be magisterially elevated, or racily colloquial, or a number of other things. Humphries' basic style is marked by brisk energy, directness, and, above all, clarity. Hardly a single word or idiom in his translation has gone out of vogue since it first appeared three decades ago. This in itself, in a translation of a poem so individually flavored as *The Aeneid,* is an impressive accomplishment. The most distinctive rhythmical and syntactic feature of Humphries' English style is his penchant for comma splices and omitted subjects of verbs, so that his constructions have a rapid, slightly breathless movement. But these are not merely personal mannerisms; rather, they are effective ways of rendering Virgil's own narrative rhythm, which, whatever the length of his sentences, works essentially through short units, with frequent main-clause verbs. (If one used *and* in English every time Virgil uses it in Latin, one would sound incoherent.) By contrast, consider the opening of Milton's *Paradise Lost,* which in sixteen lines contains only two main verbs, in lines 6 and 13. Humphries' comma splices also reflect one fundamental fact about the Latin language, namely that the subject of a verb is often contained in the verb itself rather than stated separately.

Above all, what needs to be said about Humphries is that he was himself a poet. Byron, one of the most adept of versifiers, once reminded himself and his readers that "in blank verse, Milton, Thomson, and our [British] dramatists are the beacons that shine along the deep, but warn us from the rough and barren rock on which they are kindled." Such warnings about the difficulty of writing well in unrhymed iambic pentameter deserve repeating today, when so many translators whose poetic talents can at best be called mediocre rush in like innocents to try their hands at this most difficult of meters. It is therefore gratifying and exhilarating to read such accomplished blank verse as we get in Rolfe Humphries' translation—lively and idiomatic, never prosaic or syllabically padded or merely dutiful. Every word and syllable has a job to do and does it.

A Note on the Footnotes

The notes are meant to be informational, not interpretive. They gloss not only matters having to do with the poem and ancient culture but also the very few unfamiliar words the translator uses, as well as certain matters of general information. Readers who do not need such help are asked to be indulgent.

Some of the notes deliberately repeat material from earlier ones, on the assumption that readers who need to be told once what, say, *Ausonian* means may need to be told again a hundred pages later. Cross-references between notes other than long ones have been kept to a minimum.

A few of the notes to Books I, II, III, IV, and VI are quoted or paraphrased from the notes to *The Aeneid* in *Literature of the Western World,* edited by Brian Wilkie and James Hurt (New York: Macmillan, 1984), Volume I.

BOOK I

🔲

The Landing Near Carthage

ARMS and the man I sing,[1] the first who came,
Compelled by fate, an exile out of Troy,
To Italy and the Lavinian coast,[2]
Much buffeted on land and on the deep[3]
By violence of the gods, through that long rage,
That lasting hate, of Juno's.[4] And he suffered
Much, also, in war, till he should build his town
And bring his gods to Latium,[5] whence, in time,

[1] Lines 1–16 use the standard epic opening formula, identifying the hero (the Trojan prince Aeneas), proclaiming the poem's theme and its significance, and invoking the inspiring Muse. Virgil's main models are the two preeminent Greek epics: Homer's *Iliad* and *Odyssey*, which tell, respectively, of war (the siege of Troy) and of wandering (Odysseus' long-delayed homecoming from the war). In the very first two words of his poem, *Arma virumque*, "Arms and the man," Virgil glances at the two Homeric epics, confessing his debt to them (Virgil's first six books tell of wandering, his last six of war) and implicitly promising to treat themes even loftier than those treated by Homer.

[2] The fall of Troy and the consequent emigration of Aeneas and his followers will be described in Books II and III. The Lavinian coast is in western Italy.

[3] The sea. The trials by sea are described in Books I–VI, the trials on land in Books VII–XII.

[4] Queen of the gods; consort of Jupiter. (Their Greek names are, respectively, Hera and Zeus.) The reasons for Juno's hatred of the Trojans are summarized in lines 29–36.

[5] The area of west-central Italy destined to be settled by the Trojans.

1

The Latin race, the Alban fathers, rose
10   And the great walls of everlasting Rome.[6]
     Help me, O Muse, recall the reasons: why,
Why did the queen of heaven drive a man
So known for goodness, for devotion, through
So many toils and perils? Was there slight,
Affront, or outrage? Is vindictiveness
An attribute of the celestial mind?
     There was an ancient city, Carthage, once
Founded by Tyrians, facing Italy
And Tiber's mouth, far-off, a wealthy town,
20   War-loving, and aggressive; and Juno held
Even her precious Samos in less regard.[7]
Here were her arms, her chariot, and here,
Should fate at all permit, the goddess burned
To found the empire of the world forever.
But, she had heard, a Trojan race would come,
Some day, to overthrow the Tyrian towers,
A race would come, imperious people, proud
In war, with wide dominion, bringing doom
For Libya. Fate willed it so.[8] And Juno
30   Feared, and remembered: there was the old war
She fought at Troy for her dear Greeks; her mind
Still fed on hurt and anger; deep in her heart
Paris' decision rankled, and the wrong
Offered her slighted beauty; and the hatred
Of the whole race; and Ganymede's honors—

[6] The city Alba Longa will be settled by Aeneas' son, Ascanius (also called Iulus); then, after several centuries, Rome will be founded a few miles away, by the legendary Romulus, in about 753 B.C. For fuller details, see Jupiter's prophecy in I.268–89.

[7] Carthage, a city favored by Juno, was on the north coast of Africa, near modern Tunis. It had been settled by Dido and other refugees from Tyre, a commercial center of ancient Phoenicia on what is now the coast of southern Lebanon. Carthage is called "war-loving" because it fought the three great Punic Wars against Rome in the third and second centuries B.C. The Tiber is the river of Rome. Samos, site of a major temple of Juno, is an island in the eastern Aegean Sea.

[8] The gods had only marginal influence on the superior force of Fate. The "imperious people" are the Romans. *Libya* means "Africa" or, more specifically here, Carthage.

All that was fuel to fire;[9] she tossed and harried
All over the seas, wherever she could, those Trojans
Who had survived the Greeks and fierce Achilles,[10]
And so they wandered over many an ocean,
Through many a year, fate-hounded. Such a struggle   40
It was to found the race of Rome!

They were happy
Spreading the sail, rushing the foam with bronze,
And Sicily hardly out of sight,[11] when Juno,
Still nourishing the everlasting wound,
Raged to herself: "I am beaten, I suppose;
It seems I cannot keep this Trojan king
From Italy. The fates, no doubt, forbid me.
Pallas, of course, could burn the Argive ships,
Could drown the sailors, all for one man's guilt,
The crazy acts of Ajax.[12] Her own hand   50
Hurled from the cloud Jove's thunderbolt, and shattered
Their ships all over the sea; she raised up storm
And tempest; she spiked Ajax on the rocks,
Whirled him in wind, blasted his heart with fire.
And I, who walk my way as queen of the gods,
Sister of Jove, and wife of Jove, keep warring
With one tribe through the long, long years.[13] Who cares

[9] Paris, a son of King Priam of Troy, had been asked to judge which of the three goddesses Juno (the Greek Hera), Minerva (goddess of wisdom and crafts; the Greek Athena), and Venus (goddess of love; the Greek Aphrodite) was most beautiful. He chose Venus, who rewarded him with Helen, the most beautiful of mortal women. Her flight with Paris, who had been staying as a guest with Helen and her husband Menelaus in Greece, ignited the Trojan War, fought by the Greeks to reclaim her. Ganymede was a Trojan youth who, loved by Jupiter, was caught up into heaven and promoted over Juno's daughter Hebe as cupbearer to the gods.

[10] The greatest of the Greek warriors against Troy.

[11] The story begins in the middle of the Trojans' sea journey from their fallen city to Italy. The earlier stages will be narrated in Book III. On the epic flashback, see note to II.14.

[12] Pallas Athena, or Minerva, burned the Argive (that is, Greek) ships returning from Troy, as punishment for the attempted rape of the prophetess Cassandra, at Athena's temple, by the Greek warrior Ajax.

[13] Both Jove (another name for Jupiter) and Juno were the offspring of Saturn, former king of the gods.

For Juno's godhead? Who brings sacrifice
Devoutly to her altars?"
                        Brooding, burning,
60   She sought Aeolia,[14] the storm-clouds' dwelling,
A land that sweeps and swarms with the winds' fury,
Whose monarch, Aeolus, in his deep cave rules
Imperious, weighing down with bolt and prison
Those boisterous struggling roarers, who go raging
Around their bars, under the moan of the mountain.
High over them their sceptered lord sits watching,
Soothing, restraining, their passionate proud spirit,
Lest, uncontrolled, they seize, in their wild keeping,
The land, the sea, the arch of sky, in ruin
70   Sweeping through space. This Jupiter feared; he hid them
Deep in dark caverns, with a mass of mountain
Piled over above them, and a king to give them
Most certain regulation, with a knowledge
When to hold in, when to let go. Him Juno
Approached in supplication:—"Aeolus,
Given by Jove the power to still the waters,
Or raise them with a gale, a tribe I hate
Is on its way to Italy, and they carry
Troy with them, and their household gods, once beaten.
80   Shake anger into those winds of yours, turn over
Their ships, and drown them; drive them in all directions,
Litter the sea with bodies! For such service
The loveliest nymph I have, Deiopea,
Shall be your bride forever, and you will father
Fair children on her fairness." Aeolus
Made answer: "Yours, O Queen, the task of seeking
Whatever it is you will; and mine the duty
To follow with performance. All my empire,
My sceptre, Jove's indulgence, are beholden
90   To Juno's favor, by whose blessing I
Attend the feasts of the gods and rule this storm-land."
    His spear-butt struck the hollow mountain-side,
And the winds, wherever they could, came sweeping forth,

---

[14] Aeolia, island home of Aeolus, god of the winds, was located by the
ancients near Sicily.

Whirled over the land, swooped down upon the ocean.
East, South, Southwest, they heave the billows, howl,
Storm, roll the giant combers toward the shore.
Men cry; the rigging creaks and strains; the clouds
Darken, and men see nothing; a weight of darkness
Broods over the deep; the heavy thunder rumbles
From pole to pole; the lightning rips and dazzles;   100
There is no way out but death. Aeneas shudders
In the chill shock, and lifts both hands to heaven:—
"O happy men, thrice happy, four times happy,
Who had the luck to die, with their fathers watching,
Below the walls of Troy! Ah, Diomedes,
Bravest of Greeks, why could I not have fallen,
Bleeding my life away on plains of Ilium
In our encounter there, where mighty Hector
Went down before Achilles' spear, and huge
Sarpedon lay in dust, and Simois river   110
Rolled to the sea so many noble heroes,
All drowned in all their armor?"[15] And the gale
Howls from the north, striking the sail, head on;
The waves are lifted to the stars; the oars
Are broken, and the prow slews round; the ship
Lies broadside on; a wall of water, a mountain,
Looms up, comes pouring down; some ride the crest,
Some, in the trough, can see the boil of the sand.
The South wind hurls three ships on the hidden rocks,
That sea-reef which Italians call the Altars;   120
The West takes three, sweeping them from the deep
On shoal and quicksand;[16] over the stern of one,
Before Aeneas' eyes, a great sea falls,
Washing the helmsman overboard; the ship

[15] The combat between Diomedes and Aeneas, whose mother Venus saved him from death, is related in Homer's *Iliad,* Book V. (For Virgil, this rescue was part of a providential pattern, sparing Aeneas so that he might later fulfill his role as the fountainhead of Roman history.) Ilium is another name for Troy. The death of the prince Hector, greatest of the Trojan warriors, at the hands of Achilles is related in the *Iliad,* Book XXII. Sarpedon was a king killed while fighting for the Trojans. The Simois was a river at the battlefield of Troy.

[16] The Altars were rocks between Sicily and north Africa. The treacherous shoals are the Syrtes, off the African coast near Carthage.

Whirls thrice in the suck of the water and goes down
In the devouring gulf; and here and there
A few survivors swim, the Lycian men
Whose captain was Orontes; now their arms,
Their Trojan treasures, float with the broken timbers
130   On the swing and slide of the waves. The storm, triumphant,
Rides down more boats, and more; there goes Achates;
Abas, Aletes, Ilioneus,
Receive the hostile water; the walls are broken;
The enemy pours in.
                      But meanwhile Neptune[17]
Saw ocean in a welter of confusion,
The roar of storm, and deep and surface mingled.
Troublesome business, this; he rose, majestic,
From under the waves, and saw the Trojan vessels
Scattered all over the sea by the might of the waves
140   And the wreck of sky; he recognized the anger
And cunning of his sister, and he summoned
The winds by name:—"What arrogance is this,
What pride of birth, you winds, to meddle here
Without my sanction, raising all this trouble?
I'll—No, the waves come first: but listen to me,
You are going to pay for this! Get out of here!
Go tell your king the lordship of the ocean,
The trident,[18] are not his, but mine. His realm
Reaches no further than the rocks and caverns
150   You brawlers dwell in; let him rule that palace,
Big as he pleases, shut you in, and stay there!"
    This said, he calmed the swollen sea and cloud,
Brought back the sun; Cymothoe and Triton,[19]
Heaving together, pulled the ships from the reef,
As Neptune used his trident for a lever,
Opened the quicksand, made the water smooth,
And the flying chariot skimmed the level surface.
Sometimes, in a great nation, there are riots
With the rabble out of hand, and firebrands fly

[17] God of the ocean.
[18] The three-pronged spear wielded by Neptune.
[19] Respectively, a Nereid (sea-nymph) and a sea-god. See the following note.

And cobblestones; whatever they lay their hands on   160
Is a weapon for their fury, but should they see
One man of noble presence, they fall silent,
Obedient dogs, with ears pricked up, and waiting,
Waiting his word, and he knows how to bring them
Back to good sense again. So ocean, roaring,
Subsided into stillness, as the sea-god
Looked forth upon the waters, and clear weather
Shone over him as he drove his flying horses.
   Aeneas' weary children make for harbor,
Whichever lies most near, and the prows are turned   170
To Libya's coast-line. In a bay's deep curve
They find a haven, where the water lies
With never a ripple. A little island keeps
The sea-swell off, and the waves break on its sides
And slide back harmless. The great cliffs come down
Steep to deep water, and the background shimmers,
Darkens and shines, the tremulous aspen moving
And the dark fir pointing still. And there is a cave
Under the overhanging rocks, alive
With water running fresh, a home of the Nymphs,[20]   180
With benches for them, cut from the living stone.
No anchor is needed here for weary ships,
No mooring-cable. Aeneas brings them in,
Seven weary vessels, and the men are glad
To be ashore again, to feel dry sand
Under the salt-stained limbs. Achates[21] strikes
The spark from the flint, catches the fire on leaves,
Adds chips and kindling, blows and fans the flame,
And they bring out the soaked and salty corn,
The hand-mills, stone and mortar, and make ready,   190
As best they can, for bread.
                         Meanwhile Aeneas
Climbs to a look-out, for a view of the ocean,
Hoping for some good luck; the Phrygian[22] galleys

---

[20] The Nymphs were minor nature-goddesses. They included Nereids
(of ocean), Naiads (of brooks), Dryads (of trees), and Oreads (of mountains).
[21] Aeneas' most faithful companion.
[22] Trojan (literally, of Phrygia, the region that included Troy).

Might meet his gaze, or Capys' boats, or a pennon
On a far-off mast-head flying. There is nothing,
Nothing to see out yonder, but near the water
Three stags are grazing, with a herd behind them,
A long line browsing through the peaceful valley.
He reaches for the bow and the swift arrows
200   Borne by Achates, and he shoots the leaders,
High-antlered, routs the common herd, and ceases
Only when seven are slain, a number equal
To the ships' tally, and then he seeks the harbor,
Divides the spoil, broaches the wine Acestes
Had stowed for them at Drepanum on their leaving,
A kingly present, and he calms their trouble,
Saying: "O comrades, we have been through evil
Together before this; we have been through worse,
Scylla, Charybdis, and the Cyclops' dwelling,
210   The sounding rocks.[23] This, too, the god will end.
Call the nerve back; dismiss the fear, the sadness.
Some day, perhaps, remembering even this
Will be a pleasure. We are going on
Through whatsoever chance and change, until
We come to Latium, where the fates point out
A quiet dwelling-place, and Troy recovered.
Endure, and keep yourself for better days."
He kept to himself the sorrow in the heart,
Wearing, for them, a mask of hopefulness.
220   They were ready for the feasting. Part lay bare
The flesh from the torn hides, part cut the meat,
Impaling it, still quivering, on spits,
Setting the kettles, keeping the water boiling,
And strong with food again, sprawling stretched out
On comfortable grass, they take their fill
Of bread and wine and venison, till hunger
Is gone, and the board cleared. And then they talk
For a long time, of where their comrades are,
Are, or may be, hopeful and doubtful both.

---

[23] The perils alluded to in lines 209–10 are described in Book III. The visit to Drepanum, in western Sicily, is also mentioned later, in III.703. Acestes, a Sicilian king, is presented in Book V.

Could they believe them living? or would a cry   230
Fall on deaf ears forever? All those captains,
Brave Gyas, brave Cloanthus, Amycus,
Lycus, Orontes,—in his secret heart
Aeneas mourns them.
                              Meanwhile, from the heaven
Jupiter watched the lands below, and the seas
With the white points of sails, and far-off people,
Turning his gaze toward Libya. And Venus
Came to him then, a little sadly, tears
Brimming in those bright eyes of hers. "Great father,"
She said, "Great ruler of the world   240
Of men and gods, great wielder of the lightning,
What has my poor Aeneas done?[24] what outrage
Could Trojans perpetrate, so that the world
Rejects them everywhere, and many a death
Inflicted on them over Italy?
There was a promise once, that as the years
Rolled onward, they would father Rome and rulers
Of Roman stock, to hold dominion over
All sea and land. That was a promise, father;
What changed it? Once that promise was my comfort;   250
Troy fell; I weighed one fate against another
And found some consolation. But disaster
Keeps on; the same ill-fortune follows after.
What end of it all, great king? One man, Antenor,
Escaped the Greeks, came through Illyrian waters
Safe to Liburnian regions, where Timavus
Roars underground, comes up nine times, and reaches
The floodland near the seas. One man, Antenor,
Founded a city, Padua, a dwelling
For Trojan men, a resting-place from labor,   260
And shares their quietude.[25] But we, your children,
To whom heaven's height is granted, we are betrayed,
We have lost our ships, we are kept from Italy,
Kept far away. One enemy—I tell you

---

[24] Aeneas was the son of Venus and Anchises, a mortal.

[25] Antenor was a Trojan nobleman who emigrated after the city fell.
Illyria is a region east of the Adriatic (the sea to the east of Italy), into
which the river Timavus flows. Liburnia is part of the Adriatic coast.

This is a shameful thing! Do we deserve it?
Is this our rise to power?"
                          He smiled, in answer,
The kind of smile that clears the air, and kissed her.
"Fear not, my daughter; fate remains unmoved
For the Roman generations. You will witness
270   Lavinium's[26] rise, her walls fulfill the promise;
You will bring to heaven lofty-souled Aeneas.
There has been no change in me whatever. Listen!
To ease this care, I will prophesy a little,
I will open the book of fate. Your son Aeneas
Will wage a mighty war in Italy,
Beat down proud nations, give his people laws,
Found them a city, a matter of three years
From victory to settlement. His son,
The boy Ascanius, named Ilus once,
280   When Troy was standing, and now called Iulus,
Shall reign for thirty years, and great in power
Forsake Lavinium, transfer the kingdom
To Alba Longa, new-built capital.
Here, for three hundred years, the line of Hector
Shall govern, till a royal priestess bears
Twin sons to Mars, and Romulus, rejoicing
In the brown wolf-skin of his foster-mother,
Takes up the tribe, and builds the martial walls
And calls the people, after himself, the Romans.[27]
290   To these I set no bounds in space or time;
They shall rule forever. Even bitter Juno
Whose fear now harries earth and sea and heaven
Will change to better counsels, and will cherish
The race that wears the toga,[28] Roman masters
Of all the world. It is decreed. The time
Will come, as holy years wheel on, when Troy

[26] The city Aeneas is to found, named for his second wife Lavinia. See also notes to lines 3 and 10.

[27] For more of the story of Romulus and his twin brother Remus, sons of the war-god Mars, and of the boys' being suckled by a she-wolf, see VIII.643–46 and note.

[28] The long white robe worn by Romans as civilian (as opposed to military) dress—a symbol of manhood and of membership in the freeborn class.

Will subjugate Mycenae, vanquish Phthia,
Be lord of Argos.[29] And from this great line
Will come a Trojan, Caesar, to establish
The limit of his empire at the ocean,   300
His glory at the stars, a man called Julius
Whose name recalls Iulus. Welcome waits
For him in heaven; all the spoils of Asia
Will weigh him down, and prayer be made before him.[30]
Then wars will cease, and a rough age grow gentler,
White Faith and Vesta,[31] Romulus and Remus,
Give law to nations. War's grim gates will close,
Tight-shut with bars of iron, and inside them
The wickedness of war sit bound and silent,
The red mouth straining and the hands held tight   310
In fastenings of bronze, a hundred hundred."[32]

With that, he sent down Mercury[33] from heaven
That Carthage might be kindly, and her land
And new-built towers receive them with a welcome,
And their queen, Dido, knowing the will of fate,
Swing wide her doors. On the oarage of his wings
He flies through the wide sweep of air to Libya,
Where, at the will of the god, the folk make ready
In kindliness of heart, and their queen's purpose
Is gracious and gentle.
                     All night long Aeneas   320
Had pondered many a care, and with bright morning

[29] Cities associated with the Trojans' Greek conquerors: Phthia with Achilles, Mycenae and Argos with Agamemnon, the Greek commander-in-chief.

[30] The reference is primarily to Octavian, or Caesar Augustus (63 B.C.–14 A.D.), who ruled Rome at the time when Virgil wrote *The Aeneid*. The poem is designed, among other things, to pay him tribute. After being adopted as son of Julius Caesar (100–44 B.C.), his full name became Gaius Julius Caesar Octavianus, *Augustus* being a title, conferred later. He brought peace and order to the Roman state for the first time in generations. For an account of Octavian's climactic triumph over Mark Antony and Cleopatra, see VIII.677–726.

[31] Goddess of the hearth and family. The holy fire in her temple at Rome was tended by six priestesses known as the Vestal Virgins.

[32] The gates of Janus, in Rome, kept open in wartime and closed in peacetime, were shut by Octavian in 29 B.C., for only the third time in Roman history. For a fuller description of these gates, see VII.619–36.

[33] Messenger of the gods.

Resolved to reconnoiter; the winds have brought him
To a new country: who lives in it, men
Or only beasts? The fields appear untended.
The fleet lies under a hollow cliff, surrounded
By spikes of shade, and groves arch overhead,
Ample concealment. Aeneas and Achates
Went forth together, armed, down the trail in the forest,
And there his mother met him, a girl, it seemed,
330   From Thrace or Sparta,[34] trim as any huntress
Who rides her horses hard, or outspeeds rivers
In her swift going. A bow hung over her shoulder,
Her hair blew free, her knees were bare, her garments
Tucked at the waist and knotted. As she saw them,
"Ho there, young men," she cried, "have you seen my sister
Around here anywhere? She wears a quiver,
And a spotted lynx-hide; maybe you have heard her
Hunting the boar and shouting?"
                                              But her son
Responded: "No; we have heard no sounds of hunting,
340   We have seen no one here. But tell me, maiden,
What name to call you by? In voice and feature
You are, I think, no mortal; a goddess, surely,—
Nymph, or Apollo's sister? Whoever you are,
Be kind to us, lighten our trouble, tell us
Under what sky, along what coast of the world,
We wander, knowing neither land nor people,
Driven by gales and billows. Many a victim
We shall make ready for your altar." Venus
Answered: "I have no title to such honor.
350   The Tyrian girls all wear these crimson leggings
Like mine, and carry quivers. Tyrian folk
Live here; their city is Carthage; over the border
Lies Libya, warlike people. Our queen, Dido,
Came here from Tyre; she was fleeing from her brother,—
A long and complicated story; outrage,—
No matter; here it is, in brief. Her husband
Was Sychaeus, wealthiest of all Phoenicians,
At least in land, and Dido loved him dearly

[34] Places in Greece noted for rugged physical fitness and austerity.

Since first her father gave her to him, virgin,
And then unlucky bride. She had a brother,   360
Pygmalion, king of Tyre, a monster, evil
In wickedness, and madness came between
Those men, the two of them. Pygmalion murdered
Sychaeus at the altar; he was crazy
And blind for gold and crafty; what did he care
About his sister's love? And he kept it quiet
For a long time, kept telling Dido something
To fool her with false comfort, but Sychaeus
Came to her in a dream, a ghost, unburied,
With the wounds in his breast, the story of the altar,   370
The pale lips blurting out the secret horror,
The crime in the dark of the household. *Flee,* he told her,
Forsake this land; and he told her where the treasure
Lay hidden in earth, uncounted gold and silver.
Dido was moved to flight, secured companions,
All those possessed by fear, all those whom hatred
Had made relentless; ships were standing ready,
As it so happened; they put the gold aboard,
And over the sea the greedy tyrant's treasure
Went sailing, with a woman for a captain.   380
They came here; you will see the walls arising
And the great citadel of the town called Carthage.
Here they bought ground; they used to call it Byrsa,
That being a word for bull's hide; they bought only
What a bull's hide could cover.[35] And now tell me
Who you might be yourselves? what land do you come from,
Bound for what coast?"
                        And he began his answer
With a long sigh: "O goddess, if I told you
All from the first beginning, if you had leisure
To listen to the record of our trouble,   390
It would take me all day long. From ancient Troy,
In case that name means anything, we come
Driven over many seas, and now a storm
Has whipped us on this coast. I am Aeneas,

---

[35] The purchasers made a string from the hide, cut into very thin strips,
and with this they were able to enclose a large area of land.

A good, devoted man; I carry with me
My household gods, saved from the Greeks; I am known
In heaven; it is Italy I seek,
A homeland for me there, and a race descended
From lofty Jove.[36] With a score of ships we started
400   Over the Phrygian ocean, following fate
And the way my mother pointed. Only seven
Are left us now, battered survivors, after
The rage of wind and wave. And here I wander
The wastes of Libya, unknown and needy,
Driven from Europe and Asia." And his mother
Broke in on his complaining:—"Whoever you are,
Some god must care for you, I think, to bring you
Here to the city of Carthage. Follow on,
Go to the royal palace. For, I tell you,
410   Your comrades have returned, your fleet is safe,
Brought to good haven by the turn of the winds,
Unless the augury[37] my parents taught me
Was foolish nonsense. In the heaven yonder
You see twelve swans, rejoicing in long column,
Scattered, a little while ago, and driven
By the swooping eagle, over all the sky,
But now, it seems, they light on land, or watch
Those who came down before them; as they circle
In company, and make a cheerful sound
420   With whir of wing or song, so, let me tell you,
Your ships and men already enter harbor
Or near it under full sail. Keep on, go forward
Where the path leads."
                          And as she turned, her shoulders
Shone with a radiant light; her hair shed fragrance,
Her robes slipped to her feet, and the true goddess
Walked in divinity.[38] He knew his mother,
And his voice pursued her flight: "Cruel again!

[36] Dardanus, an Italian ancestor of the Trojans, was a son of Jove (Jupiter).

[37] The art of foretelling events by interpretation of divine signs and omens.

[38] A stately gait and carriage were distinctive marks of a goddess.

Why mock your son so often with false phantoms?
Why may not hand be joined to hand, and words
Exchanged in truthfulness?" So, still reproachful,   430
He went on toward the city, with Achates,
But Venus cast dark air around their going,
A veil of mist, so that no man might see them
Or lay a hand on them, or halt them, asking
The reasons of their coming. She soared upward
To Paphos,[39] happily home to temple and altars
Steaming with incense, redolent with garlands.
    And they went on, where the little pathway led them
To rising ground; below them lay the city,
Majestic buildings now, where once were hovels,   440
A wonder to Aeneas, gates and bustle
And well-paved streets, the busy Tyrians toiling
With stones for walls and citadel, or marking
Foundations for their homes, drainage and furrow,
All under ordered process. They dredge harbors,
Set cornerstones, quarry the rock, where someday
Their theater will tower. They are like bees
In early summer over the country flowers
When the sun is warm, and the young of the hive emerge,
And they pack the molten honey, bulge the cells   450
With the sweet nectar, add new loads, and harry
The drones away from the hive, and the work glows,
And the air is sweet with bergamot[40] and clover.
"Happy the men whose walls already rise!"
Exclaims Aeneas, gazing on the city,
And enters there, still veiled in cloud—a marvel!—
And walks among the people, and no one sees him.
    There was a grove in the middle of the city,
Most happy in its shade; this was the place
Where first the Tyrians, tossed by storm and whirlwind,   460
Dug up the symbol royal Juno showed them,
The skull of a war-horse, a sign the race to come
Would be supreme in war and wealth, for ages,

[39] A city in Cyprus, sacred to Aphrodite (Venus).
[40] A fragrant oil, made from the fruit of the bergamot tree.

And Dido here was building a great temple
In Juno's honor, rich in gifts, and blessed
With the presence of the goddess. Lintel and rafter
Were bronze above bronze stairways, and bronze portals
Swung on bronze hinges. Here Aeneas first
Dared hope for safety, find some reassurance
470   In hope of better days: a strange sight met him,
To take his fear away. Waiting the queen,
He stood there watching, under the great temple,
Letting his eyes survey the city's fortune,
The artist's workmanship, the craftsman's labor,
And there, with more than wonder, he sees the battles
Fought around Troy, and the wars whose fame had travelled
The whole world over; there is Agamemnon,
Priam, and Menelaus, and Achilles,
A menace to them all. He is moved to tears.
480   "What place in all the world," he asks Achates,
"Is empty of our sorrow? There is Priam!
Look! even here there are rewards for praise,
There are tears for things, and what men suffer touches
The human heart. Dismiss your fear; this story
Will bring some safety to you." Sighing often,
He could not turn his gaze away; it was only
A picture on a wall, but the sight afforded
Food for the spirit's need. He saw the Greeks,
Hard-pressed, in flight, and Trojans coming after,
490   Or, on another panel, the scene reversed,
Achilles in pursuit, his own men fleeing;
He saw, and tears came into his eyes again,
The tents of Rhesus, snowy-white, betrayed
In their first sleep by bloody Diomedes
With many a death, and the fiery horses driven
Into the camp, before they ever tasted
The grass of Troy, or drank from Xanthus' river.[41]

---

[41] Rhesus supported the Trojans against the Greeks. According to an oracle, Troy could not fall if his horses tasted Trojan grass or drank from the Trojan river Xanthus. But before the horses could do either, Diomedes and Ulysses (the Greek Odysseus) carried them off. See Homer's *Iliad*, Book X.

Another scene showed Troilus,[42] poor youngster,
Running away, his arms flung down; Achilles
Was much too good for him; he had fallen backward   500
Out of his car, but held the reins, and the horses
Dragged him along the ground, his hair and shoulders
Bounding in dust, and the spear making a scribble.
And there were Trojan women, all in mourning,
With streaming hair, on their way to Pallas' temple,
Bearing, as gift, a robe, but the stern goddess
Kept her gaze on the ground.[43] Three times Achilles
Had dragged the body of Hector around the walls,
And was selling it for money. What a groan
Came from Aeneas' heart, seeing that spoil,   510
That chariot, and helpless Priam reaching
His hands, unarmed, across the broken body!
And he saw himself there, too, fighting in battle
Against Greek leaders, he saw the Eastern columns,
And swarthy Memnon's arms. Penthesilea,
The Amazon, blazes in fury, leading
Her crescent-shielded thousands, a golden buckle
Below her naked breast, a soldieress
Fighting with men.[44]
                       And as he watched these marvels
In one long fascinated stare of wonder,   520
Dido, the queen, drew near; she came to the temple
With a great train, all majesty, all beauty,
As on Eurotas' riverside, or where
Mount Cynthus towers high, Diana leads
Her bands of dancers, and the Oreads follow
In thousands, right and left, the taller goddess,
The quiver-bearing maiden, and Latona
Is filled with secret happiness,[45] so Dido

[42] A son of the Trojan king Priam.
[43] Pallas Athena (Minerva) sided with the Greeks against the Trojans.
[44] Memnon, an Ethiopian king, and the Amazons fought for the Trojans.
[45] Diana (the "taller goddess"), the counterpart of the Greek Artemis, was daughter of Latona (also known as Leto) and goddess of hunting. Mount Cynthus, her birthplace on the Aegean island of Delos, and the river Eurotas, in Sparta, were closely associated with her. Oreads were mountain-nymphs.

Moved in her company, a queen, rejoicing,
530   Ordering on her kingdom's rising glory.
At Juno's portal, under the arch of the temple,
She took her throne, a giver of law and justice,
A fair partitioner of toil and duty,
And suddenly Aeneas, from the crowd,
Saw Trojan men approaching, brave Cloanthus,
Sergestus, Antheus, and all those others
Whom the black storm had driven here and yonder.
This he cannot believe, nor can Achates,
Torn between fear and joy. They burn with ardor
540   To seek their comrades' handclasp, but confusion
Still holds them in the cloud: what can have happened?
They watch from the cover of mist: men still were coming
From all the ships, chosen, it seemed, as pleaders
For graciousness before the temple, calling
Aloud: what fortune had been theirs, he wonders,
Where had they left the ships; why were they coming?
They were given audience; Ilioneus,
Senior to all, began: "O Queen, whom Jove
Has given the founding of a great new city,
550   Has given to bridle haughty tribes with justice,
We, pitiful Trojans, over every ocean
Driven by storm, make our appeal: keep from us
The terrible doom of fire; protect our vessels;
Have mercy on a decent race; consider
Our lot with closer interest. We have not come
To ravish Libyan homes, or carry plunder
Down to the shore. We lack the arrogance
Of conquerors; there is no aggression in us.
There is a place which Greeks have given a name,
560   The Land in the West; it is powerful in arms,
Rich in its soil; Oenotrians used to live there,
And now, the story goes, a younger people
Inhabit it, calling themselves Italians
After their leader's name.[46] We were going there

---

[46] Italus, a legendary ruler.

When, big with storm and cloud, Orion[47] rising
Drove us on hidden quicksands, and wild winds
Scattered us over the waves, by pathless rocks
And the swell of the surge. A few of us have drifted
Here to your shores. What kind of men are these,
What barbarous land permits such attitudes?   570
We have been denied the welcome of the beach,
Forbidden to set foot on land; they rouse
All kinds of war against us. You despise,
It may be, human brotherhood, and arms
Wielded by men. But there are gods, remember,
Who care for right and wrong. Our king Aeneas
May be alive; no man was ever more just,
More decent ever, or greater in war and arms.
If fate preserves him still, if he still breathes
The welcome air, above the world of shadows,   580
Fear not; to have treated us with kindly service
Need bring you no repentance. We have cities
In Sicily as well, and King Acestes
Is one of us, from Trojan blood. We ask you
To let us beach our battered fleet, make ready
Beams from the forest timber, mend our oarage,
Seek Italy and Latium, glad at knowing
Our king and comrades rescued. But if safety
Is hopeless for him now, and Libyan water
Has been his grave, and if his son Iulus   590
Is desperate, or lost, grant us permission
At least to make for Sicily, whence we came here,
Where king Acestes has a dwelling for us."
The Trojans, as he ended, all were shouting,
And Dido, looking down, made a brief answer:
"I am sorry, Trojans; put aside your care,
Have no more fear. The newness of the kingdom
And our strict need compel me to such measures—
Sentries on every border, far and wide.
But who so ignorant as not to know   600

47 The constellation was believed to presage storms.

The nation of Aeneas, manly both
In deeds and people, and the city of Troy?
We are not as dull as that, we folk from Carthage;
The sun shines on us here. Whether you seek
The land in the west, the sometime fields of Saturn,[48]
Or the Sicilian realms and king Acestes,
I will help you to the limit; should you wish
To settle here and share this kingdom with me,
The city I found is yours; draw up your ships;
610   Trojan and Tyrian I treat alike.
Would, also, that your king were here, Aeneas,
Driven by that same wind. I will send good men
Along the coast to seek him, under orders
To scour all Libya; he may be wandering
Somewhere, in woods or town, surviving shipwreck."
      Aeneas and Achates both were eager
To break the cloud; the queen inspired their spirit
With her address. Achates asked Aeneas:—
"What do we do now, goddess-born? You see
620   They all are safe, our vessels and our comrades,
Only one missing, and we saw him drowning,
Ourselves, beneath the waves; all other things
Confirm what Venus told us." And as he finished,
The cloud around them broke, dissolved in air,
Illumining Aeneas, like a god,
Light radiant around his face and shoulders,
And Venus gave him all the bloom of youth,
Its glow, its liveliness, as the artist adds
Luster to ivory, or sets in gold
630   Silver or marble. No one saw him coming
Until he spoke:—"You seek me; here I am,
Trojan Aeneas, saved from the Libyan waves.
Worn out by all the perils of land and sea,
In need of everything, blown over the great world,
A remnant left by the Greeks, Dido, we lack

---

[48] In Roman myth, Saturn (the Greek Cronus), after being dethroned
by his son Jupiter as chief of the gods, went to Italy and presided over
a Golden Age of simplicity and goodness. Italy was also known to the
Greeks as "Hesperia" or the "land in the west."

The means to thank our only pitier
For offer of a city and a home.
If there is justice anywhere, if goodness
Means anything to any power, if gods
At all regard good people, may they give   640
The great rewards you merit. Happy the age,
Happy the parents who have brought you forth!
While rivers run to sea, while shadows move
Over the mountains, while the stars burn on,
Always, your praise, your honor, and your name,
Whatever land I go to, will endure."[49]
His hand went out to greet his men, Serestus,
Gyas, Cloanthus, Ilioneus,
The others in their turn. And Dido marvelled
At his appearance, first, and all that trouble   650
He had borne up under; there was a moment's silence
Before she spoke: "What chance, what violence,
O goddess-born, has driven you through danger,
From grief to grief? Are you indeed that son
Whom Venus bore Anchises? I remember
When Teucer came to Sidon,[50] as an exile
Seeking new kingdoms, and my father helped him,
My father, Belus, conqueror of Cyprus.
From that time on I have known about your city,
Your name, and the Greek kings, and the fall of Troy.   660
Even their enemies would praise the Trojans,
Or claim descent from Teucer's line. I bid you
Enter my house. I, too, am fortune-driven
Through many sufferings; this land at last
Has brought me rest. Not ignorant of evil,
I know one thing, at least,—to help the wretched."
And so she led Aeneas to the palace,
Proclaiming sacrifice at all the temples

[49] Aeneas' words turn out to be tragically ironic in the light of later developments in the poem and in history.

[50] This Teucer, a Greek exiled by his father, is not to be confused with the Teucer who was a legendary ancestor of the Trojans (who are therefore sometimes called Teucrians). Sidon was a city near Tyre, Dido's former home.

In honor of his welcome, and sent presents
670   To his comrades at the shore, a score of bullocks,
A hundred swine, a hundred ewes and lambs
In honor of the joyous day. The palace,
Within, is made most bright with pomp and splendor,
The halls prepared for feasting. Crimson covers
Are laid, with fine embroidery, and silver
Is heavy on the tables; gold, engraven,
Recalls ancestral prowess, a tale of heroes
From the race's first beginnings.
                                        And Aeneas,
Being a thoughtful father, speeds Achates
680   Back to the ships, with tidings for Iulus,
He is to join them; all the father's fondness
Is centred on the son. Orders are given
To bring gifts with him, saved from the Trojan ruins,
A mantle stiff with figures worked in gold;
A veil with gold acanthus[51] running through it,
Once worn by Helen, when she sailed from Sparta
Toward that forbidden marriage, a wondrous gift
Made by her mother Leda; and the sceptre
That Ilione, Priam's eldest daughter,
690   Had carried once; a necklace hung with pearls;
A crown of gold and jewels. Toward the ships
Achates sped the message.
                                        Meanwhile Venus
Plotted new stratagems, that Cupid, changed
In form and feature, should appear instead
Of young Ascanius,[52] and by his gifts
Inspire the queen to passion, with his fire
Burning her very bones. She feared the house
Held dubious intentions; men of Tyre
Were always two-faced people, and Juno's anger
700   Vexed her by night. She spoke to her wingèd son:—
"O my one strength and source of power, my son,
Disdainful of Jove's thunderbolt,[53] to you

---

[51] A leaflike pattern.
[52] Aeneas' son is sometimes called Ascanius, sometimes Iulus (as in line 680).
[53] That is, willing (as love is) to face any danger or opposition.

I come in prayer for help. You know that Juno
Is hateful toward Aeneas, keeps him tossing
All over the seas in bitterness; you have often
Grieved with me for your brother. And now Dido
Holds him with flattering words; I do not trust
Juno's ideas of welcome; she will never
Pause at a point like this. Therefore I purpose
To take the queen by cunning, put around her   710
A wall of flame, so that no power can change her,
So that a blazing passion for Aeneas
Will bind her to us. Listen! I will tell you
How you can manage this. The royal boy,
My greatest care, has heard his father's summons
To come to the city, bringing presents, rescued
From the flames of Troy and the sea; and he is ready.
But I will make him drowsy, carry him off
In slumber over Cythera, or hide him
Deep on Idalium in a secret bower[54]   720
Before he learns the scheme or interrupts it.
You, for one night, no more, assume his features,
The boy's familiar guise, yourself a boy,
So that when Dido takes you to her bosom
During the royal feast, with the wine flowing,
And happiness abounding, you, receiving
The sweetness of her kiss, will overcome her
With secret fire and poison."
                              For his mother
Cupid put off his wings, and went rejoicing
With young Iulus' stride; the real Iulus   730
Venus had lulled in soft repose, and borne him
Warm in her bosom to Idalian groves,
Where the soft marjoram cradled him with blossom
Exhaling shadowy sweetness over his slumber.
And, with Achates leading, Cupid came
Obedient to his mother, bringing gifts.

---

[54] Cythera was the island (south of Greece) where Venus touched shore
after being born of the sea-foam (her Greek name, Aphrodite, means "goddess of the froth, or foam"). Idalium, also associated with worship of
her, was a city in Cyprus, identified by alternative traditions as the site
of her birth.

The queen receives them, on a golden couch
Below the royal tapestries, where spreads
Of crimson wait Aeneas and his Trojans.
740   Servants bring water for their hands, and bread
In baskets, and fine napkins. At the fire
Are fifty serving-maids, to set the feast,
A hundred more, girls, and a hundred boys
To load the tables, and bring the goblets round,
As through the happy halls the Tyrians throng,
Admire the Trojan gifts, admire Iulus,
The young god with the glowing countenance,
The charming words, the robe, the saffron veil
Edged with acanthus. More than all the rest,
750   Disaster-bound, the unhappy queen takes fire,
And cannot have enough of looking, moved
Alike by boy and gifts. She watches him
Cling to his father's neck, or come to her
For fondling, and her eyes, her heart, receive him,
Alas, poor queen, not knowing what a god
Is plotting for her sorrow. He remembers
What Venus told him; she forgets a little
About Sychaeus;[55] the heart unused to love
Stirs with a living passion.
760   When the first quiet settled over the tables,
And the boards were cleared, they set the great bowls down,
Crowning the wine with garlands. A great hum
Runs through the halls, the voices reach the rafters,
The burning lamps below the fretted gold,
The torches flaring, put the night to rout.
The queen commands the loving-cup of Belus,
Heavy with gems and gold, and fills it full,
And silence fills the halls before her prayer:—
"Jupiter, giver of laws for host and guest,
770   Grant this to be a happy day for all,
Both Tyrians and travellers from Troy,
And something for our children to remember!
May Bacchus,[56] giver of joy, attend, and Juno

---

[55] Dido's late husband; see lines 356–74.
[56] God of wine.

Be kind, and all my Tyrians be friendly!"
She poured libation[57] on the table, touched
The gold rim with her lips, passed on the bowl
To Bitias, who dove deep, and other lords
Took up the challenge. And a minstrel played
A golden lyre, Iopas, taught by Atlas:[58]
Of the sun's labors and the wandering moon 780
He sang, whence came the race of beasts and man,
Whence rain and fire, the stars and constellations,
Why suns in winter hasten to the sea,
Or what delay draws out the dawdling nights.
The Tyrians roar, applauding, and the Trojans
Rejoice no less, and the poor queen prolongs
The night with conversation, drinking deep
Of her long love, and asking many questions
Of Priam, Hector; of the arms of Memnon;
How big Achilles was; and Diomedes, 790
What were his horses like? "Tell us, my guest,"
She pleads, "from the beginning, all the story,
The treachery of the Greeks, the wanderings,
The perils of the seven tiresome years."

---

[57] A drink-offering to the gods.
[58] The bard Iopas sings of astronomical science, which is associated with Atlas, the gigantic being who in mythology supports the heavens on his shoulders.

BOOK II

◻

The Fall of Troy

THEY all were silent, watching. From his couch
Aeneas spoke: "A terrible grief, O Queen,
You bid me live again, how Troy went down
Before the Greeks, her wealth, her pitiful kingdom,
Sorrowful things I saw myself, wherein
I had my share and more. Even Ulysses,
Even his toughest soldiery might grieve
At such a story.[1] And the hour is late
Already; night is sliding down the sky
And setting stars urge slumber. But if you long   10
To learn our downfall, to hear the final chapter
Of Troy, no matter how I shrink, remembering,
And turn away in grief, let me begin it.

Broken in war, set back by fate,[2] the leaders
Of the Greek host, as years went by, contrived,

---

[1] Ulysses is the Greek Odysseus, a prominent warrior in Homer's *Iliad* and the protagonist of his *Odyssey*, which tells of Odysseus' ten years of struggle to return after the war to his home, the island of Ithaca west of Greece. Homer presents Odysseus as bold, courageous, tough-minded, pragmatic, and, above all, ingeniously resourceful, a master of strategy. It was typical of him that, having originally resisted joining the expedition against Troy, he served with single-minded zeal once he was committed to the campaign. The Romans took a dimmer view of Odysseus, however: as despicable, treacherous, even cowardly.

[2] Tradition calls for epics to leap *in medias res*, "into the middle of things," supplying earlier events through long flashback narratives such as the story Aeneas here begins to relate. Virgil's main model is the long account of Odysseus' Mediterranean adventures that the hero narrates to the Phaeacians in Books IX through XII of Homer's *Odyssey*.

27

With Pallas' help, a horse as big as a mountain.
They wove its sides with planks of fir, pretending
This was an offering for their safe return,
At least, so rumor had it. But inside
20 They packed, in secret, into the hollow sides
The fittest warriors; the belly's cavern,
Huge as it was, was filled with men in armor.
There is an island, Tenedos, well-known,
Rich in the days of Priam; now it is only
A bay, and not too good an anchorage
For any ship to trust.[3] They sailed there, hid
On the deserted shore. We thought they had gone,
Bound for Mycenae,[4] and Troy was very happy,
Shaking off grief, throwing the gates wide open.
30 It was a pleasure, for a change, to go
See the Greek camp, station and shore abandoned;
Why, this was where Achilles camped, his minions,
The Dolopes, were here; and the fleet just yonder,
And that was the plain where we used to meet in battle.
Some of us stared in wonder at the horse,
Astounded by its vastness, Minerva's gift,
Death from the virgin goddess, had we known it.
Thymoetes, whether in treachery,[5] or because
The fates of Troy so ordered, was the first one
40 To urge us bring it in to the heart of the city,
But Capys, and some others, knowing better,
Suspicious of Greek plotting, said to throw it
Into the sea, to burn it up with fire,
To cut it open, see what there was inside it.
The wavering crowd could not make up its mind.

And, at that point, Laocoön came running,
With a great throng at his heels, down from the hilltop

---

[3] Ancient Troy was located on the eastern shore of the Aegean Sea, in what is now Turkey, at the southwestern end of the Dardanelles strait. Tenedos was an island near the mainland a little to the south.

[4] The home of Agamemnon, the Greek commander-in-chief; by extension, Greece.

[5] Thymoetes nursed a grudge against Priam, the Trojan king.

As fast as ever he could, and before he reached us,
Cried in alarm: 'Are you crazy, wretched people?
Do you think they have gone, the foe? Do you think that
    any   50
Gifts of the Greeks lack treachery? Ulysses,—
What was his reputation? Let me tell you,
Either the Greeks are hiding in this monster,
Or it's some trick of war, a spy, or engine,
To come down on the city. Tricky business
Is hiding in it. Do not trust it, Trojans,
Do not believe this horse. Whatever it may be,
I fear the Greeks, even when bringing presents.'
With that, he hurled the great spear at the side
With all the strength he had. It fastened, trembling,   60
And the struck womb rang hollow, a moaning sound.
He had driven us, almost, to let the light in
With the point of the steel, to probe, to tear, but something
Got in his way, the gods, or fate, or counsel,
Ill-omened, in our hearts; or Troy would be standing
And Priam's lofty citadel unshaken.

Meanwhile, some Trojan shepherds, pulling and hauling,
Had a young fellow, with his hands behind him,
Tied up, and they were dragging him to Priam.
He had let himself be taken so, on purpose,   70
To open Troy to the Greeks, a stranger, ready
For death or shifty cunning, a cool intriguer,
Let come what may. They crowd around to see him,
Take turns in making fun of him, that captive.
Listen, and learn Greek trickiness; learn all
Their crimes from one.
He stopped in the middle, frightened and defenceless,
Looked at the Trojan ranks,—'What land, what waters,
Can take me now?' he cried, 'There is nothing, nothing
Left for me any more, no place with the Greeks,   80
And here are the Trojans howling for my blood!'
Our mood was changed. We pitied him, poor fellow,
Sobbing his heart out. We bade him tell his story,
His lineage, his news: what can he count on,

The captive that he is? His fear had gone
As he began: 'O King, whatever happens,
I will tell the truth, tell all of it; to start with,
I own I am a Greek. Sinon is wretched,
Fortune has made him so, but she will never
90   Make him a liar. You may perhaps have heard
Rumors of Palamedes, son of Belus,[6]
A man of glorious fame. But the Greeks killed him,—
He was against the war, and so they killed him,
An innocent man, by perjury and lying
False witness. Now that he is dead they mourn him.
My father, his poor relative, had sent me
To soldier in his company; I was then
Scarcely beyond my boyhood. Palamedes
Held, for some time, some influence and standing
100   In royal councils, and we shared his glory,
But, and all men know this, Ulysses' hatred,
His cunning malice, pulled him down; thereafter
I lived in darkness, dragging out a lifetime
In sorrow for my innocent lord, and anger,
And in my anger I was very foolish,
I talked; I vowed, if I got home to Argos,
I would have vengeance: so I roused Ulysses
To hate me in his turn, and that began it,
Downfall and evil, Ulysses always trying
110   To frighten me with hint and accusation,
With rumors planted where the crowd would listen;
Oh yes, Ulysses knew what he was doing,
He never stopped, until with Calchas[7] working
Hand in glove with him—why am I telling this,
And what's the use? I am stalling. All the Greeks,
You think, are all alike; what more do you want?
Inflict the punishment. That would be something
Ulysses would rejoice in, and some others
Pay handsome money for!'

[6] Not to be confused with the Belus (Dido's father) mentioned in I.658.
Palamedes was hated by Ulysses because he had seen through and exposed
Ulysses' attempts to pose as mad and thus avoid the war.
[7] As a Greek prophet and priest, Calchas was expected to discover and
reveal the will of the gods.

But we were all on fire to hear him further.   120
Pelasgian[8] craft meant nothing to our folly.
Trembling and nervous, he resumed his lying:
'The Greeks were tired of the long war; they often
Wanted to sail from Troy for home. Oh, would
That they had only done it! But a storm
Would cut them off, or the wrong wind terrify them.
Especially, just after the horse was finished,
With the joined planks of maple, all the heaven
Roared loud with storm-clouds. In suspense and terror
We sent Eurypylus to ask Apollo   130
What could be done; the oracle was gloomy,
Foreboding: "Blood, O Greeks, and a slain virgin
Appeased the winds when first you came here; blood
Must pay for your return, a life be given,
An Argive life."[9] The word came to our ears
With terror in it, our blood ran cold in our veins,
For whom was fate preparing? who would be
The victim of Apollo? Then Ulysses
Dragged Calchas into our midst, with a great uproar,
Trying his best to make the prophet tell us   140
What the gods wanted. And there were many then
Who told me what was coming, or kept silent
Because they saw, and all too well, the scheme
Ulysses had in mind. For ten days Calchas
Said nothing at all, hid in his tent, refusing
To have a word of his pronounce the sentence,
And all the time Ulysses kept on shouting,
Till Calchas broke, and doomed me to the altar.
And all assented; what each man had feared
In his own case, he bore with great composure   150
When turned another way.
The terrible day was almost on me; fillets[10]

---

[8] Here a synonym for *Greek*.

[9] Apollo was the prophet-god; the main center of prophecy for the Greeks was his temple at Delphi, where his oracles were pronounced. The "slain virgin" was Agamemnon's daughter Iphigenia, who was sacrificed to appease divine anger and thus gain for the Greeks favorable winds when they first set out for Troy. *Argive* here means *Greek*.

[10] Headbands, worn by the sacrificial victim.

Were ready for my temples, the salted meal
Prepared, the altars standing. But I fled,
I tore myself away from death, I admit it,
I hid all night in sedge and muddy water
At the edge of the lake, hoping, forever hoping,
They might set sail. And now I hope no longer
To see my home, my parents, or my children,
160   Poor things, whom they will kill because I fled them,
Whom they will murder for my sacrilege.
But oh, by the gods above, by any power
That values truth, by any uncorrupted
Remnant of faith in all the world, have pity,
Have pity on a soul that bears such sorrow,
More than I ever deserved.'
He had no need to ask us. Priam said,
Untie him, and we did so with a promise
To spare his life. Our king, with friendly words,
170   Addressed him, saying, 'Whoever you are, forget
The Greeks, from now on. You are ours; but tell me
Why they have built this monstrous horse? who made it,
Who thought of it? What is it, war-machine,
Religious offering?' And he, instructed
In every trick and artifice, made answer,
Lifting his hands, now free: 'Eternal fires,
Inviolable godhead, be my witness,
You altars, you accursèd swords, you fillets
Which I as victim wore, I had the right
180   To break those solemn bonds, I had the right
To hate those men, to bring whatever they hide
Into the light and air; I am bound no longer
To any country, any laws, but, Trojans,
Keep to the promise, if I tell the truth,
If I pay back with interest.
All the Greek hope, since first the war began,
Rested in Pallas, always. But Ulysses,
The crime-contriver, and the son[11] of Tydeus

---

[11] Diomedes.

Attacked Minerva's temple, stole her image
Out of the holy shrine, and slew the guards,   190
And laid their bloody hands upon the goddess,[12]
And from that time the Danaan[13] hopes were broken,
Faltered and failed. It was no doubtful anger
Pallas revealed; she gave them signs and portents.
From her image in the camp the upraised eyes
Shot fire, and sweat ran salty down the limbs,
Thrice from the ground she seemed to flash and leap
With vibrant spear and clashing shield. The priest,
Calchas, made prophecy: they must take to flight
Over the sea, and Troy could not be taken   200
Without new omens; they must go to Argos,
Bring back the goddess again, whom they have taken
In curved ships over the sea. And if they have gone,
They are bound for home, Mycenae, for new arms,
New gods, new soldiers; they will be here again
When least expected. Calchas' message warned them,
And so they built this image, to replace
The one they had stolen, a gigantic offering
For a tremendous sacrilege. It was Calchas,
Again, who bade them build a mass so mighty   210
It almost reached the stars, too big to enter
Through any gate, or be brought inside the walls.
For if your hands should damage it, destruction,
(May God avert it) would come upon the city,
But if your hands helped bring it home, then Asia
Would be invading Greece, and doom await
Our children's children.'
                              We believed him, we
Whom neither Diomede nor great Achilles
Had taken, nor ten years, nor that armada,
A thousand ships of war. But Sinon did it   220

[12] That is, upon the statue of Pallas Athena, or Minerva, which the two
men thus defiled. It was believed that the security of Troy depended on
the preservation of this statue.
[13] Greek (From *Danaus,* the name of a legendary ruler of Argos, in
Greece).

By perjury and guile.
                      Then something else,
Much greater and more terrible, was forced
Upon us, troubling our unseeing spirits.
Laocoön, allotted priest of Neptune,
Was slaying a great bull beside the altars,
When suddenly, over the tranquil deep
From Tenedos,—I shudder even now,
Recalling it—there came a pair of serpents
With monstrous coils, breasting the sea, and aiming
230   Together for the shore. Their heads and shoulders
Rose over the waves, upright, with bloody crests,
The rest of them trailing along the water,
Looping in giant spirals; the foaming sea
Hissed under their motion. And they reached the land,
Their burning eyes suffused with blood and fire,
Their darting tongues licking the hissing mouths.
Pale at the sight, we fled. But they went on
Straight toward Laocoön, and first each serpent
Seized in its coils his two young sons, and fastened
240   The fangs in those poor bodies. And the priest
Struggled to help them, weapons in his hand.
They seized him, bound him with their mighty coils,
Twice round his waist, twice round his neck, they squeezed
With scaly pressure, and still towered above him.
Straining his hands to tear the knots apart,
His chaplets[14] stained with blood and the black poison,
He uttered horrible cries, not even human,
More like the bellowing of a bull when, wounded,
It flees the altar, shaking from the shoulder
250   The ill-aimed axe. And on the pair went gliding
To the highest shrine, the citadel of Pallas,
And vanished underneath the feet of the goddess
And the circle of her shield.
                            The people trembled
Again; they said Laocoön deserved it,

---

[14] Bands or garlands for the head; part of the priest's ritual dress. There
is a famous statue, in the Vatican, depicting the struggle of Laocoön with
the two serpents.

Having, with spear, profaned the sacred image.
It must be brought to its place, they cried, the goddess
Must be appeased. We broke the walls, exposing
The city's battlements, and all were busy
Helping the work, with rollers underfoot
And ropes around the neck. It climbed our walls,   260
The deadly engine. Boys, unwedded girls
Sang alleluias round it, all rejoicing
To have a hand on the tow-rope. It came nearer,
Threatening, gliding, into the very city.
O motherland! O Ilium,[15] home of gods,
O walls of Troy! Four times it stopped, four times
The sound of arms came from it, and we pressed on,
Unheedful, blind in madness, till we set it,
Ill-omened thing, on the citadel we worshipped.
And even when Cassandra gave us warning,   270
We never believed her; so a god had ordered.[16]
That day, our last, poor wretches, we were happy,
Garlanding the temples of the gods
All through the town.
              And the sky turned, and darkness
Came from the ocean, the great shade covering earth
And heaven, and the trickery of the Greeks.
Sprawling along the walls, the Trojans slumbered,
Sleep holding their weary limbs, and the Greek armada,
From Tenedos, under the friendly silence
Of a still moon, came surely on. The flagship   280
Blazed at the masthead with a sudden signal,
And Sinon, guarded by the fates, the hostile
Will of the gods, swung loose the bolts; the Greeks
Came out of the wooden womb. The air received them,
The happy captains, Sthenelus, Ulysses,
Thessandrus, Acamas, Achilles' son
Called Neoptolemus, Thoas, Machaon,
Epeos, who designed the thing,—they all
Came sliding down the rope, and Menelaus

---

[15] Another name for Troy.
[16] Cassandra was a daughter of the Trojan royal family; Apollo gave her powers to prophesy the truth but, in revenge for her rejection of his love, doomed her to be always disbelieved.

290 Was with them in the storming of a city
Buried in sleep and wine. The watch was murdered,
The open doors welcome the rush of comrades,
They marshal the determined ranks for battle.
    It was the time when the first sleep begins
For weary mortals, heaven's most welcome gift.
In sleep, before my eyes, I seemed to see
Hector, most sorrowful, black with bloody dust,
Torn, as he had been, by Achilles' car,
The thong-marks on his swollen feet.[17] How changed
300 He was from that great Hector who came, once,
Triumphant in Achilles' spoil, from hurling
Fire at the Grecian ships. With ragged beard,
Hair matted with his blood, wearing the wounds
He earned around the walls of Troy, he stood there.
It seemed that I spoke first:—'O light of Troy,
Our surest hope, we have long been waiting for you,
What shores have kept you from us? Many deaths,
Much suffering, have visited our city,
And we are tired. Why do I see these wounds?
310 What shame has caused them?' Those were foolish questions;
He made no answer but a sigh or a groan,
And then: 'Alas, O goddess-born! Take flight,
Escape these flames! The enemy has the walls,
Troy topples from her lofty height; enough
Has been paid out to Priam and to country.
Could any hand have saved them, Hector's would have.
Troy trusts to you her household gods, commending
Her holy things to you; take them, companions
Of destiny; seek walls for them, and a city
320 To be established, a long sea-wandering over.'
From the inner shrine he carried Vesta's chaplets
In his own hands, and her undying fire.[18]

    Meanwhile, the city is all confusion and sorrow;
My father Anchises' house, remote and sheltered

---

[17] For the death of Hector, see I.507–12.
[18] The hearth-fire (of which Vesta is goddess) is to be transported to a new city.

Among its trees, was not so far away
But I could hear the noises, always clearer,
The thickening din of war. Breaking from sleep,
I climb to the roof-top, listening and straining
The way a shepherd does on the top of a mountain
When fire goes over the corn, and the winds are roaring,   330
Or the rush of a mountain torrent drowns the fields
And the happy crops and the work of men and oxen
And even drags great trees over. And then I knew
The truth indeed; the craft of the Greeks was hidden
No longer from my sight. The house of a neighbor,
Deiphobus, went up in flames; next door,
Ucalegon was burning. Sigeum's water
Gave back the glow.[19] Men shouted, and the trumpets
Blared loud. I grab my arms, with little purpose,
There was no sense in it, but my heart was burning   340
To mass a band for war, rush to the hilltop
With comrades at my side. Anger and frenzy
Hurry me on. A decent death in battle
Is a helpful thought, sometimes.

    And here came Panthus, running from the weapons,
Priest of Apollo, and a son of Othrys,
With holy relics in his hands, and dragging
His little grandson, here came Panthus, running
In madness to my door. 'How goes it, Panthus?
What stronghold still is ours?' I had hardly spoken,   350
When he began, with a groan: 'It has come, this day
Will be our last, and we can not escape it.
Trojans we have been, Troy has been, and glory
Is ours no more. Fierce Jupiter has taken
Everything off to Argos, and Greeks lord it
In a town on fire. The horse, high in the city,
Pours out armed men, and Sinon, arrogant victor,
Lights up more fires. The gates are standing open,
And men are there by the thousands, ever as many
As came once from Mycenae; others block   360

[19] The death of Deiphobus, who succeeded Paris as Helen's husband,
is described more fully, in his own words, in VI.518–61. Ucalegon was
one of the king Priam's advisors. Sigeum was a cape near Troy.

The narrow streets, with weapons drawn; the blades
Flash in the dark; the point is set for murder.
A few of the guards are trying, striking blindly,
For all the good it does.'

   His words, or the gods' purpose, swept me on
Toward fire and arms, where the grim furies call,
And the clamor and confusion, reaching heaven.
Ripheus joined me, Epytus, mighty in arms,
Came to my side in the moonlight, Hypanis, Dymas,
370   And young Coroebus, Mygdon's son, poor youngster,
Mad with a hopeless passion for Cassandra,
He wanted to help Priam, but never heeded
The warnings of his loved one.
                    As they ranged
Themselves for battle, eager, I addressed them:
'O brave young hearts, it will do no good; no matter.
Even if your will is fixed, to follow a leader
Taking the final risk, you can't help seeing
The fortune of our state. The gods have gone,
They have left their shrines and altars, and the power
380   They once upheld is fallen. You are helping
A town already burnt. So let us die,
Rush into arms. One safety for the vanquished
Is to have hope of none.
                They were young, and angry.
Like wolves, marauders in black mist, whom hunger
Drives blindly on, whose whelps, abandoned, wait them
Dry-jawed, so we went on, through foes, through weapons,
To certain death; we made for the heart of the city,
Black night around us with its hollow shadow.
Who could explain that night's destruction, equal
390   Its agony with tears? The ancient city,
A power for many years, comes down, and corpses
Lie littering the streets and homes and altars.
Not only Trojans die. The old-time valor
Returns to the vanquished heart, and the Greek victors
Know what it is to fall. Everywhere sorrow,
Everywhere panic, everywhere the image
Of death, made manifold.

Out of a crowd of Greeks comes one Androgeos,
Thinking us allies, hailing us as friendly:
'Why men, where have you been, you dawdling fellows?   400
Hurry along! Here is plunder for the taking,
Others are busy at it, and you just coming
From the high ships!' And then he knew he had blundered;
He had fallen in with foes, who gave no answer.
He stopped, stepped back, like a man who treads on a serpent
Unseen in the rough brush, and then in panic
Draws back as the purple neck swells out in anger.
Even so, Androgeos pulled away in terror.
We rush them, swarm all over them; they are frightened,
They do not know their ground, and fortune favors   410
Our first endeavor. Coroebus, a little crazy
With nerve and luck, cries out: 'Comrades, where fortune
First shows the way and sides with us, we follow.
Let us change our shields, put on the Grecian emblems!
All's fair in war: we lick them or we trick them,
And what's the odds?' He takes Androgeos' helmet,
Whose plume streams over his head, takes up the shield
With proud device, and fits the sword to his side.
And Ripheus does the same, and so does Dymas,
And all the others, happily, being armed   420
With spoil, new-won. We join the Greeks, all going
Under no gods of ours, in the night's darkness
Wade into many a fight, and Greeks by the dozens
We send to hell. And some of them in panic
Speed to the ships; they know that shore, and trust it,
And some of them—these were the abject cowards—
Climb scrambling up the horse's sides, again
Take refuge in the womb.

It is not for men to trust unwilling gods.
Cassandra was being dragged from Pallas' temple,   430
Her hair loosed to the wind, her eyes turned upward
To heaven for mercy; they had bound her hands.
Coroebus could not bear that sight; in madness
He threw himself upon them, and he died.
We followed, all of us, into the thick of it,
And were cut down, not only by Greeks; the rooftops,

Held by our friends, rained weapons: we were wearing
Greek crests and armor, and they did not know us.
And the Greeks came on, shouting with anger, burning
440   To foil that rescue; there was Menelaus,
And Agamemnon, and the savage Ajax,
And a whole army of them. Hurricanes
Rage the same way, when winds from different quarters
Clash in the sky, and the forest groans, and Neptune
Storms underneath the ocean. Those we routed
Once in the dark came back again from the byways
And alleys of the town; they mark our shields,
Our lying weapons, and our foreign voices.
Of course we are outnumbered. Peneleus
450   It was, who slew Coroebus, at the altar
Sacred to Pallas. Ripheus fell, a man
Most just of all the Trojans, most fair-minded.
The gods thought otherwise. Hypanis, Dymas,
Were slain by their own men, and Panthus' goodness
Was no protection, nor his priestly office.
I call to witness Troy, her fires, her ashes,
And the last agonies of all our people
That in that hour I ran from no encounter
With any Greek, and if the fates had been
460   For me to fall in battle, there I earned it.
The current swept me off, with two companions,
One, Iphitus, too slow with age, the other,
Pelias, limping from Ulysses' wound.
The noise kept calling us to Priam's palace.

There might have been no fighting and no dying
Through all the city, such a battle raged
Here, from the ground to roof-top. At the threshold
Waves of assault were breaking, and the Greeks
Were climbing, rung by rung, along the ladders,
470   Using one hand, the right one up and forward
Over the battlements, the left one thrust
In the protecting shield. And over their heads
The Trojans pried up towers and planking, wrecking
The building; gilded beams, the spoils of their fathers,

Were ample weapons for the final moment.
Some had the doorways blocked, others, behind them,
Were ready with drawn swords. We had a moment
When help seemed possible: new reinforcement
Might yet relieve the palace.
There was a secret entrance there, a passage   480
All the way through the building, a postern gate,
Where, while the kingdom stood, Andromache
Would go, alone, or bring the little boy,
Astyanax, to Hector's father and mother.[20]
I climbed to the top of the roof, where the poor Trojans
Were hurling down their unavailing darts.
A tower stood on the very edge, a look-out
Over all Troy, the ships and camp of the Greeks.
This we attacked with steel, where the joints were weakest,
And pried it up, and shoved it over. It crashed,   490
A noisy ruin, over the hostile columns;
But more kept coming up; the shower of stones
And darts continued raining.
Before the entrance, at the very threshold,
Stood Pyrrhus,[21] flashing proudly in bronze light,
Sleek as a serpent coming into the open,
Fed on rank herbs, wintering under the ground,
The old slough cast, the new skin shining, rolling
His slippery length, reaching his neck to the sun,
While the forked tongue darts from the mouth. Automedon   500
Was with him, Periphas, Achilles' driver,
A giant of a man, and the host from Scyros,[22]
All closing in on the palace, and hurling flames.
Among the foremost, Pyrrhus, swinging an axe,
Burst through, wrenched the bronze doors out of their
      hinges,
Smashed through the panelling, turned it into a window.
The long halls came to view, the inner chambers
Of Priam and the older kings; they see

---

[20] Andromache was the wife of Hector and mother of Astyanax. Hector's
parents were Priam and Hecuba, king and queen of Troy.
[21] Achilles' son, fierce like his war-loving father.
[22] An island east of Greece; the home of Pyrrhus.

Armed warriors at the threshold.
510 Within, it is all confusion, women wailing,
Pitiful noise, groaning, and blows; the din
Reaches the golden stars. The trembling mothers
Wander, not knowing where, or find a spot
To cling to; they would hold and kiss the doors.
Pyrrhus comes on, aggressive as his father;
No barrier holds him back; the gate is battered
As the ram[23] smashes at it; the doors come down.
Force finds a way: the Greeks pour in, they slaughter
The first ones in their path; they fill the courtyard
520 With soldiery, wilder than any river
In flood over the banks and dikes and ploughland.
I saw them, Pyrrhus, going mad with murder,
And Atreus' twin sons,[24] and Hecuba
I saw, and all her daughters, and poor old Priam,
His blood polluting the altars he had hallowed.
The fifty marriage-chambers,[25] the proud hope
Of an everlasting line, are violated,
The doors with the golden spoil are turned to splinters.
Whatever the fire has spared the Greeks take over.
530   You would ask, perhaps, about the fate of Priam?
When he saw the city fall, and the doors of the palace
Ripped from the hinge, and the enemy pouring in,
Old as he was, he went and found his armor,
Unused so many years, and his old shoulders
Shook as he put it on. He took his sword,
A useless weapon, and, doomed to die, went rushing
Into the midst of the foe. There was an altar
In the open court-yard, shaded by a laurel
Whose shadow darkened the household gods, and here
540 Hecuba and her daughters had come thronging,
Like doves by a black storm driven. They were praying
Here at the altar, and clinging to the gods,
Whatever image was left. And the queen saw Priam

[23] The battering-ram.
[24] Agamemnon and Menelaus.
[25] The quarters of Priam's fifty sons and their wives. Priam also had
fifty daughters.

In the arms of his youth. 'O my unhappy husband,'
She cried, 'have you gone mad, to dress yourself
For battle, so? It is all no use; the time
Needs better help than yours; not even my Hector
Could help us now. Come to me, come to the altar;
It will protect us, or at least will let us
Die all together.' And she drew him to her.   550
   Just then through darts, through weapons, came Polites,
A son of Priam, fleeing deadly Pyrrhus,
Down the long colonnades and empty hallways,
Wounded, and Pyrrhus after him, vicious, eager
For the last spear-thrust, and he drives it home;
Polites falls, and his life goes out with his blood,
Father and mother watching. And then Priam,
In the very grip of death, cried out in anger:—
'If there is any righteousness in heaven,
To care about such wickedness, the gods   560
Will have the right reward and thanks to offer
A man like this, who has made a father witness
The murder of his son, the worst pollution!
You claim to be Achilles' son. You liar!
Achilles had some reverence, respected
A suppliant's right and trust; he gave me back
My Hector's lifeless body for the tomb,
And let me go to my kingdom.'[26] With the word
He flung a feeble spear, which dropped, deflected
From the rough bronze; it had hung there for a moment.   570
And Pyrrhus sneered: 'So, go and tell my father
The latest news: do not forget to mention,
Old messenger-boy, my villainous behavior,
And what a bastard Pyrrhus is. Now die!'
He dragged the old man, trembling, to the altar,
Slipping in his son's blood; he grabbed his hair
With the left hand, and the right drove home the sword
Deep in the side, to the hilt. And so fell Priam,

[26] In *The Iliad*, Book XXIV, Homer tells how Achilles, after slaying Hector, agreed to return the corpse to his father Priam. Achilles himself was later slain, by an arrow from Paris' bow.

Who had seen Troy burn and her walls come down, once
    monarch,
580 Proud ruler over the peoples and lands of Asia.
He lies, a nameless body, on the shore,
Dismembered, huge, the head torn from the shoulders.
    Grim horror, then, came home to me. I saw
My father when I saw the king, the life
Going out with the cruel wound. I saw Creusa[27]
Forsaken, my abandoned home, Iulus,
My little son. I looked around. They all
Had gone, exhausted, flung down from the walls,
Or dead in the fire, and I was left alone.
590   And I saw Helen,[28] hiding, of all places,
At Vesta's shrine,[29] and clinging there in silence,
But the bright flames lit the scene. That hated woman,
Fearing both Trojan anger and Greek vengeance,
A common fury to both lands, was crouching
Beside the altar. Anger flared up in me
For punishment and vengeance. Should she then,
I thought, come home to Sparta safe, uninjured
Walk through Mycenae,[30] a triumphant queen?
See husband, home, parents and children, tended
600 By Trojan slave-girls? This, with Priam fallen
And Troy burnt down, and the shore soaked in blood?
Never! No memorable name, I knew,
Was won by punishing women, yet, for me,
There might be praise for the just abolition

---

[27] Aeneas' wife.

[28] There is some question about the authenticity of the Helen episode
in lines 590–607, which are absent from the earliest manuscripts of *The
Aeneid* and were provided by Servius, an ancient commentator. According
to him, the lines were deleted from Virgil's manuscript by the men directed
to edit the poem (which Virgil never put into finished form) after the
poet died—their reasons, Servius argued, being that Aeneas' wrath toward
a woman is unchivalrous and that the passage is inconsistent with the
description of Helen in VI.538–59. The lines may well be the work of
Virgil, but how he meant to work them into the poem is uncertain.

[29] It is ironic that the adulteress Helen should seek safety in the temple
of Vesta, goddess of the hearth and thus the symbol of home and family.

[30] That is, Greece, signified here by the home city of Agamemnon, the
Greek commander and Helen's brother-in-law. Helen's own home was
Sparta, the city of her husband Menelaus.

Of this unholiness, and satisfaction
In vengeance for the ashes of my people.
All this I may have said aloud, in frenzy,
As I rushed on, when to my sight there came
A vision of my lovely mother, radiant
In the dark night, a goddess manifest,   610
As tall and fair as when she walks in heaven.
She caught me by the hand and stopped me:—'Son,
What sorrow rouses this relentless anger,
This violence?[31] Do you care for me no longer?
Consider others first, your aged father,
Anchises; is your wife Creusa living?
Where is Iulus? Greeks are all around them,
Only my love between them, fire and sword.
It is not for you to blame the Spartan woman,
Daughter of Tyndareus, or even Paris.   620
The gods are the ones, the high gods are relentless,
It is they who bring this power down, who topple
Troy from the high foundation. Look! Your vision
Is mortal dull, I will take the cloud away,—
Fear not a mother's counsel. Where you see
Rock torn from rock, and smoke and dust in billows,
Neptune is working, plying the trident, prying
The walls from their foundations. And see Juno,
Fiercest of all, holding the Scaean gates,[32]
Girt with the steel, and calling from the ships   630
Implacable companions. On the towers,—
Turn, and be certain—Pallas takes command
Gleaming with Gorgon and storm-cloud.[33] Even Jove,
Our father, nerves the Greeks with fire and spirit,
And spurs the other gods against the Trojans.
Hasten the flight, my son; no other labor
Waits for accomplishment. I promise safety
Until you reach your father's house.' She had spoken

---

[31] Although she is Aeneas' mother, Venus as goddess of love naturally
protects Helen, the most beautiful of all women.

[32] The principal gates of Troy, which had faced the Greek besiegers.

[33] On the *aegis*, the shield or breastplate of Pallas Athena (Minerva),
was depicted the head of Medusa, one of the female monsters known as
Gorgons; Medusa turned to stone anyone who gazed on her.

And vanished in the thickening night of shadows.
640   Dread shapes come into vision, mighty powers,
Great gods at war with Troy, which, so it seemed,
Was sinking as I watched, with the same feeling
As when on mountain-tops you see the loggers
Hacking an ash-tree down, and it always threatens
To topple, nodding a little, and the leaves
Trembling when no wind stirs, and dies of its wounds
With one long loud last groan, and dirt from the ridges
Heaves up as it goes down with roots in air.
Divinity my guide, I leave the roof-top,
650   I pass unharmed through enemies and blazing,
Weapons give place to me, and flames retire.

    At last I reached the house, I found my father,
The first one that I looked for. I meant to take him
To the safety of the hills, but he was stubborn,
Refusing longer life or barren exile,
Since Troy was dead. 'You have the strength,' he told me,
'You are young enough, take flight. For me, had heaven
Wanted to save my life, they would have spared
This home for me. We have seen enough destruction,
660   More than enough, survived a captured city.
Speak to me as a corpse laid out for burial,
A quick farewell, and go. Death I shall find
With my own hand;[34] the enemy will pity,
Or look for spoil. The loss of burial
Is nothing at all.[35] I have been living too long
Hated by gods and useless, since the time
Jove blasted me with lightning wind and fire.'[36]
He would not move, however we wept, Creusa,
Ascanius, all the house, insistent, pleading
670   That he should not bring all to ruin with him.
He would not move, he would not listen. Again
I rush to arms, I pray for death; what else

[34] Anchises means that he will go down fighting.

[35] Failure to receive proper burial was in fact considered a calamitous misfortune; see the Palinurus episode in Books V and VI.

[36] The god took revenge because Anchises boasted of Venus' love for him.

Was left to me? 'Dear father, were you thinking
I could abandon you, and go? what son
Could bear a thought so monstrous? If the gods
Want nothing to be left of so great a city,
If you are bound, or pleased, to add us all
To the wreck of Troy, the way is open for it—
Pyrrhus will soon be here; from the blood of Priam
He comes; he slays the son before the father,   680
The sire at the altar-stone; O my dear mother,
Was it for this you saved me, brought me through
The fire and sword, to see our enemies
Here in the very house, and wife and son
And father murdered in each other's blood?
Bring me my arms; the last light calls the conquered.
Let me go back to the Greeks, renew the battle,
We shall not all of us die unavenged.'
    Sword at my side, I was on the point of going,
Working the left arm into the shield. Creusa   690
Clung to me on the threshold, held my feet,
And made me see my little son:—'Dear husband,
If you are bent on dying, take us with you,
But if you think there is any hope in fighting,
And you should know, stay and defend the house!
To whom are we abandoned, your father and son,
And I, once called your wife?' She filled the house
With moaning outcry. And then something happened,
A wonderful portent. Over Iulus' head,
Between our hands and faces, there appeared   700
A blaze of gentle light; a tongue of flame,
Harmless and innocent, was playing over
The softness of his hair, around his temples.
We were afraid, we did our best to quench it
With our own hands, or water, but my father
Raised joyous eyes to heaven, and prayed aloud:—
'Almighty Jupiter, if any prayer
Of ours has power to move you, look upon us,
Grant only this, if we have ever deserved it,
Grant us a sign, and ratify the omen!'   710
He had hardly spoken, when thunder on the left
Resounded, and a shooting star from heaven

Drew a long trail of light across the shadows.
We saw it cross above the house, and vanish
In the woods of Ida,[37] a wake of gleaming light
Where it had sped, and a trail of sulphurous odor.
This was a victory: my father rose
In worship of the gods and the holy star,
Crying: 'I follow, son, wherever you lead;

720   There is no delay, not now; Gods of my fathers,
Preserve my house, my grandson; yours the omen,
And Troy is in your keeping. O my son,
I yield, I am ready to follow.' But the fire
Came louder over the walls, the flames rolled nearer
Their burning tide. 'Climb to my shoulders, father,
It will be no burden, so we are together,
Meeting a common danger or salvation.
Iulus, take my hand; Creusa, follow
A little way behind. Listen, you servants!

730   You will find, when you leave the city, an old temple
That once belonged to Ceres;[38] it has been tended
For many years with the worship of our fathers.
There's a little hill there, and a cypress tree;
And that's where we shall meet, one way or another.
And one thing more: you, father, are to carry
The holy objects and the gods of the household,
My hands are foul with battle and blood, I could not
Touch them without pollution.
                                        I bent down
And over my neck and shoulders spread the cover

740   Of a tawny lion-skin, took up my burden;
Little Iulus held my hand, and trotted,
As best he could, beside me; Creusa followed.
We went on through the shadows. I had been
Brave, so I thought, before, in the rain of weapons
And the cloud of massing Greeks. But now I trembled
At every breath of air, shook at a whisper,
Fearful for both my burden and companion.
    I was near the gates, and thinking we had made it,

[37] A mountain near Troy.
[38] Goddess of grain and the harvest (hence our word *cereal*).

But there was a sound, the tramp of marching feet,
And many of them, it seemed; my father, peering   750
Through the thick gloom, cried out:—'Son, they are coming!
Flee, flee! I see their shields, their gleaming bronze.'
Something or other took my senses from me
In that confusion. I turned aside from the path,
I do not know what happened then. Creusa
Was lost; she had missed the road, or halted, weary,
For a brief rest. I do not know what happened,
She was not seen again; I had not looked back,
Nor even thought about her, till we came
To Ceres' hallowed home. The count was perfect,   760
Only one missing there, the wife and mother.
Whom did I not accuse, of gods and mortals,
Then in my frenzy? What worse thing had happened
In the city overthrown? I left Anchises,
My son, my household gods, to my companions,
In a hiding-place in the valley; and I went back
Into the city again, wearing my armor,
Ready, still one more time, for any danger.
I found the walls again, the gate's dark portals,
I followed my own footsteps back, but terror,   770
Terror and silence were all I found. I went
On to my house. She might, just might, have gone there.
Only the Greeks were there, and fire devouring
The very pinnacles. I tried Priam's palace;
In the empty courtyards Phoenix and Ulysses
Guarded the spoils piled up at Juno's altar.[39]
They had Trojan treasure there, loot from the altars,
Great drinking-bowls of gold, and stolen garments,
And human beings. A line of boys and women
Stood trembling there.   780
I took the risk of crying through the shadows,
Over and over, 'Creusa!' I kept calling,
'Creusa!' and 'Creusa!' but no answer.
No sense, no limit, to my endless rushing
All through the town; and then at last I saw her,
Or thought I did, her shadow a little taller

[39] Phoenix had been a friend and mentor of Achilles.

Than I remembered. And she spoke to me
Beside myself with terror:—'O dear husband,
What good is all this frantic grief? The gods
790   Have willed it so, Creusa may not join you
Out of this city; Jupiter denies it.
Long exile lies ahead, and vast sea-reaches
The ships must furrow, till you come to land
Far in the West; rich fields are there, and a river
Flowing with gentle current; its name is Tiber.[40]
And happy days await you there, a kingdom,
A royal wife. Banish the tears of sorrow
Over Creusa lost. I shall never see
The arrogant houses of the Myrmidons,[41]
800   Nor be a slave to any Grecian woman;
I am a Dardan[42] woman; I am the wife
Of Venus' son; it is Cybele who keeps me
Here on these shores.[43] And now farewell, and love
Our son.' I wept, there was more to say; she left me,
Vanishing into empty air. Three times
I reached out toward her, and three times her image
Fled like the breath of a wind or a dream on wings.
The night was over; I went back to my comrades.
    I was surprised to find so many more
810   Had joined us, ready for exile, pitiful people,
Mothers, and men, and children, streaming in
From everywhere, looking for me to lead them
Wherever I would. Over the hills of Ida
The morning-star was rising; in the town
The Danaans held the gates, and help was hopeless.
I gave it up, I lifted up my father,
Together we sought the hills.

---

[40] The river of Rome.

[41] The Greek soldiers who had been led by Achilles.

[42] Trojan (From *Dardanus*, the name of the founder of the Trojan royal line).

[43] Cybele was a goddess associated with the region of Troy. She was called the "mother of the gods," being identified with Rhea, mother of Jupiter by Cronos (the Roman Saturn). Creusa apparently has not died a normal death but rather has been inducted into the heavenly service of the goddess.

BOOK III

□

The Wanderings
of Aeneas

"A FTER the gods' decision to overthrow
The Asian world, the innocent house of Priam,
And the proud city, built by Neptune,[1] smoked
From the ruined ground, we were driven, different ways,
By heaven's auguries, seeking lands forsaken.
Below Antandros, under Phrygian Ida,[2]
We built a fleet, and gathered men, uncertain
Of either direction or settlement. The summer
Had scarce begun, when at my father's orders,
We spread our sails. I wept as I left the harbor,   10
The fields where Troy had been. I was borne, an exile,
Over the deep, with son, companions, household,
And household gods.
                    Far off there lies a land,
Sacred to Mars; the Thracians[3] used to till it,
Whose king was fierce Lycurgus; they were friendly,
Of old, to Troy, when we were prosperous. Hither

---

[1] The walls of Troy had been built by Neptune and Apollo, but the Trojan king, Laomedon, had balked at paying the gods their promised wages. See also line 248.
[2] Antandros was a city near Troy. Phrygia was the region around Troy.
[3] Inhabitants of Thrace, a region north of the Aegean Sea, northwest of the Hellespont, or Dardanelles.

51

I sailed, and on its curving shore established
A city site; Aeneadae, I called it.
This I began, not knowing fate was adverse.

20　　　I was offering my mother proper homage,
And other gods, to bless the new beginnings,
I had a white bull ready as a victim
To the king of the gods. There was a mound nearby,
Bristling with myrtle and with cornel-bushes.
I needed greenery to veil the altar,
But as I struggled with the leafy branches,
A fearful portent[4] met my gaze. Black drops
Dripped from the ends of the roots, black blood was falling
On the torn ground, and a cold chill went through me.
30　I tried again; the shoot resisted; blood
Followed again. Troubled, I prayed to the Nymphs,
To the father of the fields, to bless the vision,
Remove the curse; and down on my knees I wrestled
Once more against the stubborn ground, and heard
A groan from under the hillock, and a voice crying:
'Why mangle a poor wretch, Aeneas? Spare me,
Here in the tomb, and save your hands pollution.
You know me, I am Trojan-born, no stranger,
This is familiar blood. Alas! Take flight,
40　Leave this remorseless land; the curse of greed
Lies heavy on it. I am Polydorus,
Pierced by an iron harvest; out of my body
Rise javelins and lances.' I was speechless,
Stunned, in my terror.
　　Priam, forever unfortunate, had sent
This Polydorus on a secret mission,
Once, to the king of Thrace, with gold for hiding
When the king despaired of the siege and the city's fortune.
And when Troy fell, and Fortune failed, the Thracian
50　Took Agamemnon's side, broke off his duty,
Slew Polydorus, took the gold. There is nothing
To which men are not driven by that hunger.
Once over my fear, I summoned all the leaders,

---

[4] An omen, or sign of something to come.

My father, too; I told them of the portent,
Asked for their counsel. All agreed, a land
So stained with violence and violation
Was not for us to dwell in. Southward ho!
For Polydorus we made restoration
With funeral rites anew; earth rose again
Above his outraged mound; dark fillets made   60
The altar sorrowful, and cypress boughs,
And the Trojan women loosed their hair in mourning.
We offered milk in foaming bowls, and blood
Warm from the victims, so to rest the spirit,
And cry aloud the voice of valediction.[5]
   Then, when we trust the sea again, and the wind
Calls with a gentle whisper, we crowd the shores,
Launch ship again, leave port, the lands and cities
Fade out of sight once more.
                 There is an island
In the middle of the sea; the Nereids' mother   70
And Neptune hold it sacred.[6] It used to wander
By various coasts and shores, until Apollo,
In grateful memory, bound it fast, unmoving,
Unfearful of winds, between two other islands
Called Myconos and Gyaros. I sailed there;
Our band was weary, and the calmest harbor
Gave us safe haven. This was Apollo's city;
We worshipped it on landing. And their king,
Priest of Apollo also, came to meet us,
His temples bound with holy fillets, and laurel.   80
His name was Anius; he knew Anchises
As an old friend, and gave us joyful welcome.
   Apollo's temple was built of ancient rock,
And there I prayed: 'Grant us a home, Apollo,
Give walls to weary men, a race, a city
That will abide; preserve Troy's other fortress,
The remnant left by the Greeks and hard Achilles.
Whom do we follow? where are we bidden to go
To find our settlement? An omen, father!'

---

[5] Farewell.
[6] The island is Delos, in the middle of the Aegean Sea; the birthplace
of Apollo. The mother of the Nereids (sea-nymphs) was Doris.

90   I had scarcely spoken, when suddenly all things trembled,
        The doors, and the laurel, and the whole mountain moved,
        And the shrine was opened, and a rumbling sound
        Was heard. We knelt, most humbly; and a voice
        Came to our ears: 'The land which brought you forth,
        Men of endurance, will receive you home.
        Seek out your ancient mother. There your house
        Will rule above all lands, your children's children,
        For countless generations.' Apollo spoke,
        And we were joyful and confused, together:
100   What walls were those, calling the wanderers home?
        My father, pondering history, made answer:
        'Hear, leaders; learn your hopes. There is a land
        Called Crete, an island in the midst of the sea,
        The cradle of our race; it has a mountain,
        Ida, like ours, a hundred mighty cities,
        Abounding wealth; if I recall correctly,
        Teucer, our greatest father, came from there
        To the Rhoetean[7] shores to found his kingdom.
        Ilium was nothing then, the towers of Troy
110   Undreamed of; men lived in the lowly valleys.
        And Cybele, the Great Mother,[8] came from Crete
        With her clashing cymbals, and her grove of Ida
        Was named from that original; the silence
        Of her mysterious rites, the harnessed lions
        Before her chariot wheels, all testify
        To Cretan legend. Come, then, let us follow
        Where the gods lead, and seek the Cretan kingdom.
        It is not far; with Jupiter to favor,
        Three days will see us there.' With prayer, he made
120   Most solemn sacrifice, a bull to Neptune,
        One to Apollo, to Winter a black heifer,
        A white one for fair winds.
                                    The story ran
        That no one lived in Crete, Idomeneus
        Having left his father's kingdom, that the houses

---

[7] Trojan (from a cape near the city).
[8] On Cybele, see II.802 and note.

Were empty now, dwellings vacated for us.[9]
We sailed from Delos, flying over the water
Past Naxos, on whose heights the Bacchae revel,
Past green Donysa, snowy Paros, skimming
The passages between the sea-sown islands.[10]
No crew would yield to another; there is shouting,   130
And the cheer goes up, 'To Crete, and the land of our
    fathers!'
A stern wind follows, and we reach the land.
I am glad to be there; I lay out the walls
For the chosen city, name it Pergamea,[11]
And the people are happy. *Love your hearths,* I told them,
Build high the citadel. The ships were steadied
On the dry beach, the young were busy ploughing,
Or planning marriage, and I was giving laws,
Assigning homes. But the weather turned, the sky
Grew sick, and from the tainted heaven came   140
Pestilence and pollution, a deadly year
For people and harvest. Those who were not dying
Dragged weary bodies around; the Dog-Star[12] scorched
The fields to barrenness; grass withered, corn
Refused to ripen. 'Over the sea again!'
My father said, 'let us return to Delos,
Consult the oracle, implore Apollo
To show us kindliness; what end awaits
Our weary destiny, where does he bid us turn
For help in trouble?'   150
    Sleep held all creatures over the earth at rest;
In my own darkness visions came, the sacred
Images of the household gods I had carried

---

[9] Idomeneus had been a king of Crete who fought against Troy. In fulfillment of a vow that he would sacrifice to Neptune the first living thing he saw after returning to Crete, he killed his son. He was therefore driven away, the gods having visited a plague on Crete as punishment.

[10] Naxos, Donysa, and Paros are islands in the south Aegean Sea, passed during the southward voyage to Crete. Bacchae were women who worshipped Bacchus, god of wine.

[11] Named for Pergamum, the citadel of Troy.

[12] Sirius, the brightest star in the sky; its rising was considered to herald the hot days of late summer.

With me from Troy, out of the burning city.[13]
I saw them plain, in the flood of light, where the moon
Streamed through the dormers. And they eased me, saying:
'Apollo would tell you this, if you went over
The sea again to Delos; from him we come
To you, with willing spirit. We came with you
160 From the burnt city, we have followed still
The swollen sea in the ships; in time to come
We shall raise your sons to heaven, and dominion
Shall crown their city. Prepare to build them walls,
Great homes for greatness; do not flee the labor,
The long, long toil of flight. Crete, says Apollo,
Is not the place. There is a land in the West,
Called by the Greeks, Hesperia:[14] anciency
And might in arms and wealth enrich its soil.
The Oenotrians lived there once; now, rumor has it,
170 A younger race has called it Italy
After the name of a leader, Italus.
Dardanus came from there, our ancestor,
As Iasius[15] was. There is our dwelling-place.
Be happy, then, waken, and tell Anchises
Our certain message: seek the land in the West.
Crete is forbidden country.'
　　　The vision shook me, and the voice of the gods;
(It was not a dream, exactly; I seemed to know them,
Their features, the veiled hair, the living presence.)
180 I woke in a sweat, held out my hands to heaven,
And poured the pure libation for the altar,
Then, gladly, to Anchises. He acknowledged
His own mistake, a natural confusion,
Our stock was double, of course; no need of saying
We had more ancestors than one. 'Cassandra,'
Anchises said, 'alone, now I remember,
Foretold this fate; it seemed she was always talking

---

[13] The household gods, or Penates, included images of the major gods
such as Jupiter and also of the minor gods who watched over one's own
household.
[14] The western region of the world, associated with Hesperus, the evening star.
[15] Brother of Dardanus.

Of a land in the West, and Italian kingdoms, always.
But who would ever have thought that any Trojans
Would reach the shores in the West? Or, for that matter,   190
Who ever believed Cassandra?[16] Let us yield
To the warning of Apollo, and at his bidding
Seek better fortunes.' So we obeyed him,
Leaving this place, where a few stayed, and sailing
The hollow keels over the mighty ocean.
    We were in deep water, and the land no longer
Was visible, sky and ocean everywhere.
A cloud, black-blue, loomed overhead, with night
And tempest in it, and the water roughened
In shadow; winds piled up the sea, the billows   200
Rose higher; we were scattered in the surges.
Clouds took away the daylight, and the night
Was dark and wet in the sky, with lightning flashing.
We wandered, off our course, in the dark of ocean,
And our pilot, Palinurus, swore he could not
Tell day from night, nor the way among the waters.
For three lost days, three starless nights, we rode it,
Saw land on the fourth, mountains and smoke arising.
The sails came down, we bent to the oars; the sailors
Made the foam fly, sweeping the dark blue water.   210
I was saved from the waves; the Strophades received me
(The word means Turning-point in the Greek language),[17]
Ionian islands where the dire Celaeno
And other Harpies live, since Phineus' house
Was closed to them, and they feared their former tables.[18]

[16] On the credibility of Cassandra, see II.270–71 and note.
[17] The Strophades are small islands west of Greece, in the Ionian Sea.
Turning-point refers to the fact that two sons of Boreas, the North Wind,
who were driving the Harpies away from Phineus (see the following note),
were turned back at these islands and prevented from further pursuing
them. The Trojans have now rounded the southwest corner of Greece;
from this time until shortly after they leave Helenus and Andromache
later in Book III, their course will be northwest, along the shore and
among the islands of Greece (including those named in lines 269–71)
that face Sicily and southern Italy.
[18] The Harpies (originally conceived of in myth as personifying storm
winds) were foul monsters sent by Jove (Jupiter) to punish Phineus, a
Thracian king, who had blinded his sons. Afterward, the Harpies were
driven from Thrace to the Strophades. Celaeno is their leader.

No fiercer plague of the gods' anger ever
Rose out of hell, girls with the look of birds,
Their bellies fouled, incontinent, their hands
Like talons, and their faces pale with hunger.
220   We sailed into the harbor, happy to see
Good herds of cattle grazing over the grass
And goats, unshepherded. We cut them down
And made our prayer and offering to Jove,
Set trestles on the curving shore for feasting.
Down from the mountains with a fearful rush
And a sound of wings like metal came the Harpies,
To seize our banquet, smearing dirtiness
Over it all, with a hideous kind of screaming
And a stinking smell. We found a secret hollow
230   Enclosed by trees, under a ledge of rock,
Where shade played over; there we moved the tables
And lit the fire again; the noisy Harpies
Came out of somewhere, sky, or rock, and harried
The feast again, the filthy talons grabbing,
The taint all through the air. *Take arms,* I ordered,
We have to fight them. And my comrades, hiding
Their shields in the grass, lay with their swords beside them,
And when the birds swooped screaming, and Misenus
Sounded the trumpet-signal, they rose to charge them,
240   A curious kind of battle, men with sword-blades
Against the winged obscenities of ocean.
Their feathers felt no blow, their backs no wound,
They rose to the sky as rapidly as ever,
Leaving the souvenirs of their foul traces
Over the ruined feast. And one, Celaeno,
Perched on a lofty rock, squawked out a warning:—
'Is it war you want, for slaughtered goats and bullocks,
Is it war you bring, you sons of liars,[19] driving
The innocent Harpies from their father's kingdom?
250   Take notice, then, and let my words forever
Stick in your hearts; what Jove has told Apollo,
Apollo told me, and I, the greatest fury,

---

[19] See note to line 3.

Shove down your throats; it is Italy you are after,
And the winds will help you, Italy and her harbors
You will reach, all right; but you will not wall the city
Till, for the wrong you have done us, deadly hunger
Will make you gnaw and crunch your very tables!'[20]
She flew back to the forest. My companions
Were chilled with sudden fear; their spirit wavered,
They call on me, to beg for peace, not now   260
With arms, but vows and praying, filthy birds
Or ill-foreboding goddesses, no matter.
Anchises prayed with outstretched hands, appeasing
The mighty gods with sacrifice:—'Be gracious,
Great gods, ward off the threats, spare the devoted!'
He bade us tear the cable from the shore,
Shake loose the sails. And a wind sprang up behind us,
Driving us northward; we passed many islands,
Zacynthus, wooded, Dulichium, and Same,
The cliffs of Neritus, Laertes'[21] kingdom,   270
With a curse as we went by for Ithaca,
Land of Ulysses. Soon Leucate's[22] headland
Came into view, a dreadful place for sailors,
Where Apollo had a shrine. We were very weary
As we drew near the little town; the anchor
Was thrown from the prow, the sterns pulled up on the
    beaches.
    This was unhoped-for land; we offered Jove
Our purifying rites, and had the altars
Burning with sacrifice. We thronged the shore
With games of Ilium. Naked, oiled for wrestling,   280
The young held bouts, glad that so many islands,
Held by the Greeks, were safely passed. A year
Went by, and icy winter roughened the waves
With gales from the north. A shield of hollow bronze,

[20] For the upshot of this prophecy, see VII.104–24.
[21] Father of Ulysses (Odysseus).
[22] A promontory off western Greece; it was associated in Virgil's time
with the great victory of Octavian (Caesar Augustus) over Mark Antony
and Cleopatra at nearby Actium, in 31 B.C. For more about this battle,
see VIII.677–726.

Borne once by Abas,[23] I fastened to the door-posts,
And set a verse below it: *Aeneas won*
These arms from the Greek victors. I gave the order
To man the thwarts and leave this harbor; all
Obeyed, swept oars in rivalry. We left
290 Phaeacia's airy heights, coasting Epirus,
Drawn to Buthrotum, a Chaonian harbor.[24]
   And here we met strange news, that Helenus,
The son of Priam, was ruling Grecian cities,
Having won the wife of Pyrrhus and his crown,
And that Andromache once more had married
A lord of her own race. Amazed, I burn
With a strange longing to seek out that hero,
To learn his great adventures. It so happened,
Just as I left the landing, that was the day
300 Andromache, in a grove before the city,
By the waters of a river that resembled
The Simois at home, was offering homage,
Her annual mourning-gift to Hector's ashes,
Calling his ghost to the place which she had hallowed
With double altars, a green and empty tomb.
I found her weeping there, and she was startled
At the sight of me, and Trojan arms, a shock
Too great to bear: she was rigid for a moment,
And then lost consciouness, and a long time later
310 Managed to speak: 'Is it real, then, goddess-born?
What are you, living messenger or phantom,
Mortal or ghost? If the dear light has left you,
Tell me where Hector is.' I was moved, so deeply
I found it hard to answer to her tears
And through my own, but I did say a little:—
'I am alive; I seem to keep on living
Through all extremes of trouble; do not doubt me,

[23] Not the Trojan mentioned in the storm-scene of Book I (line 132) but rather a Greek hero. His shield was taken either from him or from another warrior killed at Troy.
[24] Phaeacia is the idyllic land visited by Ulysses in Homer's *Odyssey*, Books V to XIII; it is frequently identified with the modern Corfu, a large island near Albania. Buthrotum was on the coast of Chaonia in Epirus, an area of Greece near what today is the Albanian border.

I am no apparition. And what has happened
To you, dear wife of Hector? Could any gain
Atone for such a loss? Has fortune tried   320
To even matters at all? Does Pyrrhus still
Presume on you as husband?' With lowered gaze
And quiet voice she answered:—'Happy the maiden
Slain at the foeman's tomb, at the foot of the walls;
Happy the daughter of Priam, who never knew
The drawing of the lots,[25] nor came to the bed
Of a conqueror, his captive. After the fire
I travelled different seas, endured the pride
Achilles filled his son with, bore him children
In bondage, till he tired of me and left me   330
For Leda's daughter and a Spartan marriage.
He passed me on to Helenus, fair enough,
Slave-woman to slave-man; but then Orestes,
Inflamed with passion for his stolen bride,
And maddened by the Furies of his vengeance,
Caught Pyrrhus off-guard, and slew him at the altar
In his ancestral home.[26] And Pyrrhus dying,
Part of the kingdom came to Helenus,
Who named the fields Chaonian, the land
Chaonia, after a man from Troy,   340
And filled the heights, as best he could, with buildings
To look like those we knew. But what of yourself?
What winds, what fate, have brought you here, or was it
Some god? Did you know you were on our coast? How is
The boy Ascanius, living still, whom Troy
Might have—does he ever think about his mother?
Does he want to be a hero, a manly spirit,
Such as his father was, and his uncle Hector?'
She was in tears again, when the son of Priam,
Helenus, with an escort, came from the city,   350

[25] For the division of the women among the conquerors.
[26] Pyrrhus, the son of Achilles and slayer of the Trojan king Priam
(II.551–78), married Hermione, the daughter of Menelaus and Helen.
(Hermione was Leda's granddaughter, strictly speaking, not her daughter,
Leda being Helen's mother.) Pyrrhus was killed by Agamemnon's son
Orestes, who had been engaged to Hermione.

Happy to recognize us, bringing us in
With tears and greeting mingled. I went on,
Seeing a little Troy, low walls that copied
The old majestic ramparts, a tiny river
In a dry bed, trying to be the Xanthus,
I found the Scaean gates, to hold and cling to.
My Trojans, too, were fond of the friendly town,
Whose king received them in wide halls; libations
Were poured to the gods, and feasts set on gold dishes.
360   Day after day went by, and the winds were calling
And the sails filling with a good south-wester.
I put my questions to the king and prophet:
'O son of Troy, the god's interpreter,
Familiar with the tripod and the laurel
Of great Apollo, versed in stars and omens,
Bird-song and flying wing,[27] be gracious to me,
Tell me,—for Heaven has prophesied a journey
Without mischance, and all the gods have sent me
The counsel of their oracles, to follow
370   Italy and a far-off country; one,
But one, Celaeno, prophesied misfortune,
Wrath and revolting hunger,—tell me, prophet,
What dangers first to avoid, what presence follow
To overcome disaster?'

                                  Bullocks slain
With proper covenant, and the chaplets loosened,
He led me to the temple of Apollo,
The very gates, where the god's presence awed me,
And where he spoke, with eloquent inspiration:—
'O goddess-born, the journey over the sea
380   Holds a clear sanction for you, under Jove,
Who draws the lots and turns the wheel of Fate.
I will tell you some few things, not all, that safely
You may go through friendly waters, and in time

---

[27] Aeneas catalogues the symbols and tools associated with the prophets
of the prophet-god Apollo. The priestess of the god's greatest shrine, at
Delphi in Greece, wore a laurel crown and sat supported on a tripod;
birds revealed truths by both their voices and the direction of their flight.

Come to Ausonian[28] harborage; the rest
Helenus does not know, or, if he did,
Juno would stop his speaking. First of all,
Italy, which you think is near, too fondly[29]
Ready to enter her nearest port, is distant,
Divided from you by a pathless journey
And longer lands between. The oar must bend   390
In the Sicilian ocean, and the ships
Sail on a farther coast, beyond the lakes
Of an infernal world, beyond the isles
Where dwells Aeaean Circe,[30] not till then
Can the built city rise on friendly ground.
Keep in the mind the sign I give you now:
One day, when you are anxious and alone
At the wave of a hidden river, you will find
Under the oaks on the shore, a sow, a white one,
Immense, with a new-born litter, thirty young   400
At the old one's udders; that will be the place,
The site of the city, the certain rest from labor.[31]
And do not fear the eating of the tables,
The fates will find a way, Apollo answer.
Avoid this coast of Italy, the lands
Just westward of our own;[32] behind those walls
Dwell evil Greeks, Narycian Locri, soldiers
Of the Cretan king, Idomeneus; the plains
Are full of them; a Meliboean captain
Governs Petelia, a tiny town   410
Relying on her fortress! Philoctetes

[28] Italian.
[29] *Fondly:* "in your naïve delusion."
[30] Circe was a witch who, during Ulysses' wanderings as described in Homer's *Odyssey*, Book X, changed his men into beasts. Aeaea was her home island, located by Virgil off the western coast of Italy.
[31] This prophecy is fulfilled in VIII.43–49,83–86.
[32] In the following lines, Helenus advises Aeneas to avoid the eastern coast of Italy (infested with people hostile to the Trojans) and to sail around Sicily rather than take the short route through the narrow passage dividing Sicily from the Italian mainland. This passage (the strait of Messina) is guarded on both sides, by a rock and whirlpool mythologized as, respectively, Scylla and Charybdis, who are adapted from Homer's *Odyssey*, Book XII.

Commands her walls.[33] And furthermore, remember,
Even when the ships have crossed the sea and anchored,
When the altars stand on the shore, and the vows are paid,
Keep the hair veiled, and the robe of crimson drawn
Across the eyes, so that no hostile visage
May interfere, to gaze on the holy fire
Or spoil the sacred omens. This rite observe
Through all the generations; keep it holy.[34]
420 From that first landing, when the wind brings you down
To Sicily's coast, and narrow Pelorus[35] widens
The waters of her strait, keep to the left,
Land on the left, and water on the left,
The long way round; the right is dangerous.
Avoid it. There's a story that this land[36]
Once broke apart—(time brings so many changes)—
By some immense convulsion, though the lands
Had been one country once. But now between them
The sea comes in, and now the waters bound
430 Italian coast, Sicilian coast; the tide
Washes on severed shores, their fields, their cities.
Scylla keeps guard on the right; on the left Charybdis,
The unappeasable; from the deep gulf she sucks
The great waves down, three times; three times she belches
Them high up into the air, and sprays the stars.
Scylla is held in a cave, a den of darkness,
From where she thrusts her huge jaws out, and draws
Ships to her jagged rocks. She looks like a girl
Fair-breasted to the waist, from there, all monster,
440 Shapeless, with dolphins' tails, and a wolf's belly.
Better to go the long way round, make turning

[33] All these are enemies of Troy who migrated to southern Italy: the Locri have come from Narycium, a city near Boeotia, in east-central Greece; Idomeneus has come from Crete (see lines 122–25 and note); the great archer Philoctetes has come to Petelia in Italy from Thessaly, in northern Greece. Meliboea was a city in Thessaly.

[34] As often in the poem, Virgil gives an ancient origin for Roman religious ritual of later times.

[35] The channel near Pelorus, which lies at the northeastern corner of the triangular island Sicily, on one side of the strait of Messina.

[36] The ancient land bridge between Italy and Sicily.

Beyond Pachynus,[37] than to catch one glimpse
Of Scylla the misshapen, in her cavern,
And the rocks resounding with the dark-blue sea-hounds.
And one thing more than any, goddess-born,
I tell you over and over: pray to Juno,
Give Juno vows and gifts and overcome her
With everlasting worship. So you will come
Past Sicily and reach Italian beaches.
You will come to a town called Cumae,[38] haunted lakes,   450
And a forest called Avernus, where the leaves
Rustle and stir in the great woods, and there
You will find a priestess, in her wildness singing
Prophetic verses under the stones, and keeping
Symbols and signs on leaves. She files and stores them
In the depth of the cave; there they remain unmoving,
Keeping their order, but if a light wind stirs
At the turn of a hinge, and the door's draft disturbs them,
The priestess never cares to catch them fluttering
Around the halls of rock, put them in order,   460
Or give them rearrangement. Men who have come there
For guidance leave uncounselled, and they hate
The Sibyl's dwelling. Let no loss of time,
However comrades chide and chafe, however
The wind's voice calls the sail, postpone the visit
To this great priestess; plead with her to tell you
With her own lips the song of the oracles.
She will predict the wars to come, the nations
Of Italy, the toils to face, or flee from;
Meet her with reverence, and she, propitious,   470
Will grant a happy course. My voice can tell you
No more than this. Farewell; raise Troy to heaven.'
　　After the friendly counsel, other gifts
Were sent to our ships, carved ivory, and gold,
And heavy silver, cauldrons from Dodona,[39]
A triple breastplate linked with gold, a helmet

---

[37] The southeastern corner of Sicily.

[38] Cumae, where Aeneas will consult the Sibyl who is to conduct him
to the Lower World, is on the west coast of Italy, near modern Naples.

[39] Site, in northwestern Greece, of the great oracle of Jupiter.

Shining with crested plume, the arms of Pyrrhus.
My father, too, has gifts; horses and guides
Are added, and sailing-men, and arms for my comrades.
480   Anchises bade the fleet prepare; the wind
Was rising, why delay? But Helenus
Spoke to Anchises, in compliment and honor:—
'Anchises, worthy of Venus' couch, and the blessing
Of other gods, twice saved from Trojan ruins,[40]
Yonder behold Ausonia! Near, and far,
It lies, Apollo's offering; sail westward.
Farewell, made blest by a son's goodness. I
Am a nuisance with my talking.'
                              And his queen,
Sad at the final parting, was bringing gifts,
490   Robes woven with a golden thread, a Trojan
Scarf for Ascanius, all courteous honor
Given with these:—'Take them, my child; these are
The work of my own hands, memorials
Of Hector's wife Andromache, and her love.
Receive these farewell gifts; they are for one
Who brings my own son back to me; your hands,
Your face, your eyes, remind me of him so,—
He would be just your age.'[41]
                              I, also, wept,
As I spoke my words of parting: 'Now farewell;
500   Your lot is finished, and your rest is won,
No ocean fields to plough, no fleeing fields
To follow, you have your Xanthus[42] and your Troy,
Built by your hands, and blest by happier omens,
Far from the path of the Greeks. But we are called
From fate to fate; if ever I enter Tiber
And Tiber's neighboring lands, if ever I see
The walls vouchsafed my people, I pray these shores,
Italy and Epirus, shall be one,
The life of Troy restored, with friendly towns

---

[40] Troy had earlier been sacked by Hercules, out of anger with the city's lying king Laomedon. See also note to VIII.296.

[41] The Greeks had killed Astyanax, the son of Andromache and Hector, by throwing him from the walls of Troy.

[42] A river at Troy; see line 355.

And allied people. A common origin,   510
A common fall, was ours. Let us remember,
And our children keep the faith.'
   Over the sea we rode, the shortest run
To Italy, past the Ceraunian rocks.[43]
The sun went down; the hills were dark with shadow.
The oars assigned, we drew in to the land
For a little welcome rest; sleep overcame us,
But it was not yet midnight when our pilot
Sprang from his blanket, studying the winds,
Alert and listening, noting the stars   520
Wheeling the silent heaven, the twin Oxen,
Arcturus and the rainy Kids.[44] All calm,
He saw, and roused us; camp was broken; the sail
Spread to the rushing breeze, and as day reddened
And the stars faded, we saw a coast, low-lying,
And made out hills. 'Italy!', cried Achates,
'Italy!' all the happy sailors shouted.
Anchises wreathed a royal wine-bowl, stood
On the high stern, calling: —'Gods of earth and ocean
And wind and storm, help us along, propitious   530
With favoring breath!' And the breeze sprang up, and
      freshened;
We saw a harbor open, and a temple
Shone on Minerva's headland.[45] The sails came down,
We headed toward the land. Like the curve of a bow
The port turned in from the Eastern waves; its cliffs
Foamed with the salty spray, and towering rocks
Came down to the sea, on both sides, double walls,
And the temple fled the shore. Here, our first omen,
I saw four horses grazing, white as snow,

---

[43] A mountain range in Epirus, in western Greece. The Trojans have
been sailing along the coast, northwest from the settlement of Helenus
and Andromache at Buthrotum. Now they change their course: hereafter,
until the storm that beaches them at Carthage, they will sail southwest
past the heel and along the sole of the "boot" of southern Italy, then
clockwise around Sicily.

[44] The twin Oxen are the Big and Little Dippers; the rainy (that is,
rain-bringing) Kids are the Hyades.

[45] The headland, on the heel of the Italian "boot," is at Castrum Minervae.

540   And father Anchises cried:—'It is war you bring us,
      Welcoming land, horses are armed for war,
      It is war these herds portend. But there is hope
      Of peace as well. Horses will bend to the yoke
      And bear the bridle tamely.' Then we worshipped
      The holy power of Pallas, first to hear us,
      Kept our heads veiled before the solemn altar,
      And following Helenus' injunction, offered
      Our deepest prayer to Juno.
                                    And sailed on,
      With some misgiving, past the homes of Greeks;
550   Saw, next, a bay, Tarentum, and a town
      That rumor said was Hercules'; against it,
      The towers of Caulon rose, and Scylaceum,
      Most dangerous to ships, and a temple of Juno.[46]
      Far off, Sicilian Etna[47] rose from the waves,
      And we heard the loud sea roar, and the rocks resounding,
      And voices broken on the coast; the shoals
      Leaped at us, and the tide boiled sand. My father
      Cried in alarm:—'This must be that Charybdis
      Helenus warned us of. Rise to the oars,
560   O comrades, pull from the danger!' They responded
      As they did, always, Palinurus swinging
      The prow to the waves on the left, and all our effort
      Strained to the left, with oars and sail. One moment
      We were in the clouds, the next in the gulf of Hell;
      Three times the hollow rocks and reefs roared at us,
      Three times we saw spray shower the very stars,
      And the wind went down at sunset; we were weary,
      Drifting, in ignorance, to the Cyclops'[48] shores.
        There is a harbor, safe enough from wind,
570   But Etna thunders near it, crashing and roaring,
      Throwing black clouds up to the sky, and smoking
      With swirling pitchy color, and white-hot ashes,

---

[46] Tarentum is on the shoreline inside the arch of the Italian "boot";
the arch is formed by the Gulf of Tarentum (of *Taranto* in a modern
atlas). Caulon and Scylaceum are to the southwest, along the sole.

[47] The famous volcano, in eastern Sicily, south of the strait of Messina.

[48] One-eyed giants.

With balls of flame puffed to the stars, and boulders,
The mountain's guts, belched out, or molten rock
Boiling below the ground, roaring above it.
The story goes that Enceladus, a giant,
Struck by a bolt of lightning, lies here buried
Beneath all Etna's weight,[49] with the flames pouring
Through the broken furnace-flues; he shifts his body,
Every so often, to rest his weariness,   580
And then all Sicily seems to moan and tremble
And fill the sky with smoke. We spent the night here,
Hiding in woods, enduring monstrous portents,
Unable to learn the cause. There were no stars,
No light or fire in the sky; the dead of the night,
The thick of the cloud, obscured the moon.
                                        And day
Arrived, at last, and the shadows left the heaven,
And a man came out of the woods, a sorry figure,
In hunger's final stages, reaching toward us
His outstretched hands. We looked again. His beard   590
Unshorn, his rags pinned up with thorns, and dirty,
He was, beyond all doubt of it, a Greek,
And one of those who had been at Troy in the fighting.
He saw, far off, the Trojan dress and armor,
Stopped short, for a moment, almost started back
In panic, then, with a wild rush, came on,
Pleading and crying:—'By the stars I beg you,
By the gods above, the air we breathe, ah Trojans,
Take me away from here, carry me off
To any land whatever; that will be plenty.   600
I know I am one of the Greeks, I know I sailed
With them, I warred against the gods of Ilium,
I admit all that; drown me for evil-doing,
Cut me to pieces, scatter me over the waves.
Kill me. If I must die, it will be a pleasure
To perish at the hands of men.' He held
Our knees and clung there, grovelling before us.

---

[49] Enceladus had fought against Jupiter, who blasted him with a thunderbolt and then pinned him under the volcano.

We urged him tell his story, his race, his fortune.
My father gave him his hand, a pledge of safety,
And his fear died down a little.
610   'I come,' he said,
'From Ithaca, a companion of Ulysses;
My name is Achaemenides; my father,
His name was Adamastus, was a poor man,
And that was why I came to Troy. My comrades
Left me behind here, in their terrible hurry,
To leave these cruel thresholds.[50] The Cyclops live here
In a dark cave, a house of gore, and banquets
Soaking with blood. It is dark inside there, monstrous.
He hits the stars with his head—Dear gods, abolish
620   This creature from the world!—he is not easy
To look at; he is terrible to talk to.
His food is the flesh of men, his drink their blood.
I saw him once myself, with two of our men
In that huge fist of his; he lay on his back
In the midst of the cave, and smashed them on a rock,
And the whole place swam with blood; I watched him chew
        them,
The limbs with black clots dripping, the muscles, warm,
Quivering as he bit them. But we got him!
Ulysses did not stand for this; he kept
630   His wits about him, never mind the danger.
The giant was gorged with food, and drunk, and lolling
With sagging neck, sprawling all over the cavern
Belching and drooling blood-clots, bits of flesh,
And wine all mixed together. And we stood
Around him, praying, and drew lots,—we had found a stake
And sharpened it at the end,—and so we bored
His big eye out; it glowered under his forehead
The size of a shield, or a sun. So we got vengeance
For the souls of our companions. But flee, I tell you,
640   Get out of here, poor wretches, cut the cables,
Forsake this shore. There are a hundred others
As big as he is, and just like him, keeping

---

[50] The story told in lines 616–80 is largely repeated from Homer's *Odyssey*,
Book IX.

Sheep in the caves of the rocks, a hundred others
Wander around this coast and these high mountains.
I have managed for three months, hiding in forests,
In the caves of beasts, on a rocky look-out, watching
The Cyclops, horribly frightened at their cries
And the tramp of their feet. I have lived on plants and berries,
Gnawed roots and bark. I saw this fleet come in,
And I did not care; whatever it was, I gladly   650
Gave myself up. At least, I have escaped them.
Whatever death you give is more than welcome.'
And as he finished, we saw that very giant,
The shepherd Polyphemus, looming huge
Over his tiny flock; he was trying to find
His way to the shore he knew, a shapeless monster,
Lumbering, clumping, blind in the dark, with a stumble,
And the step held up with trunk of a pine. No comfort
For him, except in the sheep. He reached the sand,
Wading into the sea, and scooped up water   660
To wash the ooze of blood from the socket's hollow,
Grinding his teeth against the pain, and roaring,
And striding into the water, but even so
The waves were hardly up to his sides. We fled,
Taking on board our Greek; we cut the cable,
Strained every nerve at the oars. He heard, and struggled
Toward the splash of the wave, but of course he could not
      catch us,
And then he howled in a rage, and the sea was frightened,
Italy deeply shaken, and all Etna
Rumbled in echoing terror in her caverns.   670
Out of the woods and the thicket of the mountains
The Cyclops came, the others, toward the harbor,
Along the coast-line. We could see them standing
In impotent anger, the wild eye-ball glaring,
A grim assortment, brothers, tall as mountains
Where oak and cypress tower, in the groves
Of Jove or great Diana. In our speed
And terror, we sailed anywhere, forgetting
What Helenus had said: Scylla, Charybdis,
Were nothing to us then. But we remembered   680
In time, and a north wind came from strait Pelorus,

We passed Pantagia,[51] and the harbor-mouth
Set in the living-rock, Thapsus, low-lying,
The bay called Megara: all these were places
That Achaemenides knew well, recalling
The scenes of former wanderings with Ulysses.
    An island faces the Sicanian[52] bay
Against Plemyrium, washed by waves; this island
Has an old name, Ortygia. The story
690   Tells of a river, Alpheus, come from Elis,[53]
By a secret channel undersea, to join
The Arethusan fountains, mingling here
With the Sicilian waters. Here we worshipped
The land's great gods; went on, to pass Helorus,
A rich and marshy land; and then Pachynus
Where the cliffs rose sharp and high; and Camerina,
With firm foundation; the Geloan plains,
And Gela, named for a river; then Acragas,
A towering town, high-walled, and sometime famous
700   For its breed of horses; the city of palms, Selinus;
The shoals of Lilybaeum, where the rocks
Are a hidden danger; so at last we came
To Drepanum,[54] a harbor and a shoreline
That I could not rejoice in, a survivor
Of all those storms of the sea. For here I lost
My comforter in all my care and trouble,
My father Anchises. All the storms and perils,
All of the weariness endured, seemed nothing
Compared with this disaster; and I had
710   No warning of it; neither Helenus,
Though he foretold much touble, nor Celaeno,

---

[51] The places named in lines 682–701 are located on the east and south coasts of Sicily.

[52] Sicilian. The bay is that of the great ancient city of Syracuse, in southeastern Sicily.

[53] Part of western Greece; thus the river Alpheus must flow under the Ionian sea to join the fountain Arethusa. According to the myth, Alpheus was a river-god and Arethusa a nymph he was in love with.

[54] Drepanum, at the western end of Sicily, lies almost directly opposite Carthage on the north-African coast, across a narrow part of the Mediterranean Sea, and is thus approximately where the action of Book I begins.

That evil harpy, prophesied this sorrow.
There was nothing more to bear; the long roads ended
At that unhappy goal; and when I left there,
Some god or other brought me to your shores."

And so he told the story, a lonely man
To eager listeners, destiny and voyage,
And made an end of it here, ceased, and was quiet.

BOOK IV

□

Aeneas and Dido

BUT the queen finds no rest. Deep in her veins
The wound is fed; she burns with hidden fire.
His manhood, and the glory of his race,
Are an obsession with her, like his voice,
Gesture and countenance. On the next morning,
After a restless night, she sought her sister:
"I am troubled, Anna, doubtful, terrified,
Or am I dreaming? What new guest is this
Come to our shores? How well he talks, how brave
He seems in heart and action! I suppose   10
It must be true; he does come from the gods.
Fear proves a bastard spirit. He has been
So buffeted by fate. What endless wars
He told of! Sister, I must tell you something:
Were not my mind made up, once and for all,
Never again to marry, having been
So lost when Sychaeus left me for the grave,
Slain by my murderous brother at the altar,[1]
Were I not sick forever of the torch[2]
And bridal bed, here is the only man   20
Who has moved my spirit, shaken my weak will.

---

[1] The story of what took place in Tyre between Dido's late husband,
Sychaeus, and her murderous brother, Pygmalion, and of Dido's flight
to Carthage, is told in I.351–85.

[2] Carried in wedding processions; an emblem of marriage. The image
of fire climaxes in Dido's funeral pyre at the end of Book IV.

75

I might have yielded to him. I recognize
The marks of an old fire. But I pray, rather,
That earth engulf me, lightning strike me down
To the pale shades and everlasting night,
Before I break the laws of decency.
My love has gone with Sychaeus; let him keep it,
Keep it with him forever in the grave."
She ended with a burst of tears. "Dear sister,
30   Dearer than life," Anna replied, "why must you
Grieve all your youth away in loneliness,
Not know sweet children, or the joys of love?
Is that what dust demands, and buried shadows?
So be it. You have kept your resolution
From Tyre to Libya, proved it by denying
Iarbas and a thousand other suitors
From Africa's rich kingdoms. Think a little.
Whose lands are these you settle in? Getulians,
Invincible in war, the wild Numidians,
40   Unfriendly Syrtes, ring us round, and a desert
Barren with drought, and the Barcaean rangers.[3]
Why should I mention Tyre, and wars arising
Out of Pygmalion's threats? And you, my sister,
Why should you fight against a pleasing passion?
I think the gods have willed it so, and Juno
Has helped to bring the Trojan ships to Carthage.
What a great city, sister, what a kingdom
This might become, rising on such a marriage!
Carthage and Troy together in arms, what glory
50   Might not be ours? Only invoke the blessing
Of the great gods, make sacrifice, be lavish
In welcome, keep them here while the fierce winter
Rages at sea, and cloud and sky are stormy,
And ships still wrecked and broken."

                     So she fanned
The flame of the burning heart; the doubtful mind
Was given hope, and the sense of guilt was lessened.

---

[3] The idea is that Dido is dangerously isolated on all sides: hemmed
in on land by potentially hostile peoples and on the north by the treacherous Syrtes, the shoals off the coast.

And first of all they go to shrine and altar
Imploring peace; they sacrifice to Ceres,
Giver of law, to Bacchus, to Apollo,
And most of all to Juno, in whose keeping   60
The bonds of marriage rest. In all her beauty
Dido lifts up the goblet, pours libation
Between the horns of a white heifer, slowly,
Or, slowly, moves to the rich altars, noting
The proper gifts to mark the day, or studies
The sacrificial entrails for the omens.
Alas, poor blind interpreters! What woman
In love is helped by offerings or altars?
Soft fire consumes the marrow-bones, the silent
Wound grows, deep in the heart.   70
Unhappy Dido burns, and wanders, burning,
All up and down the city, the way a deer
With a hunter's careless arrow in her flank
Ranges the uplands, with the shaft still clinging
To the hurt side. She takes Aeneas with her
All through the town, displays the wealth of Sidon,[4]
Buildings projected; she starts to speak, and falters,
And at the end of the day renews the banquet,
Is wild to hear the story, over and over,
Hangs on each word, until the late moon, sinking,   80
Sends them all home. The stars die out, but Dido
Lies brooding in the empty hall, alone,
Abandoned on a lonely couch. She hears him,
Sees him, or sees and hears him in Iulus,
Fondles the boy, as if that ruse might fool her,
Deceived by his resemblance to his father.
The towers no longer rise, the youth are slack
In drill for arms, the cranes and derricks rusting,
Walls halt halfway to heaven.
                              And Juno saw it,
The queen held fast by this disease, this passion   90
Which made her good name meaningless. In anger
She rushed to Venus:—"Wonderful!—the trophies,

---

[4] Of Carthage (from Sidon, a great city in Dido's former homeland).

The praise, you and that boy of yours[5] are winning!
Two gods outwit one woman—splendid, splendid!
What glory for Olympus! I know you fear me,
Fear Carthage, and suspect us. To what purpose?
What good does all this do? Is there no limit?
Would we not both be better off, to sanction
A bond of peace forever, a formal marriage?
100   You have your dearest wish; Dido is burning
With love, infected to her very marrow.
Let us—why not?—conspire to rule one people
On equal terms; let her serve a Trojan husband;
Let her yield her Tyrian people as her dowry."
      This, Venus knew, was spoken with a purpose,
A guileful one, to turn Italian empire
To Libyan shores: not without reservation
She spoke in answer: "Who would be so foolish
As to refuse such terms, preferring warfare,
110   If only fortune follows that proposal?
I do not know, I am more than a little troubled
What fate permits: will Jupiter allow it,
One city for the Tyrians and Trojans,
This covenant, this mixture? You can fathom
His mind, and ask him, being his wife. I follow
Wherever you lead." And royal Juno answered:
"That I will tend to. Listen to me, and learn
How to achieve the urgent need. They plan,
Aeneas, and poor Dido, to go hunting
120   When sunlight floods the world to-morrow morning.
While the rush of the hunt is on, and the forest shaken
With beaters[6] and their nets, I will pour down
Dark rain and hail, and make the whole sky rumble
With thunder and threat. The company will scatter,
Hidden or hiding in the night and shadow,
And Dido and the Trojan come for shelter
To the same cave. I will be there and join them
In lasting wedlock; she will be his own,
His bride, forever; this will be their marriage."

---

[5] Cupid, who for a time had taken the form of Iulus.
[6] Men assigned to flush the game animals from cover.

Venus assented, smiling, not ungracious—   130
The trick was in the open.[7]
   Dawn, rising, left the ocean, and the youth
Come forth from all the gates, prepared for hunting,
Nets, toils, wide spears, keen-scented coursing hounds,
And Dido keeps them waiting; her own charger
Stands bright in gold and crimson; the bit foams,
The impatient head is tossed. At last she comes,
With a great train attending, gold and crimson,
Quiver of gold, and combs of gold, and mantle
Crimson with golden buckle. A Trojan escort   140
Attends her, with Iulus, and Aeneas
Comes to her side, more lordly than Apollo
Bright along Delos' ridges in the springtime
With laurel in his hair and golden weapons
Shining across his shoulders. Equal radiance
Is all around Aeneas, equal splendor.
   They reach the mountain heights, the hiding-places
Where no trail runs; wild goats from the rocks are started,
Run down the ridges; elsewhere, in the open,
Deer cross the dusty plain, away from the mountains.   150
The boy Ascanius, in the midst of the valley,
Is glad he has so good a horse, rides, dashing
Past one group or another: deer are cowards
And wild goats tame; he prays for some excitement,
A tawny lion coming down the mountain
Or a great boar with foaming mouth.
                      The heaven
Darkens, and thunder rolls, and rain and hail
Come down in torrents. The hunt is all for shelter,
Trojans and Tyrians and Ascanius dashing
Wherever they can; the streams pour down the mountains.   160
To the same cave go Dido and Aeneas,
Where Juno, as a bridesmaid, gives the signal,[8]
And mountain nymphs wail high their incantations,

---

[7] Having been told by Jupiter (I.268–311) of the destined future of Trojans and Romans, Venus is aware that Juno's plan will fail.
  [8] Juno provides the ceremonial wedding torch, in the form of lightning flashes.

First day of death, first cause of evil. Dido
Is unconcerned with fame, with reputation,
With how it seems to others. This is marriage
For her, not hole-and-corner guilt; she covers
Her folly with this name.
                            Rumor goes flying
At once, through all the Libyan cities, Rumor
170 Than whom no other evil was ever swifter.
She thrives on motion and her own momentum;
Tiny at first in fear, she swells, colossal
In no time, walks on earth, but her head is hidden
Among the clouds. Her mother, Earth, was angry,
Once, at the gods, and out of spite produced her,
The Titans' youngest sister, swift of foot,
Deadly of wing, a huge and terrible monster,
With an eye below each feather in her body,
A tongue, a mouth, for every eye, and ears
180 Double that number; in the night she flies
Above the earth, below the sky, in shadow
Noisy and shrill; her eyes are never closed
In slumber; and by day she perches, watching
From tower or battlement, frightening great cities.
She heralds truth, and clings to lies and falsehood,
It is all the same to her. And now she was going
Happy about her business, filling people
With truth and lies: Aeneas, Trojan-born,
Has come, she says, and Dido, lovely woman,
190 Sees fit to mate with him, one way or another,
And now the couple wanton out the winter,
Heedless of ruling, prisoners of passion.
They were dirty stories, but the goddess gave them
To the common ear, then went to King Iarbas
With words that fired the fuel of his anger.
    This king was Ammon's son, a child of rape
Begotten on a nymph from Garamantia;[9]
He owned wide kingdoms, had a hundred altars
Blazing with fires to Jove, eternal outposts

---

[9] Iarbas, a rejected African suitor of Dido's (line 36), is son of Jupiter, whom the Romans equated with the Egyptian and Libyan god Ammon. The Garamantes were an African tribe.

In the gods' honor; the ground was fat with blood,   200
The temple portals blossoming with garlands.
He heard the bitter stories, and went crazy,
Before the presences of many altars
Beseeching and imploring:—"Jove Almighty,
To whom the Moorish[10] race on colored couches
Pours festive wine, do you see these things, or are we
A pack of idiots, shaking at the lightning
We think you brandish, when it is really only
An aimless flash of light, and silly noises?
Do you see these things? A woman, who used to wander   210
Around my lands, who bought a little city,
To whom we gave some ploughland and a contract,
Disdains me as a husband, takes Aeneas
To be her lord and master, in her kingdom,
And now that second Paris,[11] with his lackeys,
Half-men, I call them, his chin tied up with ribbons,
With millinery on his perfumed tresses,
Takes over what he stole, and we keep bringing
Gifts to your temples, we, devout believers,
Forsooth, in idle legend."
                              And Jove heard him   220
Making his prayer and clinging to the altars,
And turned his eyes to Carthage and the lovers
Forgetful of their better reputation.
He summoned Mercury:[12] —"Go forth, my son,
Descend on wing and wind to Tyrian Carthage,
Speak to the Trojan leader, loitering there
Unheedful of the cities given by fate.
Take him my orders through the rapid winds:
It was not for this his lovely mother saved him
Twice from Greek arms;[13] she promised he would be   230
A ruler, in a country loud with war,
Pregnant with empire; he would sire a race

[10] The word here means, simply, *African.*
[11] That is, another effeminate playboy and seducer come from Troy.
[12] Mercury (Roman equivalent of the Greek god Hermes) was the messenger of the gods.
[13] First in a combat with Diomedes (Homer's *Iliad,* Book V), then at the sack of Troy.

From Teucer's[14] noble line; he would ordain
Law for the world. If no such glory moves him,
If his own fame and fortune count as nothing,
Does he, a father, grudge his son the towers
Of Rome to be? What is the fellow doing?
With what ambition wasting time in Libya?
Let him set sail. That's all; convey the message."

240   Before he ended, Mercury made ready
To carry out the orders of his father;
He strapped the golden sandals on, the pinions[15]
To bear him over sea and land, as swift
As the breath of the wind; he took the wand, which summons
Pale ghosts from Hell, or sends them there, denying
Or giving sleep, unsealing dead men's eyes,
Useful in flight through wind and stormy cloud,
And so came flying till he saw the summit
And towering sides of Atlas,[16] rugged giant

250   With heaven on his neck, whose head and shoulders
Are dark with fir, ringed with black cloud, and beaten
With wind and rain, and laden with the whiteness
Of falling snow, with rivers running over
His agèd chin, and the rough beard ice-stiffened.
Here first on level wing the god paused briefly,
Poised, plummeted to ocean, like a bird
That skims the water's surface, flying low
By shore and fishes' rocky breeding-ground,
So Mercury darted between earth and heaven

260   To Libya's sandy shore, cutting the wind
From the home of Maia's[17] father.
Soon as the winged sandals skim the rooftops,
He sees Aeneas founding towers, building
New homes for Tyrians; his sword is studded
With yellow jasper; he wears across his shoulders
A cloak of burning crimson, and golden threads
Run through it, the royal gift of the rich queen.

[14] Original ancestor of the Trojans; father-in-law of Dardanus.
[15] Wings.
[16] The mountain in Africa, here personified as the giant (who, in mythology, held up the sky).
[17] Daughter of Atlas and mother of Mercury.

Mercury wastes no time:—"What are you doing,
Forgetful of your kingdom and your fortunes,
Building for Carthage? Woman-crazy fellow,   270
The ruler of the gods, the great compeller
Of heaven and earth, has sent me from Olympus
With no more word than this: what are you doing,
With what ambition wasting time in Libya?
If your own fame and fortune count as nothing,
Think of Ascanius at least, whose kingdom
In Italy, whose Roman land, are waiting
As promise justly due." He spoke, and vanished
Into thin air. Appalled, amazed, Aeneas
Is stricken dumb; his hair stands up in terror,   280
His voice sticks in his throat. He is more than eager
To flee that pleasant land, awed by the warning
Of the divine command. But how to do it?
How get around that passionate queen? What opening
Try first? His mind runs out in all directions,
Shifting and veering. Finally, he has it,
Or thinks he has: he calls his comrades to him,
The leaders, bids them quietly prepare
The fleet for voyage, meanwhile saying nothing
About the new activity; since Dido   290
Is unaware, has no idea that passion
As strong as theirs is on the verge of breaking,
He will see what he can do, find the right moment
To let her know, all in good time. Rejoicing,
The captains move to carry out the orders.
    Who can deceive a woman in love? The queen
Anticipates each move, is fearful even
While everything is safe, foresees this cunning,
And the same trouble-making goddess, Rumor,
Tells her the fleet is being armed, made ready   300
For voyaging. She rages through the city
Like a woman mad, or drunk, the way the Maenads
Go howling through the night-time on Cithaeron[18]
When Bacchus' cymbals summon with their clashing.

[18] A mountain in Greece where the Maenads (female worshippers of
Bacchus, god of wine) conducted their orgiastic rites.

She waits no explanation from Aeneas;
She is the first to speak: "And so, betrayer,
You hoped to hide your wickedness, go sneaking
Out of my land without a word? Our love
Means nothing to you, our exchange of vows,
310   And even the death of Dido could not hold you.
The season is dead of winter, and you labor
Over the fleet; the northern gales are nothing—
You must be cruel, must you not? Why, even,
If ancient Troy remained, and you were seeking
Not unknown homes and lands, but Troy again,
Would you be venturing Troyward in this weather?
I am the one you flee from: true? I beg you
By my own tears, and your right hand—(I have nothing
Else left my wretchedness)—by the beginnings
320   Of marriage, wedlock, what we had, if ever
I served you well, if anything of mine
Was ever sweet to you, I beg you, pity
A falling house; if there is room for pleading
As late as this, I plead, put off that purpose.
You are the reason I am hated; Libyans,
Numidians, Tyrians, hate me; and my honor
Is lost, and the fame I had, that almost brought me
High as the stars, is gone. To whom, O guest—
I must not call you husband any longer—
330   To whom do you leave me? I am a dying woman;
Why do I linger on? Until Pygmalion,
My brother, brings destruction to this city?
Until the prince Iarbas leads me captive?
At least if there had been some hope of children
Before your flight, a little Aeneas playing
Around my courts, to bring you back, in feature
At least, I would seem less taken and deserted."
    There was nothing he could say. Jove bade him keep
Affection from his eyes, and grief in his heart
340   With never a sign. At last, he managed something:—
"Never, O Queen, will I deny you merit,
Whatever you have strength to claim; I will not
Regret remembering Dido, while I have
Breath in my body, or consciousness of spirit.

I have a point or two to make. I did not,
Believe me, hope to hide my flight by cunning;
I did not, ever, claim to be a husband,
Made no such vows. If I had fate's permission
To live my life my way, to settle my troubles
At my own will, I would be watching over   350
The city of Troy, and caring for my people,
Those whom the Greeks had spared, and Priam's palace
Would still be standing; for the vanquished people
I would have built the town again. But now
It is Italy I must seek, great Italy,
Apollo orders, and his oracles
Call me to Italy. There is my love,
There is my country. If the towers of Carthage,
The Libyan citadels, can please a woman
Who came from Tyre, why must you grudge the Trojans   360
Ausonian[19] land? It is proper for us also
To seek a foreign kingdom. I am warned
Of this in dreams: when the earth is veiled in shadow
And the fiery stars are burning, I see my father,
Anchises, or his ghost, and I am frightened;
I am troubled for the wrong I do my son,
Cheating him out of his kingdom in the west,
And lands that fate assigns him. And a herald,
Jove's messenger—I call them both to witness—
Has brought me, through the rush of air, his orders;   370
I saw the god myself, in the full daylight,
Enter these walls, I heard the words he brought me.
Cease to inflame us both with your complainings;
I follow Italy not because I want to."
    Out of the corner of her eye she watched him
During the first of this, and her gaze was turning
Now here, now there; and then, in bitter silence,
She looked him up and down; then blazed out at him:—
"You treacherous liar! No goddess was your mother,
No Dardanus the founder of your tribe,   380
Son of the stony mountain-crags, begotten
On cruel rocks, with a tigress for a wet-nurse!

[19] Italian.

Why fool myself, why make pretense? what is there
To save myself for now? When I was weeping
Did he so much as sigh? Did he turn his eyes,
Ever so little, toward me? Did he break at all,
Or weep, or give his lover a word of pity?
What first, what next? Neither Jupiter nor Juno
Looks at these things with any sense of fairness.
390   Faith has no haven anywhere in the world.
He was an outcast on my shore, a beggar,
I took him in, and, like a fool, I gave him
Part of my kingdom; his fleet was lost, I found it,
His comrades dying, I brought them back to life.
I am maddened, burning, burning: now Apollo
The prophesying god, the oracles
Of Lycia,[20] and Jove's herald, sent from heaven,
Come flying through the air with fearful orders,—
Fine business for the gods, the kind of trouble
400   That keeps them from their sleep. I do not hold you,
I do not argue, either. Go. And follow
Italy on the wind, and seek the kingdom
Across the water. But if any gods
Who care for decency have any power,
They will land you on the rocks; I hope for vengeance,
I hope to hear you calling the name of Dido
Over and over, in vain. Oh, I will follow
In blackest fire, and when cold death has taken
Spirit from body, I will be there to haunt you,
410   A shade, all over the world. I will have vengeance,
And hear about it; the news will be my comfort
In the deep world below." She broke it off,
Leaving the words unfinished; even light
Was unendurable; sick at heart, she turned
And left him, stammering, afraid, attempting
To make some kind of answer. And her servants
Support her to her room, that bower of marble,
A marriage-chamber once; here they attend her,
Help her lie down.
          And good Aeneas, longing

---

[20] A region in Asia Minor; Apollo had a great shrine there.

To ease her grief with comfort, to say something   420
To turn her pain and hurt away, sighs often,
His heart being moved by this great love, most deeply,
And still—the gods give orders, he obeys them;
He goes back to the fleet. And then the Trojans
Bend, really, to their work, launching the vessels
All down the shore. The tarred keel swims in the water,
The green wood comes from the forest, the poles are lopped
For oars, with leaves still on them. All are eager
For flight; all over the city you see them streaming,
Bustling about their business, a black line moving   430
The way ants do when they remember winter
And raid a hill of grain, to haul and store it
At home, across the plain, the column moving
In thin black line through grass, part of them shoving
Great seeds on little shoulders, and part bossing
The job, rebuking laggards, and all the pathway
Hot with the stream of work.
                          And Dido saw them
With who knows what emotion: there she stood
On the high citadel, and saw, below her,
The whole beach boiling, and the water littered   440
With one ship after another, and men yelling,
Excited over their work, and there was nothing
For her to do but sob or choke with anguish.
There is nothing to which the hearts of men and women
Cannot be driven by love. Break into tears,
Try prayers again, humble the pride, leave nothing
Untried, and die in vain:—"Anna, you see them
Coming from everywhere; they push and bustle
All up and down the shore: the sails are swelling,
The happy sailors garlanding the vessels.   450
If I could hope for grief like this, my sister,
I shall be able to bear it. But one service
Do for me first, dear Anna, out of pity.
You were the only one that traitor trusted,
Confided in; you know the way to reach him,
The proper time and place. Give him this message,
Our arrogant enemy: tell him I never
Swore with the Greeks at Aulis to abolish

The Trojan race, I never sent a fleet
460   To Pergamus,[21] I never desecrated
The ashes or the spirit of Anchises:
Why does he, then, refuse to listen to me?
What is the hurry? Let him give his lover
The one last favor: only wait a little,
Only a little while, for better weather
And easy flight. He has betrayed the marriage,
I do not ask for that again; I do not
Ask him to give up Latium and his kingdom.
Mere time is all I am asking, a breathing-space,
470   A brief reprieve, until my luck has taught me
To reconcile defeat and sorrow. This
Is all I ask for, sister; pity and help me:
If he grants me this, I will pay it ten times over
After my death." And Anna, most unhappy,
Over and over, told her tears, her pleading;
No tears, no pleading, move him; no man can yield
When a god stops his ears. As northern winds
Sweep over Alpine mountains, in their fury
Fighting each other to uproot an oak-tree
480   Whose ancient strength endures against their roaring
And the trunk shudders and the leaves come down
Strewing the ground, but the old tree clings to the mountain,
Its roots as deep toward hell as its crest toward heaven,
And still holds on—even so, Aeneas, shaken
By storm-blasts of appeal, by voices calling
From every side, is tossed and torn, and steady.
His will stays motionless, and tears are vain.
    Then Dido prays for death at last; the fates
Are terrible, her luck is out, she is tired
490   Of gazing at the everlasting heaven.
The more to goad her will to die, she sees—
Oh terrible!—the holy water blacken,
Libations turn to blood, on ground and altar,

---

[21] Before sailing to Troy, the Greeks assembled their forces at the port of Aulis; it was there that the daughter of Agamemnon, Iphigenia, was sacrificed so that the gods would grant favorable winds for the sailing. Pergamus here means Troy, though strictly speaking it was the citadel of Troy.

When she makes offerings. But she tells no one,
Not even her sister. From the marble shrine,
Memorial to her former lord, attended,
Always, by her, with honor, fleece and garland,
She hears his voice, his words, her husband calling
When darkness holds the world, and from the house-top
An owl sends out a long funereal wailing,   500
And she remembers warnings of old seers,
Fearful, foreboding. In her dreams Aeneas
Appears to hunt her down; or she is going
Alone in a lost country, wandering,
Trying to find her Tyrians, mad as Pentheus,
Or frenzied as Orestes, when his mother
Is after him with whips of snakes, or firebrands,
While the Avengers menace at the threshold.[22]
    She was beaten, harboring madness, and resolved
On dying; alone, she plotted time and method;   510
Keeping the knowledge from her sorrowing sister,
She spoke with calm composure:—"I have found
A way (wish me good luck) to bring him to me
Or set me free from loving him forever.
Near Ocean[23] and the west there is a country,
The Ethiopian land, far-off, where Atlas
Turns on his shoulders the star-studded world;
I know a priestess there; she guards the temple
Of the daughters of the Evening Star; she feeds
The dragon there, and guards the sacred branches,[24]   520
She sprinkles honey-dew, strews drowsy poppies,
And she knows charms to free the hearts of lovers
When she so wills it, or to trouble others;
She can reverse the wheeling of the planets,
Halt rivers in their flowing; she can summon
The ghosts of night-time; you will see earth shaking

[22] Pentheus was driven to insanity by Bacchus for opposing the worship
of the god. Orestes was haunted by the Furies (*Avengers*) in revenge for
his killing of his mother, Clytemnestra, who had murdered his father,
Agamemnon.
[23] The waters believed to surround the world.
[24] The "daughters of the Evening Star" were the Hesperides, who, along
with a dragon, watched over the golden apples in a garden at the western
edge of the world.

Under her tread, and trees come down from mountains.
Dear sister mine, as heaven is my witness,
I hate to take these arts of magic on me!
530   Be secret, then; but in the inner courtyard,
Raise up a funeral-pyre, to hold the armor
Left hanging in the bower, by that hero,
That good devoted man, and all his raiment,
And add the bridal bed, my doom: the priestess
Said to do this, and it will be a pleasure
To see the end of all of it, every token
Of that unspeakable knave."

                       And so, thought Anna,
Things are no worse than when Sychaeus perished.
She did not know the death these rites portended,
540   Had no suspicion, and carried out her orders.

    The pyre is raised in the court; it towers high
With pine and holm-oak, it is hung with garlands
And funeral wreaths, and on the couch she places
Aeneas' sword, his garments, and his image,
Knowing the outcome. Round about are altars,
Where, with her hair unbound, the priestess calls
On thrice a hundred gods, Erebus, Chaos,
Hecate, queen of Hell, triple Diana.
Water is sprinkled, from Avernus fountain,[25]
550   Or said to be, and herbs are sought, by moonlight
Mown with bronze sickles, and the stem-ends running
With a black milk, and the caul[26] of a colt, new-born.
Dido, with holy meal and holy hands,
Stands at the altar, with one sandal loosened
And robes unfastened, calls the gods to witness,
Prays to the stars that know her doom, invoking,
Beyond them, any powers, if there are any,

---

[25] Erebus, Chaos, and Hecate (who was often represented as having three bodies and faces) were deities or powers associated with death and magic. Hecate was identified with Luna (the moon) in the sky, Diana on the earth, and Proserpina the queen of the Lower World. The entrance to the Lower World was near the lake of Avernus, in Italy.

[26] A membrane that sometimes envelops a newborn animal. Many commentators think, however, that Virgil is referring to the *hippomanes*, a growth on the head of newborn colts said to have power as a love-charm.

Who care for lovers in unequal bondage.
  Night: and tired creatures over all the world
Were seeking slumber; the woods and the wild waters   560
Were quiet, and the silent stars were wheeling
Their course half over; every field was still;
The beasts of the field, the brightly colored birds,
Dwellers in lake and pool, in thorn and thicket,
Slept through the tranquil night, their sorrows over,
Their troubles soothed. But no such blessèd darkness
Closes the eyes of Dido; no repose
Comes to her anxious heart. Her pangs redouble,
Her love swells up, surging, a great tide rising
Of wrath and doubt and passion. "What do I do?   570
What now? Go back to my Numidian suitors,
Be scorned by those I scorned? Pursue the Trojans?
Obey their orders? They were grateful to me,
Once, I remember. But who would let them take me?
Suppose I went. They hate me now; they were always
Deceivers: is Laomedon[27] forgotten,
Whose blood runs through their veins? What then? Attend
    them,
Alone, be their companion, the loud-mouthed sailors?
Or with my own armada follow after,
Wear out my sea-worn Tyrians once more   580
With vengeance and adventure? Better die.
Die; you deserve to; end the hurt with the sword.
It is your fault, Anna; you were sorry for me,
Won over by my tears; you put this load
Of evil on me. It was not permitted,
It seems, for me to live apart from wedlock,
A blameless life. An animal does better.
I vowed Sychaeus faith. I have been faithless."
So, through the night, she tossed in restless torment.
  Meanwhile Aeneas, on the lofty stern,   590
All things prepared, sure of his going, slumbers
As Mercury comes down once more to warn him,

---

[27] The notoriously dishonest former king of Troy. See III.3, III.248,
and notes.

Familiar blond young god: "O son of Venus,
Is this a time for sleep? The wind blows fair,
And danger rises all around you. Dido,
Certain to die, however else uncertain,
Plots treachery, harbors evil. Seize the moment
While it can still be seized, and hurry, hurry!
The sea will swarm with ships, the fiery torches
600   Blaze, and the shore rankle with fire by morning.
Shove off, be gone! A shifty, fickle object
Is woman, always." He vanished into the night.
And, frightened by that sudden apparition,
Aeneas started from sleep, and urged his comrades:—
"Hurry, men, hurry; get to the sails and benches,
Get the ships under way. A god from heaven
Again has come to speed our flight, to sever
The mooring-ropes. O holy one, we follow,
Whoever you are, we are happy in obeying.
610   Be with us, be propitious; let the stars
Be right in heaven!" He drew his sword; the blade
Flashed, shining, at the hawser; and all the men
Were seized in the same restlessness and rushing.
They have left the shore, they have hidden the sea-water
With the hulls of the ships; the white foam flies, the oars
Dip down in dark-blue water.
                    And Aurora[28]
Came from Tithonus' saffron couch to freshen
The world with rising light, and from her watch-tower
The queen saw day grow whiter, and the fleet
620   Go moving over the sea, keep pace together
To the even spread of the sail; she knew the harbors
Were empty of sailors now; she struck her breast
Three times, four times; she tore her golden hair,
Crying, "God help me, will he go, this stranger,
Treating our kingdom as a joke? Bring arms,
Bring arms, and hurry! follow from all the city,
Haul the ships off the ways, some of you! Others,
Get fire as fast as you can, give out the weapons,
Pull oars! What am I saying? Or where am I?

---

[28] Goddess of the dawn; mate of Tithonus.

I must be going mad. Unhappy Dido,   630
Is it only now your wickedness strikes home?
The time it should have was when you gave him power.
Well, here it is, look at it now, the honor,
The faith of the hero who, they tell me, carries
With him his household gods, who bore on his shoulders
His aged father! Could I not have seized him,
Torn him to pieces, scattered him over the waves?
What was the matter? Could I not have murdered
His comrades, and Iulus, and served the son
For a dainty at the table of his father?[29]   640
But fight would have a doubtful fortune. It might have,
What then? I was going to die; whom did I fear?
I would have, should have, set his camp on fire,
Filled everything with flame, choked off the father,
The son, the accursèd race, and myself with them.
Great Sun, surveyor of all the works of earth,
Juno, to whom my sorrows are committed,
Hecate, whom the cross-roads of the cities
Wail to by night, avenging Furies, hear me,
Grant me divine protection, take my prayer.[30]   650
If he must come to harbor, then he must,
If Jove ordains it, however vile he is,
False, and unspeakable. If Jove ordains,
The goal is fixed. So be it. Take my prayer.
Let him be driven by arms and war, an exile,
Let him be taken from his son Iulus,
Let him beg for aid, let him see his people dying
Unworthy deaths, let him accept surrender
On unfair terms, let him never enjoy the kingdom,
The hoped-for light, let him fall and die, untimely,   660
Let him lie unburied on the sand. Oh, hear me,
Hear the last prayer, poured out with my last blood!
And you, O Tyrians, hate, and hate forever

---

[29] This atrocity is committed in a number of ancient Greek myths. It
was, for example, an ancestral crime that formed part of a chain of evil
leading to the murder of Agamemnon on his return from the Trojan
war. The story is told in Aeschylus' great dramatic trilogy *The Oresteia*.

[30] Much of this curse is fulfilled in later parts of the poem (where, however, the death of Aeneas is not described).

The Trojan stock. Offer my dust this homage.
No love, no peace, between these nations, ever!
Rise from my bones, O great unknown avenger,[31]
Hunt them with fire and sword, the Dardan settlers,
Now, then, here, there, wherever strength is given.
Shore against shore, wave against wave, and war,
670 War after war, for all the generations."
    She spoke, and turned her purpose to accomplish
The quickest end to the life she hated. Briefly
She spoke to Barce, Sychaeus' nurse; her own
Was dust and ashes in her native country:—
"Dear nurse, bring me my sister, tell her to hurry,
Tell her to sprinkle her body with river water,
To bring the sacrificial beast and offerings,
And both of you cover your temples with holy fillets.
I have a vow to keep; I have made beginning
680 Of rites to Stygian[32] Jove, to end my sorrows,
To burn the litter of that Trojan leader."
Barce, with an old woman's fuss and bustle,
Went hurrying out of sight; but Dido, trembling,
Wild with her project, the blood-shot eyeballs rolling,
Pale at the death to come, and hectic[33] color
Burning the quivering cheeks, broke into the court,
Mounted the pyre in madness, drew the sword,
The Trojan gift, bestowed for no such purpose,
And she saw the Trojan garments, and the bed
690 She knew so well, and paused a little, weeping,
Weeping, and thinking, and flung herself down on it,
Uttering her last words:—
"Spoils that were sweet while gods and fate permitted,
Receive my spirit, set me free from suffering.
I have lived, I have run the course that fortune gave me,
And now my shade, a great one, will be going
Below the earth. I have built a noble city,

---

[31] Virgil is thinking of Hannibal (247–183 B.C.), the great Carthaginian general who led an invading army against Rome. Dido's curse anticipates the three Punic wars between Carthage and Rome in the third and second centuries B.C.

[32] Of the Styx, a river in the Lower World. Its ruler is Pluto or Hades (the "Stygian Jove").

[33] Feverish.

I have seen my walls, I have avenged a husband,
Punished a hostile brother. I have been
Happy, I might have been too happy, only   700
The Trojans made their landing." She broke off,
Pressed her face to the couch, cried:—"So, we shall die,
Die unavenged; but let us die. So, so,—
I am glad to meet the darkness. Let his eyes
Behold this fire across the sea, an omen
Of my death going with him."
                              As she spoke,
Her handmaids saw her, fallen on the sword,
The foam of blood on the blade, and blood on the hands.
A scream rings through the house; Rumor goes reeling,
Rioting, through the shaken town; the palace   710
Is loud with lamentation, women sobbing,
Wailing and howling, and the vaults of heaven
Echo the outcry, as if Tyre or Carthage
Had fallen to invaders, and the fury
Of fire came rolling over homes and temples.
Anna, half lifeless, heard in panic terror,
Came rushing through them all, beating her bosom,
Clawing her face:—"Was it for this, my sister?
To trick me so? The funeral pyre, the altars,
Prepared this for me? I have, indeed, a grievance,   720
Being forsaken; you would not let your sister
Companion you in death? You might have called me
To the same fate; we might have both been taken,
One sword, one hour. I was the one who built it,
This pyre, with my own hands; it was my voice
That called our fathers' gods, for what?—to fail you
When you were lying here. You have killed me, sister,
Not only yourself, you have killed us all, the people,
The town. Let me wash the wounds with water,
Let my lips catch what fluttering breath still lingers."   730
She climbed the lofty steps, and held her sister,
A dying woman, close; she used her robe
To try to stop the bleeding. And Dido tried
In vain to raise her heavy eyes, fell back,
And her wound made a gurgling hissing sound.
Three times she tried to lift herself; three times

Fell back; her rolling eyes went searching heaven
And the light hurt when she found it, and she moaned.
    At last all-powerful Juno, taking pity,
740 Sent Iris[34] from Olympus, in compassion
For the long racking agony, to free her
From the limbs' writhing and the struggle of spirit.
She had not earned this death, she had only sought it
Before her time, driven by sudden madness,
Therefore, the queen of Hades had not taken
The golden lock, consigning her to Orcus.
So Iris, dewy on saffron wings, descending,
Trailing a thousand colors through the brightness,
Comes down the sky, poises above her, saying,
750 "This lock I take as bidden, and from the body
Release the soul," and cuts the lock; and cold
Takes over, and the winds receive the spirit.[35]

---

[34] The rainbow-goddess; Juno's messenger.

[35] Orcus was another name for Pluto or Hades, king of the dead. His queen, Proserpina, would normally take a lock of Dido's hair and thus consecrate her to the powers of the Lower World, but Dido's suicide prevents the goddess from doing so; Iris must perform the rite instead of her.

BOOK V

□

The Funeral
Games for
Anchises

MEANWHILE Aeneas and the fleet were holding
The sure course over the sea, cutting the waters
That darkened under the wind. His gaze went back
To the walls of Carthage, glowing in the flame
Of Dido's funeral pyre. What cause had kindled
So high a blaze, they did not know, but anguish
When love is wounded deep, and the way of a woman
With frenzy in her heart, they knew too well,
And dwelt on with foreboding.

    They were out of sight of land, with only sea   10
Around them on all sides, alone with ocean,
Ocean and sky, when a cloud, black-blue, loomed over
With night and tempest in it; the water roughened
In shadow,[1] and the pilot Palinurus
Cried from the lofty stern. "What clouds are these
Filling the sky? What threat is father Neptune
Preparing over our heads? Trim ship,"[2] he ordered,
"Bend to the oars, reef down the sail." The course

[1] Lines 10–14 are a near-repetition of III.196–200.
[2] Haul in the ship's tackle (as protection from the high winds).

Was changed, on a slant across the wind, and the pilot
20   Turned to Aeneas: "With a sky like this,
I'd have no hope of reaching Italy,
Even if Jove himself should guarantee it.
The winds have changed, they roar across our course
From the black evening,[3] thickening into cloud.
We have no strength for headway. Luck is against us,
Let us change the course, and follow. I remember
Fraternal shores near by, the land of Eryx,
Sicilian harbors;[4] we were here before
If I recall my stars."

              Aeneas answered:
30   "I saw it long ago, the will of the winds,
The uselessness of struggle. Change the course,
Steer to the land most welcome to me; there
My friend Acestes dwells, and there my father
Anchises lies at rest. What better land
To rest our weary ships?" They made for the harbor,
With favoring wind, a swift run over the water,
A happy turn to a familiar shore.

    High on a hill-top look-out, king Acestes,
Son of a Trojan mother and Crinisus,
40   A river-god,[5] saw friendly vessels coming,
With wonder and delight, came hurrying toward them,
With a bear-skin over his shoulder, and javelins
Bristling in his grasp, and he remembered
The old relationship, and gave them welcome
With all his rustic treasure, a glad returning,
Friendly assurance for their weariness.
A good night's rest, and a bright morning followed,
And from the shore Aeneas called his comrades,
Stood on a little rise of ground, and told them:
50   "Great sons of Dardanus, heaven-born,[6] a year

---

[3] From the west. The wind drives the Trojans toward Sicily once more.

[4] Eryx, the founder of the nearby Sicilian town, was, like Aeneas, the son of Venus; hence the shores are "fraternal."

[5] Acestes' mother had been sent to Sicily by her father, to protect her from a monster that had been preying on the maidens of Troy. The Sicilian ruler Acestes has been mentioned earlier, in I.204.

[6] Dardanus, legendary king and ancestor of the Trojans, was the son of Jupiter.

Draws to an end, a year ago we buried
My father in this land, and consecrated
Sorrowful altars to his shade. The day
Comes round again, which I shall always cherish,
Always lament, with reverence, in the mourning,
For the gods' will. If I were held, an exile,
In the Gaetulian[7] quicksands, or a captive
In some Greek ship or city, I would honor
This day with solemn rites, and pile the altars
With sacrificial offering. But now,— 60
This must be heaven's purpose—we have entered
A friendly harbor. Come, then, all of us,
Let us be happy in our celebration,
Let us pray for winds, and that the god[8] hereafter
Receive his rites in temples for his honor
Built in the city we found. Two heads of oxen
Acestes gives each vessel; bring the gods
Of our own household, and the ones Acestes
Pays worship to. Nine days from now, if dawn
Comes bright and shining over the world of men, 70
There will be games, a contest for the boats,
A foot-race, javelin-throw or archery, a battle
With rawhide gloves; let all attend, competing
For victory's palm and prize.[9] And now, in silence,
Garland the brow with leaves."

                  He bound his temples
With Venus' myrtle, and the others followed,
Acestes, Helymus,[10] and young Iulus,
And the other lads, and Aeneas, from the meeting,
Moved to Anchises' tomb, and many thousands
Came thronging there. He poured libation,[11] duly, 80
Bowls of pure wine, and milk, and victim-blood,
And strewed bright flowers, praying: "Holy father,

    [7] African (from the name of a people dwelling in what is now Morocco).
    [8] The deified Anchises.
    [9] The athletic games in the following episode are modeled on the funeral games celebrated by the Greeks in honor of Achilles' dead friend Patroclus in Homer's *Iliad*, Book XXIII.
    [10] Helymus, a young friend of Acestes, was a Trojan emigrant to Sicily and the legendary ancestor of one of its tribes.
    [11] Drink-offering to the gods or the spirits.

Hail, once again; hail once again, O ashes,
Regained in vain; hail, holy shade and spirit!
Hail, from a son, destined to seek alone
The fated fields, Italian soil, alone
To seek, whatever it is, Ausonian[12] Tiber."
And as he finished speaking, a huge serpent
Slid over the ground, seven shining loops, surrounding
90   The tomb, peacefully gliding around the altars,
Dappled with blue and gold, such iridescence
As rainbow gives to cloud, when the sun strikes it.
Aeneas stood amazed; and the great serpent
Crawled to the bowls and cups, tasted the offerings,
And slid again, without a hint of menace,
Under the altar-stone.[13] Intent, Aeneas
Resumed the rites; the serpent might have been,
For all he knew, a guardian of the altar,
Or some familiar spirit[14] of Anchises.
100   Two sheep he sacrificed, two swine, two heifers,
Poured wine, invoked the spirit of his father,
And the shade loosed from Acheron.[15] His comrades
Also bring gifts, whatever they can, slay bullocks,
Load altars high; others prepare the kettles,
Sprawl on the greensward, keep the live coals glowing
Under the roasting-spits, and the meat turning.
    And the day came, the ninth they had awaited
With eagerness, bright and clear, and the crowd gathered
Under Acestes' sanction; they were eager
110   To see the Trojans, or to join the contests.
There were the prizes, tripods, and green garlands,
And palms for the winners, armor, crimson garments,
Talents[16] of silver and gold. And a trumpet heralds
The start of the games.
For the first contest

---

[12] Italian; Latin.

[13] This benevolent serpent contrasts with the serpents that had crushed Laocoön and his sons in II.221–53.

[14] Attendant spirit, of the kind that serve gods.

[15] Released the spirit (shade) of Anchises from the land of the dead (symbolized by the Acheron, a river in the Lower World), so that the spirit could be present at the rites.

[16] A talent was a unit of weight—here, a considerable one.

Four ships are entered, heavy-oared, and chosen,
The pick of the fleet. Mnestheus is one captain,
His ship the *Dragon,* and his crew is eager,—
(Later the Memmian line will call him father[17]).
Gyas commands the big *Chimaera,* a vessel
Huge as a town; it takes three tiers of oarsmen   120
To keep her moving. Then there is Sergestus
Riding the *Centaur,* and the sea-blue *Scylla*
Cloanthus leads. (The Sergian house at Rome
Descends from one, Cluentians from the other.)
     Far out in the water, facing the foaming shores,
There lies a rock, which the swollen waves beat over
On stormy days when gales blot out the stars,
But quiet in calm weather, a level landing
For the sun-loving sea-gulls. Here Aeneas
Sets a green bough of holm-oak, as a signal   130
To mark the turning-point; to this the sailors
Must row, then turn, and double back. The places
Are chosen by lot; the captains are set off,
Shining in gold and purple; all the sailors
Wear poplar-wreaths,[18] and their naked shoulders glisten
With the smear of oil. They are at their places, straining
Arms stretched to the oars, waiting the word, and their chests
Heave, and their hearts are pumping fast; ambition
And nervousness take hold of them. The signal!
They shoot away; the noise goes up to the heavens,   140
The arms pull back to the chests, the water is churned
To a foam like snow; the start is very even,
The sea gapes open under the rush of the beaks
And the pull of the oars. The racers go no faster
When the chariots take the field, and the barrier[19] springs
Cars into action, and the drivers lash
Whipping and shaking the reins. Applause and shouting
Volley and ring, and shrill excitement rises

[17] Virgil adopts the custom of tracing the roots of contemporary Roman families (such as the Memmian clan) to Trojan ancestors who, as it were, came over with the Conqueror or on the Mayflower.

[18] Poplar leaves were funereal emblems; the tree was also associated with Hercules, patron of athletes.

[19] The equivalent of the starting gate in a modern horse race.

From some with bets on the issue; all the woodland
150   Resounds, the shores are loud, and the beaten hillside
Sends back the uproar.
                      Gyas beats the others
In the rush of the starting sprint; Cloanthus follows,
With a better crew, but a slower, heavier vessel;
Behind them come the *Dragon* and the *Centaur,*
With no advantage either way; first one,
And then the other, has it, moving even
With long keels through salt water; and the leader
Has almost reached the rock, the turn; that's Gyas,
The captain, yelling loudly at his pilot:—
160   "Menoetes, what the hell! Why are you steering
So far off to the right? Bring her in closer,
This way, let the oars just miss the rocks, hug shore,
Cut her close here on the left; let the other fellows
Stay out as far as they like." Menoetes, though,
Feared unseen rocks, and made for open water.
"Why so far off the course? The rock, Menoetes,
Keep close to the rock!" And while he shouted, Gyas
Could see Cloanthus coming up behind him
Inside him, on the left, and gaining, gaining.
170   Between the roar of the rock and the ship of Gyas,
Cloanthus grazed his way, and passed the leader,
Made the turn safely, and reached open water.
Then Gyas really was burnt up; he was crying
In rage; to hell with pride, to hell with safety!
He grabbed that cautious pilot of his, and heaved him
Over the stern, he took the rudder over,
Steering for shore, and yelling at the sailors,
As old Menoetes slowly came to the surface,
His heavy garments dripping, clawing and scrambling
180   Up to the top of the rock, to perch there, drying,
A good laugh for the Trojans, as they watched him
Taking his header, coming up, and swimming,
And spitting out salt water.
                         The two last ones,
Mnestheus and Sergestus, were encouraged;
Gyas was easy now; Sergestus managed

To get ahead, a little; he neared the rock,
Less than a length ahead; the rival *Dragon*
Was lapped on him, and up and down, amidships,
Went Mnestheus, cheering on his crew:—"Get going,
Rise to the oars, my comrades, men of Hector   190
Whom I picked out for mine in Troy's last moment.
Show the old spirit and the nerve that took us
Through the Gaetulian sands, Ionian waters,
Off Cape Malea![20] We can't hope to win it,—
Let Neptune look to that!—maybe—at least,
Whatever we do, don't come in last! We could not
Bear any such disgrace." They did their utmost,
Straining with all their might, the bronze deck shaking
Under the effort, and the quiet ocean
Streamed under and past them. Arms and legs were weary,   200
Wobbly, shaking; breath came hard, they gulped
And gasped for air, and sweat ran down in rivers,
And they had some luck. Sergestus, out of his senses,
Drove in, too close, and piled up on the rock,
Which almost bounced as he hit there, and the oars
Were sheared away, and the bow hung up, and the sailors,
Shouting like mad, pushed hard with pikes or boat-hooks,
Or the wreck of the oars, to shove them off. And Mnestheus
Easier now, and with exalted spirit
From this much victory, with a prayer to the winds   210
And the oars' swift drive, was running down-hill waters,
Over the open ocean, as a dove
Suddenly startled out of her nest in a cavern
Where the young brood waits, wings to the fields in fright,
Flapping on anxious pinions, and recovers,
And skims down peaceful air, with never a motion
Of wing in the lifting air, so Mnestheus sped,
So sped the *Dragon,* racing home, and the sweep
Of her own speed made a wind. She passed Sergestus
Struggling, rock-bound, in shallow water, howling   220
For help, in vain, and learning how to manage

[20] Cape Malea was a headland at the southernmost tip of Greece; a
navigational peril, it would have been passed by the Trojans in their journey
related in Book III.

A boat when the oars are broken. She overhauled
Gyas, in the *Chimaera,* wallowing heavy
Without a pilot. Only Cloanthus was left;
They were after him with all their might, the clamor
Rose twice as loud; they were cheering the pursuer,
And the sky was a crash of shouting. On the *Scylla*
They would give their lives to hold their place, they have
        won it,
The glory and honor are theirs already, almost;
230   And Mnestheus' men take courage from their nearness;
They can because they think they can. They would have,
Perhaps, or tied, at least, had not Cloanthus
Taken to prayer:—"Gods of the seas, whose waters
I skim, whose empire lifts me up, I gladly
Promise you sacrifice, a snow-white bullock
At altars on this shore, and wine for the ocean,
And the entrails flung to the flood!" Under the waves
The Nereids heard him, Phorcus, Panopea
The maiden, and Portunus, the big-handed,
240   Boosted him on his way.[21] Swifter than arrow,
Swifter than wind, the ship swept into the harbor.
    The herald's cry proclaimed Cloanthus victor,
When all were summoned, and Anchises' son
Put the green bay leaf on his temples, silver
And wine for the ships, a steer for each. The captains
Have special prizes; the winner has a mantle,
Woven with gold, and a double seam of crimson,
With a story in the texture, Ganymede
Hunting on Ida, breathless, tossing darts
250   And racing after the deer, and caught and carried
In the talons of Jove's eagle, soaring skyward,
While the boy's old guardians reach their hands up, vainly,
And the hounds set up a cry.[22] Mnestheus, second,
Has a coat of mail, with triple links of gold,

---

[21] Phorcus was a sea-monster, Panopea a Nereid, or sea-nymph, Portunus
a god of harbors.
[22] Ganymede was a Trojan prince desired by Jupiter for his beauty; while
hunting, he was swept up into heaven to be cupbearer of the gods. See
I.35 for Juno's resentment of him.

A trophy of Demoleos; Aeneas
Had beaten him at Troy, by Simois river,
And taken the armor, glory and guard in battle.
The servants, Sagaris and Phegeus, hardly
Can lift it up, but when Demoleos wore it,
He could go, full-speed, after the flying Trojans.   260
The third award is a pair of brazen[23] caldrons,
And bowls embossed in silver.
                               They had their prizes
And went their way, proud of their wealth, and shining
With foreheads garlanded, when with much effort,
Scraped off the rock, oars lost, and one bank crippled,
Here came Sergestus, butt of jeering laughter,
Like a snake with a broken back, which a wagon-wheel
Runs over on the road, or a traveller smashes
With the weight of a stone, and, crushed, it writhes and
    struggles,
Looping the coils, and half of it is angry   270
With fiery eyes and hissing mouth, and half
Keeps dragging back the rest and doubles over
On useless muscles, powerless; Sergestus
Came home like such a serpent, maimed and broken,
But the sail went bravely up as they made the harbor,
And Aeneas kept his promise to the captain,
Glad for the ship's return, and the safe sailors.
A slave-girl, Pholoe from Crete, accomplished
At weaving, was his prize, and her twin children,
Boy-infants, at the breast.   280
The boat-race over, Aeneas makes his way
To a grassy plain, with wooded hills surrounding
The race-course in the valley. All the crowd
Come trooping after, group themselves around
The central prominence. Rewards and prizes
Draw the competitors, travellers and natives,
Trojans, Sicilians; in the foremost ranks
Are Nisus and Euryalus, the latter
Conspicuous in the flower of youth and beauty,

---

[23] Made of brass.

290   Whom Nisus follows with entire devotion:
       Diores, of the royal house of Priam,
       Was ready; Salius, an Acarnanian;
       Patron, Tegean-born; and two Sicilians,
       Panopes, Helymus, trained to the forests,
       Companions of Acestes; and many others
       Whose fame by now the darkness hides. Aeneas
       Speaks to their hope:—"No one goes unrewarded:
       To each I give two Cretan arrows, gleaming
       With polished steel, and a double-bitted axe
300   Embossed with silver. Everybody wins
       These prizes, but the first three runners also
       Shall wear the wreath of olive, and the winner
       Ride home a horse equipped with splendid trappings;
       For second place, an Amazonian quiver
       With Thracian arrows,[24] a broad belt of gold
       With jeweled buckle; and this Argive helmet
       For the one who comes in third."
                                    They take their places,
       And when the signal is given, away they go,
       Like rain from storm-cloud, bodies leaning forward,
310   Eyes on the goal. And for the lead it's Nisus,
       Swifter than winds or lightning; running second,
       A good way back, comes Salius; and the third one,
       Third at some distance, is Euryalus,
       Helymus next; right on his heels Diores.
       There's a little crowding there, the course too narrow,
       Diores, full of run, is in a pocket,
       He can't get through. The race is almost over,
       Their breath comes hard, they are almost at the finish,—
       There's a pool of blood on the ground, where the slain
            bullocks
320   Fell in the sacrifice, a slippery puddle
       Red on green ground, and Nisus does not see it,
       Nisus, still leading, thinking himself the winner,
       Is out of luck, his feet slide out from under,
       He wobbles, totters, recovers himself a little,

---

[24] The Amazons, great women warriors, and the Thracians were renowned archers allied with the Trojans.

Slips and goes forward, in a beautiful header
Through blood and mud. But he keeps his wits about him,
Does not forget his friend Euryalus; rising,
And sort of accidentally on purpose,
Gets in the way of Salius and spills him,
A cartwheel, head over heels on the flying sand.   330
Euryalus flashes past, an easy winner
Thanks to his friend's assistance, and they cheer him;
Helymus second; in third place, Diores.
   Immediately there's a loud howl of protest,
Salius shrieking in the elders' faces
With cries of *Foul!* and *Outrage!* "I was robbed,
Give me first prize!" But all the popular favor
Sides with Euryalus, who is young, and weeping,
And better-looking; and Diores backs him,
Loudly, of course, since who would get the helmet   340
If Salius was first? Aeneas ends it:—
"The race will stand as run; you get your prizes
As first proposed; no one will change the order;
But one thing I can do, and will do,—offer
A consolation to our innocent friend."
With this, he gives a lion-skin to Salius,
Heavy with shaggy hair, and the claws gilded.
Nisus is heard from:—"If you're giving prizes
For falling down, what's good enough for Nisus?
I would have won it surely, only Fortune   350
Gave me the same bad deal she handed Salius!"
And with the words he made a sudden gesture
Showing his muddy face. Aeneas, laughing,
Ordered another prize, a shield for him,
The work of Didymaon, stolen by Greeks
From Neptune's temple sometime, but recovered,
A worthy prize for a distinguished hero.
   Next is a boxing-bout. "Whoever has courage
And fighting spirit in his heart, step forward
And put the gloves on!" There are double prizes,   360
For the winner a bullock, decked with gold and ribbons,
A sword and shining helmet for the loser.
Without delay, Dares gets up; a murmur
Runs through the crowd as this big man comes forward.

They know that he was Paris' sparring-partner,[25]
And they recall his famous match with Butes
At Hector's tomb, where he knocked out that champion
And stretched him dying on the yellow sand.
Now Dares holds his head up for the battle,
370 Shakes his broad shoulders loose, warms up a little,
A left, a right, a left, in shadow-boxing.
Who will oppose him? No one puts the gloves on,
No one, from all that throng, is in a hurry
To take on Dares. So, exultant, thinking
Himself a winner by default, he grabs
The bullock by one horn, says to Aeneas:—
"If no man, goddess-born, is taking chances,
How long must I keep standing here? How long
Hang around waiting? Give the order, let me
380 Lead home my prize!" The Trojans all applaud him.
But king Acestes, sprawling on the greensward
Beside Entellus, nudges him a little:—
"What was the use, Entellus, of being a hero,
Of having been our bravest, under Eryx?
Where is that old Sicilian reputation,
And all those prizes hanging from the rafters?
Does Dares get away with this, no contest,
And all those prizes, and you sit here tamely?"
Entellus answers, "Oh, I still love glory
390 And praise; there's nothing the matter with my courage,
But I'm too old, the blood is slow and colder,
The strength not what it used to be. That bragger
Has one thing, youth, and how he revels in it!
If I had what he has, I'd not need prizes,
Bullocks or helmets either, to get me fighting."
From somewhere he produced the gloves of Eryx
And tossed them into the ring, all stiff and heavy,
Seven layers of hide, and insewn lead and iron.
The people stand amazed, and Dares shudders,
400 Wanting no part of gloves like these; Aeneas

[25] Paris, the Trojan abductor of Helen, though not a formidable warrior,
had according to some traditions been a skilled boxer.

Inspects them, turning them slowly, over and over,
And old Entellus adds a word of comment:—
"Why, these are nothing! What if you had seen
The gloves of Hercules? He used to fight here.
These are the gloves that Eryx wore against him.[26]
You still can see the blood and a splash of brains
That stained them long ago. I used to wear them
Myself when I was younger, and unchallenged
By Time, that envious rival. But if Dares
Declines these arms, all right, make matters equal,   410
Don't be afraid; I waive the gloves of Eryx,
You put the Trojan gloves aside; Aeneas
Will see fair play, Acestes be my second."
He throws the double cloak from off his shoulders,
Strips down to the great limbs, great bones, great muscles,
A giant in the ring. Aeneas brings them
Matched pairs of gloves.
                    They take their stand, each rising
On the balls of his feet, their arms upraised, and rolling
Their heads back from the punch. They spar, they lead,
They watch for openings. Dares, much the younger,   420
Is much the better in footwork; old Entellus
Has to rely on strength; his knees are shaky,
His wind not what it was. They throw their punches,
And many miss; and some, with a solid thump,
Land on the ribs or chest; temples and ears
Feel the wind of a miss, or the jaws rattle
When a punch lands. Entellus stands flat-footed,
Wasting no motion, just a slip of the body,
The watchful eyes alert. And Dares, feinting,
Like one who artfully attacks a city,   430
Tries this approach, then that, dancing around him
In varied vain attack. Entellus, rising,
Draws back his right (in fact, he telegraphs it),
And Dares, seeing it coming, slips aside;
Entellus lands on nothing but the wind
And, thrown off balance, heavily comes down

---

[26] In the bout, Eryx had been killed by Hercules.

Flat on his face, as falls on Erymanthus[27]
A thunder-smitten oak, and so on, and so on.
Roaring, the Trojans and Sicilians both
440   Rise to their feet; the noise goes up to heaven;
Acestes rushes in, to raise his comrade
In pity and sorrow. But that old-time fighter
Is not slowed down a bit, nor made more wary;
His rage is terrible, and his shame awakens
A consciousness of strength. He chases Dares
All over the ring, left, right, left, right, the punches
Rattle like hailstones on a roof; he batters Dares,
Spins him halfway around with one hand, clouts him
Straight with the other again. At last Aeneas
450   Steps in and stops it, with a word of comfort
For the exhausted Dares:—"Luckless fellow,
Yield to the god! What madness blinds your vision
To strength beyond your own?" They rescue Dares,
And drag him to the ships, with his knees caving,
Head rolling side to side, spitting out blood
And teeth; he hardly sees the sword and helmet.
They leave the palm and bullock for Entellus,
Who, in the pride of victory, cries aloud:
"Look, goddess-born! Watch, Trojans, and discover
460   Two things—how strong I was when I was younger,
And what a death you've kept away from Dares!"
And, with the word, he faced his prize, the bullock,
Drew back his right hand, poised it, sent it smashing
Between the horns, shattering the skull, and splashing
Brains on the bones, as the great beast came down, lifeless.
"This life, a better one than Dares', Eryx,
I vow as sacrifice, and so, victorious,
Retire, and lay aside the gloves forever."
          Next comes an archery contest. Aeneas offers
470   Prizes and summons; on Serestus' vessel
The mast is raised, and from its top a cord
With a fluttering dove bound to it as the mark.
Four enter; a bronze helmet takes the lots,

---

[27] A mountain in Arcadia, in Greece.

Hippocoön's leaps out first; then Mnestheus follows,
Green with the olive garland, sign and token
Of ship well driven; and third was Pandarus' brother,
Eurytion; Pandarus was the archer
Who once broke truce with the Greeks, firing an arrow
In the days of peace;[28] and last came king Acestes,
Willing to try his hand with younger men.   480
    They bend the pliant bows, each archer straining,
Draw shaft from quiver. First from the twanging string
Hippocoön's arrow flew, through sky, through wind,
Reaching its mark in the wood of the mast, which trembled
And the bird flapped wings in terror, and the crowd
Rang with applause. Mnestheus took his stand,
Drawing the bow back, aiming a little higher,
And missed the bird, but severed knot and tether,
And the dove sped free to the south. Eurytion, waiting
And ready, called in prayer upon his brother,   490
Let the dart fly, brought down the bird, exulting,
From under the dark of the cloud. She came down lifeless,
Pierced by the arrow still. No prize was left
For king Acestes, but he fired his arrow,
High as he could, to prove his skill. And a wonder
Came to their eyes; it proved an omen later
When seers explained its meaning.[29] The shaft caught fire
Flying amid the clouds, a course of flame,
Vanishing into space, as comets stream
Sweeping across the heaven, their long train flying   500
Behind them through the sky. All hearts were shaken,
Sicilian, Trojan, both, and all men prayed
To the powers on high. Aeneas hailed the omen,
Embraced Acestes, loaded him with presents,
Saying, "Receive them, father; for the king
Of heaven has willed it so, unusual honors

---

[28] This episode of truce-breaking, in which Pandarus shoots at Menelaus, is described in Homer's *Iliad,* Book IV. The truce had been agreed on so that Paris and Menelaus, Helen's lover and her husband, could resolve the war through single combat.

[29] Virgil never explains this reference; we are left to wonder what the omen was later understood to mean.

For skill surpassing. This bowl, with graven figures,
Anchises owned, given him by a Thracian,
King Cisseus,[30] memorial and token
510   Of everlasting friendship." On his brows
He bound green laurel, hailing Acestes victor
Over the rest, and no one grudged the honor,
Not even Eurytion, who had shot the dove;
Mnestheus, for the cutting of the tether,
Took his reward, and the one who hit the mast,
Hippocoön, was not forgotten either.
    But while the shoot was on, Aeneas called
Epytides, Iulus' guardian, to him,
With words for a loyal ear:—"Go, tell Iulus,
520   If the boys are ready, and the horses marshalled,
To lead them, for Anchises' sake, presenting
Himself in arms." And he bade the throng draw back,
Leaving the long course clear and the field open.
The boys rode in, shining on bridled ponies
Before their fathers' eyes, in true formation,
To a murmur of delight. The garlands weighed
The young hair down, they carried cornel spear-wands
With iron at the tip; and some had quivers
Bright-polished, at their shoulders; torques[31] of gold
530   Looped high on the breast in pliant rings. Three leaders
Led, each, three squadrons, and a dozen followed
Each gay young captain. One of them was Priam,
Son of Polites, and King Priam's grandson,
On a piebald Thracian, white of brow and fetlock.[32]
Young Atys led another line—(The Atii,
In Latium, claim descent from him)—young Atys,
Iulus' special friend.[33] And last, most handsome,

---

[30] Regarded by Virgil as father of Queen Hecuba of Troy.

[31] The torque was a military decoration, of twisted metal, worn around the neck and across the breast.

[32] The area above the hoof.

[33] This is one of Virgil's many glances at his own age: Julius Caesar, who had adopted Octavian, had belonged to the clan Julia, while Octavian (Caesar Augustus) belonged to the clan Atia. The equestrian maneuvers in the present episode anticipate the *Lusus Troiae*, or *Ludus Troianus* (Trojan Games), a Roman ceremony sponsored in the poet's era by both Caesars.

Iulus rode a Carthaginian courser,
Queen Dido's gift. Sicilian horses carried
The other riders, who rode up to the cheering,   540
Shy, as they heard the sound, and the fond welcome
Of crowds that saw the fathers in the children.
They rode full circle once, and then a signal,
A crack of the whip, was given, and they parted
Into three groups, went galloping off, recalled,
Wheeled, made mock charge, with lances at the ready,
Made march and counter-march, troops intermingled
With troops, to right and left, in mimic battle,
Mimic retreat, and mimic peace, a course
Confusing as the Labyrinth in Crete   550
Whose path runs through blind walls, where craft has hidden
A thousand wandering ways, mistake and error
Threading insoluble mazes,[34] so the children,
The sons of Troy, wove in and out, in conflict
In flight and sport, as happy as dolphins leaping
Through the Carpathian waters.[35] This was a custom
Ascanius, when grown, himself established
At Alba Longa,[36] his own town, and taught there
What he had learned in boyhood, and the Albans
In turn informed their children, and the Romans   560
Keep this ancestral rite; the boys are Troy,
And the game Trojan, to this very day,
From its first observance, in Anchises' honor.
    Here fortune changed, not keeping faith; for Juno,
While the ritual of sport went on, sent Iris,
With a fair wind, to the Trojan fleet. She was angry,
Still, and the ancient grudge unsatisfied,
And Iris, over her thousand-colored rainbow,
Ran her swift path, unseen, beheld the crowd,
Surveyed the shore, harbor and fleet deserted,   570
While far off on the lonely coast the women

---

[34] The famous labyrinth of Crete was built by the master craftsman Daedalus to conceal the Minotaur, a monster born of the Cretan queen Pasiphae after she made love with a bull. For a fuller version of the story, see VI.13–37 and note.

[35] The sea separating Crete from the mainland of Asia Minor.

[36] The city, forerunner of Rome, to be founded by Ascanius.

Mourned for Anchises lost, weeping and watching
The unfathomable deep. "For weary people,
Alas! how much remains, of shoal and ocean!"
So ran the common sigh. They crave a city,
They are tired of bearing the vast toil of sailing,
And into their midst came Iris, versed in mischief,
Laying aside her goddess-guise, becoming
Old Beroe, Doryclus' wife, who sometime
580   Had children, fame, and lineage. Now Iris,
Resembling her, came down to the Trojan mothers.
"Alas for us!" she cried, "on whom the Greeks
Never laid hands, to drag us down to death
Before our native walls! Unfortunate people,
For what is fortune saving us, what doom,
What dying? It is seven weary summers
Since Troy's destruction, and still we wander over
All lands, all seas, with rocks and stars forever
Implacable, as we go on pursuing
590   A land that flees forever over the waters.
Here lived our brother Eryx, here we find
A welcomer, king Acestes; who forbids us
To found the walls, to build our city here?
O fatherland, O household gods in vain
Saved from the Greeks, will there never be any walls
For Troy again? No Simois or Xanthus,
The rivers Hector loved? Come with me, burn
These vessels of ill-omen. Let me tell you,
I have been given warnings; in a dream
600   I saw Cassandra,[37] she was giving me firebrands,
Here seek your Troy, here is your home, she told me;
It is time for us to act, be quick about it!
Neptune himself, with fire on these four altars,
Provides the method, and the resolution."
    She was the first to seize a brand; she raised it
Above her head, and swung it, streaming and glowing,

---

[37] The doomed Trojan prophetess; compare II.270,430–34; III.185–91.
Her fictitious prophetic utterance here is persuasive as her authentic ones
never had been while she lived.

And flung it forth. The women, for a moment,
Stood in bewilderment, and one, the oldest,
Named Pyrgo, nurse to Priam's many children,
Cried out:—"This is no Beroe, I tell you,   610
Mothers! Look at her flashing eyes, her spirit,
Her stride, her features; every mark of the goddess
Attends her presence. Beroe I myself
Have just now come from; she lies ill and grieving
All by herself, in sorrow for her absence
From reverence for Anchises."
                              As they gazed
Doubtfully at the ships, with sullen eyes,
Distracted, torn between a sickly yearning
For present land and rest, and the kingdoms calling
Them fatefully over the sea, the goddess, cleaving   620
The air on her bright pinions,[38] rose to heaven.
They were shaken then, amazed, and frenzy-driven;
They cried aloud; tore fire from the hearths and altars;
Made tinder of the altar-decorations,
The garlandry and wreaths. And the fire, let loose,
Rioted over thwarts and oars and rigging.
   To theatre and tomb Eumelus brought
Word of the ships on fire; and the men could see
The black ash billowing in the smoky cloud,
And first Ascanius, as full of spirit   630
As when he led the games, rushed to the trouble
As fast as he could ride; no troubled masters
Could hold him back. "Poor things, what are you doing?
What craziness is this? what are you up to?
It is no Greek camp, no enemy you're burning
But your own hopes! Look at me! Here I am,
Your own Ascanius!" And before their feet
He flung the helmet he had worn when leading
The little war-game. And Aeneas hurried
With others to the troubled camp. The women   640
Scattered and fled along the shore, in terror
And guilt, wherever they could, to hiding-places

[38] Wings.

In woods or caves in the rock; they are ashamed
Of daylight and their deed; Juno is shaken
Out of their hearts, and they recognize their own.
That does not stop the fire; it burns in fury
Under wet oak, tow smoulders, and the stubborn
Steam eats the keels away, destruction seizing
On deck and hull, and water can not quench it,
650 Nor any strength of men. Tearing his garment
Loose from his shoulders, Aeneas prays to heaven:—
"Almighty Jove, if the Trojans are not hateful
To the last man, if any record of goodness
Alleviates human trouble, let our fleet
Escape this flame, O father; save from doom
This little Trojan remnant; or with lightning,
If I deserve it, strike us down forever!"
He had scarcely spoken, when a cloudburst fell
Full force, with darkness and black tempest streaming,
660 And thunder rumbling over plain and hillock,
The whole sky pouring rain; the ships were drowned
With water from above, the half-burnt timbers
Were soaked, and the hiss of steam died out; four vessels
Were gone, the others rescued from disaster.
   And now Aeneas, stunned by the bitter evil,
Was troubled at heart, uncertain, anxious, grieving:
What could be done? forget the call of the fates
And settle here in Sicily, or keep on
To the coast of Italy? An old man, Nautes,
670 Whom Pallas[39] had instructed in deep wisdom,
Gave him the answer. "Goddess-born, wherever
Fate pulls or hauls us, there we have to follow;
Whatever happens, fortune can be beaten
By nothing but endurance. We have here
A friend, Acestes, Trojan-born, divine
In parentage; make him an ally in counsel,
Partner in enterprise; to him hand over
The ones whose ships are lost, and all the weary,
The sick and tired, the old men, and the mothers

[39] Pallas Athena, or Minerva, goddess of wisdom. Nautes, according to
a tradition, was her priest, who helped introduce her rites to Rome.

Who have had too much of the sea, and the faint-hearted,   680
Whose weariness may find a city for them
Here in this land; Acesta, let them call it."
The old man's words still troubled him; the mind
Was torn this way and that. Night rode the heavens
In her dark chariot, and there came from the darkness
The image of Anchises, speaking to him
In words of comfort:—"Son, more dear to me
Than life, when life was mine; son, sorely troubled
By Trojan fate, I come at Jove's command,
Who drove the fire away, and from the heaven   690
Has taken pity. Obey the words of Nautes,
He gives the best of counsel; the flower of the youth,
The bravest hearts, lead on to Italy.
There will be trouble there, a rugged people
Must be subdued in Latium. Come to meet me,
First, in the lower world; come through Avernus[40]
To find me, son. Tartarus' evil prison
Of gloomy shades I know not, for I dwell
Among the happy spirits in Elysium.
Black sheep are good for sacrifice. The Sibyl,   700
A holy guide, will lead the way, foretelling
The race to come, the given walls. Farewell,
My son; the dewy night is almost over,
I feel the breath of the morning's cruel horses."
He spoke, and vanished, smoke into airy thinness,
From the cries of his son, who woke, and roused the embers
Of the drowsing altar-fires, with meal and censer
Propitiating Vesta,[41] making worship
To Trojan household gods.
             And called Acestes
And the Trojan counsellors, told them of Jove   710
And his good father's orders, the decision
He has reached at last. They all agree, Acestes
Accepts the trust. They make a roll for the city,
The women-folk, the people willing to linger,
The unadventurous; and they make ready

[40] The lake near the entrance to the Lower World of the dead; also, the Lower World itself. Aeneas will visit it in Book VI.
[41] Goddess of the hearth and home; compare I.306 and II.591.

The thwarts again, replace the fire-scorched timbers,
Fit out new oars and rigging. There are not many,
But a living company, for war brave-hearted.
Aeneas ploughs the limits for the city,
720 Sets out new homes, Ilium, again, and Troy,
A kingdom welcome to Acestes, senate
And courts, and laws, established; and a shrine
High on the crest of Eryx, is given Venus,
Near the high stars, and a priest assigned as warden
To the wide boundaries of Anchises' grove.
    Nine days they hold farewells, one tribe together
For the last time, with honor at the altars,
And seas are calm, and winds go down, and the whisper
Of a little breeze calls to the sail; the shore
730 Hears a great wail arise; they cling to each other
All through the night and day. Even the mothers,
The weary men, to whom the face of the sea
Once seemed so cruel, and its very name
A menacing monster, want to go now, willing
For all the toil of exile. These Aeneas
Comforts with friendly words, and bids Acestes
Be their good brother. Then he slays to Eryx
Three bullocks, and a lamb to the gods of storm-cloud.
It is time to loose the cables. At the bow
740 He stands, his temples garlanded with olive,
Makes to the sea libation of wine and entrails,
And the wind comes up astern, and they sweep the waters
In happy rivalry.
                      But meanwhile Venus,
Driven by worry, went to Neptune, pouring
Complaints from a full heart:—"Neptune, the anger
Of Juno, her insatiable vengeance,
Which neither time nor any goodness softens,
Drives me to humble prayer. She never weakens
For Jove's command, nor the orders of the fates;
750 It is not enough for her that the Trojan city
Is quite consumed by hatred, and the remnants
Of that poor town harried all over the world
With every kind of punishment; she still follows
Even their bones and ashes. She may know

The reasons for that wrath of hers. Remember
How great a weight of water she stirred up lately
In the Libyan seas, confusing sky and ocean,
With Aeolus conspiring, and in your kingdom!
And now her crime has driven the Trojan mothers 760
To burn their ships, to give their comrades over
To a coast unknown. Let what is left come safely
Over the sea, to reach Laurentian[42] Tiber,
If what I ask is just, if those are walls
Due them by fate's decree."
     And Neptune answered:—
"None has a better right to trust my kingdom
Than the goddess born of the sea-foam. And I have earned
This confidence. I have often checked the anger
Of sea and sky. And the rivers of Troy are witness
I have helped on land as well, and saved Aeneas.
When thousands died at Troy, with fierce Achilles 770
In hot pursuit, and the rivers groaned, and Xanthus
Could hardly find the sea, I formed a cloud
Around Aeneas, when he met Achilles
With the gods adverse, and no great strength to help him,
I rescued him, in spite of my own anger
At the perjury of Troy, in spite of my passion
To raze the walls I had built.[43] Now too my purpose
Remains; have done with fear; he will reach in safety
The haven of Avernus; the prayer is granted.
Let one be lost in the flood, one life alone 780
Be given for the many."
    This comfort given,
To bring the goddess joy, he yoked his horses,
Gold bridle, foaming bit, and sent them flying
With the lightest touch of the reins, skimming the surface
In the bright blue car; and the waves went down, the axle
Subdued the swell of the wave, and storm-clouds melted

---

[42] Latin (from Laurentum, a kingdom in west-central Italy prominent in the latter half of the poem).

[43] The rescue of Aeneas by Neptune (Poseidon) is described in Homer's *Iliad*, Books XX and XXI. The "perjury of Troy" refers to the refusal by the early Trojan king Laomedon to pay Neptune what he had been promised for helping to build the city's walls.

To nothing in the sky, and his attendants
Followed along, great whales, and ancient Glaucus,
Palaemon, Ino's son, and the rushing Tritons,
790   The army of Phorcus, Melite and Thetis
Watching the left, and the maiden Panopea,
Cymodoce and Thalia and Spio,[44]
So that Aeneas, in his turn, was happy,
Less anxious at heart. The masts are raised, and sail
Stretched from the halyards; right and left they bend
The canvas to fair winds: at the head of the fleet
Rides Palinurus, and the others follow,
As ordered, close behind him; dewy night
Has reached mid-heaven, while the sailors, sleeping,
800   Relax on the hard benches under the oars,
All calm, all quiet. And the god of Sleep,
Parting the shadowy air, comes gently down,
Looking for Palinurus, bringing him,
A guiltless man, ill-omened dreams. He settles
On the high stern, a god disguised as a man,
Speaking in Phorbas'[45] guise, "O Palinurus,
The fleet rides smoothly in the even weather,
The hour is given for rest. Lay down the head,
Rest the tired eyes from toil. I will take over
810   A little while." But Palinurus, barely
Lifting his eyes, made answer: "Trust the waves,
However quiet? trust a peaceful ocean?
Put faith in such a monster? Never! I
Have been too often fooled by the clear stars
To trust Aeneas to their faithless keeping."
And so he clung to the tiller, never loosed
His hand from the wood, his eyes from the fair heaven.
But lo, the god over his temples shook
A bough that dripped with dew from Lethe, steeped
820   With Stygian magic,[46] so the swimming eyes,
Against his effort, close, blink open, close
Again, and slumber takes the drowsy limbs.

[44] The names in these five lines are those of sea-gods and sea-nymphs.
[45] A friend of Palinurus.
[46] Lethe, the river of forgetfulness, and Styx, the river of death, are
part of the landscape of the Lower World, described in Book VI.

Bending above him, leaning over, the god
Shoves him, still clinging to the tiller, calling
His comrades vainly, into the clear waves.
And the god is gone like a bird to the clear air,
And the fleet is going safely over its journey
As Neptune promised. But the rocks were near,
The Siren-cliffs, most perilous of old,
White with the bones of many mariners,   830
Loud with their hoarse eternal warning sound.[47]
Aeneas starts from sleep, aware, somehow,
Of a lost pilot, and a vessel drifting,
Himself takes over guidance, with a sigh
And heartache for a friend's mishap, "Alas,
Too trustful in the calm of sea and sky,
O Palinurus, on an unknown shore,
You will be lying, naked."

---

[47] The Sirens, as described in Homer's *Odyssey*, Book XII, were females who enchanted sailors with their beautiful songs, luring them to destruction. Virgil associates this peril with certain actual rocks in the sea near modern Naples.

BOOK VI

□

The
Lower World

MOURNING for Palinurus, he drives the fleet
To Cumae's[1] coast-line; the prows are turned, the anchors
Let down, the beach is covered by the vessels.
Young in their eagerness for the land in the west,
They flash ashore; some seek the seeds of flame
Hidden in veins of flint, and others spoil
The woods of tinder, and show where water runs.
Aeneas, in devotion, seeks the heights
Where stands Apollo's temple, and the cave
Where the dread Sibyl dwells, Apollo's priestess,   10
With the great mind and heart, inspired revealer
Of things to come. They enter Diana's grove,
Pass underneath the roof of gold.[2]
                                        The story
Has it that Daedalus fled from Minos' kingdom,
Trusting himself to wings he made, and travelled
A course unknown to man, to the cold north,

---

[1] A city, near the modern Naples, where Aeneas is to visit the Sibyl
named Deiphobe, mythical prophet and priestess of Apollo, in preparation
for his visit to the Lower World.

[2] The temple and its environs were sacred to both Apollo and Diana,
his full sister. In her alter ego as Hecate, she was goddess of the Lower
World and was sometimes associated with witchcraft.

Descending on this very summit; here,
Earth-bound again, he built a mighty temple,
Paying Apollo homage, the dedication
20   Of the oarage of his wings. On the temple doors
He carved, in bronze, Androgeos' death, and the payment
Enforced on Cecrops' children, seven sons
For sacrifice each year: there stands the urn,
The lots are drawn—facing this, over the sea,
Rises the land of Crete: the scene portrays
Pasiphae in cruel love, the bull
She took to her by cunning, and their offspring,
The mongrel Minotaur, half man, half monster,
The proof of lust unspeakable; and the toil
30   Of the house is shown, the labyrinthine maze
Which no one could have solved, but Daedalus
Pitied a princess' love, loosened the tangle,
Gave her a skein to guide her way. His boy,
Icarus, might have been here, in the picture,
And almost was—his father had made the effort
Once, and once more, and dropped his hands; he could
    not
Master his grief that much.[3] The story held them;
They would have studied it longer, but Achates[4]
Came from his mission; with him came the priestess,

---

[3] Minos was king of Crete. His wife Pasiphae, in a bovine disguise fabricated by the craftsman Daedalus, made love with a bull and then gave birth to the Minotaur, half bull and half human. (Compare V.550–53.) Minos then forced Daedalus to construct a labyrinth to contain the Minotaur. After the Athenians killed Androgeos, the son of Minos, the king in revenge forced them (the "children" of Cecrops, an early king of Athens) to sacrifice to the Minotaur, each year, the lives of seven young men and seven young women, chosen by lots drawn from an urn. The Athenian hero Theseus went to Crete and succeeded in killing the monster that was devouring his compatriots. In this enterprise he was helped by Daedalus and the love-smitten Ariadne, Minos' daughter, who gave Theseus a thread to guide him back out of the labyrinth. Imprisoned for his part in this feat, Daedalus with his son Icarus escaped from Crete on wings the father had constructed; Icarus, however, died when he flew too close to the sun, which melted the wax fastenings of his wings. Daedalus, after reaching Italy, built the temple and executed the carvings that Aeneas is examining, though Virgil represents the artist as having been incapable, in his grief, of representing his son's tragic story.
[4] Aeneas' most faithful friend.

Deiphobe, daughter of Glaucus,[5] who tends the temple   40
For Phoebus and Diana; she warned Aeneas:
"It is no such sights the time demands; far better
To offer sacrifice, seven chosen bullocks,
Seven chosen ewes, a herd without corruption."
They were prompt in their obedience, and the priestess
Summoned the Trojans to the lofty temple.
  The rock's vast side is hollowed into a cavern,
With a hundred mouths, a hundred open portals,
Whence voices rush, the answers of the Sibyl.
They had reached the threshold, and the virgin cried: 50
"It is time to seek the fates; the god is here,
The god is here, behold him." And as she spoke
Before the entrance, her countenance and color
Changed, and her hair tossed loose, and her heart was
    heaving,
Her bosom swollen with frenzy; she seemed taller,
Her voice not human at all, as the god's presence
Drew nearer, and took hold on her. "Aeneas,"
She cried, "Aeneas, are you praying?
Are you being swift in prayer? Until you are,
The house of the gods will not be moved, nor open   60
Its mighty portals." More than her speech, her silence
Made the Trojans cold with terror, and Aeneas
Prayed from the depth of his heart: "Phoebus Apollo,
Compassionate ever, slayer of Achilles
Through aim of Paris' arrow,[6] helper and guide
Over the seas, over the lands, the deserts,
The shoals and quicksands, now at last we have come
To Italy, we hold the lands which fled us:
Grant that thus far, no farther, a Trojan fortune
Attend our wandering. And spare us now,   70
All of you, gods and goddesses, who hated
Troy in the past, and Trojan glory. I beg you,
Most holy prophetess, in whose foreknowing
The future stands revealed, grant that the Trojans—

---

[5] Glaucus was a sea-god gifted with prophetic powers.

[6] Apollo, patron of archers, helped Paris to slay Achilles by shooting
him in the heel, the only part of his body not supernaturally protected.

I ask with fate's permission—rest in Latium
Their wandering storm-tossed gods. I will build a temple,
In honor of Apollo and Diana,
Out of eternal marble, and ordain
Festivals in their honor, and for the Sibyl
80   A great shrine in our kingdom, and I will place there
The lots and mystic oracles for my people
With chosen priests to tend them.[7] Only, priestess,
This once, I pray you, chant the sacred verses
With your own lips; do not trust them to the leaves,
The mockery of the rushing wind's disorder."[8]
      But the priestess, not yet subject to Apollo,
Went reeling through the cavern, wild, and storming
To throw the god, who presses, like a rider,
With bit and bridle and weight, tames her wild spirit,
90   Shapes her to his control. The doors fly open,
The hundred doors, of their own will, fly open,
And through the air the answer comes:—"O Trojans,
At last the dangers of the sea are over;
That course is run, but graver ones are waiting
On land. The sons of Dardanus will reach
The kingdom of Lavinia—be easy
On that account—the sons of Dardanus, also,
Will wish they had not come there. War, I see,
Terrible war, and the river Tiber foaming
100 With streams of blood. There will be another Xanthus,
Another Simois, and Greek encampment,
Even another Achilles, born in Latium,
Himself a goddess' son. And Juno further
Will always be there: you will beg for mercy,
Be poor, turn everywhere for help. A woman
Will be the cause once more of so much evil,
A foreign bride, receptive to the Trojans,
A foreign marriage.[9] Do not yield to evil,

---

[7] The Sibylline books, venerated in Virgil's day, were supposed to contain prophetic oracles important to the guidance of Rome.

[8] See Helenus' instructions to Aeneas in III.455–63,466–67.

[9] In short, it will be the Trojan war all over again. Xanthus and Simois were rivers at Troy. The second Achilles will be the Italian hero Turnus

(Continued)

Attack, attack, more boldly even than fortune
Seems to permit. An offering of safety,—   110
Incredible!—will come from a Greek city."[10]
    So, through the amplifiers of her cavern,
The hollow vaults, the Sibyl cast her warnings,
Riddles confused with truth; and Apollo rode her,
Reining her rage, and shaking her, and spurring
The fierceness of her heart. The frenzy dwindled,
A little, and her lips were still. Aeneas
Began:—"For me, no form of trouble, maiden,
Is new, or unexpected; all of this
I have known long since, lived in imagination.   120
One thing I ask: this is the gate of the kingdom,
So it is said, where Pluto reigns, the gloomy
Marsh where the water of Acheron[11] runs over.
Teach me the way from here, open the portals
That I may go to my belovèd father,
Stand in his presence, talk with him. I brought him,
Once, on these shoulders, through a thousand weapons
And following fire, and foemen. He shared with me
The road, the sea, the menaces of heaven,
Things that an old man should not bear; he bore them,   130
Tired as he was. And he it was who told me
To come to you in humbleness. I beg you
Pity the son, the father. You have power,
Great priestess, over all; it is not for nothing
Hecate gave you this dominion over
Avernus' groves. If Orpheus could summon
Eurydice from the shadows with his music,
If Pollux could save his brother, coming, going,
Along this path,—why should I mention Theseus,

(son of the nymph Venilia as Achilles had been the son of the nymph
Thetis), who will become Aeneas' rival for the princess Lavinia. Thus
woman will again be at the root of the troubles, as with Helen and (it
may be implied) Dido.
    [10] Pallanteum, a city on the site of the future Rome; it had been founded
by Evander, king of Arcadia (in Greece), who had emigrated to Italy. See
Book VIII.
    [11] One of the rivers of the Lower World.

140   Why mention Hercules?[12] I, too, descended
From the line of Jupiter." He clasped the altar,
Making his prayer, and she made answer to him:
"Son of Anchises, born of godly lineage,
By night, by day, the portals of dark Dis
Stand open: it is easy, the descending
Down to Avernus.[13] But to climb again,
To trace the footsteps back to the air above,
There lies the task, the toil. A few, beloved
By Jupiter, descended from the gods,
150   A few, in whom exalting virtue burned,
Have been permitted. Around the central woods
The black Cocytus glides, a sullen river;
But if such love is in your heart, such longing
For double crossing of the Stygian lake,[14]
For double sight of Tartarus,[15] learn first
What must be done. In a dark tree there hides
A bough, all golden, leaf and pliant stem,
Sacred to Proserpine. This all the grove
Protects, and shadows cover it with darkness.
160   Until this bough, this bloom of light, is found,
No one receives his passport to the darkness
Whose queen requires this tribute. In succession,
After the bough is plucked, another grows,

[12] The legendary musician Orpheus was allowed to lead his dead wife Eurydice out of the Lower World (though he lost her after all, being unable to obey the command not to look back as she followed him). Pollux, an immortal who was half-brother to the mortal Castor, wished to die with him but could not; Jupiter, however, agreed to let them exchange places daily, each living alternately in the heavens and in the world of the dead. Theseus and Pirithous had tried to abduct Proserpine, queen of the dead. (She is also called Proserpina and Persephone.) The most difficult of Hercules' famous "labors" was the theft of Cerberus, the three-headed dog guarding the Lower World. (See lines 415–21.)

[13] Dis, like Hades (Greek) and Orcus, is another name for the god Pluto, and also for his realm, the Lower World. Avernus in this passage also means the Lower World, named for a sulfurous volcanic lake near Cumae. See also line 136.

[14] The four rivers of the Lower World (besides Lethe, the river of forgetfulness) were Styx, Acheron, Cocytus, and Phlegethon.

[15] The place in the Lower World where evil was punished. Aeneas actually sees only the walls of Tartarus, but it is described, in lines 573–660. *Tartarus* can also mean the Lower World in general.

Gold-green with the same metal. Raise the eyes,
Look up, reach up the hand, and it will follow
With ease, if fate is calling; otherwise,
No power, no steel, can loose it. Furthermore,
(Alas, you do not know this!), one of your men
Lies on the shore, unburied, a pollution
To all the fleet, while you have come for counsel   170
Here to our threshold.[16] Bury him with honor;
Black cattle slain in expiation for him
Must fall before you see the Stygian kingdoms,
The groves denied to living men."
                                Aeneas,
With sadness in his eyes, and downcast heart,
Turned from the cave, and at his side Achates
Accompanied his anxious meditations.
They talked together: who could be the comrade
Named by the priestess, lying there unburied?
And they found him on dry sand; it was Misenus,   180
Aeolus' son, none better with the trumpet
To make men burn for warfare. He had been
Great Hector's man-at-arms; he was good in battle
With spear as well as horn, and after Hector
Had fallen to Achilles, he had followed
Aeneas, entering no meaner service.
Some foolishness came over him; he made
The ocean echo to the blare of his trumpet
That day, and challenged the sea-gods to a contest
In martial music, and Triton, jealous, caught him,   190
However unbelievable the story,
And held him down between the rocks, and drowned
    him
Under the foaming waves.[17] His comrades mourned,
Aeneas most of all, and in their sorrow
They carry out, in haste, the Sibyl's orders,

---

[16] An unburied corpse was offensive for religious reasons. See the meeting with Palinurus later in Book VI.

[17] Triton was a sea-deity, son of Neptune, and was often portrayed as blowing a conch-shell trumpet. The classical gods did not like to be challenged at their own specialties. Appropriately, the father of the trumpeter Misenus (line 181) is the namesake of the god of the winds, Aeolus.

Construct the funeral altar, high as heaven,
They go to an old wood, and the pine-trees fall
Where wild beasts have their dens, and holm-oak rings
To the stroke of the axe, and oak and ash are riven
200   By the splitting wedge, and rowan-trees come rolling
Down the steep mountain-side. Aeneas helps them,
And cheers them on; studies the endless forest,
Takes thought, and prays: "If only we might see it,
That golden bough, here in the depth of the forest,
Bright on some tree. She told the truth, our priestess,
Too much, too bitter truth, about Misenus."
No sooner had he spoken than twin doves
Came flying down before him, and alighted
On the green ground. He knew his mother's birds,
210   And made his prayer, rejoicing,—"Oh, be leaders,
Wherever the way, and guide me to the grove
Where the rich bough makes rich the shaded ground.
Help me, O goddess-mother!" And he paused,
Watching what sign they gave, what course they set.
The birds flew on a little, just ahead
Of the pursuing vision; when they came
To the jaws of dank Avernus, evil-smelling,
They rose aloft, then swooped down the bright air,
Perched on the double tree, where the off-color
220   Of gold was gleaming golden through the branches.
As mistletoe, in the cold winter, blossoms
With its strange foliage on an alien tree,
The yellow berry gilding the smooth branches,[18]
Such was the vision of the gold in leaf
On the dark holm-oak, so the foil was rustling,
Rattling, almost, the bract[19] in the soft wind
Stirring like metal. Aeneas broke it off
With eager grasp, and bore it to the Sibyl.
      Meanwhile, along the shore, the Trojans mourned,
230   Paying Misenus' dust the final honors.
A mighty pyre was raised, of pine and oak,

---

[18] Mistletoe is a parasite with hardly visible roots, so that in winter it contrasts in appearance with the tree it grows on and seems to live a strange, self-sustaining life.
[19] A botanical term translating *brattea,* a thin metallic leaf.

The sides hung with dark leaves, and somber cypress
Along the front, and gleaming arms above.
Some made the water hot, and some made ready
Bronze caldrons, shimmering over fire, and others
Lave and anoint the body, and with weeping
Lay on the bier his limbs, and place above them
Familiar garments, crimson color; and some
Take up the heavy burden, a sad office,
And, as their fathers did, they kept their eyes   240
Averted, as they brought the torches nearer.
They burn gifts with him, bowls of oil, and viands,
And frankincense; and when the flame is quiet
And the ashes settle to earth, they wash the embers
With wine, and slake the thirsty dust. The bones
Are placed in a bronze urn by Corynaeus,
Who, with pure water, thrice around his comrades
Made lustral cleansing, shaking gentle dew
From the fruitful branch of olive; and they said
Hail and farewell! And over him Aeneas   250
Erects a mighty tomb, with the hero's arms,
His oar and trumpet, where the mountain rises
Memorial for ever, and named Misenus.[20]
    These rites performed, he hastened to the Sibyl.
There was a cavern, yawning wide and deep,
Jagged, below the darkness of the trees,
Beside the darkness of the lake. No bird
Could fly above it safely, with the vapor
Pouring from the black gulf (the Greeks have named it
Avernus, or A-Ornos, meaning *birdless*[21]),   260
And here the priestess for the slaughter set
Four bullocks, black ones, poured the holy wine
Between the horns, and plucked the topmost bristles
For the first offering to the sacred fire,
Calling on Hecate, a power in heaven,
A power in hell. Knives to the throat were driven,
The warm blood caught in bowls. Aeneas offered

[20] The promontory at the southwestern end of the Bay of Naples is
still called Cape Miseno.
[21] Most authoritative manuscripts of *The Aeneid* omit this parenthetical
statement.

A lamb, black-fleeced, to Night and her great sister,
A sterile heifer for the queen;[22] for Dis
270   An altar in the night, and on the flames
The weight of heavy bulls, the fat oil pouring
Over the burning entrails. And at dawn,
Under their feet, earth seemed to shake and rumble,
The ridges move, and bitches bay in darkness,
As the presence neared. The Sibyl cried a warning,
"Keep off, keep off, whatever is unholy,
Depart from here![23] Courage, Aeneas; enter
The path, unsheathe the sword. The time is ready
For the brave heart." She strode out boldly, leading
280   Into the open cavern, and he followed.
    Gods of the world of spirit, silent shadows,
Chaos and Phlegethon, areas of silence,
Wide realms of dark, may it be right and proper
To tell what I have heard, this revelation
Of matters buried deep in earth and darkness!
    Vague forms in lonely darkness, they were going
Through void and shadow, through the empty realm
Like people in a forest, when the moonlight
Shifts with a baleful glimmer, and shadow covers
290   The sky, and all the colors turn to blackness.
At the first threshold, on the jaws of Orcus,
Grief and avenging Cares have set their couches,
And pale Diseases dwell, and sad Old Age,
Fear, evil-counselling Hunger, wretched Need,
Forms terrible to see, and Death, and Toil,
And Death's own brother, Sleep, and evil Joys,
Fantasies of the mind, and deadly War,
The Furies' iron chambers,[24] Discord, raving,
Her snaky hair entwined in bloody bands.
300   An elm-tree loomed there, shadowy and huge,

[22] The sister of Night (Nox) was Earth (Tellus). The "queen" is Proserpine.
[23] At Roman religious ceremonies, the ritual dismissal of the uninitiated; here applied to Aeneas' companions, who must now leave him. The approaching "presence" (line 275) is that of the goddess Hecate, accompanied by her hounds.
[24] The Furies were primitive female agents of revenge and punishment for crime.

The aged boughs outspread, beneath whose leaves,
Men say, the false dreams cling, thousands on thousands.
And there are monsters in the dooryard, Centaurs,
Scyllas, of double shape, the beast of Lerna,
Hissing most horribly, Briareus,
The hundred-handed giant, a Chimaera
Whose armament is fire, Harpies, and Gorgons,
A triple-bodied giant.[25] In sudden panic
Aeneas drew his sword, the edge held forward,
Ready to rush and flail, however blindly,   310
Save that his wise companion warned him, saying
They had no substance, they were only phantoms
Flitting about, illusions without body.
    From here, the road turns off to Acheron,
River of Hell; here, thick with muddy whirling,
Cocytus boils with sand. Charon is here,
The guardian of these mingling waters, Charon,
Uncouth and filthy, on whose chin the hair
Is a tangled mat, whose eyes protrude, are burning,
Whose dirty cloak is knotted at the shoulder.   320
He poles a boat, tends to the sail, unaided,
Ferrying bodies in his rust-hued vessel.
Old, but a god's senility is awful
In its raw greenness. To the bank come thronging
Mothers and men, bodies of great-souled heroes,
Their life-time over, boys, unwedded maidens,
Young men whose fathers saw their pyres burning,
Thick as the forest leaves that fall in autumn
With early frost, thick as the birds to landfall
From over the seas, when the chill of the year compels them   330
To sunlight. There they stand, a host, imploring

[25] These lines are a catalogue of many of the most famous or fearsome
monsters of ancient fable. Centaurs were half man, half horse; Scylla was
a six-headed monster (described in III.432–44) who devoured sailors in
the straits of Messina; the beast of Lerna was the Hydra, a gigantic many-
headed serpent; Briareus, as the text states, was a giant with a hundred
hands; the fire-breathing Chimaera was a combination of lion, goat, and
serpent; the Harpies were foul bird-women (described in III.213–57); the
Gorgons (Medusa and her two sisters) were snake-haired female monsters
who literally petrified men who gazed on them; the triple-bodied giant
was named Geryon.

To be taken over first. Their hands, in longing,
Reach out for the farther shore. But the gloomy boatman
Makes choice among them, taking some, and keeping
Others far back from the stream's edge. Aeneas,
Wondering, asks the Sibyl, "Why the crowding?
What are the spirits seeking? What distinction
Brings some across the livid stream, while others
Stay on the farther bank?" She answers, briefly:
340   "Son of Anchises, this is the awful river,
The Styx, by which the gods take oath; the boatman,
Charon; those he takes with him are the buried,
Those he rejects, whose luck is out, the graveless.
It is not permitted him to take them over
The dreadful banks and hoarse-resounding waters
Till earth is cast upon their bones. They haunt
These shores a hundred restless years of waiting
Before they end postponement of the crossing."
Aeneas paused, in thoughtful mood, with pity
350   Over their lot's unevenness; and saw there,
Wanting the honor given the dead, and grieving,
Leucaspis, and Orontes, the Lycian captain,
Who had sailed from Troy across the stormy waters,
And drowned off Africa, with crew and vessel,[26]
And there was Palinurus, once his pilot,
Who, not so long ago, had been swept over,
Watching the stars on the journey north from Carthage.[27]
The murk was thick; Aeneas hardly knew him,
Sorrowful in that darkness, but made question:
360   "What god, O Palinurus, took you from us?
Who drowned you in the deep? Tell me. Apollo
Never before was false, and yet he told me
You would be safe across the seas, and come
Unharmed to Italy; what kind of promise
Was this, to fool me with?" But Palinurus
Gave him assurance:—"It was no god who drowned me,[28]

[26] For Orontes, see I.127–30. Leucaspis is not mentioned there, however.
[27] See V.796–838.
[28] Palinurus is ignorant of the role of the god of Sleep in casting him overboard. Apollo's promise is not mentioned elsewhere in the poem.

No falsehood on Apollo's part, my captain,
But as I clung to the tiller, holding fast
To keep the course, as I should do, I felt it
Wrenched from the ship, and I fell with it, headlong.   370
By those rough seas I swear, I had less fear
On my account than for the ship, with rudder
And helmsman overboard, to drift at the mercy
Of rising seas. Three nights I rode the waters,
Three nights of storm, and from the crest of a wave,
On the fourth morning, sighted Italy,
I was swimming to land, I had almost reached it, heavy
In soaking garments; my cramped fingers struggled
To grasp the top of the rock, when barbarous people,
Ignorant men, mistaking me for booty,[29]   380
Struck me with swords; waves hold me now, or winds
Roll me along the shore. By the light of heaven,
The lovely air, I beg you, by your father,
Your hope of young Iulus, bring me rescue
Out of these evils, my unconquered leader!
Cast over my body earth—you have the power—
Return to Velia's[30] harbor,—or there may be
Some other way—your mother is a goddess,
Else how would you be crossing this great river,
This Stygian swamp?—help a poor fellow, take me   390
Over the water with you, give a dead man
At least a place to rest in." But the Sibyl
Broke in upon him sternly:—"Palinurus,
Whence comes this mad desire? No man, unburied,
May see the Stygian waters, or Cocytus,
The Furies' dreadful river; no man may come
Unbidden to this bank. Give up the hope
That fate is changed by praying, but hear this,
A little comfort in your harsh misfortune:
Those neighboring people will make expiation,   400
Driven by signs from heaven, through their cities
And through their countryside; they will build a tomb,

[29] A man carrying valuable goods.
[30] A town near Cumae.

Thereto bring offerings yearly, and the place
Shall take its name from you, Cape Palinurus."[31]
So he was comforted a little, finding
Some happiness in the promise.

                             And they went on,
Nearing the river, and from the stream the boatman
Beheld them cross the silent forest, nearer,
Turning their footsteps toward the bank. He challenged:—

410   "Whoever you are, O man in armor, coming
In this direction, halt where you are, and tell me
The reason why you come. This is the region
Of shadows, and of Sleep and drowsy Night;
I am not allowed to carry living bodies
In the Stygian boat; and I must say I was sorry
I ever accepted Hercules and Theseus
And Pirithous, and rowed them over the lake,
Though they were sons of gods and great in courage.
One of them dared to drag the guard of Hell,

420   Enchained, from Pluto's throne, shaking in terror,
The others to snatch our queen from Pluto's chamber."[32]
The Sibyl answered briefly: "No such cunning
Is plotted here; our weapons bring no danger.
Be undisturbed: the hell-hound in his cavern
May bark forever, to keep the bloodless shadows
Frightened away from trespass; Proserpine,
Untouched, in pureness guard her uncle's threshold.[33]
Trojan Aeneas, a man renowned for goodness,
Renowned for nerve in battle, is descending

430   To the lowest shades; he comes to find his father.
If such devotion has no meaning to you,
Look on this branch at least, and recognize it!"
And with the word she drew from under her mantle
The golden bough; his swollen wrath subsided.
No more was said; he saw the bough, and marvelled
At the holy gift, so long unseen; came sculling

---

[31] As with Misenus and modern Cape Miseno (line 253), Palinurus' name
is still given today to a promontory on the Italian coast (Point Palinuro).
[32] See lines 139–41 and note.
[33] Proserpine's husband, Pluto, was also her uncle, since she was the
daughter of Jupiter, Pluto's brother.

The dark-blue boat to the shore, and drove the spirits,
Lining the thwarts, ashore, and cleared the gangway,
And took Aeneas aboard; as that big man
Stepped in, the leaky skiff groaned under the weight,   440
And the strained seams let in the muddy water,
But they made the crossing safely, seer and soldier,
To the far margin, colorless and shapeless,
Grey sedge and dark-brown ooze. They heard the baying
Of Cerberus, that great hound, in his cavern crouching,
Making the shore resound, as all three throats
Belled horribly; and serpents rose and bristled
Along the triple neck. The priestess threw him
A sop with honey and drugged meal; he opened
The ravenous throat, gulped, and subsided, filling   450
The den with his huge bulk. Aeneas, crossing,
Passed on beyond the bank of the dread river
Whence none return.
                A wailing of thin voices
Came to their ears, the souls of infants crying,
Those whom the day of darkness took from the breast
Before their share of living. And there were many
Whom some false sentence brought to death. Here Minos
Judges them once again;[34] a silent jury
Reviews the evidence. And there are others,
Guilty of nothing, but who hated living,   460
The suicides. How gladly, now, they would suffer
Poverty, hardship, in the world of light!
But this is not permitted; they are bound
Nine times around by the black unlovely river;
Styx holds them fast.
              They came to the Fields of Mourning,
So-called, where those whom cruel love had wasted
Hid in secluded pathways, under myrtle,
And even in death were anxious. Procris, Phaedra,
Eriphyle, displaying wounds her son
Had given her, Caeneus, Laodamia,   470
Caeneus, a young man once, and now again

[34] This Minos, who had given laws to and ruled Crete, seems to be identical with the one mentioned in line 14 (see note to line 37), but possibly his grandfather is intended.

A young man, after having been a woman.[35]
And here, new come from her own wound, was Dido,
Wandering in the wood. The Trojan hero,
Standing near by, saw her, or thought he saw her,
Dim in the shadows, like the slender crescent
Of moon when cloud drifts over. Weeping, he greets her:—
"Unhappy Dido, so they told me truly
That your own hand had brought you death. Was I—
480   Alas!—the cause? I swear by all the stars,
By the world above, by everything held sacred
Here under the earth, unwillingly, O queen,
I left your kingdom. But the gods' commands,
Driving me now through these forsaken places,
This utter night, compelled me on. I could not
Believe my loss would cause so great a sorrow.
Linger a moment, do not leave me; whither,
Whom, are you fleeing? I am permitted only
This last word with you."

                      But the queen, unmoving
490   As flint or marble, turned away, her eyes
Fixed on the ground: the tears were vain, the words,
Meant to be soothing, foolish; she turned away,
His enemy forever, to the shadows
Where Sychaeus, her former husband, took her
With love for love, and sorrow for her sorrow.
And still Aeneas wept for her, being troubled
By the injustice of her doom; his pity
Followed her going.

                  They went on. They came
To the farthest fields, whose tenants are the warriors,
500   Illustrious throng. Here Tydeus came to meet him,

[35] Some of these figures (all women) were evil, some admirable. Procris'
jealousy of her husband led to his killing her by accident; Phaedra nursed
a guilty, unrequited love for her stepson; Eriphyle, having been bribed,
sent her husband to his death in war and was then, in return, killed by
her son; Laodamia, on the other hand, was the faithful wife of the first
man to die at Troy and gave up her life to be with him after his death.
The sex-changed Caeneus had been seduced, as a maiden named Caenis,
by Neptune. The translator omits two other women named here by Virgil:
Pasiphae (for her unnatural love, see line 26 and note) and Evadne, a
wife who immolated herself on her husband's funeral pyre.

Parthenopaeus came, and pale Adrastus,[36]
A fighter's ghost, and many, many others,
Mourned in the world above, and doomed in battle,
Leaders of Troy, in long array; Aeneas
Sighed as he saw them: Medon; Polyboetes,
The priest of Ceres; Glaucus; and Idaeus
Still keeping arms and chariot;[37] three brothers,
Antenor's sons; Thersilochus; a host
To right and left of him, and when they see him,
One sight is not enough; they crowd around him,   510
Linger, and ask the reasons for his coming.
But Agamemnon's men, the Greek battalions,
Seeing him there, and his arms in shadow gleaming,
Tremble in panic, turn to flee for refuge,
As once they used to, toward their ships, but where
Are the ships now? They try to shout, in terror;
But only a thin and piping treble issues
To mock their mouths, wide-open.
                                         One he knew
Was here, Deiphobus, a son of Priam,
With his whole body mangled, and his features   520
Cruelly slashed, and both hands cut, and ears
Torn from his temples, and his nostrils slit
By shameful wounds. Aeneas hardly knew him,
Shivering there, and doing his best to hide
His marks of punishment; unhailed, he hailed him:—
"Deiphobus, great warrior, son of Teucer,
Whose cruel punishment was this? Whose license
Abused you so? I heard, it seems, a story
Of that last night, how you had fallen, weary
With killing Greeks at last; I built a tomb,   530
Although no body lay there, in your honor,
Three times I cried, aloud, over your spirit,
Where now your name and arms keep guard. I could
      not,
Leaving my country, find my friend, to give him
Proper interment in the earth he came from."

[36] Three of the seven heroes who led a famous siege of the city of Thebes.
[37] Idaeus had been charioteer to Priam, king of Troy.

And Priam's son replied:—"Nothing, dear comrade,
Was left undone; the dead man's shade was given
All ceremony due. It was my own fortune
And a Spartan woman's[38] deadliness that sunk me
540   Under these evils; she it was who left me
These souvenirs. You know how falsely happy
We were on that last night; I need not tell you.
When that dread horse came leaping over our walls,
Pregnant with soldiery, she led the dancing,
A solemn rite, she called it, with Trojan women
Screaming their bacchanals;[39] she raised the torches
High on the citadel; she called the Greeks.
Then—I was worn with trouble, drugged in slumber,
Resting in our ill-omened bridal chamber,
550   With sleep as deep and sweet as death upon me—
Then she, that paragon of helpmates, deftly
Moved all the weapons from the house; my sword,
Even, she stole from underneath my pillow,
Opened the door, and called in Menelaus,
Hoping, no doubt, to please her loving husband,
To win forgetfulness of her old sinning.
It is quickly told: they broke into the chamber,
The two of them, and with them, as accomplice,
Ulysses came, the crime-contriving bastard.[40]
560   O gods, pay back the Greeks; grant the petition
If goodness asks for vengeance! But you, Aeneas,
A living man—what chance has brought you here?
Vagrant of ocean, god-inspired,—which are you?
What chance has worn you down, to come, in sadness,
To these confusing sunless dwelling-places?"
    While they were talking, Aurora's rosy car
Had halfway crossed the heaven;[41] all their time
Might have been spent in converse, but the Sibyl

[38] Helen, who had left her husband Menelaus and run off to Troy with
Paris; after his death she had become the wife of Deiphobus.

[39] Wild revels in honor of Bacchus, god of wine. Helen carried one of
the torches customary in such revels but used it treacherously, as a signal
to the Greeks.

[40] The insult is meant literally by Deiphobus, suggesting actual infidelity
by Ulysses' mother.

[41] Aurora was goddess of the dawn. It is now past noon on earth.

Hurried them forward:—"Night comes on, Aeneas;
We waste the hours with tears. We are at the cross-road,   570
Now; here we turn to the right, where the pathway leads
On to Elysium, under Pluto's ramparts.
Leftward is Tartarus, and retribution,
The terminal of the wicked, and their dungeon."
Deiphobus left them, saying, "O great priestess,
Do not be angry with me; I am going;
I shall not fail the roll-call of the shadows.
Pride of our race, go on; may better fortune
Attend you!" and, upon the word, he vanished.
    As he looked back, Aeneas saw, to his left,   580
Wide walls beneath a cliff, a triple rampart,
A river running fire, Phlegethon's torrent,
Rocks roaring in its course, a gate, tremendous,
Pillars of adamant,[42] a tower of iron,
Too strong for men, too strong for even gods
To batter down in warfare, and behind them
A Fury, sentinel in bloody garments,
Always on watch, by day, by night. He heard
Sobbing and groaning there, the crack of the lash,
The clank of iron, the sound of dragging shackles.   590
The noise was terrible; Aeneas halted,
Asking, "What forms of crime are these, O maiden?
What harrying punishment, what horrible outcry?"
She answered:—"O great leader of the Trojans,
I have never crossed that threshold of the wicked;
No pure soul is permitted entrance thither,
But Hecate, by whose order I was given
Charge of Avernus' groves, my guide, my teacher,
Told me how gods exact the toll of vengeance.
The monarch here, merciless Rhadamanthus,[43]   600
Punishes guilt, and hears confession; he forces
Acknowledgment of crime; no man in the world,
No matter how cleverly he hides his evil,
No matter how much he smiles at his own slyness,
Can fend atonement off; the hour of death

---

[42] An extremely hard metal.
[43] Brother of Minos and, like him, a judge in the Lower World.

Begins his sentence. Tisiphone, the Fury,
Leaps at the guilty with her scourge; her serpents
Are whips of menace as she calls her sisters.
Imagine the gates, on jarring hinge, rasp open,
610   You would see her in the doorway, a shape, a sentry,
Savage, implacable. Beyond, still fiercer,
The monstrous Hydra dwells; her fifty throats
Are black, and open wide, and Tartarus
Is black, and open wide, and it goes down
To darkness, sheer deep down, and twice the distance
That earth is from Olympus.[44] At the bottom
The Titans crawl, Earth's oldest breed, hurled under
By thunderbolts; here lie the giant twins,
Aloeus' sons, who laid their hands on heaven
620   And tried to pull down Jove; Salmoneus here
Atones for high presumption,—it was he
Who aped Jove's noise and fire, wheeling his horses
Triumphant through his city in Elis, cheering
And shaking the torch, and claiming divine homage,
The arrogant fool, to think his brass was lightning,
His horny-footed horses beat out thunder!
Jove showed him what real thunder was, what lightning
Spoke from immortal cloud, what whirlwind fury
Came sweeping from the heaven to overtake him.
630   Here Tityos, Earth's giant son, lies sprawling
Over nine acres, with a monstrous vulture
Gnawing, with crooked beak, vitals and liver
That grow as they are eaten; eternal anguish,
Eternal feast.[45] Over another hangs
A rock, about to fall; and there are tables
Set for a banquet, gold with royal splendor,
But if a hand goes out to touch the viands,

[44] The dwelling-place of the gods.

[45] The Titans, giant offspring of Heaven and Earth, fought alongside Saturn in his unsuccessful struggle against his son Jupiter. The sons of Aloeus, Otus and Ephialtes, were giants who tried to assault the gods by piling the mountains Ossa and Pelion on top of Olympus. Salmoneus imitated Jove's thunder, in a city sacred to Jove, by driving a brass chariot over a brass bridge. Tityos had sexually assaulted the goddess Latona, who was avenged by her children Apollo and Diana.

The Fury drives it back with fire and yelling.
Why name them all, Pirithous, the Lapiths,
Ixion?[46] The roll of crime would take forever.   640
Whoever, in his lifetime, hated his brother,
Or struck his father down; whoever cheated
A client, or was miserly—how many
Of these there seem to be!—whoever went
To treasonable war, or broke a promise
Made to his lord, whoever perished, slain
Over adultery, all these, walled in,
Wait here their punishment. Seek not to know
Too much about their doom. The stone is rolled,
The wheel keeps turning; Theseus forever   650
Sits in dejection; Phlegyas, accursed,
Cries through the halls forever: *Being warned,*
Learn justice; reverence the gods![47] The man
Who sold his country is here in hell; the man
Who altered laws for money; and a father
Who knew his daughter's bed. All of them dared,
And more than dared, achieved, unspeakable
Ambitions. If I had a hundred tongues,
A hundred iron throats, I could not tell
The fullness of their crime and punishment."   660
And then she added:—"Come: resume the journey,
Fulfill the mission; let us hurry onward.
I see the walls the Cyclops[48] made, the portals
Under the archway, where, the orders tell us,
Our tribute must be set." They went together
Through the way's darkness, came to the doors, and halted,
And at the entrance Aeneas, having sprinkled
His body with fresh water, placed the bough
Golden before the threshold. The will of the goddess

---

[46] Ixion, king of the Lapiths, had attempted a sexual assault on Juno;
for Pirithous (son of Ixion), see lines 139–40 and note and lines 415–
21.

[47] Theseus is punished, presumably, for his attempt to abduct Proserpine
(see lines 415–21). Phlegyas (father of Ixion) had burned Apollo's temple
at Delphi.

[48] The Cyclops labored in the forge of Vulcan, the blacksmith god of
fire.

670   Had been performed, the proper task completed.
            They came to happy places, the joyful dwelling,
        The lovely greenery of the groves of the blessèd.
        Here ampler air invests the fields with light,
        Rose-colored, with familiar stars and sun.
        Some grapple on the grassy wrestling-ground
        In exercise and sport, and some are dancing,
        And others singing; in his trailing robe
        Orpheus strums the lyre; the seven clear notes
        Accompany the dance, the song.[49] And heroes
680   Are there, great-souled, born in the happier years,
        Ilus, Assaracus; the city's founder,
        Prince Dardanus.[50] Far off, Aeneas wonders,
        Seeing the phantom arms, the chariots,
        The spears fixed in the ground, the chargers browsing,
        Unharnessed, over the plain. Whatever, living,
        The men delighted in, whatever pleasure
        Was theirs in horse and chariot, still holds them
        Here under the world. To right and left, they banquet
        In the green meadows, and a joyful chorus
690   Rises through groves of laurel, whence the river
        Runs to the upper world.[51] The band of heroes
        Dwell here, all those whose mortal wounds were suffered
        In fighting for the fatherland; and poets,
        The good, the pure, the worthy of Apollo;
        Those who discovered truth and made life nobler;
        Those who served others—all, with snowy fillets
        Binding their temples, throng the lovely valley.
        And these the Sibyl questioned, most of all
        Musaeus,[52] for he towered above the center
700   Of that great throng:—"O happy souls, O poet,
        Where does Anchises dwell? For him we come here.
        For him we have traversed Erebus'[53] great rivers."

---

[49] For Orpheus, see lines 136–37 and note. He is playing on a seven-stringed lyre, or harp.
[50] Three illustrious ancestors of the Trojans.
[51] The river is Eridanus, believed in fable and folklore to be the underground source of the river Po.
[52] Legendary poet, taught by Orpheus.
[53] God of darkness; more generally, the Lower World itself.

And he replied:—"It is all our home, the shady
Groves, and the streaming meadows, and the softness
Along the river-banks. No fixed abode
Is ours at all; but if it is your pleasure,
Cross over the ridge with me; I will guide you there
By easy going." And so Musaeus led them
And from the summit showed them fields, all shining,
And they went on over and down.   710
    Deep in a valley of green, father Anchises
Was watching, with deep earnestness, the spirits
Whose destiny was light, and counting them over,
All of his race to come, his dear descendants,
Their fates and fortunes and their works and ways,
And as he saw Aeneas coming toward him
Over the meadow, his hands reached out with yearning,
He was moved to tears, and called:—"At last, my son,—
Have you really come, at last? and the long road nothing
To a son who loves his father? Do I, truly,   720
See you, and hear your voice? I was thinking so,
I was hoping so, I was counting off the days,
And I was right about it. O my son!
What a long journey, over land and water,
Yours must have been! What buffeting of danger!
I feared, so much, the Libyan realm would hurt you."
And his son answered:—"It was your spirit, father,
Your sorrowful shade, so often met, that led me
To find these portals. The ships ride safe at anchor,
Safe in the Tuscan sea. Embrace me, father;   730
Let hand join hand in love; do not forsake me."
And as he spoke, the tears streamed down. Three times
He reached out toward him, and three times the image
Fled like the breath of the wind or a dream on wings.
    He saw, in a far valley, a separate grove
Where the woods stir and rustle, and a river,
The Lethe, gliding past the peaceful places,
And tribes of people thronging, hovering over,
Innumerable as the bees in summer
Working the bright-hued flowers, and the shining   740
Of the white lilies, murmuring and humming.
Aeneas, filled with wonder, asks the reason

For what he does not know, who are the people
In such a host, and to what river coming?
Anchises answers:—"These are spirits, ready
Once more for life; they drink of Lethe's water
The soothing potion of forgetfulness.
I have longed, for long, to show them to you, name them,
Our children's children; Italy discovered,
750   So much the greater happiness, my son."
"But, O my father, is it thinkable
That souls would leave this blessedness, be willing
A second time to bear the sluggish body,
Trade Paradise for earth? Alas, poor wretches,
Why such a mad desire for light?" Anchises
Gives detailed answer: "First, my son, a spirit
Sustains all matter, heaven and earth and ocean,
The moon, the stars; mind quickens mass, and moves it.
Hence comes the race of man, of beast, of wingèd
760   Creatures of air, of the strange shapes which ocean
Bears down below his mottled marble surface.
All these are blessed with energy from heaven;
The seed of life is a spark of fire, but the body
A clod of earth, a clog, a mortal burden.
Hence humans fear, desire, grieve, and are joyful,
And even when life is over, all the evil
Ingrained so long, the adulterated mixture,
The plagues and pestilences of the body
Remain, persist. So there must be a cleansing,
770   By penalty, by punishment, by fire,
By sweep of wind, by water's absolution,
Before the guilt is gone. Each of us suffers
His own peculiar ghost.[54] But the day comes
When we are sent through wide Elysium,
The Fields of the Blessed, a few of us, to linger
Until the turn of time, the wheel of ages,
Wears off the taint, and leaves the core of spirit

---

[54] This notoriously elusive aphorism, typical of the formidable difficulties in translating Virgil, probably means something like "Each endures his own penance and lives with his own purgatorial consciousness" (though other meanings have been suggested).

Pure sense, pure flame.[55] A thousand years pass over
And the god calls the countless host to Lethe
Where memory is annulled, and souls are willing   780
Once more to enter into mortal bodies."
   The discourse ended; the father drew his son
And his companion toward the hum, the center
Of the full host; they came to rising round
Where all the long array was visible,
Anchises watching, noting, every comer.
"Glory to come, my son, illustrious spirits
Of Dardan lineage, Italian offspring,
Heirs of our name, begetters of our future!
These I will name for you and tell our fortunes:[56]   790
First, leaning on a headless spear, and standing
Nearest the light, that youth, the first to rise
To the world above, is Silvius; his name
Is Alban; in his veins Italian blood
Will run with Trojan; he will be the son
Of your late age; Lavinia will bear him,
A king and sire of kings; from him our race
Will rule in Alba Longa. Near him, Procas,
A glory to the Trojan race; and Capys,
And Numitor, and Silvius Aeneas,   800
Resembling you in name, in arms, in goodness,
If ever he wins the Alban kingdom over.
What fine young men they are! What strength, what prowess!
The civic oak already shades their foreheads.
These will found cities, Gabii, Fidenae,
Nomentum; they will crown the hills with towers
Above Collatia, Inuus fortress, Bola,

[55] Certain rare and noble spirits remain in Elysian bliss rather than being reincarnated. Anchises is one of these.

[56] In lines 791–808, Anchises describes the Trojan lineage in Italy up to the time of Romulus, legendary founder (in 753 B.C., several centuries after Aeneas) of Rome proper. Alba Longa, forerunner of Rome, was the city founded by Ascanius (as we are told in I.278–83). Silvius was third in the line to rule after Aeneas and Ascanius/Iulus. The persons listed in lines 798–800 were subsequent Alban kings (one of whom, Silvius Aeneas, was denied the throne for a long time). The aboriginal towns mentioned in lines 805–08 were near Rome.

Cora, all names to be, thus far ungiven.
    "And there will be a son of Mars; his mother
810 Is Ilia, and his name is Romulus,
Assaracus' descendant. On his helmet
See, even now, twin plumes; his father's honor
Confers distinction on him for the world.
Under his auspices Rome, that glorious city,
Will bound her power by earth, her pride by heaven,
Happy in hero sons, one wall surrounding
Her seven hills, even as Cybele, riding
Through Phrygian cities, wears her crown of towers,
Rejoicing in her offspring, and embracing
820 A hundred children of the gods, her children,
Celestials, all of them, at home in heaven.[57]
Turn the eyes now this way; behold the Romans,
Your very own. These are Iulus' children,[58]
The race to come. One promise you have heard
Over and over: here is its fulfillment,
The son of a god, Augustus Caesar, founder
Of a new age of gold, in lands where Saturn
Ruled long ago;[59] he will extend his empire
Beyond the Indies, beyond the normal measure
830 Of years and constellations, where high Atlas
Turns on his shoulders the star-studded world.[60]
Maeotia[61] and the Caspian seas are trembling
As heaven's oracles predict his coming,
And all the seven mouths of Nile are troubled.
Not even Hercules, in all his travels,
Covered so much of the world, from Erymanthus
To Lerna; nor did Bacchus, driving his tigers

[57] Cybele, a Phrygian (Trojan) deity considered the mother of the gods, was associated with the building and fortifying of cities.
[58] Iulus, Aeneas' son, was regarded as the progenitor of the Julian clan of Virgil's time, and thus of the line of Caesars.
[59] Augustus was "son of a god" because Julius Caesar, of whom Augustus was the adopted son, was deified at his death. Saturn, after being deposed by his son Jupiter, was supposed to have reigned in Italy during the mythical Age of Gold.
[60] The giant Atlas (sometimes identified with the north-African mountain) was imagined as supporting the heavens on his shoulders.
[61] Region north of the Black Sea.

From Nysa's summit.[62] How can hesitation
Keep us from deeds to make our prowess greater?
What fear can block us from Ausonian[63] land?   840
    "And who is that one yonder, wearing the olive,
Holding the sacrifice? I recognize him,
That white-haired king of Rome, who comes from Cures,
A poor land, to a mighty empire, giver
Of law to the young town. His name is Numa.
Near him is Tullus; he will rouse to arms
A race grown sluggish, little used to triumph.
Beyond him Ancus, even now too boastful,
Too fond of popular favor.[64] And then the Tarquins,
And the avenger Brutus, proud of spirit,   850
Restorer of the balance. He shall be
First holder of the consular power; his children
Will stir up wars again, and he, for freedom
And her sweet sake, will call down judgment on them,
Unhappy, however future men may praise him,
In love of country and intense ambition.[65]
    "There are the Decii, and there the Drusi,
A little farther off, and stern Torquatus,
The man with the axe, and Camillus, the regainer
Of standards lost. And see those two, resplendent   860
In equal arms, harmonious friendly spirits
Now, in the shadow of night, but if they ever
Come to the world of light, alas, what warfare,
What battle-lines, what slaughter they will fashion,
Each for the other, one from Alpine ramparts

[62] Erymanthus, a mountain range, and Lerna, a lake, were in Greece;
among the Twelve Labors of Hercules were victories over monsters inhabit-
ing these places. The mountain Nysa (located in India, according to one
tradition) was the boyhood home of Bacchus, the god of wine, whose
chariot was drawn by tigers.

[63] Italian.

[64] The religious and civic lawgiver Numa Pompilius, the warlike Tullus,
and Ancus (according to Virgil, a demagogue) were, respectively, the second, third, and fourth kings of Rome (Romulus having been the first).

[65] Brutus (not to be confused with the Brutus who assassinated Julius
Caesar centuries later) expelled the last (seventh) of the Roman kings,
Tarquinius Superbus, and founded the Roman republic in 509 B.C. He
had his sons executed for attempting to restore the old monarchical line.

Descending, and the other ranged against him
With armies from the east, father and son
Through marriage, Pompey and Caesar.[66] O my children,
Cast out the thoughts of war, and do not murder
870 The flower of our country. O my son,
Whose line descends from heaven, let the sword
Fall from the hand, be leader in forbearing!
　　"Yonder is one who, victor over Corinth,
Will ride in triumph home, famous for carnage
Inflicted on the Greeks; near him another,
Destroyer of old Argos and Mycenae
Where Agamemnon ruled; he will strike down
A king descended from Achilles; Pydna
Shall be revenge for Pallas' ruined temple,
880 For Trojan ancestors. Who would pass over,
Without a word, Cossus, or noble Cato,
The Gracchi, or those thunderbolts of warfare,
The Scipios, Libya's ruin, or Fabricius
Mighty with little, or Serranus, ploughing
The humble furrow? My tale must hurry on:
I see the Fabii next, and their great Quintus
Who brought us back an empire by delaying.[67]
Others, no doubt, will better mould the bronze
To the semblance of soft breathing, draw, from marble,

----

[66] The Decii, Torquatus, and Camillus were military or civic heroes of
the fourth and third centuries B.C. The Drusi were ancestors of Livia,
wife of Caesar Augustus. The civil war (49–45 B.C.) between the forces
of Julius Caesar and those of his son-in-law Pompey, in Virgil's own lifetime, had been part of the chain of events culminating in the accession
of Augustus.

[67] The "victor over Corinth" (line 873) was Mummius; the "another"
of line 875 was probably Paullus (both second century B.C.). The latter,
by defeating a Greek opponent, descended from Achilles, at the battle
of Pydna, avenged Greek desecration of the Trojan temple of Pallas Athena
during the Trojan War; see I.48–50, II.430–32. These two heroes, along
with the other men named in lines 881–87, were among the greatest of
the Roman military and political figures from the fifth through the
second centuries B.C. The legacy of the episode with Dido is hinted at through
the mention of the two Scipios and Quintus Fabius Maximus ("Cunctator,"
or "Delayer," famous for his drawn-out avoidance tactics), all three of
whom won victories over Carthage in the Punic Wars (third and second
centuries B.C.).

The living countenance; and others plead   890
With greater eloquence, or learn to measure,
Better than we, the pathways of the heaven,
The risings of the stars: remember, Roman,
To rule the people under law, to establish
The way of peace, to battle down the haughty,
To spare the meek. Our fine arts, these, forever."[68]
    Anchises paused a moment, and they marvelled,
And he went on:—"See, how Marcellus[69] triumphs,
Glorious over all, with the great trophies
Won when he slew the captain of the Gauls,   900
Leader victorious over leading foeman.
When Rome is in great trouble and confusion
He will establish order, Gaul and Carthage
Go down before his sword, and triple trophies
Be given Romulus in dedication."
    There was a young man going with Marcellus,
Brilliant in shining armor, bright in beauty,
But sorrowful, with downcast eyes. Aeneas
Broke in, to ask his father: "Who is this youth[70]
Attendant on the hero? A son of his?   910
One of his children's children? How the crowd
Murmurs and hums around him! what distinction,
What presence, in his person! But dark night
Hovers around his head with mournful shadow.
Who is he, father?" And Anchises answered:—
"Great sorrow for our people! O my son,
Ask not to know it. This one fate will only
Show to the world; he will not be permitted
Any long sojourn. Rome would be too mighty,

---

[68] In these memorable lines, one of the most famous passages in all of literature, the "Others" (line 888), with whose accomplishments Anchises is comparing those of the Romans, are primarily the Greeks. In oratory the Greeks were not in fact superior, but Anchises concedes even this area, so as to keep the distinction between the two peoples clean and emphatic.

[69] Roman general of the third century B.C.

[70] The Younger Marcellus—descendant of the Marcellus just described, nephew and son-in-law of Caesar Augustus, and presumed successor to him—died of malaria in 23 B.C. at the age of nineteen.

920 Too great in the gods' sight, were this gift hers.
What lamentation will the field of Mars[71]
Raise to the city! Tiber, gliding by
The new-built tomb, the funeral state, bear witness!
No youth from Trojan stock will ever raise
His ancestors so high in hope, no Roman
Be such a cause for pride. Alas for goodness,
Alas for old-time honor, and the arm
Invincible in war! Against him no one,
Whether on foot or foaming horse, would come
930 In battle and depart unscathed. Poor boy,
If you should break the cruel fates; if only—
You are to be Marcellus. Let me scatter
Lilies, or dark-red flowers, bringing honor
To my descendant's shade; let the gift be offered,
However vain the tribute."
        So through the whole wide realm they went together,
Anchises and his son; from fields of air
Learning and teaching of the fame and glory,
The wars to come, the toils to face, or flee from,
940 Latinus' city and the Latin peoples,
The love of what would be.
                                    There are two portals,
Twin gates of Sleep, one made of horn, where easy
Release is given true shades, the other gleaming
White ivory, whereby the false dreams issue
To the upper air. Aeneas and the Sibyl
Part from Anchises at the second portal.[72]
He goes to the ships, again, rejoins his comrades,
Sails to Caieta's[73] harbor, and the vessels
Rest on their mooring-lines.

---

[71] The Campus Martius, site of Marcellus' tomb.

[72] Why Aeneas should emerge through the gate of falsehood is one of the most mystifying problems in the entire poem. Virgil may mean no more than that Aeneas ends his visit to the Lower World early in the night, since dreams dreamt at that time were considered deceiving. (The reliable dreams were those dreamt just before waking.) But other interpreters scorn this notion, as too trivial to suit the apparently deliberate effect of high-solemn mystery.

[73] A town about 35 miles up the coast from Cumae and the modern Naples.

BOOK VII

▣

Italy: The Outbreak of War

Here on our shores a woman died, Caieta,
Nurse of Aeneas, and her name still guards
Her resting-place with honor, if such glory
Is comforting to dust.
               Her funeral mound
Was raised, and solemn rites performed; Aeneas,
When the deep water quieted, set sail.
The wind held fair to the night, and the white moon
Revealed the way over the tremulous water.
They skimmed the shores of Circe's island;[1] there
The sun's rich daughter made the secret groves   10
Ring with continual singing, and the halls
Were bright with cedar burning through the night,
And the strident shuttle ran across the weaving.
Off shore, they heard the angry growl of lions
Trying to shake their shackles off, and roaring
In the late darkness, bristling boars, and bears
Coughing in cages, and the great wolves howling.

---

[1] The encounters of Odysseus and his men with the witch Circe, daughter
of the Sun, are major episodes in Homer's *Odyssey*, Books X and XII.

All these were men, whom cruel Circe's magic
Changed into animals. But Neptune kept
20   The Trojans safely seaward, filled the sails,
Carried them safely past these anxious harbors.
    And now the sea is crimson under the dawn,
Aurora glowing in her ruddy car,
And the winds go down, and the air is very still,
The slow oars struggle in the marble sea,
As from the ship Aeneas sees a grove
And through its midst a pleasant river running,
The Tiber, yellow sand and whirling eddy,
Down to the sea. Around, above and over,
30   Fly the bright-colored birds, the water-haunters,
Charming the air with song. The order given,
The Trojans turn their course to land; they enter
The channel and the shade.
                  Help me, Erato,[2]
To tell the story: who were kings in Latium,
What was the state of things, when that strange army
First made for shore? Dear goddess, help the poet!
There is much to tell of, the initial trouble,
The grim development of war, the battles,
The princes in their bravery driven to death,
40   Etruscan[3] cohorts, all the land in the west
Marshalled in armor. This is a greater mission,
A greater work, that moves me.[4]
                King Latinus
Was an old man, long ruler over a country
Blessed with the calm of peace.[5] He was, they tell us,

---

   [2] Erato was one of the inspiring Muses, usually associated with lyric, especially love, poetry. Why Virgil addresses her, since he is writing epic poetry about war and not lyric poetry about love, is something of a puzzle. Love is the theme in the last six books only in the sense that the war involves the question of which suitor Lavinia will marry.

   [3] Of west-central Italy. The Etruscans, who had an advanced art and civilization, dominated Italy in the seventh and sixth centuries B.C.

   [4] Greater, that is, than what was narrated in the first half of the poem. The imminent alliances and battles will decide the future of Rome.

   [5] Laurentum, the city and region ruled by Latinus, was southwest of Rome, near the mouth of the Tiber.

The son of Faunus; Marica was his mother,
A nymph, Laurentian-born. And Faunus' father
Was Picus, son of Saturn, the line's founder.[6]
Latinus had no sons; they had been taken,
By fate, in their young manhood; an only daughter
Survived to keep the house alive, a girl   50
Ripe for a husband. She had many suitors
From Latium, from Ausonia. Most handsome,
Most blessed in ancestry, was the prince Turnus,
Whom the queen mother favored, but the portents
Of the high gods opposed. There was a laurel
In the palace courtyard, tended through the years
With sacred reverence, which king Latinus,
When first he built the city, had discovered,
And hallowed to Apollo, and the people
Were called Laurentians, from its name. A marvel,   60
So runs the story, occurred here once, a swarm
Of bees, that came, loud-humming through clear air
To settle in the branches, a dense jumble
All through the leafy boughs. "We see a stranger,"
The prophet cried, "and a strange column coming
On the same course to the same destination,
We see him lord it over the height of the city."
Another time Lavinia was standing
Beside her father at the altar, bringing
The holy torch to light the fire, when—horror!—   70
Her hair broke out in flame, sparks leaped and crackled
From diadem and coronal; her progress
Was a shower of fire, as she moved through the palace
Robed with gray smoke and yellow light, a vision
Fearful and wonderful. She would be glorious,
They said, in fame and fortune, but the people
Were doomed, on her account, to war.
                                        Latinus
Was troubled by such prophecies, and turned
To Faunus, his prophetic father, seeking
His oracles for help, in Albunean   80

---

[6] Faunus and Picus were primitive rural gods of Italy.

Woodland and forest, where the holy fountain
Makes music, breathing vapor from the darkness.[7]
Italian men, Oenotrian[8] tribes, in trouble
Come here for answers; here the priesthood, bringing
The offerings for sacrifice, by night-time
Slumbers on fleece of victims, seeing visions,
Hearing strange voices, meeting gods in converse,
Deep down in Acheron.[9] Hither Latinus
Came, pilgrim and petitioner; the fleeces
90   Were spread for him, a hundred woolly victims,
And as he lay, half waking and half sleeping,
From the deep grove he heard a voice:—"My son,
Seek not a Latin husband for the princess;
Distrust this bridal; stranger sons are coming
To wed our children, to exalt our title
High as the stars, and from that marriage offspring
Will see, as surely as sun looks down on ocean,
The whole world at their feet." These answers Faunus
Gave to his son, warnings in night and silence;
100   Latinus may have said no word, but Rumor
Had spread the news, all up and down the cities
Throughout Ausonia, by the time the Trojans
Tied up their vessels at the grassy landing.
    Aeneas and the captains and Iulus
Sprawled in the shade; a feast was spread; they placed
The wheels of hardtack[10] on the ground, and on them
Morsels of food, and sliced or quartered apples,
And after these were eaten, hunger drove them
To break the disks beneath with teeth and fingers.
110   "Ho!" cries Iulus, "We are eating our tables!"
A boy's joke, nothing more. But the spoken word
Meant something more, and deeper, to Aeneas,
An end of hardship. He caught up the saying,
Felt the god's presence. "Hail!" he cried, remembering,

---

[7] The exact location of Albunea is uncertain.

[8] Italian (more exactly, south-Italian).

[9] Here, the powers associated with the Lower World, considered as a source of prophetic visions.

[10] A crude form of bread.

"Hail, O my destined land! All hail, ye faithful
Gods of our homeland! Here our country lies.
Now I remember what Anchises told me:
My son, when hunger overtakes you, driven
To unknown shores, and the food seems so little
You find it best to gnaw the tables also,   120
There hope for home, there build, however weary,
The city walls, the moat, the ditch, the rampart.[11]
This must have been that hunger, and the ending
Of our misfortunes. Come then, let us gladly
Explore what lands these are, what people hold them.
Now pour your cups to Jove, in the light of morning,
Pray to Anchises; let the wine again
Go round in happiness." He wreathed his temples
With forest greenery, and made his prayers,
To the genius of the place,[12] to the nymphs, to Earth,   130
Oldest of goddesses, to the unknown rivers,
To Night, and all her rising stars, to Jove,
To Cybele, to his parents, in heaven or Hades.[13]
And the almighty father thrice made thunder
From the clear sky, and a bright cloud blazed above them
With rays of burning light, and a sudden rumor
Runs through the Trojan ranks that the day has come
To build the city due them. Cheered by the omen,
They hurry on the feast, set out the wine-bowls,
Crown them with garlands.

And on the next bright morning   140
As light streamed over the earth, they took the bearings
For city and land and coast-line; here they found
Numicius' fountain,[14] here the river Tiber,
Here the brave Latins dwell. A hundred envoys,

---

[11] It was not Anchises but a Harpy, Celaeno, who made this prophecy;
see III.254–57. There are a good many such inconsistencies in *The Aeneid*,
probably owing to Virgil's failure to give the poem its final revisions before
he died.

[12] Every place was believed to have its own "genius," or presiding spirit.

[13] The Trojan goddess Cybele was "mother of the gods." (See VI.817–
21.) Aeneas' mother, the goddess Venus, is in heaven; his late father,
the mortal Anchises, is in the Lower World (Hades).

[14] A small river, in legend the place where Aeneas died.

Picked men of every station, Aeneas orders
To go to King Latinus' noble city:
They must bear gifts, be crowned with leaves of olive,
Appeal for peace. They hurry at his bidding.
Aeneas himself marks where the walls shall rise,
150   With a shallow trench, studies the site, and circles
The settlement, like a camp, with moat and rampart.
And his ambassadors had made their journey;
They were seeing, now, the Latin towers and roof-tops,
And, on suburban plains, young men in training,
Breaking their steeds to saddle or car, or drawing
The bow, or hurling darts, daring each other
To fights and races. A courier, at the gallop,
Brought the king word that foreigners were coming,
Big men, in strange attire. He bade them welcome,
160   And took his place, high on the throne, before them.
    That was a mighty palace, rising high
Over the city, with a hundred columns;
Picus had ruled from there, and the place was holy
With sacred forest and revered tradition.
Here kings received the sceptre, here uplifted
The bundled rods of power;[15] here was their senate,
Their banquet-hall, their temple; here the elders
Made sacrifice, faced the long line of tables.
And here were statues of the ancient fathers,
170   Carved out of cedar, Italus, Sabinus,
The planter of the vine, whose image guarded
The curving sickle, and Saturn, and two-faced Janus,
All standing in the hallways;[16] and other kings
From the very first beginning; and warriors wounded
Fighting for homeland. On the door were hanging
The consecrated arms; and there were chariots,
Trophies of battle, curving axes, helmets

[15] The *fasces*, a Roman symbol of authority projected by Virgil into the past, consisted of a bundle of sticks from which an axe protruded. (This became the symbol of the twentieth-century Fascist party in Italy.)

[16] Italus and Sabinus were mythical forerunners of later Italian peoples (the Sabines being, among other things, winemakers). Saturn, father of Jupiter, came to be identified with the primitive Italian god Saturnus. Janus, the early Italian god of gateways, was presented as looking both forward and to the rear. (Hence the name of our first month, January.)

And helmet-plumes, bars wrenched from gates, and javelins,
And shields, and beaks of captured ships. Quirinus,
The god (on earth the hero, Romulus),[17]   180
Was seated, holding the sacred staff of office,
Wearing the augur's robe; and near him Picus,
Tamer of horses, whom that lovesick woman,
Circe, his wife, had struck with her golden wand,
And changed by magic spells into a bird
Whose wings were of many colors.[18]

                          In this temple,
Latinus, from his father's throne, gave summons,
And the Trojans entered, and he made them greeting
In courteous oration: "Tell me, Trojans—
We know, you see, your city and race, your voyage   190
Across the oceans—tell me your petition.
What cause, what need, has brought you here? You have
    come
Over the blue-green waters to Ausonia.
Were you off your course, or driven by storm? Mischances
On the high seas are not unknown to sailors.
No matter: you have entered peaceful rivers,
You rest in a good harbor. We bid you welcome.
Do not avoid our friendship. We must tell you
We Latins come from Saturn; we are people
Whose sense of justice comes from our own nature   200
And the custom of our god. No law, no bondage,
Compels our decency.[19] And I remember,
Though it was long ago, some story told us
By older men; it seems that Dardanus,
An ancestor of yours, was born here, left here
For towns in Phrygian Ida,[20] and Thracian Samos,
Or Samothrace, they call it now. He left here,
When he departed, from his Tuscan dwelling

---

[17] Romulus was the mythical founder of Rome; see VI.809–16. Romulus/
Quirinus was Rome's first augur (sacred forecaster of events).
[18] Picus was identified with the woodpecker, a bird linked with augury.
For Circe, see lines 9–19.
[19] In the Age of Gold, under Saturn, the world was still innocent and
unsophisticated.
[20] That is, the region of Troy, Ida being a mountain there.

Called Corythus, and now the golden palace
210   Of starry sky receives him, throned in heaven,
A god, who multiplies their count of altars."
    Ilioneus answered:—"Son of Faunus,
Great king, no tempest and no blackness drove us
Over the waves to shelter here; no star,
No shore, has fooled us in our voyage.
We came on purpose, and with willing hearts,
To this your city, exiled from a kingdom,
The greatest, once, that ever the sun looked down on.
We come from Jove; in Jove as ancestor
220   The sons of Troy rejoice; our king, Aeneas,
Himself is sprung from Jove; it is he who sent us
To seek your threshold. No one in all the world,
Whether he lives on the farthest edge of ocean,
Whether he lives in the deepest heart of the tropics,
No one, I think, but knows how fierce a storm-cloud
Broke from Mycenae[21] over the plains of Ida,
And how two worlds, Europe and Asia, battled,
Driven by fate to war. We have been driven
By that great tidal wave across vast oceans,
230   And now we ask a little home, a harbor—
We will do no damage—for our country's gods,
We ask for nothing more than all should have,
For air and water. You need not be sorry,
We shall do nothing shameful in your kingdom,
Your fame, your kindness, as we tell the story,
Will grow in greatness. Ausonia, I promise,
Will not regret receiving Troy. I swear it
On our captain's fate and honor, proven often
In loyalty, in war. There are many nations,
240   Nations and people both, who have often sought us,
Wanted us for their allies—do not scorn us
For coming as petitioners, with garlands,
With suppliant words—it was the will of heaven
That drove us to your shores. Dardanus came
From here, and over and over again Apollo guides us
To Tiber and Numicia's sacred fountain.

[21] The city of Agamemnon, Greek commander-in-chief.

Our king is sending presents, little tokens
Of former fortune, relics and remainders
Rescued from Troy on fire. This gold Anchises
Used when he poured libations at the altar,   250
This sceptre and this diadem were Priam's,
Who wore these robes, the work of Trojan women,
When he gave laws to the assembled people."
    Latinus, at his words, was grave; he held
His gaze downcast, but his anxious eyes kept turning.
It was not the crimson color, nor Priam's sceptre,
That moved him so; he was thinking of his daughter,
Her marriage, and the oracle of Faunus.
This one might be the man, this stranger, coming
From a far-off land, might be his son, a ruler   260
Called, by the fates, to share his power, to father
Illustrious children, masters of the world.
He spoke, in gladness:—"Bless, O gods, our project
And your own augury! It will be given,
O Trojan, as you ask. I do not scorn
The gifts you bring. Never, while I am ruling,
Shall you be lacking fruitful land in plenty,
And Troy's abundance shall be yours forever.
And as for king Aeneas, if you bring us
True tidings of his longing for our friendship,   270
Our hospitality, and our alliance,
Let him appear in person, let him never
Shrink from our friendly gaze. To King Latinus
It will be pact and covenant to meet him,
To take him by the hand. Give him my answer:
I have a daughter; prodigies from heaven
Innumerable, and my father's warnings,
Delivered through his oracle, forbid me
To give my daughter to a native husband.
They tell me that my son-to-be is coming   280
From foreign shores, to raise our name to heaven.
Such is the prophecy they make for Latium.
Your king, I think, must be the man they promise,
If I have any sense of divination.[22]

[22] The art of foretelling the future by interpreting omens.

He is the one I choose."
                              And he brought horses,
The pick of his stables, out of all his hundreds,
Assigned them to the Trojans in due order,
Swift runners they were, caparisoned with crimson,
With saddle-cloths of gold, and golden halters
290 Swung at their shoulders, and the bits were golden.
He chose a chariot for Aeneas; with it
Two stallions breathing fire, immortal horses
Sprung from the stock which Circe, in her cunning,
Had stolen from the sun, her father, and bred them
To her own mares. The Trojans rode back happy
With gifts and peace and welcome from Latinus.
     And here was Juno coming back from Argos,[23]
Riding the air, and fierce as ever, seeing,
As far away as Sicily and Pachynus,[24]
300 Aeneas and the Trojan fleet rejoicing.
She saw them building homes, she saw them trusting
The friendly land, she saw their ships forsaken.
She stopped, she tossed her head, in hurt and hatred,
Speaking, with none to listen:—"There they are,
The race I hate, the fates that fight my own.
They could not die on Sigean fields;[25] they could not
Be captured, and stay captured. Troy went down,
It seems, in fire, and they rose from the ashes.
Armies and flame were nothing; they found the way.
310 Whereas my power, no doubt, lies weak and weary,
I have hated them enough, I am tired of hating,
I have earned my rest. Or have I? I dared to follow
Those exiles over the water with deadly hatred,
Used up all threats of sea and sky against them,
And what good did it do? Scylla, Charybdis,
The Syrtes,[26] all availed me nothing. Tiber
Shelters them in his channel now, in safety.
What do they care for me, or the threats of ocean?

[23] A Greek city where Juno was specially honored.
[24] The southernmost cape of Sicily.
[25] Sigeum was a cape near Troy.
[26] Treacherous waters north of Africa, where the storm at the beginning
of Book I occurred. For Scylla and Charybdis, see III.428–44,555–66.

Mars could destroy the giant race of Lapiths,
Jupiter put a curse on Calydon   320
To soothe Diana's anger;[27] what had either,
Calydon or the Lapiths, done to merit
The vengeance of the gods? But I, great queen
Of heaven, wife of Jove, I keep enduring,
Dare everything, turn everywhere, for nothing—
I am beaten by Aeneas! So, if my power
Falls short of greatness, I must try another's,
Seek aid where I can find it. If I cannot
Bend Heaven, I can raise Hell. It will not be given,—
I know, I know—to keep him from his kingdom,   330
To keep him from his bride: Lavinia, Latium,
Will come to him in time. It is permitted
To keep that time far off. It is permitted
To strike their people down. It will cost them something,
Their precious father and son. As for the bride,
Bloodshed will be her dowry, and Bellona[28]
Matron of honor. Hecuba bore one firebrand,
And Venus' issue shall be such another,
A funeral torch for Troy re-born."[29]
                                   She came

Earthward, with that, and summoned, in her anger,   340
One of the evil goddesses, Allecto,
Dweller in Hell's dark shadows, sorrow-bringer,
Lover of gloom and war and plot and hatred.
Even her father hates her, even her sisters,
She takes so many forms, such savage guises,
Her hair a black and tangled nest of serpents.[30]

[27] The Centaurs, drunken guests at the wedding feast of Pirithous (king of the Lapiths), were according to this version incited by Mars to attack and kill their hosts. Diana's anger was aroused against the city of Calydon because its ruler accidentally failed to sacrifice to her; Jupiter allowed her to get revenge by sending a boar to prey on the inhabitants.

[28] Goddess of war, the female counterpart of Mars.

[29] The Trojan queen, Hecuba, dreamed that she would give birth to a firebrand, or torch; the dream was realized in her son Paris, who carried off Helen and thus ignited the Trojan war. Venus' issue is, of course, Aeneas.

[30] Allecto was one of the Furies, three infernal sisters who punished the guilty; the other two were Tisiphone and Megaera. Their father, or
(Continued)

And Juno whets the knife-edge of her passion:—
"Daughter of Night, grant me a boon, a service,
To keep my pride and honor undefeated.
350 Stop it, this Trojan swindle of Latinus
With marriages, this ravage of his kingdom!
You have the power: when brothers love each other
You know the way to arm them, set them fighting,
You can turn houses upside down with malice,
Bring under one roof the lash, the funeral torches,
You have a thousand names of evil-doing,
A thousand ways and means. Invent, imagine,
Contrive—break up the peace, sow seeds of warfare,
Let arms be what they want; in the same moment
Let arms be what they seize."

360   Therewith Allecto,
Infected with her Gorgon poison,[31] travelled
To Latium and the palace, where the queen,
Amata, brooded, womanly resentment
Burning within her heart, for Turnus' marriage,
And, fuel on fire, the coming of the Trojans.
From her own dark hair, Allecto pulled one serpent
Meant for the queen, her intimate heart, her bosom,
Corruption, evil, frenzy, for the household.
Between the robe and the smooth breasts the serpent
370 Went gliding deep, unseen, unfelt; the woman
Received the viperous menace. The snake grew larger,
Became a collar of gold, became a ribbon
Wound through the hair, entwining, sliding smoothly
Over the limbs, mercurial poison, working
With slow infection, no great passionate fury,
So that the queen, at first, spoke low and softly,
As mothers do, protesting to Latinus
And weeping for her daughter's Trojan marriage:—
"Must she be given, my lord, to Trojan exiles?
380 Have you no pity for her, for yourself,

---

master, was Pluto, god of the Lower World. In the present passage Allecto
is primarily an agent and personification of hatred uncontrolled.

[31] Poison like that of Medusa, one of the Gorgons (another set of three
monstrous sisters), who turned gazers to stone.

No pity for a mother? He will desert us,
This faithless pirate, with our child as booty,
At the first turn of the wind. That was the way—
Remember?—the Phrygian shepherd came to Sparta
And went away with Leda's daughter, Helen.[32]
A solemn pledge—does that amount to nothing?
You loved your people once; you were bound to Turnus.
Our son[33] must be a stranger; Faunus says so.
If Faunus speaks, so be it. I remind you
All lands, not ours, are foreign; and prince Turnus,   390
By the letter of the oracle, an alien.
Trace back his ancestry—Acrisius' daughter
Founded his line, and what could be more foreign
Than the heart of Greece, Mycenae?"[34]

                                        But she found
Her words were vain: Latinus had decided,
She saw she could not move him. And the poison
By now had taken hold, a wild excitement
Coursing the veins; her bones were turned to water;
Poor queen, there was no limit to her raging,
Streeling,[35] one end of the city to another.   400
You know how schoolboys, when a top is spinning,
Snap at it with a whiplash, in a circle
Around an empty court, and keep it going,
Wondering at the way it keeps on whirling,
Driven by blows in this or that direction,
So, through the midst of cities and proud people,
Amata drives, is driven. Madness and guilt upon her,
She flies to the mountains, tries to hide her daughter
Deep in the woods, acts like a drunken woman,
Cries, over and over, "This girl is meant for Bacchus,   410

---

[32] Amata refers to Paris, who had grown up as a shepherd, having been exiled from the Trojan palace because of Hecuba's ill-omened dream. Helen's mother, Leda, was ravished by Zeus (Jupiter) in the form of a swan.

[33] That is, son-in-law.

[34] Acrisius was a king of Argos, near Mycenae in Greece. His daughter was Danaë, who emigrated to Italy and there founded Ardea, the capital city of the Rutulians, an ancient Italian people. Their ruler is Turnus, who will be Aeneas' chief adversary in the latter half of the poem.

[35] Wandering distractedly, as if mad.

And not for any Trojans, only Bacchus
Is worthy of her; she honors him in dancing,
Carries his wand, and keeps for him the sacred
Lock of her hair!"[36] And Rumor, flying over,
Excites the other wives to leave their houses.
They come with maddened hearts, with their hair flying,
Their necks bare to the winds; they shriek to the skies,
Brandish the vine-bound spears, are dressed as tigers,
Circle and wheel around their queen, whose frenzy
420   Tosses the burning pine-brand high, in gesture
To suit the marriage-hymn: "O Latin mothers,
Listen, wherever you are: if any care
For poor Amata moves you, or any sense
Of any mother's rights, come join the revels,
Loosen the hair, exult!" Allecto drives her
To the dens of the beasts; her eyes are stained and bloodshot,
Rolled upward to the white.

                 So, thought Allecto,
That should suffice: the palace of Latinus,
And all the king intended, in confusion.
430   She flew on dusky wings, a gloomy goddess,
To the bold Rutulian's walls, that city, founded,
Men say, by Danaë and Acrisian settlers,
A place once called Ardea, and it keeps
Its ancient name; its glory has departed.
And here, in his high palace, Turnus slumbered.
In the dead of night, Allecto changed her features,
Her limbs, transformed her glowering, her grimness,
To an old woman's wrinkles, bound a ribbon
Around gray hair, worked in a wreath of olive,
440   And she was Calybe then, an aged priestess
Of Juno's temple, and so she came to Turnus:—
"Turnus! Can this be borne, so many labors
Wasted, the kingdom given to the Trojans?
The king denies you all, the bride, the dowry

---

[36] Bacchus (the Greek Dionysus) was god of wine. He was especially
worshipped by women (Bacchantes), in wild, frenzied rites. These women
often kept a lock of hair sacred to the god.

Bought with your blood;[37] his heir must be a stranger.
They mock you; never mind. Go forth, protect them,
Save them from dangers, see what thanks they give you,
Lay low the Tuscan ranks, hold over the Latins
The shield of peace. I tell you, Juno told me,
And you so calmly slumbering all through it,   450
Rise up, be doing something, and be happy
To see the young men armed, and get them going
Out of the gates! There are ships to burn, and captains
To set on fire: the mighty gods command it.
Let King Latinus know it, let him reckon
With Turnus in arms, unless he keeps his promise."
But Turnus, smiling at her, answered:—"Mother,
You tell me nothing new; I know a fleet
Has come to Tiber's waters; do not scare me
With fears imagined; Juno, I am certain,   460
Has not forgotten me. Your age, old woman,
Worn-down, truth-weary,[38] harries you with worries,
Makes you ridiculous, a busybody,
Nervous for nothing in the wars of kings.
Back to the temple, mind your proper business,
Leave war and peace where they belong, with warriors."
Allecto blazed with anger: Turnus, speaking,
Was suddenly afraid, so wild her features,
So fierce her flaming eyes, the snakes of the Fury
Hissing disaster. She shoves him back; he falters,   470
Tries to say more; she plies her whip, she doubles
The rising serpents, and her wild mouth cries,
"See me for what I am, worn down, truth-weary,
Nervous for nothing in the wars of kings!
See what I am, see where I come from, bringing
War, war and death, from the Grim Sisters' home."
She flung the firebrand at him, torch and terror
Smoking with lurid light. The body, sweating,
Is torn from sleep; he cries for arms, he seeks

[37] Turnus has presumably fought as an ally of Latinus in some campaign
not otherwise mentioned in the poem.
[38] Having exhausted, through old age, her prophetic powers to see truth.

480 Arms at his bedside, through the hallways, lusting
For sword and steel, war's wicked frenzy mounting
To rampant rage. Even so a caldron bubbles
When fire burns hot beneath, and water seethes,
Stirs, shifts, breaks out in boiling, and the cloud
Of steam goes toward the sky. The peace is broken.
The call to arms is given; let the captains
March on Latinus, drive the foe from Latium,
Protect the fatherland. Turnus is coming;
No matter who they are, Trojans or Latins,
490 Turnus will take them on. And his example,
His frenzied prayer, shook his Rutulian comrades,
All eagerness for war. They all admired him,
For handsome bearing, youth, or deeds of courage,
Or kingly birth: boldness engenders boldness.

    Allecto, meanwhile, took a new direction,
To the Trojans now; she had found a place for mischief
Along the shore, she had seen Iulus hunting;
His hounds were driven to madness; the scent was rank,
Hot in their nostrils; away they went, the pack
500 In full cry after the deer, and that pursuit
Was the first cause of trouble; that first kindled
The countryside to violence. That deer,
A handsome animal, with mighty antlers,
Belonged, a pet, to Tyrrhus and his children,
Who had raised him from a fawn. Tyrrhus, the father,
Was keeper of the royal herds, and Silvia,
The daughter, used to comb the beast, and wash him,
Twine garlands in his horns, caress and love him,
And he, grown used to her, would wander freely
510 Over the woods and meadows, and come home
At nightfall to the friendly door and stable.
This was the deer Iulus' hounds had started,
Floating downstream, reclining by the river
For coolness' sake, where young Ascanius, burning
For a huntsman's praise, saw him, and loosed the arrow
That pierced the belly and side, so the poor creature
Came wounded to the house he knew, and moaning
Crept into his stall, bleeding, and like a person

Asking for help, filled all the house with sorrow.
First Silvia came, beating her arms, and others,   520
Summoned for help, equipped themselves for vengeance,
With Allecto lurking in the silent forest.
A knotted club, a sharpened stake, a firebrand,
Whatever comes to hand will serve, when anger
Is looking for a weapon. Tyrrhus calls them,
They are warriors now, not farmers; they leave the logging,
The quartered oak, the wedges; in breathless anger
Tyrrhus grabs up the axe. A perfect moment
For the goddess on her watch-tower!—she comes flying
To the stable roof; she sounds the shepherds' call,   530
Straining her hellish voice on the curved horn
Till grove and woodland echo. Diana's lake
Hears, and Velinus' fountain, and white Nar,
The spring of sulphur;[39] and mothers, in their panic,
Hold their young children close. But swift to the sound,
The dire alarum, came the farmers, running;
They call no man their master; they snatch up weapons.
And on the other side the youth of the Trojans
Pour through the open gates to help Iulus.
They are drawn up now; no more a rustic quarrel   540
With stakes and clubs, the double-bladed steel
Decides the issue, swords are drawn, the harvest
Is black and spiky; bronze defies the sunlight,
Tossing its luster cloudward. As waves at sea
At first are little whitecaps under the wind,
And slowly turn to billows, and then great combers,
So rose the swell of war. Young Almo fell,
Eldest of Tyrrhus' sons; a whirring arrow,
Piercing the throat, choked him in his own blood.
And many around him fell, among them one,   550
A good old man, Galaesus, who had come forward
To plead for peace, and died; he was most just
Of all Ausonia's men, and wealthy, counting
Five flocks of sheep and cattle; a hundred ploughs

---

[39] The lake was near a temple of Diana. Velinus was a Sabine lake, Nar
a stream that flowed into the Tiber north of Rome.

Furrowed his acres.
                    So they fought together,
And neither won,—Allecto had kept her promise:
She had soaked the war in blood, she had made beginning
Of death in battle. She left the western land,
She soared to Juno in heaven, proud of her triumph:—
560   "There it is for you, perfect, war created
From disagreement! Tell them to join in friendship,
Let them make treaties, now my hand has spattered
The Trojans with Ausonian blood! And still
I can do more, if you desire it: cities
Near-by, I can plague to war with rumors, burn them
With wild desire for battle, bring in allies
From everywhere; I will sow the land with armies."
But Juno answered:—"That is plenty, thank you;
They can not stop it now; man battles man;
570   Fresh blood is on the arms that chance first gave.
Now let them stage that bridal feast, that wedding,
Venus' distinguished son, and king Latinus!
Olympus' ruler would be most unwilling
To let you roam thus freely in the heavens;
Be gone from here; whatever more is needed,
I will attend to." So spoke Saturn's daughter,
And the serpents hissed as the Fury raised her wings,
Flew up, swooped down, to Hell. Under high hills
In Italy's heart, there lies a vale, Ampsanctus,[40]
580   Well known in many lands. Dark forests hide it
On every side, and in its very centre
A roaring torrent over the rocks goes brawling,
And there is a cavern here, a breathing hole
For terrible Dis, and a gorge, where Acheron river[41]
Opens the deadly jaws; and here Allecto
Sank out of sight, relieving earth and heaven.
    And Juno gave the war the final touches.
The shepherds came to the city from the battle,
Bearing young Almo, slain, and old Galaesus,

---

[40] A foul-smelling place, because of underground gases emitted.
[41] One of the rivers of the Lower World, ruled by Dis or Pluto.

His peaceful face defiled; they cry to the gods,   590
They call on King Latinus. Turnus is there,
As they cry murder, fuel to their fire,
Making their terror double: *the kingdom falls*
To the men of Troy, he shouts; *our blood is tainted;*
I am degraded here! And the Latin mothers,
Trooping the pathless woods in Bacchic orgies,
Amata's cause being their cause, assemble
From every side; it is Mars for whom they clamor,
Not Bacchus any more. And all the people,
Against the omens, against the will of the gods,   600
Cry out for wicked war. They fight each other,
Almost, to siege and storm Latinus' palace.
He is a rock in the sea; he stands like a sea-rock
When a crash of water comes, and it is steadfast
Against the howl of the waves, and the roar is useless,
And the sea-weed, flung at the side, goes dripping back.
But even so Latinus could not conquer
Their blind determination. Things were going
As Juno willed. He invoked the empty air,
He invoked the gods, in vain. "Alas, we are broken!   610
We are broken by fate, we are swept away by storm.
You will pay for this, you will pay for it with bloodshed,
O my poor people! And punishment is waiting,
Turnus, for you; you will find it very bitter,
And then you will pray, and it will be too late.
My rest is won, my voyage almost over;
I lose a happy death." He said no more,
Shut himself in his palace, and relinquished
The reins of power.
                        There was a Latin custom,
Cherished, thereafter, by the Alban cities,[42]   620
As now by Rome, great empress—when they rouse
The god of war to battle, against the Getans,
Arabians, Hyrcanians, no matter;

---

[42] Virgil describes Alba Longa as the successor to the earliest Trojan
community and forerunner of Rome during the three centuries before
Rome was founded by Romulus in 753 B.C. See I.278–85, VI.791–808.

Whether they march on India, or strive
To win back captured standards from the Parthians,[43]
The custom holds. There are twin gates of Mars,
Held in both awe and reverence; they are fastened
By bolts of bronze, a hundred, by the eternal
Solidity of iron, and their guardian
630   Is Janus, always watchful at the threshold.
These, when the fathers vote for war, the consul,
Girt in the dress of Romulus, and belted
Gabinian-wise, with his own hand must open,
Must swing the portals wide, with his own voice
Cry war, and the others follow, and the trumpets
Give tongue in bronze agreement.[44] So Latinus
Was called on, by that custom, for announcement
Of war against the Trojans, for the opening
Of those grim gates. But he refused to touch them,
640   Fled from the task he loathed, hid in the darkness,
And Juno, coming from heaven, shoved them open
With her own hand; the turning hinges grated,
The iron was loosed for war. And all Ausonia,
Listless till then, unmoved, blazed out in fury:
On foot they came, on horseback; through the dust
The cry rang out *To arms!* They oil the shields,
They make the javelins shine, they hone the axes,
They love the sight of banner, the sound of trumpet.
In five great cities, Tibur, Crustumerium,
650   Antemnae, and Atina, and Ardea,[45]
Strong towns, and proud, and turret-crowned, they forge
New weapons on their anvils; they carve out helmets,

---

[43] The Getans lived in what is now Romania and Hungary, the Hyrcanians and Parthians near the Caspian Sea. The Parthians had humiliated Rome in 53 B.C. by badly defeating a Roman army and capturing its standards. (Augustus negotiated their return in 20 B.C.)

[44] Virgil is referring to an arched passage in Rome, the gates of Janus (god of gateways). (See I.307–11, VII.172.) When the consul (chief magistrate of Rome) opened these gates of war, he ritually wore his toga in the "Gabinian" fashion, with one fold wrapped tightly in order to free the arm. After he thus proclaimed war, it was necessary for the people to endorse the decision.

[45] Cities in Latium, the region in central Italy surrounding Rome.

Make wicker covers for the shields; they hammer
Breastplates of bronze, or greaves[46] of pliant silver.
They beat their ploughshares into swords; the furnace
Gives a new temper to the blades of their fathers.
Alarum sounds, password is whispered. Helmets
Come down from the wall; the yoke weighs down the horses;
A man puts on his armor, picks up his shield,
Buckles his sword to his side.
                Open the mountain,[47]   660
Muses, release the song!—what kings were hurried
Hot-haste to war, who filled their battle-lines,
How Italy blossomed with men, and burned with weapons,
For you remember, Muses, and you have power
To make us all remember, deeds that rumor,
Far-off and faint, brings to our recollection.
   First from the Tuscan shore came fierce Mezentius,
Arming his columns, the man who scorned the gods.[48]
Beside him, handsomer than any other,
Save only Turnus, stood his son, young Lausus,   670
Tamer of horses, huntsman, from Agylla,[49]
Leading a thousand warriors, a vain mission;
He was worthy, Lausus, of a happier fortune
Than being his father's subject; he was worthy
Of a better father.
              Near them, Aventinus
Paraded over the field his horses, victors
In many a fight, his chariots, crowned with palm-leaves.
His shield portrayed a hundred snakes, and the Hydra,

[46] Armor for the lower legs.

[47] Mount Helicon (in Greece), home of the inspiring Muses. The remainder of Book VII is Virgil's response, much more creative and varied than in Homer, to the catalogue of Greek and Trojan combatants in *The Iliad*, Book II. The persons and places Virgil names represent many areas of Italy and are drawn from a combination of antiquarian tradition, legend, myth, and Virgilian invention. Several of the persons in the catalogue emerge at greater length in later parts of the poem. The piling-up of proper names, as in this passage, is also a feature of epic style.

[48] Tuscany is the region surrounding modern Florence, in northwest Italy. More of Mezentius' background is revealed in Book VIII.

[49] Agylla (in Etruria, the region northwest of Latium) was later called Caere.

Serpent-surrounded, a token of his father,
680 For this was Hercules' son, whose manly beauty
Was like his father's. His mother was a priestess,
Rhea, whom Hercules had known when, victor,
He had slain Geryon, reached Laurentian country,
And bathed Iberian cattle in the Tiber.[50]
His birthplace was the forest on the hillside
That men call Aventine; his birth was secret.
His men go into battle with pikes and javelins,
Fight with the tapering sabre, and a curious
Sabellan type of dart. And Aventinus
690 Strode out on foot, the skin of a lion swinging
Across his shoulders; the bristling mane was shaggy,
And the head rose above it like a helmet,
With the white teeth bared and snarling. So he entered
The royal halls, and everything about him
Gave sign of Hercules.

                Next came two brothers,
Twins from the town of Tibur,[51] named Catillus
And Coras; through the throng of spears they entered
As Centaurs, born from clouds, come down the mountains,
Crashing through wood and thicket in their onrush.
700   There was Caeculus, the founder of Praeneste,[52]
A king who, legend says, was born to Vulcan
In a country that raised cattle, found, untended,
Beside a campfire. His men were country fellows
From every here and there, from steep Praeneste,
From Juno's Gabian fields, from the cold river,
The Anio, Anagnia, Amasenus,
Hernician rocks, and dewy stream and meadow.
Some of them had no arms, no shields, no chariots,
Their weapons, for the most part, being slingshots
710 And bullets of dull lead, but some of them carried
A couple of darts apiece, and for their headgear

---

[50] Hercules' great Labors included killing the many-headed Hydra and stealing the cattle belonging to Geryon, an Iberian (Spanish) giant.
[51] Tibur is the present-day Tivoli, a suburb about twenty miles east of Rome.
[52] An ancient town in Latium, twenty miles southeast of Rome.

Wore tawny wolfskins; they kept the left foot bare,
They wore a rawhide shinguard on the other.
    And there was Messapus,[53] a son of Neptune,
A tamer of horses, a man whom none in battle
Could hurt with fire or sword; his people came
To war from years and years of peaceful living,
Men from Fescennium, Soracte's mountains,
Flavinian fields, Ciminus' lake and hillside,
Capena's groves. They sang as they were marching,   720
Hailing their king in measured step and rhythm,
Their music like the sound of swans, bound home,
White through white cloud, as they return from feeding,
And the long throats pour echoing music over
Meadow and river. You would not think of warriors,
Marshalled in bronze, in that array, but a cloud
Of raucous birds, driven from sea to shore.
    Clausus, a host in himself, led a great host
Of Sabine blood; the Claudian tribe at Rome
Of Sabine origin owes to him its name.[54]   730
His followers came from many cities, Cures,
Eretum, Amiternum, and Mutusca,
Renowned for olives, Tetrica, Nomentum,
Velinus' countryside and Mount Severus,
Casperia and Foruli; many rivers
Had served their thirst, the Fabaris, the Tiber,
Himella's stream, chill Nursia, and Allia,
A name of evil omen: they came like waves
Rolling to Africa's coast when fierce Orion
Sinks in the wintry ocean,[55] as thick as grain   740
Turned brown in early summer on Hermus' plain
Or Lydia's yellow acres. The earth trembles
Under their feet; the shields clang on their shoulders.
    And there was Agamemnon's son, Halaesus,[56]

---

[53] Messapus will appear often in later episodes, as one of the principal leaders of the Italians. His followers come from places north of the Tiber (lines 718–20).

[54] The Sabines lived northeast of Rome.

[55] The constellation Orion was associated with storms.

[56] Halaesus leads men from the northern part of Campania, which is the region surrounding Naples in southwest Italy.

A hater of the Trojan name; for Turnus
He yoked his steeds, he brought a thousand peoples,
Men who hoe Massic vineyards, men from hills,
Men from the plains; men from Volturnus' river,
Men from the town of Cales; Oscan people,
750   Saticulan hosts. Their weapon is the javelin,
Wound with the whiplash; an old-fashioned shield
Covers their left; for work, close-in, they carry
Sharp-bladed scimitars.
                          And Oebalus[57]
Was with him, son of Telon and Sebethis,
Born by that nymph when Telon, old, was ruling
Over Capri, a realm his son extended
Over Sarrastrian tribes, over the plainland
The Sarnus waters; Batulum, Celemna,
Rufrae, were all his towns, and high Abella,
760   Rich in its apple-trees. These warriors carried
Some kind of German dart; they used for headgear
Bark of the cork-tree: shields and swords were bronze.
     From Nersae Ufens came,[58] a man distinguished
In arms and reputation; his tribe were huntsmen,
Farmers, after a fashion; they wore their armor
Even when ploughing. Rugged soil they lived on;
They loved to raid and live on what they raided.
     Archippus, the Marruvians' king, had sent
A warrior-priest, Umbro, renowned in courage.
770   His helmet carried olive leaves; he knew
The arts of charming serpents and of healing
Their venomous wounds; he had no magic, later,
Against the Trojan spear-point, and the herbs,
Gathered on Marsian hills, availed him little
In days of war;[59] his native groves and waters
Mourned his untimely death.
                          And Virbius came,

---

[57] Oebalus leads men from farther south in Campania.
[58] Ufens leads hill people from north and east of Rome, in the Apennine Mountains.
[59] The Marsi, living around the town Marruvium, were also hill people, from east of Rome.

Aricia's handsome son, raised in the groves,
The marshy shores around Diana's altar,
Most rich, most gracious.[60] Hippolytus, his father,
Had once been slain, the story runs, a victim   780
Of Phaedra's hate and passion, and the vengeance
His father took; he had been drawn and quartered
By Theseus' stallions, but Apollo's magic,
Diana's love, had given him life again
Under the stars and the fair light of heaven,
And Jupiter, angry that any mortal
Should rise from shadow to life, struck down his healer,
Apollo's son, with a fearful blast of thunder,
Hippolytus being hidden by Diana
In a secret place, where the nymph Egeria tended   790
Her sacred grove; there he lived out, alone,
In the Italian woods, the days of his life
With no renown; he took another name,
Virbius, meaning, *Twice a man;* no horses
Ever came near that grove, that holy temple,
Seeing that horses on an earlier shore
Had overturned his chariot in panic
And been his death, driven to panic terror
By monsters from the ocean. But his son,
Virbius the younger, had no fear of horses,   800
Driving and riding to war.
                              Among the foremost,
Taller than any, by a head, was Turnus,

[60] Virbius, of Latium, was the son of another Virbius who under his earlier name, Hippolytus, had died and then been restored to life. In Virgil's version of the story, which elaborates on the Greek myth, the chaste young outdoorsman Hippolytus (a protégé of Diana, goddess of the hunt) had been the object of his stepmother Phaedra's desire. After being rebuffed by him, she killed herself, leaving behind a message accusing Hippolytus of making advances to her. The Athenian king Theseus, Phaedra's husband and father of Hippolytus, called on Neptune to punish his son; the god responded by sending a monster out of the ocean which caused Hippolytus' horses to bolt and drag him to his death. But through Diana's influence he was restored to life by Aesculapius, a great healer and son of Apollo. The healer was then struck down by Jupiter for violating the laws of life and death. The rest of the story is told in lines 789–99.

Gripping the sword; his helmet, triple-crested,
Had a Chimaera on it, breathing fire
From gaping jaws; the bloodier the battle,
The hotter the fight, the redder that reflection,
And on his shield, in gold, the story of Io,
The heifer, once a girl; you could see her guardian,
Argus, the hundred-eyed, and her poor father,
810   The river-god with streaming urn, Inachus.[61]
And a cloud of warriors on foot behind him,
Columns with shields, the Argives and Auruncans,
Rutulians,[62] old Sicanians, Labicians
With colored shields, Sacranians, men from Tiber,
Ploughmen of Circe's ridge, soldiers from Anxur,
Sons of Feronia, that land of greenness
Where Satura's marsh lies dark, and the cold river
Runs seaward through the valley.
                              And last of all
Camilla rode,[63] leading her troops on horseback,
820   Her columns bright with bronze, a soldieress,
A woman whose hands were never trained to weaving,
To the use of wool, to basketry, a girl
As tough in war as any, in speed afoot
Swifter than wind. She could go flying over
The tips of the ears of the wheat, and never bruise them,
So light her way, she could run on the lift of the wave,
Dry-shod; and they came from the houses and fields to
        wonder,

---

[61] On the helmet of Turnus, the greatest of the Latin heroes, was a likeness of the Chimaera, a fire-breathing monster that was part lion, part goat, and part serpent. On his shield was depicted an emblem of his people's connection with the Argives of Greece (see note to line 394): the story of Io, daughter of the Argive king and river-god Inachus. Jupiter desired Io, but the jealous Juno changed the girl into a heifer and set the hundred-eyed Argus to keep watch over her. (In some versions Jupiter himself caused Io's metamorphosis.)

[62] On the Rutulians, see note to line 394.

[63] Camilla's people were the Volscians, natives of the hills in the southern part of Latium. Largely, probably entirely, invented by Virgil, she is the counterpart for him of Penthesilea, a queen of the Amazons (women warriors) who, according to a tradition later than Homer, fought for Troy in the Trojan war.

To gaze at her going, young men, and matrons thronging,
Wide-eyed and with parted lips, at the glory of royal crimson
Over her shoulders' smoothness, the clasp of the gold   830
In her hair, and the way she carried the Lycian quiver,[64]
The heft of the pastoral myrtle, the wand with the
    spear-point.

[64] The Lycians, of Asia Minor, were renowned archers.

BOOK VIII

□

Aeneas
at the Site
of Rome

As Turnus raised war's banner, and the trumpets
Blared loud above Laurentum's citadel,
And fiery horses reared, and arms were clashing,
Confusion reigned: all Latium joined alliance,
The youth were mad for war. Messapus, Ufens,
And that despiser of the gods, Mezentius,
Brought forces in from everywhere; wide fields
Were stripped of countrymen. They sent a message
By Venulus, to Diomede in Arpi:[1]
Come to our aid; the Trojans are in Latium;
Aeneas with a fleet and vanquished gods
Proclaims himself a king; it is fate, he says;
And many tribes are joining him; his name
Spreads far and wide in Latium. Diomede
(The message says), better than many others,
Should know the outcome, if the grace of fortune

---

[1] Diomede was one of the foremost Greek warriors who fought against
Troy. He has emigrated to Italy and now rules Arpi, or Argyripa, a city
in Apulia, the southeastern region forming the "heel" of the boot of Italy.
Venulus is one of the men of Tibur, a city founded by Greeks.

181

Follows Aeneas in the scheme he nurtures.
He knows the Trojans; he can judge them better
Than Turnus or Latinus.
                              So, in Latium,
20   Events were shaping, and Aeneas knew it,
And saw it all, and turned and tossed in torment
On a great sea of trouble. The swift mind
Went searching, probing, veering with every shift,
As when in a bronze bowl the light of water,
Reflected by the sun or moonlight, wavers,
Dances and flits about, from wall to ceiling.
Night: over all the world the weary creatures,
The beasts and birds, were deep in sleep; Aeneas,
With warfare in his heart, stretched out for rest
30   Where the cold sky was awning over the river,
And sleep came late. Before him rose an image,
An aged head amid the poplar leaves,
A mantle of gray, and shady reeds around him,
Tiber, the river-god, in consolation
And comfort speaking:—"Son of the gods, redeemer
Of Troy from overseas, her savior ever,
O long-awaited on Laurentian fields,
Here is your home, be sure of it; here dwell
Your household gods, be sure. Do not turn back,
40   Do not be frightened by the threats of war:
The swollen rage of Heaven has subsided.
Soon—do not take my words for idle phantoms,
Illusions of a dream—under the holm-oaks
Along the shore, you will find a huge sow lying,
White, with a new-born litter at her udders,
Thirty of them, all white, a certain token
Of a new city, in thirty years. Your son
Will found it; he will call it the White City,
A glorious name, beyond all doubt whatever.[2]
50   Further, I have a word or two of guidance
To speed you through the pressure of the moment
Toward ultimate victory. Inland a little

---

[2] Compare the prophecy of Helenus in III.396–402. The White City is
Alba Longa (*alba* means "white").

Arcadian people live, a race descended
From Pallas' line; their king is called Evander,
Under whose banner they have built a city,
High on the hills; its name is Pallanteum.[3]
They wage continual warfare with the Latins;
Take them as allies, in covenant and treaty.
And I myself will guide you there, upstream
Along the banks, the oars against the current.   60
Rise, goddess-born; when the stars set, make prayer
To Juno first, with suppliant vows appeasing
Her threats and anger. As for me, my tribute
May wait your triumph. I am blue-green Tiber,
The river most dear to Heaven, I am the river
You see, brim-full to these rich banks, this ploughland:
This is my home, the source of lofty cities."
    So spoke the river-god, to his deep pool diving.
Slumber and night were gone. Aeneas rose,
Faced eastern sunlight, took up river water   70
In the hollow of his hands, and made his prayer:—
"Laurentian Nymphs, to whom the rivers owe
Their essence, father Tiber, holy river,
Receive Aeneas, be his shield in danger.
Wherever your presence dwells, in pool or fountain,
Whatever land its flowing bounty graces,
O comforter in time of trouble, surely
Our gifts will bring their meed of honor, always,
To the horned ruler of the western waters.
Only be with us, give us confirmation!"   80
He had made his prayer; two ships were quickly chosen
Out of the fleet, equipped, and the crews made ready.
    And then a marvel struck their eyes, a wonder!
White in the wood, on the green ground, there lay
A sow with her white litter, and Aeneas
Brought them in sacrifice to Juno's altar.
All that long night, the Tiber calmed his flood;
The silent wave, retreating, lay as still
As pool or mere or watery plain; the oars

---

[3] Pallas was an ancient hero from Arcadia, in Greece. (Evander's son
is also named Pallas.) Pallanteum is on the site of the Palatine hill, in
what later will be Rome.

90   Dipped without strain; the voyage went with laughter
      And cheerful shouting; over the waters rode
      The oily keels; and waves and woods in wonder
      Beheld the shields of men, the colored vessels,
      Divide the flood. Day turns to night. They traverse
      The winding bends, with green shade arching over,
      Parting the green woods in the quiet water,
      Till it is noon, and they see walls and houses,
      Evander's town, which Roman power later
      Made equal to the city, a mighty empire,
100   But it was little then. They turned to the shore,
      Drew near the city.
                          On that day, it happened,
      The king was paying customary homage,
      In a grove before the city, to the gods,
      To Hercules, most of all. And his son Pallas
      Was with him there, and the leaders of the people,
      The lowly senate, bringing gifts of incense
      Where the warm blood was smoking at the altars.
      They saw the tall ships come, they saw them gliding
      Upstream, through the dark wood, the feathered oar-blades
110   Making no noise at all, and they were frightened,
      They rose; they would have left the feast, but Pallas,
      Unterrified, forbade them; he seized a weapon,
      Rushed out in challenge, calling from a hillock:—
      "What cause, young men, has brought you here, exploring
      Ways that you do not know? Where are you going?
      What is your race? Where do you come from? Are you
      Bringers of peace or war?" Aeneas answered
      From the high stern, raising the branch of olive:—
      "We are men from Troy; we are armed against the Latins,
120   Whose arrogant war we flee. We seek Evander.
      Take him this message: tell him chosen leaders,
      Dardanus' sons, have come, to seek for friendship,
      For allied arms." And Pallas, in amazement
      At hearing that great name, cried, "Come and join us,
      Whoever you are, speak to my father, enter,
      O guest, into our household!" And his hand
      Reached out to greet and guide them. They left the river,

Drew near the grove; with friendly words Aeneas
Spoke to Evander:—"Best of the sons of Greeks,
To whom, at fortune's will, I bring petition,   130
Bearing the branch of peace, I have not been frightened
To come to you, a Danaan chief, related
To Atreus' twin sons.[4] In my own right
I am worth something; we are bound together
By the god's holy oracles, by the old
Ancestral kinship, by your own renown
Widespread through all the world. I am glad to follow
The will of fate. Dardanus, our great father,
Was father of Troy; his mother was Electra,
Daughter of Atlas, who carries on his shoulders   140
The weight of heaven. Mercury is your father,
Born, on Cyllene's chilly peak, to Maia,
And Maia, if legend is credible, the daughter
Of Atlas, who carries heaven on his shoulders.
A common blood runs in our veins, and therefore
I sent no embassies, I planned no careful
Tentative overtures; myself, I came here
My life at your disposal, in supplication
Before your threshold. We are harried in war
By the same race that harries you, the sons   150
Of Daunus;[5] nothing, so they think, will stop them,
If we are beaten, from complete dominion
Over the western land and both her oceans.
Receive and give alliance: our hearts are brave,
Our spirit tried and willing."
                                    He had finished.
Evander had been watching him, expression,
Gesture, and mood, and bearing. He made answer:—
"How gladly, bravest man of all the Trojans,
I recognize and welcome you! Your father,
The great Anchises, speaks to me again,—   160
These are the words, the voice, the very features

[4] *Danaan* means "Greek." The sons of Atreus were Menelaus, husband
of Helen, and Agamemnon, the Greek commander-in-chief at Troy.
[5] Daunus was Turnus' father; his "sons" were Turnus' people, the Rutulians.

That I recall so well. Once Priam came here,
Faring to Salamis,[6] his sister's kingdom.
I was a young man then; I stared in wonder
At the chiefs of Troy, at Priam, but Anchises
Towered above them all, and my heart was burning
To clasp his hand, to speak with him: I met him,
I led him, proudly, to Pheneus' city,[7]
And when he left, he gave me a fine quiver
170 With Lycian arrows, a cloak with gold embroidered,
A pair of golden bridles; my son Pallas
Rejoices in them now. The bond you ask for
Is given, the treaty made. To-morrow morning
My escort will attend your leave, my riches
Be at your service. Meanwhile, since you come here
As friends of ours, join us in celebrating
These yearly rites of ours. It is not permitted
Our people to postpone them. In your kindness,
Become accustomed to your allies' tables."

180   He gave the orders for the feast's renewal.
Once more the cups are set; the king, in person,
Conducts his guests to places on the greensward,
Reserving for Aeneas, in special honor,
A maple throne, draped with the skin of a lion.
Chosen attendants and the priest of the altar
Bring the roast portions, pile the bread in baskets,
Serve Bacchus' wine. Aeneas and the Trojans
Feast on the consecrated food.

                                   When hunger
Was satisfied, and the wine went round, Evander
190 Told them a story:—"No vain superstition,
No ignorance of the gods, enjoins upon us
These solemn rites, this feast, this deep devotion
To a mighty power's altar. O Trojan guest,
We are grateful men, saved from a cruel danger,
We pay these rites each year, each year renewing
A worship justly due. Look up at the cliff
Hung on the high rocks yonder, see the scattered

---

[6] A Greek island, near Athens. The visit described obviously took place
before Evander and his people migrated to Italy.
[7] One of Evander's own cities, in Arcadia.

Rubble of rock, the ruin of a dwelling,
The jumble of toppled crags. There was a cave there
Once on a time; no man had ever measured   200
Its awful depth, no sunlight ever cheered it.
The half-man, Cacus, terrible to look at,
Lived in that cave, and the ground was always reeking
With the smell of blood, and nailed to the doors, the faces
Of men hung pale and wasted. Vulcan fathered
This monster; you would know it if you saw him
With the black fire pouring from mouth and nostrils,
A bulk of moving evil. But time at last
Brought us the help we prayed for; a great avenger,
A god, came to our rescue, Hercules,   210
Proud in the death and spoil of triple Geryon,
Drove his huge bulls this way, the great herd filling
Valley and river.[8] And the crazy Cacus,
Who never would lose a chance for crime or cunning,
Made off with four of the bulls and four sleek heifers,
Dragging them by their tails; the tracks would never
Prove he had driven them to his rocky cavern.
He hid them in the darkness; whoever looked
Would think they had gone not to, but from, the cave.
Meanwhile, as Hercules drove the well-fed herd   220
Out of the stables to the road again,
Some of them lowed in protest; hill and grove
Gave back the sound, and from the cave one heifer
Lowed in return. That was the doom of Cacus.
Black bile[9] burned hot in Hercules; he grabbed
His weapons, his great knotted club, went rushing
Up to the mountain-top. Never before
Had men seen terror in the eyes of Cacus.
Swifter than wind, he dove into his cavern,
Shut himself in, shattered the links of iron   230
That held aloft the giant boulder, dropped it
To block the doorway, and Hercules came flinging
His angry strength against it, to no purpose.

[8] Hercules had carried off the cattle belonging to Geryon, a triple-bodied
monster who ruled over Spain.
[9] In ancient medical science, one of the four "humours"; bad temper,
a "black" mood.

This way he faced, and that, and gnashed his teeth
In sheer frustration; he went around the mountain
Three times, in burning rage; three times he battered
The bulkhead of the door; three times he rested,
Breathless and weary, on the floor of the valley.
Above the cavern ridge, a pointed rock,
240   All flint, cut sharp, with a sheer drop all around it,
Rose steep, a nesting place for kites and buzzards.
It leaned a little leftward toward the river.
This Hercules grabbed and shook, straining against it;
His right hand pushed and wrenched it loose; he shoved
    it,
With a sudden heave, down hill, and the heaven thundered,
The river ran backward and the banks jumped sideways,
And Cacus' den stood open, that great palace
Under the rock, the chambered vault of shadows.
An earthquake, so, might bring to light the kingdoms
250   Of the world below the world, the pallid regions
Loathed by the gods, the gulf of gloom, where phantoms
Shiver and quake as light descends upon them.
So there was Cacus, desperate in the light,
Caught in the hollow rock, howling and roaring
As Hercules rained weapons down upon him,
Everything he could use, from boughs to millstones,
But Cacus still had one way out of the danger:
A cloud of smoke rolled out of his jaws; the cave
Darkened to utter blackness, thick night rolling
260   With fitful glints of fire. This was too much
For Hercules in his fury; he jumped down through it,
Through fire, where the smoke came rolling forth the
    thickest,
Where the black billows seethed around the cavern.
And Cacus, in the darkness, to no purpose
Poured forth his fire and smoke. Hercules grabbed him,
Twisted him into a knot, hung on and choked him
Till the eyes bulged out and the throat was dry of blood.
He tore the doors loose, and the house was open;
People could see the lost and stolen plunder,
270   And Hercules dragged the shapeless ugly carcass
Out by the feet, a fascinating object

For the gaze of men, the terrible eyes, the muzzle,
The hairy chest, and the fire dead in the gullet.
Ever since then we keep this day, rejoicing
In honor of our deliverance; Potitius
Was founder of the rite, Pinaria's household
Custodian of the service.[10] In this grove
We set our altar, calling it the greatest,
And greatest it shall be, to me, forever.
Join with us, then, in honor of all that glory,   280
Bind wreaths around your temples, reach the wine-cup,
Call with good-will upon our common god."
He veiled his hair with the two-colored poplar
In Hercules' honor,[11] and held out the goblet;
All made libation and prayer.
                        And evening came,
And the priests went forth, Potitius first; they wore
The skins of beasts, and they were bearing torches.
The feast renewed, they brought the welcome viands
To a second table, loading, too, the altars.
And the Dancing Priests around the sacred altars   290
Lit fire and sang their songs. They too wore poplar,
Both groups, one old, one young, and chanted verses
In praise of Hercules, his deeds, his glories,
How first he strangled in his grip twin serpents,
The monsters Juno sent;[12] how, great in war,
Troy and Oechalia went down before him;[13]
How, under King Eurystheus, he bore
A thousand heavy toils, at Juno's order.[14]

---

[10] The Potitii and the Pinarii were families that, in later Roman history, were devoted to a cult of Hercules.

[11] The poplar (sacred to Hercules) has leaves that are white or silvery underneath.

[12] Hercules was Jupiter's son by Alcmene; the jealous Juno sent two serpents to attack Hercules in his cradle, but the infant killed the serpents instead.

[13] Hired to save Troy from a monster preying on it, Hercules was denied his pay and therefore destroyed the city. He also destroyed the east-Grecian city of Oechalia when he was denied the king's daughter Iole after he won an archery competition for which she was to be the winner's prize.

[14] Hercules' famous Labors, which he was required to perform for Eurystheus, king of the Greek city Tiryns, actually numbered twelve by the
(Continued)

"Hail, O unvanquished hero, whose hand brought low
300   Pholus, Hylaeus, the cloud-born double shapes,
Monsters of Crete and the Nemean lion.
The Stygian lakes trembled at Hercules' crossing,
And Cerberus was frightened, in his cavern,
Lying on bones half-eaten. O unafraid
Of any monster, even Typhoeus, towering
High in his arms, even the snake of Lerna
With all its hissing heads,—hail, son of Jove,
Hail, glorious addition to the heavens!
Favor our rites and yours with gracious blessing!"
310   So they sang praises, and they crowned the service
With the tale of Cacus, that fire-breathing monster,
And hill and woodland echoed to the singing.

      Then back to the city again; and old Evander
Kept his son Pallas near him and Aeneas,
Talking of various matters; so the journey
Was lightened, and the landscape charmed Aeneas,
Who wondered as he watched the scene, and questioned,
And learned its early legend. King Evander
Began the story:—"Native Nymphs and Fauns[15]
320   Dwelt in these woodlands once, and a race of men
Sprung from the trunks of trees, or rugged oak,
Men primitive and rude, with little culture:
They had no knowledge of ploughing, none of harvest;
The fruits of the wild trees, the spoils of hunting,
Gave them their nourishment. Then Saturn came here,
Fleeing Jove's arms, an exile from his kingdom.
He organized this race, unruly, scattered

---

traditional count. Some of them are mentioned in the following lines:
the defeat of Pholus, Hylaeus, and other Centaurs (who were half man,
half horse, and whose race was fathered by Ixion on a cloud shaped like
Juno); the salvation of Crete from a mad bull and of the Nemean valley,
in Greece, from a lion (which Hercules strangled); the theft of the dog
Cerberus who guarded the Lower World (see VI.415–21); and the defeat
of the many-headed Hydra (the "snake of Lerna," in Greece), a monster
that regenerated two heads for each one cut off. Not generally classed
with the Labors was the help Hercules gave the gods when they were
threatened by the fiery giant Typhoeus, another many-headed monster.
      [15] Deities of the countryside. Fauns were similar to the Greek satyrs.

Through the high mountains, gave them law and order.
He gave the place a name; Latium, he called it,
Since once he lay there safely, hiding in shelter.[16]   330
Under his rule there came those golden ages
That people tell of, all the nations dwelling
In amity and peace. But little by little
A worse age came, lack-luster in its color,
And the madness of war, and the evil greed of having.
Then came the Ausonian bands, Sicanian peoples,
And the land of Saturn took on other names,
And the kings came, and the fierce giant Thybris
For whom we named our river;[17] we forgot
Its older title, Albula. Here I came   340
An exile from my country, over the seas,
Driven by fate and fortune, which no man
Can cope with or escape. The nymph Carmentis,
My mother, led me here with solemn warnings
Under Apollo's guidance."
              So Evander
Finished the tale, resumed the walk. They came,
First, to an altar and a gate: Carmental
The Romans call it, in honor of that nymph
Who first foretold the greatness of the Romans,
The glory of Pallanteum.[18] Past the portal   350

[16] In Latin, *latere* means "to be hidden."

[17] The Ausonians were Italians; the Sicanians were Sicilians; the Thybris river was the Tiber.

[18] Lines 346–69, identifying the early sites of landmarks of later Rome, such as the Carmental gate near the Capitol of Virgil's day, are typical of his brand of patriotism: proud and yet eager to celebrate and implicitly preach the simple primitive virtues that Romans should keep alive. The "sanctuary" of line 351, also near the Capitol, was the Asylum, which Romulus, the founder of Rome, established as a center for regional refugees. The Lupercal was a cave by the Palatine hill (where Caesar Augustus resided), believed to be the den of the wolf (Latin *lupus*, "wolf") that had nursed Romulus; the Greek nature god Pan (worshipped especially in Evander's home country of Arcadia) was sometimes called Pan Lycaeus, an epithet that also means "wolf." The "wood of Argiletum" was on a site near what would be the Forum; legend derived its name from that of a treacherous guest (Argus) of Evander's who had been killed there. The Tarpeian house, named for a tall rock, was on the site of the Capitol,

(Continued)

They came to a spreading grove, a sanctuary
Restored by Romulus, and under the cold cliff
The Lupercal, named, in Arcadian fashion,
For the great god Pan. And then Evander showed him
The wood of Argiletum, and told the legend
Of the death of Argus, once a guest. From there
They went to the Tarpeian house, and a place
Golden as we now know it, once a thicket,
Once brush and briar, and now our Capitol.
360   Even then men trembled, fearful of a presence
Haunting this wood, this rock. "A god lives here,"
Evander said, "what god, we are not certain,
But certainly a god. Sometimes my people
Think they have seen, it may be, Jove himself
Clashing the darkening shield, massing the storm-cloud.
Here you can see two towns; the walls are shattered,
But they remind us still of men of old,
Two forts, one built by Janus, one by Saturn,
Janiculum, Saturnia."
                So they came,
370   Conversing with each other, to the dwelling
Where poor Evander lived, and saw the cattle
And heard them lowing, through the Roman forum,
The fashionable section of our city,
And as they came to the house itself, Evander
Remembered something,—"Hercules," he said,
"Great victor that he was, bent head and shoulders
To enter here, and this house entertained him.
Dare, O my guest, to think of wealth as nothing,
Make yourself worthy of the god, and come here
380   Without contempt for poverty." He led him,
The great Aeneas, under the low rafters,
Found him a couch, nothing but leaves, and the bedspread
A Libyan bear-skin. And night came rushing down
Dark-wingèd over the earth.
                  And Venus' heart

---

where in Virgil's time Jupiter and other gods had rich temples. The Ianicu-
lum (named for Janus, god of gateways) was a hill in Virgil's Rome that
was considered an archaeological site even in his day. The "darkening
shield" of line 365 is the *aegis;* see 451–55 and note.

Was anxious for her son, and with good reason,
Knowing the threats and tumult of the Latins.
She spoke to Vulcan, in that golden chamber
Where they were wife and husband, and her words
Were warm with love:—"When the Greek kings were tearing
Troy's towers as they deserved, and the walls were fated   390
To fall to enemy fire, I sought no aid
For those poor people, I did not ask for weapons
Made by your art and power; no, dearest husband,
I would not put you to that useless labor,
Much as I owed to Priam's sons,[19] however
I sorrowed for my suffering Aeneas.
But now, at Jove's command, he has made a landing
On the Rutulian coast; I come, a suppliant
To the great power I cherish, a mother asking
Arms for her son. If Thetis and Aurora   400
Could move you with their tears,[20] behold what people
Unite against me, what cities sharpen weapons
Behind closed gates, intent on our destruction!"
So Venus pleaded, and as she saw him doubtful,
The goddess flung her snowy arms around him
In fondlement, in soft embrace, and fire
Ran through him; warmth, familiar to the marrow,
Softened his sternness, as at times in thunder
Light runs through cloud. She knew her charms, the goddess,
Rejoicing in them, conscious of her beauty,   410
Sure of the power of love, and heard his answer:—
"No need for far-fetched pleading, dearest goddess;
Have you no faith in me? You might have asked it
In those old days; I would have armed the Trojans,
And Jupiter and the fates might well have given
Another ten years of life to Troy and Priam.
Now, if your purpose is for war, I promise
Whatever careful craft I have, whatever

---

[19] Paris, the Trojan prince, had given the prize (a golden apple) to Venus, judging her to be more beautiful than Juno and Minerva—an incident that sowed the first seed of the Trojan war.

[20] Thetis, mother of Achilles, had persuaded Vulcan to make arms for him (Homer's *Iliad,* Book XVIII); Aurora, goddess of the dawn, had done the same thing for her son Memnon.

Command I have of iron or electrum,[21]
420   Whatever fire and air can do. Your pleading
Is foolish; trust your power!" And he came to her
With the embrace they longed for, and on her bosom
Sank, later, into slumber.
                    And rose early
When night was little more than half way over,
The way a housewife must, who tends the spindle,
Rising to stir and wake the drowsing embers,
Working by night as well as day, and keeping
The housemaids at the task, all day, till lamplight,
A faithful wife, through toil, and a good mother,
430   Even so, like her, with no more self-indulgence,
The Lord of Fire rose early, from soft pillows
To the labor of the forge.
                  An island rises
Near the Sicanian coast and Lipare,
Aeolian land, steep over smoking rocks.
Below them roars a cavern, hollow vaults
Scooped out for forges, where the Cyclops pound
On the resounding anvils;[22] lumps of steel
Hiss in the water, and the blasts of fire
Pant in the furnaces; here Vulcan dwells,
440   The place is called Vulcania, and here
The Lord of Fire comes down. In the great cave
The smiths were working iron; a thunderbolt
Such as Jove hurls from heaven, was almost finished,
Shaped by the hands of Brontes, Steropes,
And naked-limbed Pyracmon. They had added
Three rods of twisted rain and three of cloud,
And three of orange fire and wingèd wind,
And now they were working in the flash, the sound,

[21] An alloy, gold and silver mixed.
[22] The "island" of line 432 is the one now called Vulcano, about fifty miles from the famous volcano Mt. Etna (on the Sicilian mainland). Vulcano and Lipare (where the god of the winds, Aeolus, had his dwelling) are among the Lipari, volcanic islands north of Sicily. Vulcan's laborers, the Cyclops, are conceived here as wholly different from the one-eyed monsters of III.616–80. Their names, in lines 444–45, mean Thunder, Lightning, and Fire-Anvil.

The fear, the anger, the pursuing flame.
Elsewhere a chariot for Mars was building   450
To harry men and cities; and for Pallas
An awful shield, with serpent scales of gold,
Snakes interwoven, and the Gorgon's head,
Awaiting polish. The neck was severed, the eyes
Already seemed to roll,[23] when Vulcan came
Crying, "Away with this! Another task
Demands your toil, your thought. Arms for a warrior!
Use all your strength, you need it now; exert
The flying hands, ply all your master skill,
Break off delay!" And all, obedient, bent   460
To the great task; the bronze, the golden ore
Run down like rivers, and the wounding steel
Melts in the furnace as they shape the shield,
Welding it, orb on orb, a sevenfold circle
Made one, for all the weapons of the Latins.
Some keep the bellows panting, others dip
The hissing bronze in water, and the anvil
Groans under the hammer-stroke. In turn they raise
Their arms in measured cadence, and the tongs
Take hold of the hot metal, twist and turn it.   470
So sped the work on Lemnos.[24]
                  And Evander
Was wakened by the kindly light of morning
And bird-song under the eaves, and the old man rose,
Donned simple tunic and sandals, and hung on
His simple sword, and over his shoulders twisted
The panther hide, out of the way of the hilt.
Two hounds were all his bodyguard; he came,
So, to Aeneas' cabin; he remembered
His words and promised service, found his guest

[23] The *aegis*, the name given to the shield (or possibly breast-armor) of Zeus, was also borne by his daughter Pallas Athena (Minerva). Medusa, one of the Gorgons often depicted on shields, was a female monster, with snakes for hair, who turned anyone to stone who gazed on her; Perseus, with the help of a mirror, cut off her head.

[24] Lemnos was the island in the Aegean Sea frequented by Hephaestus, the Greek counterpart of Vulcan, who landed there after being hurled from heaven by Zeus (Jupiter). It was on Lemnos that some traditions located the workshop of the blacksmith-god.

480   An early riser also; hand met hand,
And soon companions joined them, young prince Pallas,
Loyal Achates. They stroll a while, then settle
Themselves for conversation, and Evander
Is first to speak:—"Great captain of the Trojans,
I cannot, while you live, consider Troy
A beaten town, I cannot see her people
As anything but victors. I am sorry
Our power to help is meager. On one side
A river hems us in, and on the other
490   Rutulian armies thunder at our walls.
Still, I can find you, or I think so, allies,
Great people, an encampment rich in kingdoms,
An unexpected aid. The fates have brought you
To the right place. Not far away, Agylla,
A city built of ancient stone, lies waiting,
A town the Lydians founded;[25] you know the race,
Renowned in war. It was a prosperous city
For many years, until Mezentius ruled it,
A cruel, arrogant man, sadist and savage.
500   God pay him back in kind! I cannot tell you
All his foul deeds: this will suffice;—he fastened
Live men to dead men, strapped their hands together,
Tied face to face, and killed them, slowly, slowly,
In the waste and stain and clasp of that long death.
They suffered long, his subjects, but at last
They rose in arms against him, his mad household,
Hurled fire to his roof-top, slaughtered his companions.
He fled that ruin to Rutulian fields,
Where Turnus' weapons shielded him. Now all
510   Etruria, risen in arms, demands,
With threat of war, the king for punishment,
And you shall be the leader of those thousands
Who throng the shore with ships, whose cry is *Forward!*
But an old prophet holds them back, those warriors,

---

[25] Agylla (or Caere) was a city north of Rome in Etruria, which is the region surrounding modern Florence. Lydia is a region of Asia Minor on the Aegean Sea. Virgil apparently follows the tradition that the ancient Etruscans, or Etrurians, originally came from this area.

The pride and glory of an ancient people,
Whom a just grievance and a righteous anger
Inflames against Mezentius. *It is not fated,*
He says, *for any native-born Italian*
To tame a race so proud. Choose foreign leaders!
And so the Etruscan battle-lines have settled   520
Unwarlike on the plain, through heaven's warning.
Tarchon himself has sent me envoys, bearing
The crown and sceptre, urging me to his camp,
Bidding me take the throne.[26] But cold old age,
And years too thin for battle, these begrudge me
The high command. I would send my son, but Pallas
Comes from a Sabine mother; he is partly
A native-born Italian. You, Aeneas,
Possess the proper strength, the proper lineage,
The summons of the gods. Take up the burden!   530
My Pallas will go with you, my hope and comfort.
You are the one to teach him a soldier's duty,
How to endure; let him learn from you in action,
Behold your deeds, and, in his youth, admire them.
I will give two hundred horsemen, young Arcadians,
The flower of our manhood; and two hundred
Will go with you besides in the name of Pallas."
    Aeneas and Achates, listening, brooded
With downcast gaze, in troubled speculation
Prolonging bitter thoughts, but Venus gave them   540
A sign from the bright heaven: a flash of thunder
Came from the cloudless sky, a blare of trumpets,
And all things suddenly shaken. They looked up swiftly;
Again, again, they heard the roar and rumble,
They saw arms redden in the clear of heaven,
Listened to thunder in cloud. And some were frightened;
Not so the Trojan: he knew his mother's promise.
"Ask not, O friend, the meaning of the portent,"
He cried, "Olympus[27] summons me; I know it.
This was the sign my goddess-mother promised   550

---

[26] Tarchon is presumably the deposed Mezentius' successor.
[27] That is, the gods (from the name of the mountain where they dwell).

When war was near; she would bring me arms from Vulcan,
She said, to help us all.[28] Alas! what slaughter
Waits for the Latins now! How costly, Turnus,
The price that must be paid me! Shields and helmets
And bodies of brave men, swept under Tiber.
Now let them call for battle, and break treaties!"
    He rose and at his quickening the altars
Blazed into sudden fire; he paid his honors
To Hercules, to all the gods of household,
560 And all made sacrifice, sheep duly chosen.
Aeneas sought, once more, his ships, his comrades,
Chose, to attend him, those most brave in battle,
Despatched the rest down stream again with tidings
To take Ascanius of his father's fortunes.
Horses are brought for all the Trojan leaders,
And for Aeneas the best, a charger, golden
With lion-skin caparison, claws gilded.
    And rumor flies about the little city
Spreading the news of horsemen on their mission
570 To Tarchon's shores, and mothers, in a panic,
Double their prayers, and fear comes nearer danger
With Mars' great image looming large. Evander
Holds Pallas by the hand, cannot release him,
Speaks through his tears:—"If Jupiter would only
Bring me my lost years back, make me the man
I used to be, I was once, at Praeneste
Where I struck down the foremost ranks, and burned
The piled up shields! That day I was a hero,
A conqueror, and Erulus went down,
580 By this right hand, to hell. His mother gave him
Three lives, and threefold armor; I had to kill him
Three times, and did, and thrice I stripped his armor.[29]
If I were what I used to be, my son,
They would never take you from me; and Mezentius
Would never have heaped those insults on his neighbor,

---

[28] The poem has not actually told of such a promise by Venus.
  [29] This episode from Evander's younger days is not further explained
in the poem.

Never have made a widow of the city.[30]
But you, great gods on high, and you, great king
Of the high gods, take pity on a father,
Hear the Arcadian king. I pray for life
As long as Pallas lives, I pray to see him   590
If you will spare him; if he comes back safely
I pray to meet him once again. No more
I ask; how hard my life may be, no matter.
But if there is in fortune any menace,
Something I cannot speak of, let me die
Before I know the worst, while I can hope
However I doubt, while still I have my Pallas,
My late and only pleasure, here beside me,
And never news for the worse!" And so they parted,
And servants helped the old man into the palace.   600

    They had gone from the gates, the horsemen, and Aeneas,
Achates and the Trojans, and in the centre
Pallas, a blaze of light, like Lucifer
Whom Venus loves beyond all fiery stars,
The glory risen from the ocean wave,
Dissolver of the shadows.[31] On the walls
The mothers, trembling, watched them go, the squadrons
Bright in their bronze, and the cloud of dust behind them,
So, out of sight, where the road turns off to forest,
They go, the men in arms, and a shout arises,   610
And the column forms, and the echo of the gallop
Comes clopping back through the ground where the dust
     is rising.
    The cold stream, Caere, has a grove beside it,
Much reverenced of old, where the curve of the hills
And the dark firs make a shelter: the old people,
So rumor says, held grove and feast-day sacred
Here in Silvanus' honor, god of the fields,

---

[30] It is not entirely clear whether the city intended here is Mezentius'
own former city, Agylla, or Evander's city, Pallanteum; probably it is the
latter.
[31] Here *Lucifer* (literally, "light-bearer") means the morning star, which
is most commonly Venus.

God of the fold. Tarchon and his Etruscans
Were camped not far from here, and from the hill-top
620   Watchers could see their legions, tented safely
Through the wide plain. In Caere's grove Aeneas
Rested his horses and his weary warriors.

      And the bright goddess through the clouds of heaven
Came bringing gifts, seeing her son alone
By the cold river in the quiet valley,
And spoke to him:—"Behold, the gifts made ready
By Vulcan's promised skill. Fear not, my son,
To face the wars with Turnus and the Latins!"
After the word, the embrace. She placed the armor,
630   All shining in his sight, against an oak-tree;
Rejoicing in the gift, the honor, he turned
His eyes to these, over and over again,
Could not be satisfied, took in his hands
The helmet with the terrible plumes and flame,
The fatal sword, the breastplate, made of bronze,
Fire-colored, huge, shining the way a cloud,
Dark-blue, turns crimson under the slanting sun,
The greaves of gold refined and smooth electrum,
The spear, the final masterpiece, the shield.
640   Hereon the great prophetic Lord of Fire
Had carved the story out, the stock to come,
The wars, each one in order, all the tale
Of Italy and Roman triumph.[32] Here
In Mars' green cave the she-wolf gives her udders
To the twin boys, turning half round to lick them,
And neither is afraid, and both are playing.[33]
Another scene presents the Circus-games,
When Romans took their Sabine brides, and war
Broke out between old Tatius and the sons

[32] The divinely-made shield of Achilles in Homer's *Iliad,* Book XVIII,
contains in pictures a synopsis of the ways of human life, in fairly universal
terms. Virgil's equivalent, for Aeneas, is a vision of the glories of Roman
history to come and of the Roman character.

[33] To make his usurped power secure, Amulius attempted to have his
great-nephews, the infant Romulus and his twin brother Remus, drowned
in the Tiber, but they survived, being suckled by a she-wolf in the cave
of the Lupercal on the site of Rome. Romulus grew up to found the city
and establish its line of kings.

Of Romulus, and was ended, monarchs pledging   650
Peace at the altars over sacrifice.[34]
Mettus, the false, by the wild horses drawn
And quartered, sheds his life-blood over the brambles;[35]
Porsena, the besieger, rings the city
For Tarquin's sake, exile and tyrant; Romans
Rush on the steel for freedom; Clelia breaks
Her bonds to swim the river; and Horatius
Breaks down the bridge.[36] The guardian Manlius
Holds the high capitol and that crude palace
Fresh with the straw of Romulus; the goose   660
Flutters in silver through the colonnades
Shrieking alarm; the Gauls are near in darkness,
Golden their hair, their clothing, and their necks
Gleam white in collars of gold, and each one carries
Two Alpine javelins; they have long shields.
Near them, the Fire-god sets the priests with caps
Of wool, the miracle of the shields from heaven,
The Salii dancing, the Luperci naked,
And the chaste matrons riding through the city
In cushioned chariots.[37] Far off, he adds   670

[34] The men of the newly founded city, having no women, seized them
from Sabines who had come to watch the games in honor of Neptune
being celebrated in the Circus, or amphitheater, of Rome. The seizing
of the women caused war between the Romans and Sabines (ruled by
Tatius), but it was halted through the intervention of the women, and
the two peoples became allies.

[35] Mettus Fufetius was executed in the way described when, after having
promised to fight for Rome during one of its early regional conflicts, he
treacherously withdrew his troops from battle.

[36] After the Romans expelled their savage and tyrannical king Tarquinius
Superbus, the Etrurian king Lars Porsena of Clusium attacked Rome in
an attempt to restore Tarquinius to the throne. In the face of the enemy,
Horatius held a bridge over the Tiber until it could be destroyed. This
helped save the newborn (509 B.C.) Roman republic. Clelia was a young
Roman woman who, having been taken hostage by Porsena, escaped by
swimming the Tiber, was then returned to Porsena by the Romans, and
finally was freed by Porsena, along with other prisoners, because he admired her courage.

[37] When Gauls from the Alps threatened the citadel of Rome in 390
B.C., the Roman consul Manlius was alerted to their night attack by the
cackling of the sacred geese kept at the Capitol, where the early thatched
hut of the founder Romulus was also preserved. Lines 666–70 describe
(Continued)

The seats of Hell, the lofty gates of Pluto,
Penance for sin: Catiline, with the Furies
Making him cower; farther off, the good,
With Cato giving laws.[38] And all this scene
Bound with the likeness of the swelling ocean,
Blue water and whitecap, where the dolphins playing
Leap with a curve of silver. In the center
Actium,[39] the ships of bronze, Leucate[40] burning
Hot with the glow of war, and waves on fire
680   With molten gold. Augustus Caesar stands
High on the lofty stern; his temples flame
With double fire, and over his head there dawns
His father's star.[41] Agrippa[42] leads a column
With favoring wind and god, the naval garland
Wreathing his temples. Antony assembles
Egypt and all the East; Antony, victor
Over the lands of dawn and the Red Sea,
Marshals the foes of Rome, himself a Roman,
With—horror!—an Egyptian wife. The surge
690   Boils under keel, the oar-blades churn the waters,
The triple-pointed beaks drive through the billows,

---

religious celebrations of Roman victory and also acknowledge the Roman
matrons, whose right to ride in luxury was earned by earlier contributions
of their gold and jewels to the state.

[38] We see scenes of contrasted evil and good: Catiline, who in 63 B.C.
plotted against the Roman government and is now punished in Hell by
the Furies, and Cato the Younger (95–46 B.C.), the model of old-fashioned
Roman virtue.

[39] The climactic scene, at the center of the shield, shows the naval victory
by the forces of Octavian (later Caesar Augustus) over the combined forces
of Mark Antony, his rival for power, and Cleopatra, the Egyptian queen
who had become Antony's consort. The great battle took place at Actium,
off western Greece, in 31 B.C.; it ended decades of Roman civil war. Virgil
presents this battle as a conflict between Roman virtue and Eastern luxury,
decadence, and religious barbarism. Antony's and Cleopatra's fleets returned to Egypt, after she panicked, and a year later both he and she
died defeated, leaving Octavian in sole power and bringing peace to Rome.

[40] A promontory near Actium that served as base for Octavian's fleet.

[41] A comet representing the spirit of the late Julius Caesar was supposed
to have appeared in 43 B.C. in honor of Octavian, his adopted son; thereafter Octavian wore a star on his helmet.

[42] War minister and commander of Octavian's forces at Actium.

You would think that mountains swam and battled mountains,
That islands were uprooted in their anger.
Fireballs and shafts of steel are slanting showers,
The fields of Neptune redden with the slaughter.
The queen drives on her warriors, unseeing
The double snakes of death;[43] rattle and cymbals
Compete with bugle and trumpet. Monstrous gods,
Of every form and fashion, one, Anubis,
Shaped like a dog, wield their outrageous weapons   700
In wrath at Venus, Neptune, and Minerva.
Mars, all in steel, storms through the fray; the Furies
Swoop from the sky; Discord exults; Bellona,[44]
With bloody scourge, comes lashing; and Apollo
From Actium bends his bow. Egypt and India,
Sabaeans and Arabians, flee in terror.
And the contagion takes the queen, who loosens
The sheets to slackness, courts the wind, in terror,
Pale at the menace of death. And the Nile comes
To meet her, a protecting god, his mantle   710
Spread wide, to bring a beaten woman home.
And Caesar enters Rome triumphant, bringing
Immortal offerings, three times a hundred
New altars through the city. Streets are loud
With gladness, games, rejoicing; all the temples
Are filled with matrons praying at the altars,
Are heaped with solemn sacrifice. And Caesar,
Seated before Apollo's shining threshold,
Reviews the gifts, and hangs them on the portals.
In long array the conquered file, their garments,   720
Their speech, as various as their arms, the Nomads,
The naked Africans, Leleges, Carians,
Gelonians with quivers, the Morini,
Of mortals most remote, Euphrates moving
With humbler waves, the two-mouthed Rhine, Araxes,

[43] The ill-omened double snakes are especially appropriate to Cleopatra because she afterward committed suicide by allowing herself to be bitten by asps.
[44] Goddess of war.

Chafing beneath his bridge.[45]

                All this Aeneas
Sees on his mother's gift, the shield of Vulcan,
And, without understanding, is proud and happy
As he lifts to his shoulder all that fortune,
730   The fame and glory of his children's children.   ◻

---

[45] The list of names is primarily geographical symbolism honoring Caesar Augustus and Rome. The wandering Nomads (Numidians) were from Africa, the Leleges and Carians from Asia, the Gelonians and Morini from eastern and northern Europe. The Araxes is the river Aras, in Armenia.

BOOK IX

◻

In the Absence
of Aeneas

HILE all this happened far away, queen Juno
Sent Iris down from heaven to bold Turnus.
She found him resting in a sacred valley,
Pilumnus'[1] grove, his ancestor; all radiant
She spoke to him:—"No god would promise, Turnus,
This answer to your prayers, but the turn of time
Has put it in your hands. Aeneas has gone,
Leaving the town, the fleet, and his companions,
Seeking the realm of Palatine Evander,
And more than that: he has won some cities over,
He calls the Etruscan countrymen to arms.
What are you waiting for? Now is the time
For chariot and horse. Break off delay,
Take the bewildered camp!" She spoke, and rose
Skyward on even wings, and under the clouds
Cut her great soaring arc. And Turnus knew her,
And raised his hands to the sky, and followed her flight:—
"O Iris, pride of heaven, who sent you to me
Through clouds to earth? Whence comes this storm of
    brightness?
I see the heavens part, and the stars wheeling

---

[1] An early Latin agricultural god; great-grandfather of Turnus.

205

Across the sky.² I follow these great omens,
Whoever calls to arms." And, with the word,
He went to the stream, took water up, prayed often,
Making his vows to all the gods of heaven.
   And now, over all the plain, the army was coming,
Rich in caparison,³ and rich in horses,
In gold and broidered robes, Messapus leading,
And Turnus in the center, and Tyrrhus' sons
As captains in the rear:⁴ they stream as Ganges
30   Streams when his seven quiet tides flood over,
Or Nile resents his deep confining channel.
The Trojans see the sudden cloud, black dust
Thickening over the plain, and darkness rising,
And Caicus cries from the rampart:—"What is this,
O fellow-citizens, this rolling darkness?
Bring the swords quickly, bring weapons, climb the walls,
Here comes the enemy, yea! Hurry, hurry!"
Trojans, and noise, pour through the gates together,
Men fill the walls. For so, on his departure,
40   Aeneas had given orders: if something happened,
They should not risk a battle in the open,
They should only guard the camp, protect the ramparts.
So, much as they would love to mix in battle,
Anger and shame give way to prompt obedience.
They bar the gates; protected by their towers
They wait while the foe comes on. And Turnus, riding
Impatient past his dawdling column, is there
Before the city knows it. He has twenty
Fast riders with him, his mount a piebald Thracian,
50   His helmet gold with crimson crest. He cries,
"Who will be first with me? Will anybody
Be first with me against them? Let them have it!"
And with the word, he lets the javelin fly,
First sign of battle; and they cheer and follow
And wonder a little at the Trojans, cowards

---

² This is a miraculous vision, since the time is not night but day.
³ A decorated covering draped over a horse.
⁴ For Messapus and his people, see VII.714–27. Tyrrhus is the king
Latinus' herdsman, whose eldest son was killed; see VII.502–49.

Who dare not fight in the open, man to man,
Who hug their walls for comfort. Round and round,
Turnus, a wild man, rides, seeking an entrance,
But there is no way in. He is like a wolf
Lurking about a sheep-fold, snarling at midnight   60
Beside the pens, enduring wind and rain,
While the bleating lambs are safe beneath the ewes,
And he, unable to get at them, rages
Fierce and dry-throated in the drive of hunger;
So Turnus looks at wall and camp, and passion
Burns hot within him, burns to his very bones.
How to get in? or how to yank the Trojans
Out of their cloister, smear them over the plain?
Ah, but the fleet is there, beside the camp,
Sheltered by earthworks and the flowing river: 70
There lies the chance! He calls for fire, he hurls it,
The burning torch, and his hand, almost, is burning,
And all of them pitch in—Turnus has shown them,
And Turnus eggs them on—they are armed with
    firebrands,
They rob the hearths; the tar flares lurid yellow
Against the grey of the cloud, the soot and ashes.
   What god, O Muses, turned the fire? Who saved
The Trojan ships? Remind me—the story is old,
Men have believed it long, its glory endless.
When first Aeneas built the fleet on Ida,[5]   80
Preparing for deep seas, the mother of gods,
Queen Cybele, spoke to Jove:—"Grant me, my son,
Lord of Olympus now, a mother's prayer.[6]
I had a pine-wood on the mountain-top,
And men, for many years, brought offerings there,
I loved that forest, dark with fir and maple,
But when the Trojan lacked a fleet, I gave him
My timber gladly; now my heart is troubled.
Relieve my fear, and let a mother's pleading

---

[5] The mountain near Troy.

[6] Mount Olympus was the gods' dwelling-place. Cybele, identified with
Rhea, mother of Jupiter, helped him dethrone his father Saturn.

90   Keep them from wreck on any course, unshaken
      By any whirlwind. Grown upon our mountains,
      They should have privilege." Her son, the swayer
      Of the stars of the world, replied, "What call, O mother,
      Is this you make on fate? What are you seeking?
      Should keels laid down by mortal hand have title
      To life immortal? Should Aeneas travel
      Through danger, unendangered? Such power is given
      No god in heaven. But I make this promise:
      After their course is run, after the harbors
100   In Italy receive them, safe from ocean,
      And with Aeneas landed in Laurentum,[7]
      I will take away their mortal shape, I will make them
      Goddesses of the sea, like Nereus' daughter,
      Like Galatea, the nymphs who breast the foam."
      So Jupiter promised, and, as gods do, took oath,
      By the rivers of his brother under the world,
      The banks that seethe with the black pitchy torrent,
      And made Olympus tremble with his nod.[8]
          The promised day had come, the fates had finished
110   The allotted span, when Turnus' desecration
      Warned Cybele to keep the torch and firebrand
      Far from her holy vessels. A new light blazed
      In mortal sight, and from the east a cloud
      Ran across heaven, and choirs from Ida followed,
      And a dread voice came down the air:—"O Trojans,
      Be in no hurry to defend my vessels,
      You have no need of arms; Turnus, most surely,
      Will burn the seas before he burns these pine-trees.
      Go forth in freedom, goddesses of ocean,
120   The Mother wills it so." And each ship parted
      Cable from bank, and dove to the deep water
      As dolphins dive, and reappeared as maiden,—
      Oh marvel!—and all of them bore out to ocean.
          Rutulian hearts were stunned, their captains shaken,
      Their steeds confused and frightened; even Tiber

---

[7] The region and city of king Latinus.
[8] Jupiter's brother is Pluto, god of the Lower World. To swear by the
Styx, a river there, was the most solemn oath a god could take.

Shrank back from the sea, and the murmuring stream
    protested.
But Turnus kept his nerve, his words rang loud
In challenge to their courage:—"These are portents
To make the Trojans timid; Jove has taken
Their comfort from them; the ships they always fled in   130
Run from Rutulian fire and sword; the oceans
Are pathless for the Trojans now, their hope
Of flight all gone: half of their world is taken,
And the earth is in our hands, Italians, thousands,
Thousands of us in arms. I am not frightened,
However they boast of oracles from heaven.
Venus and fate have had their share: the Trojans
Have done enough even to touch our richness,
The Ausonian fields. I have my omens, also,
To match with theirs, a sword to slay the guilty,   140
Death for the rape of brides! Not Atreus' sons,
Not only Menelaus and Mycenae,
Know what this hurt can be, this need for vengeance,
This right to take up arms.⁹ Once to have perished,
They tell us, is enough. Once to have sinned
Ought to have been enough and more. Hereafter
All women should be hateful to them, cowards
Hiding behind the sheltering moat and rampart,
The little barriers that give them courage!
Have they not seen the walls that Neptune built them   150
Sink in the fires? Which one of you is ready,
Brave hearts, to slash their barriers with the sword,
To join me in the onrush? I do not need
The arms of Vulcan, nor a thousand vessels
Against the Trojans.¹⁰ Let them have Etruria!¹¹
One thing, at least, they need not fear,—the darkness,

---

⁹ Turnus is thinking of his fiancée, Latinus' daughter Lavinia, and of
the plan to have her marry Aeneas. The enraged Turnus compares himself
to Menelaus, Helen's husband, another victim of a Trojan wife-stealer
(Paris). Menelaus was a son of Atreus; his brother Agamemnon ruled Mycenae in Greece.

¹⁰ The Greeks had sent a thousand ships to Troy. Achilles, their greatest
warrior, had been provided with armor made by the god Vulcan.

¹¹ That is, the Etruscan forces promised to the Trojans by Evander
(VIII.491–530). See also IX.10–11.

The sneaking theft of their Palladium image,[12]
Guards slain in the dark, hiders in horse's belly;
I fight in open daylight, I have fire
160   To put around their walls, I will teach them something,—
Their business now is not with those Greek heroes
Whom Hector kept at bay for ten long years.
Now day is almost over; you have done
Good work; rest now; be happy, be preparing,
Be hopeful for the battles of to-morrow."
    Meanwhile, the guards were posted, under orders
Of Messapus, their officer; and the walls
Were ringed with fire. Fourteen Rutulian captains
Led, each, a hundred men, bright in their gold,
170   Plumed in their crimson, on patrol or resting,
Or sprawling on the grass, gambling or drinking;
The fires burn bright, the sentinels are watchful.
    Above them, from the wall, the Trojans, waiting,
Maintain the heights with arms, and, anxious, test
The strength of the gates, link bridge and battlement,
Warriors in harness. Mnestheus and Serestus
Urge on the work; they were to be the leaders,
Aeneas said, in the event of trouble.
Along the walls the host mounts guard; they share
180   Relief and danger in turn, each at his post.
    Nisus, quick-handed with the javelin
And the light arrows, very keen in arms,
Stood guard beside the gate, Nisus, a son
Of Hyrtacus, sent by the huntress Ida[13]
To join Aeneas; and near-by his friend
Euryalus;[14] no Trojan was more handsome
Than he was, that first bloom of youth. They shared
Assignments always, side by side in the charge,
And side by side defenders. Here they were

----

[12] A statue of the goddess Pallas Athena, or Minerva, stolen by Ulysses
and Diomedes. See II.187-98.
   [13] A nymph (presumably Nisus' mother), named for the mountain near
Troy.
   [14] For the foot-race involving Nisus and Euryalus, back in Sicily, see
V.281-357.

Together on sentry-duty at the gate.   190
Nisus burst out:—"Euryalus, what is it?
Do the gods put this ardor in our hearts
Or does each man's desire become his god?
I want much more than this, I am not contented
With all this peace and calm; my mind keeps calling
To battle, or something big. Look! The Rutulians
Are far too confident: their lights are scattered;
They lie asleep or drunk; and all is silent.
Listen! I have a plan. People and fathers
Demand Aeneas, ask that men be sent him   200
With information. If I can make them promise
To let you go[15] —(the glory of the action
Is all I want myself)—I think that I
Can find the way around that hill, can manage
To reach the walls and fort of Pallanteum."
This shook Euryalus: a great love of praise
Spoke in his answer to his eager comrade:—
"What, Nisus? Are you planning to leave me out
In this bold scheme, planning to go alone
Into such dangers? No; no, no. I am   210
Opheltes' son, a warrior trained among
Greek terror and Trojan suffering; and I follow,
With you, great-souled Aeneas and his fortunes.
I have a spirit, not too fond of living,
Not too dissatisfied to buy with death
The honor that you strive for." Nisus answered:—
"I had no fear on your account, be certain;
That would be shameless of me: so may Jove,
Or any god that looks on this with favor,
Bring me back home triumphant. But disaster,   220
As well you know, or god, or chance, might take me:
If so, your youth being worthier, I'd have you
Be my survivor, give to earth my body,
Rescued or ransomed, or pay the final honor
To, it might be, an empty tomb. I would not

---

[15] A clearer translation would be "If I can make them promise to give
you the reward I ask for."

Cause sorrow to the only woman of many
Who scorned Acestes' city, and came on
With you, her only son."[16] But then the other
Replied:—"There is no use in all this talking.
230   My mind is fixed, and we had better hurry."
He roused the guards; new men came on; together
Euryalus and Nisus seek their leader.
    All other creatures over all the world
Were easing their troubles in slumber, and hearts forgot
Sorrow and pain; not so the Trojan leaders
Meeting in council. Here were things of moment;
What should they do? how would they reach Aeneas?
They stood there, leaning on long spears, most gravely,
Holding their shields. Euryalus and Nisus
240   Crave instant audience; the matter is urgent,
They say, and worth a little interruption.
Iulus takes the lead, meets their impatience,
Tells Nisus to speak out. "Give us a hearing,
O men of Troy," says Nisus, "do not hold
Our years against us: we have something for you.
All the Rutulians are drunk or sleeping,
They are quiet now. There is a place, we know it,
We have seen it with our eyes, a place that cunning
Can take advantage of: you know the gate
250   Nearest the sea, and how the road splits off there.
The watchfires there die down, and the black smoke rises
Dark to the sky out there. Give us a chance!
Let us go to find Aeneas and Pallanteum.
You will see us here again; it will not be long
Till we come back, weighed down with spoil. We will kill
    them.
We will not miss the way; we have seen the city
Far in the distant valleys. We go hunting
Along here often; we know all the river.
We know it all by heart." And old Aletes,
260   A wise man in a council, gave the answer:—

[16] The reference is to the weaker pilgrims who chose not to go on but
to stay behind with the ex-Trojan Acestes in Sicily. See V. 674–715. Other
parts of the poem make it clear, however, that Euryalus' mother was not
literally the only woman to keep going and arrive in Italy.

"Gods of our ancestors, under whose guidance
Troy is and has been, always, our destruction
Must be far off, seeing your care has brought us
Young men of such high heart and lofty spirit."
In deep emotion, his hands reached out for theirs,
His arms went round their shoulders. "What can I give you,
Young men," he cried, "worthy your praise and glory?
The best rewards come from the gods, the finest
From your own character, but good Aeneas
Will not forget your service, and your peer   270
In age, Ascanius, surely will remember."
And that young man broke in, "Most truly, Nisus,
I trust my fortune to you. My only safety
Lies in my sire's return. By all our gods,
I beg you both, I pray, bring back my father.
Our trouble goes when he is here. I promise
Two silver wine-cups, captured from Arisba,[17]
A pair of tripods, two great talents[18] of gold,
An ancient bowl, the present of queen Dido.
And if we capture Italy, if we live   280
To wield the sceptre and divide the spoil,
You know the horse that Turnus rides, the armor
He carries on his back, all gold—that armor,
The shield, the crimson plumes, and the war-horse, Nisus,
Are your reward; even now, I so declare them.
My father will give twelve women, beautiful captives,
And captive men, equipped with arms, and land
Now held by king Latinus; and I cherish
With all my heart, Euryalus, your courage.
Your years are near my own, and all my life   290
Your glory will be mine; in peace or war,
In word and deed, I trust in you, completely."
Euryalus replied:—"No day will ever
Prove me unworthy of brave deeds, if fortune
Is kind, not cruel, to me. I ask one thing
Better than any gift: I have a mother
Of Priam's ancient line, and she came with me,

---

[17] A city near Troy. Virgil does not specify how or when the cups were captured there.
[18] Units of weight.

Poor soul, from Troy, and king Acestes' city
Was powerless to keep her. I leave her now
300   With never a word about what I am doing,
Whatever its danger is, with no farewell.
I cannot bear a mother's tears. I beg you,
Comfort her helplessness, relieve her sorrow.
Let me take with me that much hope; it will help me
Face any risk more boldly." They were weeping
At this, the Trojans, all of them, Iulus
More deeply touched than any. And he spoke:—
"Be reassured, Euryalus; all we do
Will prove as worthy as your glorious mission.
310   Your mother shall be mine, in all but name;
Great honor waits the mother of a son
So great in honor. Whatever fortune follows,
I vow and swear it, with an oath as solemn
As any my father ever took, I promise,
When you return to us, safe and successful,
Your triumph and your glory and your prizes
Shall be for her as well, for all your house."
He spoke with tears, and from his sword-belt took
A present in farewell, the golden sword,
320   The ivory scabbard, wonderfully fashioned
By old Lycaon's[19] talent; Mnestheus gave
A lion-skin to Nisus, and Aletes
Exchanged his helmet with him. As they started,
All the great company, young men and old ones,
Went with them to the gate, and out beyond it
The hopeful prayers attended them. Iulus,
Mature beyond his years, gave many a message
To carry to Aeneas, but the winds
Bore these away and swept them off to cloudland.
330   And now they have crossed the trench, and through night's
       shadow
Invade the hostile camp; they are bound to be
The doom of many. They see the bodies sprawling
In drunken sleep, the chariots half turned over,
Men lying under the wheels and among the reins,

---

[19] One of the renowned craftsmen and arms-makers of Crete.

And Nisus whispers:—"Euryalus, we must
Be bold; the chance is given; here lies our way.
Watch and keep back, lest some one steal upon us
Along the trail behind. I lead, you follow
Where I have cut the way; it will be a broad one."
His voice was silent; and he drew the sword   340
At Rhamnes, cushioned on high covers, lying
In a deep slumber, breathing deep, a king
And Turnus' favorite augur, but his doom
No augury prevented. Nisus struck
Three slaves, and then the armor-bearer of Remus,
And Remus' charioteer—their necks were severed
With steel, and their lord Remus was beheaded.
The trunk spurts blood, the earth and couch are darkened
With blood, black-flowing. Lamyrus and Lamus
Are slain, and young Serranus, handsome gambler   350
Who had won high stakes that night, and slept contented
Smiling at the gods' favor, luckier surely
If he had lost all night. A starving lion
Loose in a sheepfold with the crazy hunger
Urging him on, gnashing and dragging, raging
With bloody mouth against the fearful feeble,
So Nisus slaughters. And his savage comrade
Keeps pace with him: Fadus is slain, Herbesus,
Rhoetus, Abaris, all of them unconscious,
Murdered in sleep. One of them, Rhoetus, wakened   360
A little, saw, and tried to hide, and crouching
Behind a wine-bowl, took the sword, and rose,
Stumbled and sprawled and belched, the red life spurting
Out of the mouth, red wine, red blood. All hotly
Euryalus went on. Messapus' quarters
Are next in line; the fires burn low, the horses,
Tether-contented, graze. Then, briefly, Nisus,
Sensing his comrade's recklessness in slaughter,
Calls:—"Light is near, our enemy; give over,
We have killed enough, we have cut the path we needed,   370
No more of this!" They left behind them armor
Of solid silver, bowls, rich-woven carpets,
But must take something: Rhamnes' golden sword-belt
Euryalus held on to, all that armor

That went with long tradition, from father to son,
From son to enemy, once more a trophy
For young Euryalus. He dons the armor,
Picks up, puts on, besides, a shapely helmet,
The spoil of Messapus, the long plume flowing.
380   They leave the camp, are on their way to safety.
        Meanwhile, sent forward from the Latin city,[20]
Horsemen were coming, while the legion rested
Behind them on the plain, three hundred horsemen
With word for Turnus, under their captain Volcens,
All armed with shields and riding at the ready.
They are near the camp, the wall, and in the distance
See two men turning left along a pathway,
And a helmet glittering among the shadows,
Euryalus' prize and foolishness. They notice
390   At once, of course, and challenge. From the column
Volcens cried out:—"Halt! Who goes there? Who are you?
What are you doing in arms? Upon what mission?"
No answer: flight to wood and trust in darkness.
But the horsemen, fanning out, block every cross-road,
Circle and screen each outlet. Wide with brambles
And dark with holm-oak spreads the wood; the briars
Fill it on every side, but the path glimmers
In the rare intervals between the shadows.
Euryalus is hindered by the branches,
400   The darkness, and the spoil he carries; terror
Makes him mistake the path. Nisus is clear,
Reaching the site that later men called Alba,[21]
Where king Latinus had his lofty stables.
He halts, looks back to find his friend: in vain.
"Euryalus, Euryalus, where are you?
Where have I lost you? How am I to follow
Back through the tangled wood, and the treacherous thickets?
Euryalus, Euryalus!" He turns,
Tries to retrace his steps, is lost in the woods,
410   And hears the horses, hears the shouts and signals

[20] From Laurentum, king Latinus' city.
[21] The city that, in the future, will be founded by Aeneas' son. See I.9
and note, I.278–85. Alba was in fact, however, some miles from the site
of the present action.

As the pursuit comes closer, and he hears
A cry, he sees Euryalus, dragged along
Out of the treason of the night and darkness,
Bewildered by the uproar, fighting vainly
In the hands of Volcens' squadron. There is nothing
Nisus can do, or is there? With what arms,
What force, redeem his friend? Or is it better
To hurl himself to death, dash in, regardless,
To glorious wounds? His spear is poised, his arm
Drawn back; he looks to the moon on high, and prays:—   420
"Dear goddess, daughter of Latona,[22] aid me,
Pride of the stars and glory of the groves,
If ever my father Hyrtacus brought honors
In my name to the altar, if ever I
Have brought gifts home from my own hunting, aid me!
Let me confound that troop, direct my weapon!"
The straining body flung the spear; it whistled
Across the shadow of night, and Sulmo took it
In his turned back; the point snaps off; it lodges
With part of the splintered wood deep in the lungs.   430
Sulmo goes down, his mouth spurts blood, his body
Sobs, straining, in the gasp and chill and shudder
Of a cold death. They look in all directions,
See nothing. And another spear is flying,
Fiercer this time. This pierces Tagus' temples,
Clings, warm, in the split brain. And Volcens rages,
And cannot find the spearman, and his anger
Has no sure place to go, but for his vengeance
Turns on Euryalus, sword drawn, and rushing
He cries:—"You will pay for both of them, your blood   440
Be the atonement." Nisus, from the darkness,
Shrieks in his terror:—"Here I am, I did it,
The guilt is mine, let him alone, come get me,
Rutulians! How could he have dared or done it?
God knows, the only thing he did was love
A luckless friend too well." But the sword is driven
Deep in the breast. Euryalus rolls over,

[22] Latona's daughter was Diana, goddess of hunting, of the moon, and of forests.

Blood veins the handome limbs, and on the shoulder
The neck droops over, as a bright-colored flower
450   Droops when the ploughshare bends it, or as poppies
Sink under the weight of heavy summer rainfall.
And Nisus rushes them; he is after Volcens,
Volcens alone. They mass around him, cluster,
Batter him back, but through them all he charges,
Whirling the blade like fire, until he drives it
Full in the face while the Rutulian, shrieking,
Goes down, and Nisus, dying, sees him die,
Falls over his lifeless friend, and there is quiet
In the utter peace of death.
                        Fortunate boys!
460   If there is any power in my verses,
You will not be forgotten in time and story
While rock stands firm beneath the Capitol,
While the imperial house maintains dominion.
    With victory and tears, with spoil and plunder,
They brought Rutulian Volcens home to camp-ground,
And a great wail arose, for Rhamnes slaughtered,
For Numa, for Serranus, for so many
Slain in one fight. They rush to see the bodies,
To heroes dead or dying, to the ground
470   Reeking with carnage, the red foaming rivers.
They recognize the spoil, the shining helmet
Brought back for Messapus, and all the trappings
It cost them sweat to win.
                  And the Dawn-goddess
Came from her husband's saffron couch, bestowing
Fresh light across the world. Turnus, in armor,
Summoned his men to arms, and every leader
Marshalled his ranks of bronze, and each man sharpens
His anger with one rumor or another.
And more than that, a pitiful sight, they fix
480   On spears upraised, and follow with loud shouting,
The heads of Nisus and Euryalus.
On the left of the wall the Trojans form their line
Whose right rests on the river. They hold the trenches,
Stand on the high towers, sorrowing; they know,

And all too well, those heads with spears for bodies,
And the black blood running down.
                    And meanwhile Rumor
Goes flying through the panic of the city,
Comes to Euryalus' mother. That poor woman
Is cold as death; the shuttle falls from her hands,
The yarn is all unwound. She rushes, shrieking,   490
Tearing her hair, out to the walls, in frenzy,
Heedless of men, heedless of darts and danger
To fill the air with terrible lamentation:—
"Is this thing you I see, Euryalus?
Could you, a poor old woman's only comfort,
Leave her to loneliness? O cruel, cruel!
To go to danger, and never a farewell word
Between the mother and son! And now you lie
On a strange land for dogs and birds to pick at,
No mother to bathe the wounds, or close the eyes,   500
To veil the body with the robe I worked on
For quite another purpose, night and day,
Comforting, so, the cares of age. Where can I
Go now, to find you? In what land are lying
The limbs, dismembered, and the mangled body?
Is this thing all you bring me from the wars,
Is this what I have followed on land and sea?
If you have anything of decent feeling,
Rutulians, kill me; hurl your weapons on me,
All of you, all of them: let steel destroy me.   510
Or, father of the gods, have pity on me
And strike with the bolt of lightning; hurl to Hell
The life I hate; no other way is left me
To break the cruel thread."[23] And at her wailing
The Trojan spirit sank, and a groan of sorrow
Passed through the ranks, their will to battle broken.
She kindles mourning; the leaders give an order,
Idaeus and Actor, taking her between them,
Lead her away.
              And the loud terrible trumpet

[23] The thread of life.

520   Blared in bronze-throated challenge, and the shouting
Rose to the sky. And on they came, the Volscians
Under their tortoise-shield,[24] in a wild hurry
To fill the moat, tear down the wall: some sought
A quick way in, or over, with scaling-ladders
Where the ring of men is thin, and light breaks in
Where no men stand. And in reply the Trojans
Rain every kind of weapon down—long war
Has taught them how the walls must be defended.
They use crude poles to push men off the ladders,
530   They roll tremendous boulders to crush the ranks
Covered by shields, and glad of that protection,
Too little now, too small for the great rock
The Trojans heave and pry and dump down on them
Where the clump of men is thickest. The back of the tortoise
Is broken, like the bodies of men beneath it.
No more blind war, like this, for the Rutulians!
They change their tactics, sweep the wall with arrows,
Mezentius, grim to look at, works with firebrands,
While Neptune's son, Messapus, tamer of horses,
540   Keeps tearing at the walls, and screaming for ladders.
    Help me, Calliope,[25] with the song: what killing
Turnus dealt out that day, the roll of victims
Whom every warrior sent to Hell: O, aid me
To unfold it all, the war's great panorama.
    There was a tower, high overhead, well chosen
To suit the ground, equipped with lofty gangways;[26]
On this the Italians spent their every effort
To tear it down, the Trojans to defend it
With stones from above, and arrows through the
      loopholes.
550   A firebrand, flung by Turnus, found a lodging
Along one side, and the wind blew and fanned it,
And lintel and planking burned, and the men huddled

---

[24] A combat formation in which men advanced huddled together under
the shell of their joined shields. The Volscians were from a region in
south Latium, southeast of Rome; their military leader was Camilla (see
VII.818–32). But apparently *Volscians* is used loosely here, to mean "Italians."

[25] The Muse who inspired epic poetry.

[26] The gangways run from the tower to the walls of the fort.

Within, and found no way to flee, and shifted
Toward the undamaged portion, when all of a sudden,
Lopsided under the weight, it toppled crashing
And filled all heaven with thunder. Half dead already
Men reached the ground, and the tower came down upon
    them,
Pierced through and through by shafts of their own making,
Their chests transfixed by jagged broken timbers.
Two manage to escape, Lycus, Helenor,   560
The latter a young warrior, the son
Of a Maeonian[27] King and a slave-girl mother,
Who sent him off to Troy in arms (forbidden,
Since arms were not for slaves), a naked sword,
A shield with no device.[28] He saw himself
Now in the midst of Turnus' thousands, marshalled
Before him and behind him. There he stood
Like a wild animal, ringed in by hunters,
Raging against their weapons, and sure of death,
Leaping upon them,—so Helenor, certain   570
To die, rushed where the weapons were the thickest.
Lycus was swifter afoot: through men, through weapons,
He gained the wall, reached up to pull himself over,
Reached up for hands to help him. But Turnus came
Hot on his heels:—"You fool," he cried in triumph,
"Did you think you were out of reach?" And as he hung
    there,
Turnus grabbed him, tore him loose, and the wall came with
    him.
An eagle, so, sweeps up again to heaven
With a white swan or rabbit in his talons;
Or so a wolf snatches a lamb from the sheepfold   580
To the bleating of the ewe. A shout arises;
Men from all sides come on; they fill the trenches,
Keep firebrands flying at the tower and rooftop.
Ilioneus knocks over one, Lucetius,
Who came to the gates with fire; he bowled him over

   [27] From Maeonia, or Lydia, a region of Asia Minor a little south of
Troy.
   [28] With no identifying emblem, since Helenor had not as yet performed
any heroic feats.

With a rock as big as a mountain. Liger slew
Emathion with a javelin; Asilas
Shot Corynaeus down. Caeneus won
Over Ortygius, lost to Turnus. Turnus
590   Killed half a dozen, Clonius, Dioxippus,
Itys, Promolus, Sagaris, and Idas.
Capys cut down Privernus: a spear had grazed him,
And the fool had flung his shield aside, to carry
His hand to his side, and an arrow pinned it there,
And went on through, a mortal wound in the bowels.
A young man in the battle, the son of Arcens,
Stood out conspicuous in arms, a tunic
Embroidered bright, Iberian[29] blue; his father
Had sent him from his mother's grove along
600   Symaethus stream and Palicus' rich altars.[30]
Mezentius saw him there, laid down his spear,
Whirled the sling thrice around his head, let fly,
And the slug of the sling-shot split the victim's temples,
Stretching his blue in the deep yellow sand.
    Then, so they say, was the first time Iulus
Brought down a man in war; he had hunted only
Wild beasts, before this time, with bow and arrows.
There was a youngster, Remulus by name,
Or, it might be, Numanus, lately married
610   To Turnus' younger sister, very proud
And pleased with his new royalty. He strode
Along the foremost battle-line, and taunted,
Shouting indecencies, a swollen hero:—
"What, once again, O Phrygians twice-besieged?
Have you no shame, to hide behind the ramparts
A second time, a second time with walls
To ward off death? Look at the silly warriors
Who claim our brides with steel! What god, what madness,
Brought you to Italy? No sons of Atreus
620   Are here, no lying glib Ulysses. We
Are a tough race, we bring our new-born sons
To the ice-cold river, dip them in to make them

[29] Spanish.
[30] The Symaethus was a river in Sicily; the Palici were deities worshipped
there.

Tough as their fathers, make them wake up early
To hunt till they wear the forests out; they ride,
They shoot, and love it; they tame the earth, they battle
Till cities fall: and all our life is iron,
The spear, reversed, prods on the ox; old age
Pulls on the helmet over the whitest hair;
We live on what we plunder, we revel in booty.
But you—O wonderful in purple and saffron![31] —   630
Love doing nothing, you delight in dancing,
And oh, those fancy clothes, sleeves on the tunics,
And ribbons in the bonnets! Phrygian women,
By God, not Phrygian men! Be gone forever
Over the heights of Dindymus; pipe and timbrel
Call you to female rites:[32] leave arms to men,
The sword to warriors!"
                    But Ascanius loosened
An arrow from the quiver, held the shaft
Nocked to the bow-string, and with arms outspread
For shot, made prayer:—"Almighty Jupiter,   640
Favor my bold beginning. I shall offer
The temple every year a snow-white bullock
With gilded horns, a young one, but already
Tall as his dam, butting with horn, and pawing
The sand with restless hoof." The father heard him,
There was thunder on the left, and in that instant
The fatal bow-string twanged. The shaft came flying
Through air, and the steel split the hollow temples
Of that young bragger Remulus. "Go on,
Mock valor with arrogant words! This is the answer   650
The Phrygians twice-besieged, the Phrygian women,
Send back to Remulus." The Trojans cheered him
With joyful shouts and spirits raised to heaven.
    And it so happened from the realm of sky
Long-haired Apollo, throned with cloud, looked down
And saw the Ausonian[33] battle-lines and city,
And had a word of blessing for Iulus:—

---

[31] Yellow-orange.
[32] The rites of the Trojan goddess Cybele ("mother of the gods"), worshipped especially by women. Dindymus was a mountain near Troy.
[33] Italian.

"Good for your prowess, youngster! That's the way
To reach the stars, a son of gods, a father
660 Of gods to be. In time the wars will end
Under that royal line.[34] Troy sets you free
For greater destinies." And he left the heaven,
Came through the stir of air, and sought Iulus,
Disguised as ancient Butes, armor-bearer,
Once, to Anchises, a guardian at his threshold,
Later Ascanius' servant. With his voice,
His grizzled hair, his color, his sounding arms,
Apollo came and spoke to the hot young warrior:—
"Let that be plenty, son of great Aeneas:
670 Numanus slain and unavenged; your arrow
Has done its work. Apollo grants this praise,
Your first, and does not envy the little archer.
But now, my son, refrain from war." He vanished,
Before the speech was ended, into thin air,
And the Trojan captains knew the god, his weapons,
The clang of the quiver of the god ascending,[35]
And at his will and order keep Ascanius
Out of the fight for which he longs, themselves
Go back to the work, charge at the jaws of danger.
680 The loud cry runs from tower to tower, all down
The avenue of the walls, and they bend the bows,
And catapults hum as the great stone goes flying.
The ground is sown with weapons; shield and helmet
Ring with the clanging; the fight is a swell and a surge
Like the rise of a wind from the west, with rainstorm pelting
Hard on the ground, thicker than hail on ocean,
When Jupiter lashes the gales and cloud-burst thunders from
        heaven.
    Two young men, tall as pine-trees, tall as hills
That gave them birth, Alcanor's sons, their mother
690 The Oread[36] Iaera, stood at the gate,
Obeying orders, Pandarus and Bitias,

---

[34] The "gods to be" are Iulus' descendants Julius Caesar and Caesar
Augustus, both considered by the Romans as deified. Augustus ended a
long period of Roman civil war; see I.298–311.
[35] Apollo was the god of archers.
[36] Mountain nymph.

And had their own idea, and flung it open,
Relying on their arms, an invitation—
Here's open house for all, come in, come in!
To right and left they stood before the towers,
Armed with the steel, and with the high plumes tossing,
Like twin oaks towering by pleasant rivers.
The Rutulians saw the entrance open, rushed in,
Were beaten back: Haemon, the son of Mars,
Tmarus the headstrong, Quercens, Aquicolus   700
Handsome in arms, fled with their columns routed,
Or perished in the gateway. And anger mounted
In all those battling spirits: the Trojans gathered,
Daring in closer combat now, and risking
Brief sallies past the walls.
                              Turnus, far off,
Raging and rioting, heard the glad tidings
Of enemies gone wild with slaughter, gates
Flung open wide. Whatever he was doing
He broke off gladly, burned with monstrous anger,
Rushed to the Trojan gate and those proud brothers.   710
Antiphates came to meet him, bastard son
Of tall Sarpedon[37] and a Theban mother,
And Turnus' javelin laid him low: it flew,
Italian cornel-wood, through the soft air,
Lodged in the throat, pierced deep into the chest.
The wound's dark hollow filled with foaming red,
The steel grew warm in the lung. And Turnus' hand
Brought down Meropes, Erymas, Aphidnus,
Then Bitias blazing-eyed and hot in spirit.
No javelin brought him down, no common javelin   720
Would ever have killed that giant, but a pikestaff,[38]
Rifled and whirring loud, driven like lightning,
Cut through the double leather, the double mail
With scales of gold, and the huge limbs sprawl and tumble,
Earth groans, and his great shield clangs down above him,

---

[37] A king and heroic ally of the Trojans, killed at Troy by Achilles' friend
Patroclus (Homer, *Iliad*, Bood XVI). *Theban* refers not to the famous Greek
city of Thebes but rather to Thebe, a city near Troy in Asia Minor.
[38] A long spear (with, in this case, a long and very heavy metal head;
normally it was fired from a machine).

The way a pillar of rock comes down, at Baiae,
When men have pried it loose and shoved it over
Into the ocean, and, crashing down in ruin,
It lies in shallow water, confusion of sea,
730   Eruption of black sand, and the shock of sound
Makes the high mountains tremble, and the earth
Shudder under the oceans.[39]
                    And Mars[40] added
New strength and spirit to the Latins, raked them
With the sharp sting of the spur, and sent the Trojans
Panic and runaway fear. The Latins, given
The chance of fight, come on, as the war-god rides them.
Pandarus, seeing his brother's fallen body,
Seeing the turn of fortune, puts his shoulder
With all his strength to the gate, and slowly, slowly,
740   Swings it on stubborn hinge, to leave his comrades,
Many of them, shut out, beyond the rampart,
Fighting in desperate battle; others he welcomes
As they come pouring in, the fool, not seeing
One of them was no Trojan! That was Turnus,
Shut up in the town, as welcome as a tiger
Penned in a flock of sheep. And Turnus' eyes
Shone with new light, his arms rang loud, his plume
Nodded blood-red, and his great shield flashed lightning.
Sudden confusion fastened on the Trojans;
750   They knew him as he was, gigantic, hateful,
But Pandarus flashed forward toward him, burning
With vengeance for a brother's death, and shouting:—
"Why, this is not Amata's[41] bridal palace,
Nor yet the center of your father's city!
This is a hostile camp you see here, Turnus,
And not a chance to leave it." Turnus only
Smiled at him with untroubled heart:—"Start something,
If there is any fighting spirit in you;

---

[39] Baiae was a town on the Italian coast, near the modern Naples; in Virgil's day many of the wealthy built homes there, extending into the sea and supported on man-made stone or concrete foundations. Artificial breakwaters were also constructed for naval purposes.

[40] God of war.

[41] Latinus' queen and mother of Lavinia, whom Turnus hoped to marry.

Come closer; I have a message for king Priam:
Tell him Achilles was here." And Pandarus flung   760
His spear, rough-knotted, the unpeeled bark still on it,
And the winds bore it off, and Juno parried
The threat of the coming wound, and it fastened, harmless,
Stuck in the wooden gate.
                    "And here's a weapon
That will not miss, seeing my right hand swings it,"
And with his answer Turnus rose full height
To the sword upraised, and brought it down, and the steel
Split the head clean apart between the temples,
And Pandarus came crashing down, and the earth
Shook underneath his weight, and he lay there, dying,   770
Limbs buckled underneath him, and his armor
Spattered with brains, and the head's halves, divided,
Dangling on either shoulder.
                    And the Trojans
Ran every way, in rout and sudden terror.
That day might well have been their last, that battle
The end of war, had Turnus ever bothered
To break the bars of the gate, let in his comrades.
But no: his fury and mad desire of slaughter
Drove him one way, and one way only, forward.
He caught Phaleris, and he hamstrung Gyges,   780
And snatched their spears and flung them at the Trojans
Who fled with nothing but their backs for target.
Juno supplied him fire and strength. He added
Halys to the dead roster of his comrades,
Pierced Phegeus through his shield and mail. Four others,
Alcander, Halius, Prytanis, Noemon,
Ignorant of his presence, roused the fighters
Along the walls, and fell before they knew it.
Lynceus, calling his comrades, came to meet him,
And Turnus, standing higher, slashed and swung,   790
Close in, and the flashing blade swept head and helmet
Together from the shoulders; then he slaughtered
Amycus, hunter of beasts, a clever craftsman
In arming darts with poison; and Aeolus' son,
Clytius; and Cretheus, the Muses' comrade,
Lover of music and song, whose theme was always

Warfare and warhorse, arms of men, and battle.
    And the Trojan leaders heard about the slaughter,
And met, Serestus, keen in arms, and Mnestheus,
800   And saw their comrades wheeling and Turnus welcomed,
And Mnestheus tried to halt them:—"Where do you aim
That flight?" he cried, "What other ramparts have you?
What walls beyond these walls? Shall one man, circled,
Hemmed in on every side, deal out destruction
Unscathed through all the city? Will you let him
Send down to Hell so many brave young fighters?
What kind of cowards are you? Have you no pity,
No shame at all, for your unhappy country,
Your ancient household gods, and great Aeneas?"
810   That gave them courage; and the column thickened,
And they were firm, and stood. And very slowly
Turnus drew back, retreating toward the river,[42]
And they came on, more boldly now, with yelling
And massing rank on rank, a crowd of hunters
With deadly spears, after a deadly lion,
And the beast they hunt is frightened, but still deadly,
Still dangerous, still glaring, and neither anger
Nor courage lets him turn his back, and forward
He cannot go, however much he wants to,
820   Through all that press of men and spears. So Turnus,
Doubtful, kept stepping back, little by little,
Burning, inside, with anger. Two more times
He made a sudden charge, sent the foe flying
Along the walls, but they came back, and Juno
Dared not assist him further; Jove had sent
Iris from heaven, with no uncertain message
If Turnus does not leave the Trojan ramparts.
He can no longer hold his own against them,
The shield and sword-arm falter; darts like hail
830   Rain down from everywhere. The helmet rings
Around his temples, and the brass cracks open
Under the storm of stones; the horsehair crest
Is shot away; the boss of the shield is dented;

---

[42] The Trojan fort lies on the riverbank; only its landward side is surrounded by walls.

Mnestheus, with lightning force, and other Trojans
Multiply spears. The sweat all over his body
Runs in a tarry stream; he cannot breathe.
At last, with one great leap, in all his armor,
He plunges into the stream, and Tiber takes him
On the yellow flood, held up by the buoyant water,
Washing away the stains of war, a hero,   840
Returning happily to his warrior-comrades.

BOOK X

◻

Arms
and the Man

MEANWHILE all-powerful Olympus flings
The palace open wide:[1] the council meets,
At Jove's command, under the starry dwelling
From which he sees all lands, the Trojan camp,
The Latin people. Between the double doors
They find their places. Jupiter speaks first:—
"Great dwellers in Heaven, why the change of heart?
Why do you fight with hostile spirit? I
Had said, I thought, that Italy and the Trojans
Were not to meet in war.[2] Why, then, this brawling
In face of my command? What fear has driven
This side or that to arms and provocation?
The proper time will come—be in no hurry—
When Carthage, fierce and wild, will loose destruction
On the heights of Rome, and spring the Alps wide open.[3]

---

[1] The opening of the gods' palace on Mount Olympus indicates the break of a new day.

[2] The apparent contradiction between this statement and Jupiter's prophecy of the war in I.274–75 may result from Virgil's failure to complete revisions of the poem before he died. But perhaps we are simply meant to understand that, although Jupiter foresaw the war, its occurrence contravenes his wishes.

[3] The prophetic reference is to the Second Punic War (218–202 B.C.), between Rome and Carthage, during which the Carthaginian general, Han-

(Continued)

Hate will be lawful then, and ravage, and battle.
But now, subside; be friendly; accept my order."
    So Jupiter spoke, briefly, but golden Venus
Was far from brief in answer:—"O great father,
20   Sovereign of men and destiny forever,
What other power is there for us to pray to?
Do you see, I ask you, these Rutulian warriors
In all their insolence? Have you noticed Turnus
Riding on horseback through their midst, all swollen,
With Mars as second? The barricaded walls
No longer shield the Trojans. The battle rages
Within the gates, on the high towers; the trenches
Swim deep in blood. Aeneas does not know it;
He is far away. Must siege go on forever?
30   Is this your will? Another enemy threatens
The walls of Troy, new-born, another army
Comes from Aetolian Arpi; Diomedes
Once more attacks the Trojans.[4] Wounds for me
Are still to come, I well believe; your daughter
Waits for a mortal outrage, not the first one.[5]
The Trojans came to Italy: was the coming
With your consent, by your design? If not,
Why, let them pay the penalty, do not help them!
Or were they following order after order
40   Given by gods above, by gods below?
If so, who dares to overturn your justice,
Who dares create new fates? Do I have to mention
The fleet on fire in Sicily, the winds
Let loose by Aeolus, their king, or Iris
Sent through the clouds? And now she[6] is even rousing—
This chance she had not yet taken—the shades of Hell,
And here is Allecto, suddenly given license
In the upper world, and ravaging and raving

---

nibal, led an army across the Alps and invaded Italy. The Romans, however,
ultimately won the war, under Scipio Africanus.
    [4] For Diomedes, see VIII.8–19 and note.
    [5] Venus had been wounded by Diomedes during one of the battles
around Troy; see Homer, *Iliad*, Book V.
    [6] Juno.

Through the Italian cities.[7] As for empire,
I care no more about it. I was hopeful   50
When fortune still existed. Let the winners
Be those you want to win: have it your way.
If that tough wife of yours will give the Trojans
No land in all the world, no realm whatever,
I beg you, father, by the smoking ruins
Of shattered Troy, let me spare one, Iulus,
Let him, at least, be saved from war. Aeneas,
Of course, will still be tossed on unknown waters,
Following any course that fortune offers.
Let me protect his son. I have Amathus,   60
High Paphus and Cythera, Idalia's groves;
There he may live, laying aside his weapons,
A long inglorious lifetime.[8] Order Carthage
To crush Ausonia with her empire; nothing
Shall interfere with Tyrian towns.[9] Much good
It did him to escape the plague of war,
To have fled through Argive[10] burning, to have exhausted
All dangers of the land and the great ocean,
Looking for Latium and a new-born Troy!
Much good indeed! It would have been much better   70
For the very soil of Troy and her last ashes
To have been the new foundation for their dwelling.
Give the poor wretches Simois and Xanthus,[11]
Father, once more; I pray you, let the Trojans
Live, once again, the fall of Troy!" And Juno
Burst out in anger:—"Why do you compel me

---

[7] For Iris and her role in the burning of Trojan ships, see V.564–664;
for the storm roused with the help of Aeolus, god of the winds, see I.59–
134; for the hatred stirred up by the infernal goddess Allecto, see VII.339–
586. All these calamities had been inflicted on the Trojans by Juno.

[8] The cities Amathus, Paphus (or Paphos), and Idalium, on the eastern-
Mediterranean island of Cyprus, and the island Cythera off southern
Greece, were favorite haunts of Venus.

[9] Carthage was founded by Dido and her fellow-refugees from Tyre
(I.351–85). Ausonia is Italy.

[10] Greek. The reference is to the destruction of Troy, narrated in Book
II.

[11] The rivers at Troy.

To break my silence, to make my sorrow vulgar
With words for the world's ear? What god, what mortal
Forced war upon Aeneas? Who advised him
80   To advance, an enemy, against Latinus?
He came to Italy at the fates' command—
So be it; but what about Cassandra's ravings?[12]
Was I the one—I must have been—who told him
To leave the camp, to trust his life to the winds?
Was I the one who told him to make a boy
The captain of the wall? Was it I who told him
To seek Etruscan allies, to hunt down people
Who meant no harm?[13] What god, what power of mine
Drove him to all his cheating? What has Juno
90   Or Iris, sent through the clouds, to do with this?
Disgraceful and disgusting, that Italians
Threaten the walls of Troy, new-born; that Turnus
Stay in his native land, Turnus, descended
Himself from king and goddess.[14] What about it?
What about this, that Trojans harry Latins
With smoking brand and violence, set their yoke
On fields not theirs, and carry off the plunder?
Who let them know whose daughters to wed, or ravish?
Who told them to hold out the hand for peace
100   And arm the ships for war? Oh, you are able,
Of course you are, to give them mist for a man,
To steal Aeneas from Greek hands; you are able
To turn their fleet to sea-nymphs, but if I
Help the Rutulians even a very little,
Is that so monstrous?[15] *Aeneas does not know it;*

[12] Cassandra, the Trojan princess and prophet whose true prophecies were always treated by her people as ravings, had predicted the Trojan settlement of Italy; see III.185–91.

[13] The Etruscan allies (that is, from Etruria) are the former subjects of the evil king Mezentius, whom they expelled. For the true story, as opposed to this distorted version of Juno's, see VIII.491–530.

[14] Through his mother, the nymph Venilia, Turnus was descended from the god Pilumnus.

[15] During one of the battles of the Trojan war, Aeneas had been rescued by Venus and Apollo, who cast a cloud around him; see Homer, *Iliad*, Book V. For the transformation of the Trojan fleet into sea-nymphs (achieved not by Venus but by Jupiter and Cybele), see IX.77–123.

He is far away. Good. Let him still not know it;
Let him still be far away. You have Amathus,
High Paphus and Cythera; so why meddle
With savage hearts and a city big with war?
And now, it seems, I am trying to pull over 110
The wobbling walls of Troy! Really! Who was it,
I, or somebody else, who flung the Trojans,
Poor things, in the path of the Greeks? What was the
    reason
For Europe and Asia to rise in arms, break treaties
Over a piece of stealing? Was it I
Who shipped the adulterer Paris out to Sparta?[16]
Was it I who armed his lust? That was the time
To have had some fear for those poor suffering Trojans.
It is too late now. You rise to the occasion
With unjust whining and shrill scolding nonsense." 120
    So Juno argued: the company of heaven
Sided with one or the other, and the sound
Was like the sound of winds caught in the forest,
And sailors, listening, know that storms are coming.
And Jupiter all-powerful, the ruler
Of all the world, began, and with his word
The lofty palace of the gods grew quiet,
The earth's foundations trembled, and the winds
Were still, and the loud ocean hushed the waters.
"Take these my words to heart; be sure to heed them. 130
It is forbidden Ausonians and Trojans
To join in concord; the arguments among you,
It seems, will never end. Therefore I tell you,
Whether a man is Trojan or Rutulian,
Whatever luck he has to-day, whatever
He hopes to have to-morrow, it does not matter,
I treat them both the same. It may be fate,
It may be Trojan foolishness and error
That keeps the camp besieged: I do not judge.
I hold Rutulians under obligation 140

---

[16] For the jealousy provoked in Juno by Paris' judgment that Venus
was more beautiful, his adultery with Helen, and the fatal consequences
for Troy, see I.31–34 and note.

As well as Trojans. In every man's beginning
His luck resides, for good or ill. I rule
All men alike. The fates will find the way."
And all Olympus trembled as he nodded
And swore by the waters of his Stygian brother,
The pitchy banks and the black seething torrent.[17]
There was no more talking. From his golden throne
Jove rose, with gods and goddesses attending
In deferential escort.

                     In the meantime
150   At every gate Rutulians drive, determined
To bring down men with steel, ring walls with flame.
The host of Troy is held inside, blockaded,
With never a hope of flight. Wretched, they stand
At the high towers, in vain; they are none too many
To stretch the circle out. Imbrasus' son,
Asius, is there; Thymoetes; two young men,
Assaracus' sons;[18] and Castor, and old Thymbris,
In the front ranks; two brothers of Sarpedon,
Clarus and Thaemon, with them; they came from Lycia.
160   One man, with every ounce of strength, is heaving
To lift a giant boulder, half a mountain:
That would be Acmon, Clytius' son: Lyrnesus,
Their home, produced enormous men—a brother,
Mnestheus, too, was something of a giant.[19]
So rocks are weapons of defense, and arrows,
And darts, and balls of fire, and fighting men
Are busy with them all, and the little Trojan,
The pet of Venus, rightly so, was with them,
Bare-headed, a handsome sight, a shining jewel

---

[17] Jupiter takes his most awesome oath, by Styx, the river in the Lower World ruled by his brother Pluto. The tenor of Jupiter's speech is (1) that the enmity between Venus and Juno makes the fact of war inevitable, and (2) that he will not intervene in the fighting but rather will be neutral, allowing events to take their course in accordance with human effort, chance, and fate.

[18] That is, named for Assaracus, a former king of Troy and great-grandfather of Aeneas.

[19] For Sarpedon, see IX.712 and note. Lycia is in the southwest of what is now Turkey. Lyrnesus was a town in Mysia, south of Troy.

Inlaid in yellow gold, or a medallion   170
Of ivory in terebinth or boxwood;[20]
So shone Iulus, whose white neck and shoulders
Seemed whiter where the blond hair fell, and the circlet
Of gold made bright the golden hair. Ismarus
Was there, an archer, whose shafts were dipped in poison,
A warrior far from his Maeonian homeland
Where Pactolus floods the fields with yellow gold.[21]
And Mnestheus was there; he had beaten Turnus
The day before, and knew it, and was proud;
And Capys fought beside him: his name was given   180
To a city, later,—Capua, south of Rome.
    So these men had been fighting, clash and conflict
In the rough shock of warfare, as Aeneas,
At midnight, cleaved the seas. He had left Evander,
He had found the Tuscan camp, he had told the king
His name, his race, his need, what help he brought him,
Told Tarchon of Mezentius, of the spirit
Of violence in Turnus; had given warning
That, always, men need help; had made appeal,
Which Tarchon promptly answered: so the people   190
Were free from fate's injunction, free for war,
Having a foreign leader.[22] Aeneas' ship
Headed the column, her figure-head a mountain
With lions at the base, familiar Ida,
Dear to the Trojan exiles. And Aeneas
Sailed on toward war and all those changing fortunes,
And Pallas stayed beside him, asking questions:
What stars were those? which was the one to guide them
Through the dark night? what fortunes had he suffered

[20] The terebinth is a small Mediterranean tree, with black wood. Boxwood is yellowish.
[21] Maeonia, or Lydia, was a region of Asia Minor south of Troy. According to the myth, the river Pactolus contained gold, since Midas, whose touch turned all things to gold, bathed in it.
[22] Aeneas is sailing back by sea, with his new reinforcements, having followed up on Evander's plan that the Trojans ally themselves with the former subjects of Mezentius. A prophecy had stipulated that they must serve under a non-Italian; in the meantime Tarchon has been their leader. See VIII.491–622.

On land and sea?
200   Fling wide the gates, O Muses,
Inspire the song: what force rides with Aeneas
From Tuscan shores, what warships sail the ocean?[23]
    Massicus leads the way in the bronze *Tiger*,
A thousand men on board; they have come from Clusium,
From Cosae's city, archers all, with quivers
Light on their shoulders, and their bows are deadly.
With them is glowering Abas; a gold Apollo
Gleams on his bowsprit, and the vessel blazes
With men in armor; the little island Ilva,[24]
210   Rich in her mines, had sent them, thrice a hundred,
And Populonia furnished twice as many.
Third comes Asilas, priest and augur, learnèd
In all the signs, diviner of stars and lightning,
Of birds and entrails; he brings a thousand spearmen
From Pisa, on Etruscan soil. And Astur
Follows, a handsome horseman, with three hundred
Stalwarts from Caere, Minio, and Pyrgi,
Proud, confident men, with arms of many colors.
And Cinyras is there, the bravest leader
220   Of all Ligurian captains, and Cupavo,
With none too many followers; his crest
Is white swan-plumage, a token of his father,
Who, so they say, loved Phaethon, and grieved
Over his fall from heaven, and made music
To heal his sorrow, under the poplar trees
Phaethon's sisters haunted, and so, singing,
Became a bird, all white and soft, and vanished
From earth, and was a crying voice in heaven,
Cygnus, the swan.[25] And now his son Cupavo

---

[23] This catalogue of Aeneas' new allies parallels the catalogue of the Italians, introduced with a similar appeal to the Muses, in VII.660–832. The geographical names in the present passage are, except for Mantua in the far north, of places in Etruria and Liguria, regions of northwest Italy. Three of the leaders described will appear later in the poem: Abas, Asilas, and Aulestes.

[24] In modern times better known as Elba, the island between Italy and Corsica from which Napoleon made his dramatic return to power in 1815.

[25] Phaethon, foolishly attempting to drive the chariot of his father, the sun-god, lost control of it. Jupiter, to keep the earth from being consumed

Comes to the wars, driving his ship, the *Centaur*,   230
Which towers high as a cliff; the long keel furrows
A wide wake over the sea.
                              And Ocnus summons
Men from his native shores, Ocnus, the son
Of a Tuscan river and a woman, Manto,
Gifted in prophecy; her name was given
To Mantua, rich in ancestors, one city,
Three races, each one master of four peoples,
And Mantua the queen of all, her power
Secure in Tuscan strength.[26] From here Mezentius
Rouses five hundred men in arms against him,   240
And Mincius, Benacus' son, crowned with grey rushes,
Brings them down to the sea.[27] On comes Aulestes,
Whose *Triton* wallows heavily in the waters,
With a hundred oars lashing the waves to foam,
And the blue waters tremble at the sea-god
Riding the prow,[28] conch at his lips, a figure
Shaped like a shaggy man, as far as the belly,
And then a fish or serpent, a great sea-monster,
Under whose weight the water sucks and gurgles.
So the bronze vessels come, thirty good ships   250
For the help of Troy, and men, and chosen leaders,
Over the salt sea plains.
                              And day had gone,
And the dear moon in her night-wandering chariot
Was halfway up the sky; Aeneas, restless,
Tended the sails and rudder, holding the course,
And a band of his own company came to meet him,

---

by fire, killed Phaethon with a thunderbolt. He fell in Liguria, in northwest
Italy, where he was mourned by his sisters, transformed into poplar trees,
and by his loving friend Cycnus (father of Cupavo), transformed into a
swan. *Cygnus,* as in the name of the constellation, is a variant spelling of
cycnus, "swan."

[26] Virgil glorifies his original home town, Mantua, by associating its ori-
gins with the prophetess Manto and the god of the river Tiber and by
presenting Mantua as the leader of a confederacy of twelve peoples.

[27] The Mincius was actually a river in northern Italy, flowing from the
lake Benacus, or Garda, past Mantua.

[28] The sea-god Triton is the figurehead at the prow of the ship named
for him.

Those goddesses, whom Cybele had ordered
To rule the seas that once they sailed. They knew him,
Their king, far off, circled his ships in greeting,
260   And Cymodocea, of them all most gifted
In ways of speech, clung to the stern; one hand
Lifted her out of the water, and the other
Kept plying under the waves. She hailed Aeneas:—
"Are you on watch, son of the gods? Be watchful,
Crowd on full sail! We are the pines of Ida,
Born from that sacred mountain. Nymphs of the sea,
We used to be your fleet. But treacherous Turnus
Drove us with fire and sword; against our will
We broke our bonds to you, and now we seek you
270   Over the deep. The mother of the gods[29]
Took pity on us, and made us goddesses,
Immortal under the waters. We have bad news; your son
Is under siege; walls hold him in, and trenches,
And the air is filled with darts, and the wild Latins
Bristle in war. The cavalry of Pallas
And the brave Etruscan allies, minding orders,
Hold their appointed station.[30] Turnus knows it,
Turnus is certain to send opposing squadrons
To keep them from the camp. Hurry, then, hurry,
280   Get the men armed by daylight; raise the shield
Given by Vulcan, the invincible armor,
Bright with its ring of gold.[31] To-morrow morning
Shall see, unless I speak in foolish error,
Great heaps of slain Rutulians." She finished speaking,
And as she left the ship, her right hand gave it
An expert shove, and it sped over the water
Swifter than javelin or flying arrow,
And the other vessels quickened pace. Aeneas
Marvelled, amazed, and the portent[32] cheered his spirit,
290   And he looked up to the vault of heaven, praying:—

---

[29] Cybele.

[30] We must assume that this part of the army allied with the Trojans has come overland, the other part having sailed with Aeneas.

[31] For the divinely-made armor of Aeneas, see VIII.623–730.

[32] Omen.

"Dear mother of the gods, Idaean queen,
Lover of tower-crowned cities, and the lions
That draw the chariot,[33] be my leader now
Before the fight begins, affirm the omen,
Favor the Trojans, goddess, with your blessing."
And as he spoke, new day broke over the ocean
In a great blaze of light, and the darkness vanished.
    It was time for the last warnings to his comrades:
Follow the signals, nerve the spirit for battle,
Make every preparation! And he stood there,   300
High on the stern, seeing, before his eyes,
The Trojans and his camp, and he lifted high
The blazing shield, and the Trojans raised a clamor
To the high stars; new hope inflamed their anger,
And the darts flew, as cranes come back to Strymon
Noisy before the southern gales.[34] But Turnus
And the Rutulian leaders were dumbfounded,—
What miracle was this?—looked back and saw
The sterns lined up to the shore, the whole great ocean
One mass of moving ships. The helmet burned,   310
The crest streamed fire, the golden boss of the shield
Poured golden radiance: even so, at night-time
The comets burn blood-red, or Sirius' fire,
Portent of drought and pestilence to mortals,
Saddens the sky with evil glare.[35]
                                    But Turnus
Never lost confidence or nerve; he would beat them
There at the shore, he knew, and stop the landing.
"Men, here is what you always prayed for; do it!
Break through with sword-arm! Mars is in your hands.[36]
Remember, every man, his wife, his household,   320

---

[33] Cybele (worshipped on Ida, the mountain at Troy) taught the art of
fortifying cities. Her chariot was regularly represented as drawn by lions.
Compare the figurehead of Aeneas' ship, in lines 192–95.

[34] The Strymon was a river in Thrace, the region north of the Aegean
Sea. In the simile, the cranes are migrating northward.

[35] By the ancients' calendar, Sirius, the brightest star in the sky, made
its annual reappearance in the hot days of late summer.

[36] Turnus probably means, "The battle is yours to win or lose" (Mars
being the god of war). The meaning is disputed, however.

His fathers' noble glories. On to meet them
At the water's edge: they tremble there, they stagger,
And luck helps men who dare." He chose his captains,
Picked men for this attack, and left to others
The duty of the siege.

              Meanwhile Aeneas
Landed his comrades, down from the tall ships,
Over the gangways. Many leapt boldly down
Catching the ebb of the sea, and others vaulted
Over the oar-blades. Tarchon, watching the shore-line,
330   Saw where the shallow water was hardly breathing,
Where never a breaker roared, where the smooth ocean
Came gliding slowly in, and he turned his prow,
Calling on comrades:—"Now is the time, bend to it,
Lean on the oars, pick up the ships and lift them!
Let the beaks split this hostile land, and keels
Plough a deep furrow: what does a shipwreck matter,
So we take hold of land?" And as he urged them
They rose to the oars, they drove the foaming ships
To the dry Latin fields, and every vessel
340   Came in, unhurt, except for one. For Tarchon
Ran up on a ledge of rock and hung there, doubtful,
Tilting now back, now forward, until he broke
Above the weary wave, and the timbers weakened,
Gave way, and the men were flung in the midst of ocean,
Among the broken oars and the floating cross-beams,
And the drag of the undertow.

                  No lazy dawdling
Held Turnus back; he hurled his lines against them,
He stopped them at the shore. Aeneas charged,
Aeneas was the first invader, Aeneas
350   Struck down the Latin countrymen, killed Theron,
The biggest of them all. That was an omen;
Theron had taken extra pains to meet him,
But the sword went through his mail and through his tunic
And pierced his side and drank his blood. Next, Lichas
Was slain, Apollo's devotee, at birth
Cut from the womb of his dead mother: the child
Escaped the steel, but not the man. Two others,

One of them tough, one huge, Cisseus, Gyas,
Went down before Aeneas. They were fighting
With clubs, as Hercules used to, and much good   360
It did them, though their father was Melampus
Who had been with Hercules through many labors.[37]
Then there was Pharus, who had his mouth wide oₗen,
For boast or taunt, and got a javelin in it,
Flung by Aeneas' hand. Cydon loved Clytius,
And followed him everywhere, his golden darling,
And would have had a lesson in forgetting
All his beloved young men, falling a victim
Under Aeneas' hand, but his seven brothers,
The sons of Phorcus, hurried to his rescue.   370
Each one let fly a dart: helmet and shield
Turned them aside, or they only grazed the body
Through Venus' help. "Achates,"[38] cried Aeneas,
"Bring up more weapons! Any I ever landed
In bodies of the Greeks, on the plains of Ilium,[39]
Will never miss Rutulians here." He snatched
A great spear up, and flung it; it went flying
Through Maeon's shield of bronze; it rent the breastplate,
It tore the breast, went through, and struck Alcanor
Through the right arm around his falling brother,   380
And pierced the arm, and kept its bloody journey
While the dead arm dangled from shoulder-sinew.
Numitor ripped the spear from his brother's body,
Aimed at Aeneas, missed, but grazed Achates.
    Clausus from Cures, proud of his young body,
Let fly, far off, a javelin,[40] which caught Dryops
Under the chin and pierced the throat and robbed him
Of voice—he tried to speak—and life together,
And Dryops' forehead hit the ground, and blood
Poured thick from mouth and wound. Three Thracians fell,   390

---

[37] On the Labors of the great hero Hercules, see VIII.297–308 and note.
[38] Aeneas' right-hand man.
[39] Troy.
[40] Clausus, and (in the following lines) Halaesus and the invulnerable Messapus, are Italian warriors. They were sketched in the catalogue of Book VII, lines 728–43, 744–53, and 714–27.

Sons of the race of Boreas, and three others,
Ismarians, sons of Idas, killed by Clausus.[41]
Halaesus came to his side, and Neptune's son,
Messapus, joined them, that famous tamer of horses.
Here, there, on every side, the struggle rages:
The cry is *Drive them back!* Here is the beach-head
For gain or loss. As warring winds in heaven
Rage at each other through that wide dominion,
Equal in will and violence, the battle
400   Doubtful and long, and nothing yields, not wind,
Not cloud, not sea, in that eternal deadlock,
So Troy meets Latium in the shock of fighting,
Foot tramples foot, man grapples man.
                              And inland,
On ground where a raging stream had sent stones rolling,
And torn the bushes from the banks, the horsemen
Had to be infantry, for the rough ground
Forbade the use of chariots. Their nerve
Was at low ebb; they fled. And Pallas saw them,[42]
And being their one hope, with scorn and prayer
410   Rallied their courage:—"Where do you flee, Arcadians?
By your own brave deeds I beg you, by your king,
By the old wars won in Evander's name,
By my own hopes to match my father's praise,
Trust not to flight. The sword must cut the way,
And where that mass of men comes thickest toward us,
That way we go, with Pallas as your leader.
Our country calls; no gods pursue us: men,
We are being chased by men, with no more hands,
With no more lives than we have. Ocean blocks us
420   With his great dam; earth offers us no haven:
Are we bound for Troy[43] or the sea?" And he dashed in
Where the enemy was thickest. Lagus came

---

[41] Boreas, god of the north wind, was associated by the Greeks with
Thrace, for them a wintry region. Ismarus was a town, near a mountain
of the same name, in Thrace.

[42] See line 277 and note. Pallas has sailed with Aeneas, but he has now,
apparently, assumed command of the cavalry forces that traveled overland
to the battle site.

[43] That is, for the Trojan camp.

To meet him; fate was far from kind to Lagus.
He was trying to lift a stone when Pallas hit him,
And the javelin stuck in the spine between the ribs
Till Pallas pulled it loose again. Then Hisbo
Hoped to surprise him and failed; he came in rushing,
Reckless and angry over the death of Lagus,
And Pallas was ready for him, and drove the sword
Deep in the swollen lung. He went for Sthenius,   430
Then Anchemolus, of Rhoetus' ancient line,
The consort of his stepmother in incest,[44]
And then he saw twin brothers, sons of Daucus,
Named Thymber and Larides, whom their kinsmen
Could never tell apart, and their own parents
Made fond mistakes about them. But Pallas made
Them different, once for all; Evander's sword
Cut off the head of Thymber; Larides' hand,
Severed, looked blindly for its arm, the fingers
Closed, quivering and dying, on the sword.   440
    So the Arcadians rallied; his example
Armed them with shame and rage. Tyres and Teuthras,
Arcadian brothers, started after Rhoeteus,
Who fled, and that saved Ilus' life, for Pallas
Had flung a spear at Ilus, but Rhoeteus, driving
Into its path, received it, rolled from the chariot,
And his heels kicked the ground in death's convulsion.
And as in summer, when a shepherd kindles
Fire here and there among the brush or forest,[45]
And waits for wind, and hears it rise, and swiftly   450
The many fires are one great blaze, and Vulcan
Takes charge of all the field, above the battle
Watching victorious, so Pallas' comrades
Swept in from all directions, bright and burning,
Toward him, their focus and centre. And Halaesus
Came on to meet them, pulling himself together,
Setting himself for battle. He killed Ladon,
Pheres, Demodocus: Strymonius threatened

---

[44] Forced to flee after committing incest with his stepmother, Anchemolus found asylum with Turnus' father.
[45] The shepherd is trying to clear land by fire.

His throat with the gleaming sword, and for his trouble
460   Got his right hand cut off, and then Halaesus
Bashed Thoas' head in with a rock and scrambled
His skull-bones, blood and brains. Halaesus' father
Knew his son's destiny and tried to spare him,
Hiding him in the woodlands, but grew old
And could not watch forever, and when his eyes
Were blind in death, the fates reached out, Halaesus
Could not avoid his doom. Pallas attacked him,
Praying before he flung the spear:—"O Tiber,
Grant to the steel I poise and hurl good fortune,
470   A pathway through the breast of tough Halaesus:
Your oak will hold his arms and spoil as trophy."
And Tiber heard the prayer; Halaesus' luck
Ran out, he had left himself exposed, to cover
Imaon with his shield, and the bare breast
Took the Arcadian lance.
                      Lausus, unfrightened,
Himself no little portion of war, fought on,[46]
Kept up the courage of his men, found Abas
And cut him down; when Abas fell, a cluster
Of stubborn fight was broken. The young men die,
480   Arcadians, Etruscans, Trojan fighters
Who had survived Greek wounds; they come to grips,
Both armies, equal in leadership and valor;
Lines become columns, columns lines: all thickens
Into confusion, a press too close for fighting.
On one side Pallas thrusts and strains, and Lausus
Struggles to meet him, two young heroes, equal,
Or nearly so, in years, in worth, in courage,
In handsome manliness; and both denied
Return to fatherland; and each forbidden
490   To meet the other; and both assured of finding
Their fate where a greater enemy is waiting.
    Meanwhile the sister of Turnus brought him warning,
Lausus needs aid![47] So, with his car, he drove
Swift through the ranks. "Break off, and give me room,"

---

[46] Lausus, son of the impious Mezentius, was introduced in VII.669–75.

[47] Turnus' sister is not a mortal woman but a nymph named Juturna.

He cried, "Room for my duel. I am bound
To battle Pallas; Pallas is my prize,
My prize alone. I only wish his father
Were here to watch!" Obedient, his comrades
Gave place, and as they yielded, Pallas stood
Astonished at this arrogance, this giant: 500
He took the whole scene in, undaunted, proud,
Fierce, high in spirit, with a ready answer
For Turnus' taunting:—"Either I win my praise
For kingly spoils or glorious death, and soon:
My father can face either: spare the threats!"
And he moved forward, and the blood ran chill
In all Arcadian hearts. Down from his car
Jumps Turnus; he comes nearer, like a lion
Who sees far-off a bull, intent on battle,
And stalks, and rushes; even so came Turnus,   510
Came within spear-throw; Pallas, watching, knew it,
Took a step forward, and, that chance might favor
However uneven his strength, prayed to the heavens:—
"If ever my father entertained a stranger
Who proved a god, and gave him food and greeting,
Aid me, O Hercules![48] Let Turnus see me
Taking the bloody armor from his body,
And his dying eyes behold me, Pallas, victor."
The young prayer touched the god: his grief was stifled
Deep in his heart, and tears were vain; his father[49]   520
Spoke to him kindly:—"Every man, my son,
Has his appointed time; life's day is short
For all men; they can never win it back,
But to extend it further by noble deeds
Is the task set for valor. Even my son,
My own, and sons of other gods have fallen
Under Troy's lofty walls. Sarpedon, Turnus,
Fate calls alike: the years for each are measured,
The goal in sight." Jupiter, having spoken,

[48] As several passages in Book VIII explain, the hero-god Hercules was closely associated with Pallas' father, Evander, and his city.

[49] Jupiter was the father of Hercules, who grieves here because he cannot save Pallas, and the father also of the heroic Sarpedon, one of Jupiter's favorites, who had been earlier killed at Troy.

530   Shifted his eyes from the Rutulian landscape.
     And Pallas flung the spear, full force, and drew
The flashing blade; the shaft sped on, it struck
Where mail and shoulder met; piercing the shield
It grazed the side of Turnus. And he poised
His long oak shaft with the sharp iron, hurled it,
And a taunt went with the toss:—"Which pierces deeper,
Your spear or mine?" So, through the plates of iron,
The plates of bronze, the overlapping leather,
Through the shield's center drives the quivering point,
540   Through stubborn mail, through the great breast. In vain
Pallas pulls out the dart, warm from the wound.
His blood, his life, come with it, and he falls
Doubled upon his wound; the armor clangs
Over his body; he strikes the hostile earth,
Dying, with bloody mouth. Above him Turnus,
Rejoicing, cries:—"Arcadians, take notice,
And let Evander know, I am sending back
Pallas as he deserved. Whatever honor
A tomb affords, whatever comfort lies
550   In burial, that much I grant, and freely:
A costly welcome, Evander's to Aeneas!"
His left foot on the body, he ripped loose
The belt's great weight, with the story of a murder
Carved in its metal, the young men foully murdered
On the bridal night, the chamber drenched in blood,
As Clonus, son of Eurytus, engraved it.[50]
And Turnus gloried in the spoil, exulting—
O ignorant mortal mind, which never knows
Of fate or doom ahead, or how, in fortune,
560   To keep in decent bounds! A time is coming
When Turnus would pay dearly, could he purchase
Pallas unharmed again, would view with loathing

[50] The fifty daughters of Danaus, king of Argos in southern Greece, married the fifty sons of Aegyptus, his brother. Danaus, however, knew a prophecy according to which he would be killed by his son-in-law, and he therefore ordered his daughters to kill their husbands on the wedding night. Except for one, Hypermnestra, the women carried out the order. The surviving husband, Lynceus, later killed Danaus to avenge the deaths of his brothers, thus also fulfilling the prophecy. Clonus is probably an invented master-artist invoked to dignify the work of art.

Those spoils, that day. But now, with tears and weeping,
Comrades lift Pallas to the shield and take him,
Great sorrow and great glory, to his father.
One day of war, one day of death, but victims,
And many, for Rutulians to remember.
   No rumor, but a runner from the battle
Comes to Aeneas, of his men endangered,
At the edge of death: they are giving way, the Trojans,   570
There is not much time. Aeneas draws the sword;
Aeneas, burning, cuts a pathway through
The nearest lines; it is Turnus he is seeking,
Turnus the arrogant, slaughter fresh upon him.
Aeneas, all imagination, sees
Pallas, Evander, and the friendly tables
To which he came, a stranger; hears the pledge
Given and taken. For another pledge
He seizes four young men, the sons of Sulmo,
And four whom Ufens fathered;[51] he takes them, living,   580
For later sacrifice, to dye with blood
The funeral pyre of Pallas. From afar,
He aimed his spear at Magus, but that warrior
Ducked under it cleverly, and the shaft flew over,
And Magus was a suppliant at his knees:—
"I beg you, by the shades of great Anchises,
By all the hope you have of young Iulus,
Spare me, a father and a son, for son
And father. I have property and treasure,
A lofty house, talents of gold and silver   590
Buried in safety, crude and minted metal.
One life like mine is nothing to the Trojans:
What difference will it make?" "Save for your sons,"
Aeneas answered, "all that gold and silver.
Turnus broke off all bargain-talk, the killer,
When Pallas fell. The shades of great Anchises
Know this, my growing son, Iulus, knows it."
His left hand grasped the helmet; Magus felt
His head drawn back, he felt throat muscles tighten,

[51] Sulmo was killed by Nisus; see IX.427–33. Ufens was introduced in
the catalogue of Italian warriors, VII.763–67.

600   And, as he pleaded still, he felt the sword
        Deep driven to the hilt.
                                     A son of Haemon
        Was standing not far off, the holy fillets[52]
        Around his temples, gleaming in the robes
        He wore as priest of Phoebus and Diana,
        Bright in his glittering arms. He fled Aeneas
        Across the field, in vain escape, and stumbled,
        And the Trojan hero, standing over his body,
        Struck down, and killed, and gave him a cloak of
             darkness,
        And Serestus took his armor, spoil for Mars.[53]
610   Caeculus, born of Vulcan's race, and Umbro,
        From Marsian mountains, rallied the ranks.[54] Aeneas
        Came storming toward them, hot from wounding Anxur,
        Who had been boasting loud, hoping that words
        Would make him more aggressive: there was no limit
        To promises he made himself, long years,
        A ripe old age—if so, he would be a cripple,
        A man with no left hand: Aeneas lopped it
        Off at the wrist, and the shield's round circle with it.
        Tarquitus, son of Dryope and Faunus,[55]
620   Proud in his gleaming arms, stood up against him
        Briefly; the spear drove through the shield's huge weight
        Nailing it to the breastplate; all in vain
        Tarquitus pleaded, stammering and choking.
        Aeneas gave his head a shove; the body,
        Still warm, turned halfway over under his foot.
        Dying, Tarquitus heard:—"Lie there, and scare me,
        Terrible warrior! No loving mother
        Will ever bury your bones, no father build
        A sepulchre above them. The birds of prey
630   Will take you, or the waters of the flood,
        And greedy fishes nibble your wounds and mouth them."

        [52] Ceremonial headbands.
        [53] Serestus was one of the Trojan leaders during Aeneas' absence; see
        IX.176–78. The armor is to be offered up to Mars, god of war.
        [54] For Caeculus and Umbro, see the catalogue, VII.700–13,768–76.
        [55] Dryope was a wood-nymph, Faunus a faun (half man, half goat), proba-
        bly not the Faunus who was Latinus' father.

Four more were slaughtered, Lucas and Antaeus,
Conspicuous in Turnus' ranks, and Numa,
And sun-burnt Camers, son of noble Volcens,[56]
Richest in land of all Ausonians, ruler
Over Amyclae, the city known for silence.[57]
Men say there was a giant once, Aegaeon,
Who had a hundred arms, and fifty mouths
From each of which came fire, and fifty swords
And fifty shields, and rattled them together,   640
Defying Heaven's thunderbolts and lightning,[58] —
Such was Aeneas now, a victor raging
All up and down the field, with one sword only
But that one hot and red. He saw Niphaeus
Driving his four swift horses, and went toward them
With terrible strides and cursing, and they bolted,
Shook off the driver, dragged the car, a ruin,
Down to the shore of the sea. And then two brothers
Bring their white chariot on, Lucagus, Liger,
Of whom Lucagus whirls the sword in fighting,   650
And Liger plies the reins; they burn with fury,
More than Aeneas can stand: he rushes, monstrous,
A giant with a spear. And Liger taunts him:—
"Whoa! This is not Achilles' car, these fields
Not Troy, these horses Diomedes'.[59]
You will get it now, the end of life and battle,
Here on this ground." Poor crazy-talking Liger!
Aeneas wastes no words; his lance comes flying,
And while Lucagus, leaning over the chariot,
Makes of his sword a whip, his left foot forward,   660
Setting himself for action, the point comes through

[56] For the cavalry captain Volcens, who, after capturing Euryalus, was killed by Nisus, see IX. 381–465.

[57] The inhabitants of Amyclae, a town on the Italian coast halfway between Rome and modern Naples, were notorious for giving false alarms and were therefore ordered to keep silent about enemy attacks. Thus, they fell easy prey to an actual attack.

[58] This giant, one of those who (in Virgil's version of the myth) warred against Jupiter, is also called Briareus.

[59] Aeneas had twice been divinely rescued, from Diomedes and from Achilles (Homer, *Iliad,* Books V and XX). He will not be as lucky this time, Liger implies.

The low rim of his shield, drives on, and pierces
The groin on the left side. Lucagus topples,
Writhes on the ground, and dies; and then Aeneas
Has words for him, and bitter ones:—"Lucagus,
Your horses have not run away; they are brave,
They are no traitors, shying at a shadow.
You are the one, it seems, the cheap deserter,
Who jump the wheels, leave the poor beasts forsaken."
670 He pulls the horses up; and down comes Liger,
His luck all gone, his hands outstretched for mercy:—
"O Trojan hero, son of mighty parents,
For their remembrance, spare my life: Oh, hear me—"
And there was more he would have said. Aeneas
Broke in:—"Liger, that's not the way you sounded
A little while ago. What? Should a brother
Leave brother in the battle? Never. Die!"
And the sword went its deadly way, exposing
The spirit's hiding-place. Such was the carnage
680 Dealt by Aeneas over the plain, a whirlwind,
A flood of black destruction. And at the city
Ascanius and the warriors broke the siege,
Came from the threatened camp.
                                And high in heaven
Jupiter spoke to Juno:—"Sister of mine,
And dearest wife, it is, as you were thinking—
You are not wrong—Venus, who helps the Trojans,
Instead of their own right hands, war-quick, or spirit
Aggressive in attack, enduring in danger."[60]
And Juno made meek answer:—"Why, dear husband,
690 Trouble me further? I am sick at heart,
I fear your sad commandments. If I only
Had what I used to have, compelling love,
You would not, all-powerful king, refuse my pleading:
You would let me rescue Turnus from the battle,
Restore him safely to his father Daunus.
That would have been my prayer; but let him die,
Let innocent blood be forfeit to the Trojans,

---

[60] Jupiter is being ironic; obviously the enraged Aeneas is doing very
well on his own.

No matter that his lineage is lofty,
His origin from our stock;[61] no matter, either,
The generous offerings he has made your altars." 700
    The king of high Olympus thus made answer:—
"If it is only respite and reprieve
You ask for this doomed youth, delay, postponement,
If that is all, and you realize I know it,
Take Turnus off by flight, snatch him from danger.
That much you are permitted. But if, beneath the prayer,
Some deeper hope lies hidden, if you are thinking
The war might change entirely, then you nourish
The silliest kind of dreaming." Juno, weeping,
Replied:—"But what if, in your heart, you granted 710
The gift your speech refuses? What if Turnus
Might still live on? No; heavy doom awaits him,
Or else I am borne along in grievous error.
I wish my fear were false and I deluded,
And that the god, who has all power, would use it
To change things for the better." And, having spoken,
She veiled herself with cloud, came down from heaven,
Driving a storm before her, and sought Laurentum,[62]
The Trojan line, the Latin camp, and fashioned
Out of a cloud a hollow man, a figure 720
Thin, weak, and curious to see, a phantom,
A false Aeneas, dressed in Trojan armor,
A mimic shield and crest, with unreal language,
Voice without purpose, the image of a stride,
Like the vain forms that flit when death is over,
Like dreams that mock the drugged and drowsy senses.
With arrogant joy this ghost went out parading
Before the warriors' ranks, brandishing weapons,
Taunting and daring Turnus, who came on,
Hurled from afar the whirring spear; the phantom 730
Turned and made off, and Turnus, in confusion,
Nourished an empty hope: Aeneas, he thought,
Had turned away, was gone. "What now, Aeneas?
Where do you flee? Do not desert the bride,

[61] For Turnus' divine lineage, see lines 93–94 and note.
[62] The region ruled by Latinus.

The marriage chamber!"[63] And he drew the sword
Glittering as he challenged, and did not notice
The winds sweep off his happiness. Near by,
Moored to a shelf of rock, a ship was standing,
Ladders let down, and gangplank set; a king
740   Had sailed therein from Clusium.[64] The ghost,
The false Aeneas, hurrying, found shelter
Deep in the hold, and Turnus followed after,
Hot-foot through all delays, leaped onto the deck,
And had no sooner reached the bow than Juno
Broke off the mooring-lines, and the ship went scudding
Over the yielding sea. The real Aeneas
Kept calling Turnus to the fight, kept killing
Any who crossed his path. But the frail image
No longer sought a hiding-place, but swept
750   High to the darker clouds, with Turnus riding
The gale far out to seaward. Ignorant still,
Ungrateful for reprieve, he looked to shore,
Raising his hands to heaven, and praying:—"Father,
What have I done, to be so tricked, so sullied?
What am I being punished for? Where am I?
Who am I, for that matter? Fugitive
And coward, will I ever see again
The camp, the walls? And all that band of heroes
Who followed me and trusted me, I leave them
760   In death unspeakable, I see them wheeling,
I hear their dying groans. What am I doing?
What gulf, what chasm, is deep enough to hide me?
Pity me, winds; dash this accursèd vessel
On rocks, on reefs, on any savage quicksands.
I, Turnus, plead with all my heart, ah, strand me
Beyond all reach, where rumor or Rutulian
May neither one pursue me." His doubting spirit,
Mad with so much disgrace, was undecided
Whether to let the sword drive through the body,
770   Or dive and swim for it, toward camp and Trojans.

---

[63] Another reference to the alleged stealing by Aeneas of Turnus' bride-
to-be, Lavinia.
[64] A city in Etruria, in northwest Italy.

Three times he tried each way, three times his hand,
His will, were stayed by Juno in her mercy
And the tall ship, on wind and tide, was carried
On to Ardea,[65] Daunus' lofty city.
   Meanwhile, at Jove's command, Mezentius, burning,
Entered the fight, swept through the cheering Trojans.[66]
The Etruscan ranks rush on; against Mezentius
All turn their hate, their weapons. But he stands
Firm as a cliff, a jutting promontory
In the great deep, exposed to the winds' anger,   780
Taking all violence of sky and ocean,
Itself unmoved, immovable. Mezentius
Slew Hebrus, son of Dolichaon, and with him
Latagus and the running Palmus; Palmus
He hamstrung from behind, and left him writhing,
And gave his arms to Lausus, mail for his shoulders,
Plumes for the helmet. A rock brought down Latagus,
Smashing his mouth, full in the face. Evanthes
Fell victim, and Paris' comrade fell, that Mimas
Whose mother gave him birth on the same evening   790
When Hecuba was delivered of her firebrand.[67]
As a wild boar, sheltered for many years
In woods of pine or tracts of marshland, nourished
On reeds thick-grown, is driven from the mountains
By the sharp-toothed hunting-dogs, and comes to the nets,
And makes a stand, and snorts in savage anger,
And bristles up his shoulders, and no one dares
Come any nearer, but they all assail him
At a safe distance, pelting him and shouting,
And he is fierce and bold and very stubborn,   800
Gnashing his teeth, and shaking off the weapons,
Even so, like that wild boar, Mezentius held them
At bay, all those who hated him; they dared not
Close with the sword; they kept their distance, shouting,
Assailing him, but out of reach, with missiles.

[65] Turnus' own city; Daunus was his father.
[66] Mezentius was the first man sketched in the catalogue of Italian leaders, VII.667–68; for the atrocities that led his people to expel him, see VIII.494–509.
[67] For Paris as Hecuba's firebrand, see VII.337–39 and note.

There was a youth named Acron, who had come
From a Greek town, leaving his bride a virgin
At home in Corythus.[68] Mezentius saw him
Bright in the ranks, flashing, maroon and crimson,
810   The colors of his bride. Mezentius saw him
The way a hungry lion sees a deer
And the jaws open and the mane is lifted
And after one great leap the claws are fastened
Deep in the flank, and the mouth is red with slaughter.
So charged Mezentius into the midst, and Acron
Went down, heels drumming on the ground, and blood
Staining the broken spear. Orodes fled,
Or tried to, but no spear for him; Mezentius
Closed in, and struck with the sword, leaned on his spear,
820   With one foot on the body, and cried aloud:—
"Here lies Orodes, men, a mighty captain,
No little bit of the war!" His comrades joined him,
Shouting applause; with his last breath Orodes
Managed an answer:—"Not for long, O foeman,
Shall I be unavenged: exult a little.
Your doom keeps watch; you will hold these fields, as I do,
Before too long." Mezentius, smiling at him,
Said only, "Die; and let the sire of the gods,
The king of men, look after me." The steel
830   Came from the body; iron sleep and heavy
Repose weighed down his eyes; they closed forever
In night's eternal dark.
                    Caedicus slaughters
Alcathous,[69] Sacrator kills Hydaspes,
Rapo cuts two men down, Parthenius, Orses,
A tough, strong fighter; Messapus slays Clonius,
Lying, defenceless, on the ground, a rider
Thrown when the bridle of the horse was broken,
And Messapus slays another, Erichaetes,
Who tried to fight on foot; and Lycian Agis
840   Attempts to fight on foot, and meets Valerus,
And finds him a stout foeman, like his fathers,

[68] A city in Etruria that had Greek roots.
[69] In the following lines Italians kill Trojan opponents, except in the
fight between Salius and the Trojan Nealces.

And falls; and Thronius falls; his victor, Salius,
Is victim of Nealces, a good fighter
With javelin and far-deceiving arrow.
The scales were balanced: Trojans and Rutulians,
Arcadians, Etruscans, died and slaughtered.
Mars was a heavy-handed god, impartial
In dealing death and wounds. Victors and vanquished
Stood firm, in death or triumph, and the gods
Pitied both sides and all that useless anger,   850
That suffering which mortals take in battle.
Venus is watching, and Saturnian Juno,
And pale Tisiphone through the hosts goes raging.[70]
    And now Mezentius, shaking his great spear,
Sweeps like a whirlwind over the plain, a giant
Huge as Orion, wading through the waters,
Towering with his shoulders over the waves,
Lugging an ancient ash-tree from the mountains,
And his head hidden in the clouds of heaven,[71]
So looms Mezentius, monstrous in his armor,   860
And, from the other side, Aeneas sees him,
And moves to meet him, and Mezentius stands there,
Unfrightened, heavy-set, waiting his foe.
He eyes the distance that the spear may need,
Indulges in mock prayer:—"Let my right hand,
That is to say, my god, and the dart I balance
Favor me now! And as a trophy, Lausus,
I vow yourself, my son, to carry, living,
The spoil stripped from this robber."[72] The spear flew on,
Glanced from the shield, wounded the knight Antores   870
Between the side and thigh; Evander's ally,
Hercules' comrade, a man from Argos, he falls,
Killed by a wound meant for another; dying,
He thinks of his dear Argos.[73] And Aeneas

[70] Tisiphone was one of the Furies; see VII.341–46 and note.

[71] Orion, for whom the great winter constellation is named, was in mythology a mighty and gigantic hunter.

[72] This speech shows Mezentius' contempt for religion; piety dictated
that the spoils taken from a defeated enemy be dedicated to one of the
gods.

[73] Argos, in Greece, was near Arcadia, from which Evander had emigrated
to Italy.

Lets drive his spear: it penetrates the shield,
The triple bronze, the layers of leather, biting
Deep in the groin, not going through. And happy
At sight of Tuscan blood, Aeneas draws
Sword from his side, comes hotly on; Mezentius
880   Staggers, and Lausus grieves; he loves his father,
The tears stream down his face.
Mezentius, dragging back, useless, disabled,
Slowly gives ground, the hostile spear still trailing,
Still fastened to the shield. Lausus runs forward,
Lifts his right arm and strikes. Aeneas parries,
Lausus is halted. But his comrades follow—
The father, with the son's protecting shield,
Has, still, a chance of safety. Missiles shower
From all sides at Aeneas: though he rages,
890   He huddles under shelter, like a farmer
When hailstones rattle down, or any traveller
Seeking what he can find, a river bank,
An overhanging rock, or any cover
Until the downpour stops, and the sun returns
Men to their daily labor: so Aeneas,
With javelins thickening, every way, against him,
Endures the storm of war, and threatens Lausus:—
"What rush to death is this? What silly daring
Beyond the limit of strength? O foolish youngster,
900   You love your father, I know, but fool yourself
With too much loving." Lausus, in his madness,
Has never a thought of stopping, and Aeneas
Feels anger rise against him, and the Fates
Tie off the ends of Lausus' thread:[74] the Trojan
Drives with the sword; it is buried in the body
Deep to the hilt. The little shield, frail armor
Against so great a menace, could not hold it.
The pliant tunic, woven by his mother
With golden thread, is no more help; the blood
910   Stains it another color, and through air

---

[74] The three Parcae, or Fates, respectively spun the thread of a human
life, measured the thread, and finally cut it off at the point representing
death.

The life went sorrowing to the shades. And now
Aeneas changes. Looking on that face
So pale in death, he groans in pity; he reaches
As if to touch him with his hand, in comfort,
Knowing, himself, how one can love a father.
"Poor boy, what tribute can Aeneas offer,
What praise for so much glory? Keep the armor
You loved so much: if there is any comfort
In burial at home, know I release you
To your ancestral shades and ashes.[75] Further,   920
You have one solace, this, that you have fallen
By great Aeneas' hand." He lifted Lausus
From the bloody ground and raised the head, that dust
And earth and blood should not defile its glory,
And called the Etruscans[76] closer, scornful of them
Over their hesitation.
    Meanwhile, Mezentius, by the wave of the river,
Propped his slumped frame against a tree-trunk, staunching
The wound with water. The bronze helmet hung,
Inverted, from the bough; the heavy arms   930
Lay quiet on the meadow. Chosen men
Were standing by. Sick, and with labored breath,
He let his chin fall forward, rubbed his neck,
While over his chest the flowing beard was streaming.
Over and over again, he asks and sends
For Lausus: bring him back, he tells the men,
Those are the orders from his unhappy father.
But they were bringing him back, a big man slain
By a big wound. Mezentius knew the sound
Of sorrow from afar, before he heard it,   940
Fouled his gray hair with dust, flung up his arms,
Clung to the body. "O my son, my son,
Was I so fond of living that I sent
You to the sword for me, saved by your wounds,
Alive when you are dead? The wound indeed
Is driven deep, the bitterness of death
Comes home. I was the one, my son, my son,

[75] To your dead ancestors and to the earthly tomb.
[76] Lausus' own men.

Who stained your name with crime, with hatred, driven
From throne and sceptre. I have owed too long
950   The debt of punishment, and here I am,
Living, and never leaving men and light,
But I shall leave." He heaved his sickened weight,
Pulling himself together, groin and all,
Slowly. The wound was deep, but he could stand.
He ordered them to bring his horse, that solace,
That pride of his, on which he used to ride
Victorious out of all the wars. He spoke,
And the beast sorrowed with his master's sorrow:—
"Rhoebus, if anything is ever long
960   For mortal beings, you and I have lived
For a long time. Today you carry back
Those bloody spoils, Aeneas' arms, avenging
The pangs of Lausus with me, or we both,
If no force clears the way, go down together,
O bravest heart, too noble to endure
The stranger's order and the Trojan rider."
He swung astride, shifted his weight a little,
The way he always did, held in both hands
A load of darts. The helmet glittered bronze,
970   The horsehair plume was bristling as he rode,
Madness and grief and shame all urging on
That singleness of purpose. He came on fast,
Calling, *Aeneas! Aeneas!* over and over,
And his voice was loud and firm. Aeneas heard,
Rejoiced, and recognized, and made his prayer:—
"Let this be true, O father of the gods,
O high Apollo!"—then, to his foe, "Come on!"
And moved to meet him with the deadly spear.
Mezentius answered:—"Do you frighten me
980   With all that fierceness, now that my son is taken?
How meaningless! That was the only way
You could destroy me. Now I fear no death,
I spare no god.[77] Be quiet; for I come
To die, but first of all I bring you this,

---

[77] Mezentius defies both Aeneas and the gods he has called on in lines
976–77.

A present from me,"—and he flung the dart,
And flung another, and another, wheeling
In a great arc. The boss of gold held strong.
Three times in circles to the left he rode
Around the steady Trojan;[78] thrice the hand
Let fly the dart, and thrice the shield of bronze
Was a great forest with its load of spears.
All this was wearisome,—too many darts,
Too much defensiveness. Aeneas broke
Out of the watchful attitude, and flung
The spear between the charger's hollow temples.
The great beast reared with fore-hooves flailing air,
Throwing the rider, and came tumbling down
Head-foremost on him, shoulder out of joint.
Trojan and Latin uproar swelled to heaven.
Aeneas, sword-blade ready, rushes in:—
"Where is the fierce Mezentius now, and where
All that wild rage of spirit?" But the king,
Raising his eyes, drank in the sky a little,
Knew a brief moment of recovery,
Enough to say:—"O bitter enemy,
Why all the tauntings and the threats of death?
There is no wrong in slaughter: neither I
Nor Lausus ever made such battle-pledges.[79]
One thing I ask, if beaten enemies
Have any claim on mercy. Let my body
Be granted burial. I know the hate
Of my own people rages round me. Keep
Their fury from me. Let me share the grave
Of my dear son." He said no more, but welcomed,
Fully aware, the sword-thrust in the throat,
And poured his life in crimson over the armor.

990

1000

1010

---

[78] The counterclockwise circling allows Mezentius to keep his left (shield) arm between himself and Aeneas and to face the unshielded right side of Aeneas' body.

[79] Mezentius means that he, and also his son Lausus when fighting as his deputy, accept the rule of war—kill your enemy or be killed by him—on a kind of abstract level that makes personal judgments irrelevant.

BOOK XI

◻

The Despair
of the Latins

MEANWHILE Aurora, rising, left the ocean.
Aeneas' heart was troubled—so much dying,
So great a need for funeral rites,—but first
Vows must be paid for victory. At dawn
He sets an oak-trunk on a mound, the branches
Stripped off on every side, and hangs upon it
Mezentius' gleaming arms, the war-god's trophy.
He adds the crest, blood-stained, the broken darts,
The riddled breast-plate; binds, to the left, the shield,
Hangs from the neck the ivory sword.[1] His comrades   10
Hail him, and gather close around, and listen:—
"The greatest task is done: as for the future,
Fear not, my heroes! Here are spoils and first-fruits
Of one proud king; Mezentius is in our hands.
We march, now, on Latinus and his cities.
Prepare your arms, your nerve; let your hopes run
Onward before the war. When the gods grant us
To raise our standards and to lead our army
Out of this camp, let no delay impede us
Through ignorance, no fear retard our courage.   20
Meanwhile, let us commit to earth the unburied bodies

---

[1] With this reverent ritual compare X.865–69 and note.

Of our dear comrades, for no other honor
Waits them below the world.[2] Go, offer homage,
The final rites to those whose blood has won us
This fatherland; let Pallas be sent home
To the mourning city of Evander: Pallas
Had courage, and the day was black that took him
To the bitterness of death."

                         He spoke with tears
And went back to the threshold, where old Acoetes,
30   An armor-bearer, once, to king Evander,
And then, less happily, guardian over Pallas,
Kept watch beside the body. A Trojan throng
Stood all around, an honor-guard, and the women
Loosened their hair in ceremonial mourning,
And when Aeneas came, the lofty portal
Sounded with groaning and with lamentation,
And wailing reached the stars. He looked at Pallas,
The pillowed head, the face as white as snow,
The jagged wound in the smooth breast, and spoke,
40   And could not check his weeping:—"Ah, poor youngster!
Fortune, a little while, was happy for us
And then turned evil and grudging, and refused me
The joy of seeing you ride back in triumph
To your father's house with news of our new kingdom.
I have not kept my promise to Evander,
Whose arms went round me when I left, who sent me
To win great empire, and who gave me warning
That these were men of spirit, tough in battle.
And now, perhaps even at this very moment,
50   The dupe of empty hope, he is making prayers,
Heaping the altars high with gifts, while we
In sorrow attend his lifeless son, with honor
As empty as the father's hope, for Pallas
Owes nothing more to any god in heaven.[3]
Unhappy Evander, our long-awaited triumph,

[2] In other words, "this is the only honor we can meaningfully render to the dead in the Lower World."

[3] By dying, Pallas has become exempt from all further debts to the gods (such as gratitude for surviving or winning in battle).

Our glorious return, comes to this only,
The bitter funeral of a son; and so
Aeneas keeps his promise!
            And yet, O king,
You will not see him slain by shameful wounds,
You will not long for a dire death to cancel   60
The memory of a son, safe, but a coward.
We have lost a great protection, all of us,
Ausonia, Iulus."
          He gave orders
To raise the pitiful body for its journey,
And chose a thousand men to honor Pallas
With this last escort, to share Evander's tears,
Poor comfort for so great a grief, but due him.
Men weave the bier with osier and soft willow
And shadow it over with leaves of oak, and Pallas
Rests on his country litter, like a flower   70
Some girl has picked and lost, a violet
Or drooping hyacinth, and all its luster
Still there, though earth is kind to it no longer.
And then Aeneas brought two robes, whose crimson
Was stiff with gold, robes that the queen of Carthage
Had woven for him, happy in her labor,
Running the gold through crimson. Over Pallas
The robes are cast, the sad and final honor,
The hair is veiled for the fire, and many trophies
Are added, prizes from the Latin battles,   80
Horses, and weapons, captured from the Latins,
And human victims, offerings to the shades,
Their blood to sprinkle funeral fire, are led
Hands bound behind them, and the names of foemen
Are cut in the trunks of trees that bear their armor.
Unhappy old Acoetes trudges with them,
Beating his breast, clawing his face, or flinging
His wretched body down in the dust. And chariots
Follow, Rutulian blood on wheel and axle,
And Pallas' war-horse Aethon, riderless,   90
Without caparison, weeps for his master,
The great tears rolling down. Other men carry

The spear and helmet only, for the rest
Turnus had taken as spoil. And then there follows
A long array of mourners, Trojans, Tuscans,
Arcadians, with arms reversed: so they pass
In long procession, comrade after comrade,
Far on and almost out of sight. Aeneas
Halts, and sighs deeply:—"The same grim fates of war
100 Call us from here to other tears. Forever
Hail, O great Pallas, and farewell forever!"
He said no more, but turned to the high walls,
Strode back to the camp.
                                    And envoys came
From the Latin city, veiled with boughs of olive,
Asking for truce: let him return the bodies
Strewn by the sword across the battlefield,
Let them be given burial. No war
Is fought with vanquished men, deprived of light:
Let him be merciful—had he not called them
110 Hosts at one time, and fathers? And good Aeneas
Granted, of right, the truce they sought, and added
Brief words:—"What evil destiny, O Latins,
Involved you in such tragic war, to flee us,
Your friends that might have been? You ask for peace,
Peace for the dead, slain by the lot of battle.
Peace? I would gladly grant it to the living.
I would not be here unless fate had given
This place, this dwelling, and I wage no war
Against your people, but your king deserted
120 Our friendliness; he had more confidence
In Turnus' weapons. Turnus, in simple justice,
Should be the one to face this death. If, truly,
He seeks to end the war, to drive the Trojans
By strength of hand from Italy, he should have
Taken my personal challenge: one of us
Would live, to whom his own right hand or heaven
Had granted life. Go now, depart in peace,
Kindle the death-fires for your luckless comrades."
He spoke, and they were silent: they had nothing
130 That could be said; they could not face him, either,

And kept their eyes and faces toward each other.
    And then old Drances,[4] always bitter and hateful,
Resentful of young Turnus, spoke in answer:—
"O great in glory, even greater in arms,
Heroic Trojan, how can I ever praise you
As highly as I should? Am I to wonder
First at your justice or your warlike prowess?
We shall be glad, indeed, to take these words
Back to our native city and, fortune willing,
Join you with king Latinus. As for Turnus,   140
Let him seek his own alliances! Our pleasure
Will be in building walls for you, as fate
Ordains, that we should carry on our shoulders
The masonry of Troy." And they all cheered him.
They pledged twelve days for peace, and in the forests
Trojans and Latins walked as friends together,
Over the ridges, peace among them. Ash-trees
Rang as the two-edged axe bit deep; the pines,
Star-towering, came down; the oak, the cedar,
Split by the wedges, filled the groaning wagons.   150
    And Rumor, messenger of all that mourning,
Came flying to Evander's home and city,
Rumor, so short a time before the herald
Of victories in Latium for young Pallas.
Out to the gates came the Arcadians; torches,
Carried aloft, after the ancient custom,
Marked off the fields from highway; the long road
Shone with the light of fire, and the Trojans, coming,
Met their lament, and when the mothers saw them,
The city itself was one great fire of mourning.   160
No force could hold Evander back: he came,
Rushing, into the sad procession's center,
And where the barrow[5] halted, clung to Pallas,
Weeping and groaning, and his voice could hardly
Manage its way through choking sobs:—"Ah, Pallas,

---

[4] Drances appears at greater length later in Book XI. An elderly man,
more skilled in scheming and words than in heroic deeds, he makes an
effective contrast to Turnus.
    [5] Bier.

You have not kept your promise to your father!
You said you would be careful in the battles!
I knew, I knew too well, how much new glory,
How much the sweet fresh pride in the first battle,
170   Could overpower discretion. Here are the first-fruits
Of your young manhood; here are the cruel lessons
Of war brought home; and all my prayers unheeded
By any god! But my dear wife is happy,
Spared, by her death, this anguish. I live on,
I have overcome my fate by living so,
A father who survives his son. I should have
Followed the Trojan arms, let the Rutulians
O'erwhelm me with their darts; I should have died,
And this procession brought me home, not Pallas.
180   It is not your fault, O Trojans; I do not blame you,
The treaties joined, the hands we clasped, in friendship.
No: this was coming to me, this was due
The lot of my old age. An early death
Took off my son; I shall rejoice, hereafter,
Knowing he led the Trojans into Latium,
Slew Volscians by the thousands. He was worthy,
Pallas, my son, of such a death. Aeneas,
The mighty Trojans, the Etruscan captains,
The Etruscan ranks, all think so. They bring trophies,
190   Great trophies, those my son brought low; and Turnus
Would be another trophy, were his years,
His strength, the same as his young enemy's.
But why am I, unhappy man, delaying
The Trojan hosts from battle? Go: remember
To tell Aeneas this: I keep on living,
However hateful life may be, with Pallas
Taken away from me, I keep on living
Because of his right hand: it owes me something,
The death of Turnus, for the son and father.
200   And this Aeneas knows, the one thing wanting
To make his praise and fortune sure. I ask
No joy in life—that is impossible—
But only this one thing, to take my son,
In the shades below, one message: Turnus has fallen."
    Meanwhile the dawn had brought to weary mortals

Her kindly light, and work again, and labors.
Along the winding shore Aeneas, Tarchon,
Set up the pyres, and all, as had their fathers,[6]
Brought bodies of their kinsmen, lit the fires
That burned, but darkly, and the light of heaven   210
Was hidden by the blackness of that shadow.
Three times, in glittering armor, they went riding
Around the funeral blaze, three times they circled
The mournful fire and cried with wailing voices.
Tears fell on earth and armor; heaven heard
The groans of men, the blare of trumpet. Spoils
Went to the fire, the handsome swords, the helmets,
Bridles and shining wheels, and well-known gifts
For men who died, their shields, their luckless weapons.
Bullocks were slain, and bristly swine, and sheep   220
From all the fields, homage to fire and death,
And all along the shore, they watched their comrades
Burn on the pyres, and guarded the dead embers,
And could not leave till day had gone, and night
Dewy with gleaming stars rolled over heaven.
     And elsewhere in the countryside the Latins
Built, as the Trojans had, pyres without number.
Many were slain, and many men were buried
Where they had fallen, and many men sent home
To their own cities, and many no one knew,   230
No one could mark with honor or distinction,
And these were given one common pyre; the fields
Rivalled each other as the fires kept burning.
Three days had gone; and over bones and ashes
They heaped the earth, still warm. Inside the walls,
Within the city of that rich king Latinus,
Grief swelled from murmur to wailing, to loud uproar,
The greatest share of sorrow. Brides and mothers,
Sisters and fatherless boys, crying and cursing,
Denounced the evil war and Turnus' marriage.   240
They call on him, on Turnus alone, to settle
The issue with the sword; he is the one,

----

[6] The dead from each of the different nations were buried in accordance
with their particular customs.

Their accusation cries, who wants the kingdom,
All Italy for himself, and the highest honors.
And Drances, savage, tips the balance further:
Turnus, alone (he says), is called on, Turnus
Alone is called to battle. But against them
Many a man has good to say of Turnus,
And the shadow of the queen's great name protects him,[7]
250   And he has been a mighty man in battle.
        And during all this swirling burning tumult,
Envoys, who came from Diomede's great city,
Brought gloomy news:[8] nothing had been accomplished
With all that toil and trouble; nothing gained
By gifts or gold or pleading, and the Latins
Were left two choices, to seek for other allies
Or ask Aeneas for peace. Under the burden
Of that great grief even Latinus falters.
Aeneas is called by fate, the will of heaven
260   Is clear, the gods are angry; the fresh graves,
Before their eyes, bear more than ample witness.
Therefore, he calls a council; all his leaders
Stream through the crowded highways to the palace,
And in their midst, the oldest man among them,
The first in power, Latinus, far from happy,
Speaks from his throne,—the messengers from Arpi
Should tell what news they bring, in proper order,
Sparing no single item. All were silent,
Obedient to his word, and Venulus
270   Gave the report:—"O citizens, we have seen
The Argive camp, and Diomede. We made
The journey safely through all kinds of perils.
We have touched the hand by which Troy fell. That hero
Has his own city now, named from his father,
In Garganus' conquered fields.[9] We entered there,

[7] On the queen Amata's opposition to Aeneas and support for Turnus
as suitor of her daughter Lavinia, see VII.360–427.

[8] The Latins had sent a diplomatic mission, headed by Venulus, to the
city of Arpi in southeastern Italy, in hopes of enlisting the support of
Diomede, the Greek hero who fought in the Trojan war; see VIII.8–19.

[9] Arpi was also called Argyripa, the name being supposedly derived from
Argos, the Greek city that had been Diomede's home. Garganus was a
mountain in southeastern Italy.

Had leave to speak, offered our gifts, and told him
Our name and country, why we came to Arpi,
Who made war on us. He listened to our story
And answered us, quite calmly. These are his words:—

'O happy people of the realm of Saturn,   280
Ancient Ausonians,[10] what chance, what fortune
Disturbs your rest, leads you to unknown warfare?
All of us, every one, who desecrated
The fields of Troy with steel—I do not mention
All that we suffered under those high walls,
Or heroes drowned in Simois—every one,
All over the world, has paid and kept on paying
All kinds of punishment, all kinds of torture,
A band that even Priam would have to pity.
Minerva knows it, with her baleful star,[11]   290
Euboea's headland knows it, and Caphereus,
That cape of vengeance. From that warfare driven
Ulysses faced the Cyclops; Menelaus
Was exiled far to the west. Idomeneus
Lost Crete: what need is there to mention Pyrrhus,
To name the Locrians on Libya's coastline?
Even the Greeks' great captain, Agamemnon,
Met shame beyond his threshold; Clytemnestra
Struck with her evil hand,—the king of men,
The conqueror of Asia, fell, a cuckold   300

[10] Saturn had reigned in Italy (Ausonia) after being dethroned by his son Jupiter.
[11] The evils that befell the Greeks after the Trojan war, referred to in the following lines, included the storm (presided over by a "baleful star") sent by Minerva (Pallas Athena), who was angered at the rape of Cassandra by Ajax (see I.48–54); a shipwreck the Greeks suffered after the king of Euboea, embittered by the Greeks' execution of his son Palamedes, displaced the navigational lights at Cape Caphereus; the ten-years' wandering endured by Ulysses, filled with perils such as his encounter with the gigantic one-eyed Cyclops (see III.588–680); the marooning of Menelaus off the coast of Egypt; the punishment of Crete and the exile of its king, Idomeneus, after his return from the war, when he killed his son (see III.122–25); the killing of Pyrrhus, Achilles' son and slayer of Priam, by his rival Orestes (see III.321–37); the dispersement of the Locrians to Africa after their king, Ajax, died; and, most dire of all, the murder of the commander-in-chief, Agamemnon, on his homecoming to Mycenae, by his wife Clytemnestra and her lover.

Murdered in his own palace, at Mycenae.
To me the gods were kinder; they would not let me
See home again, the wife I loved, the altars
Of lovely Calydon;[12] here I am, still haunted
By portents[13] horrible to see—my comrades
Lost, seeking heaven on their wings, or aimless
Along the rivers, crying in shrill voices
Around the rocks, creatures of lamentation
That once were men! The gods know how to punish.
310   This, so it seems, was what I had to hope for
Ever since that first moment of my madness
When I took steel in hand and wounded Venus.
No, no; do not invite me to such battles.
The walls of Troy have fallen; I have no quarrel
With any Trojans any more. Those evils
I have forgotten, or, if I remember,
I find no pleasure in them. Take Aeneas
The gifts you bring me from your native country.
I have stood up against his terrible weapons,
320   I have fought him hand to hand. Believe an expert,
Take it from one who knows, how huge he rises
Above that shield of his, with what a whirlwind
He rifles out that spear. If Troy had only
Two other men as good, Greece would be mourning
With doom the other way, and the towns of Argos
Admit the conqueror. For ten long years
They kept us waiting at that stubborn city,
And the Greek victory was at a standstill
Through Hector and Aeneas; both were famous
330   In spirit, both in feats of arms, Aeneas
The more devoted man. I tell you, join them
In treaty, on what terms you can. I warn you,
Beware, beware, of facing them in battle.'

So you have heard, great king, Diomede's answer

---

[12] The original home of Diomede, in northwestern Greece, before he settled in Argos.

[13] Omens—in this case visions, by which Diomede is haunted, of his men changed into birds. He fears that divine punishment may be impending, especially because during the war he had inflicted a wound on Venus.

And what he thinks of this great war."
                                  The sound
Rose, as he ended, like the sound of water
When rocks delay a flood, and the banks re-echo
The stir and protest of the angry river,
Confusion, argument, in swirl and eddy,—
So the Ausonians brawled among each other,   340
Muttered, and then subsided; and king Latinus
Spoke from his lofty throne:—"I wish, O Latins,
Decision had been taken in such matters
A long while since; that would have been much better.
This is no time for councils to be summoned.
The enemy is at the gate. We are waging
A most unhappy war against a people
Descended from the gods; we cannot beat them.
No battles wear them down; if they are conquered,
They cannot let the sword fall from the hand.   350
Whatever hope you had in Diomede,
Forget it. All your hope is what you are,
But you can see how little that amounts to.
You have it all before your eyes; you have it
In your own hands, and most of it is ruin.
I lay no blame on any man; what valor
Could do, it has done: the body of our kingdom
Has fought with all its strength. We are bled to the white.
Hear, then, what I propose; I am not yet certain
Entirely—here it is, in brief. We have   360
An ancient tract of land, far to the west,
Touching the Tuscan river,[14] where our natives,
Rutulians, Auruncans, sow and harrow
The stubborn hills, rough land and cattle country.
Let all this region and its high pine-forest
Be ceded to the Trojans out of friendship;
Let us make fair terms and have them share our kingdom,
Here they may build and settle if they want to.
But if their minds are bent on other borders,
On any other nation, if they are able   370

[14] The Tiber, which flows down from the north. *Tuscan* here means
"Etruscan," i.e., having to do with Etruria, the region to the northwest.

To leave our soil, let us build a navy for them,
Twenty good ships of oak, more if they need them.
We have the timber at the water's edge;
All they need tell us is what kind, how many,
For us to give them workmen, bronze, and dockyards.
A hundred spokesmen from the noblest Latins
Should go with boughs of olive, bearing presents,
Talents of gold and ivory, the robe,
The throne, of state, symbols of our dominion.
380   Consult together; help our weary fortunes."
       Then Drances, hostile still, whom Turnus' glory
Goaded with envy's bitter sting, arose,
A man of wealth, better than good with his tongue;
If not so fierce in war, no fool in council,
A trouble-maker, though; his mother was noble,
His father no-one much. He spoke in anger:—
"Good king, you ask our guidance in a matter
Obscure to none, needing no word of ours.
All know, admit they know, what fortune orders,
390   Yet mutter rather than speak. Let him abate
That bluster of his, through whose disastrous ways
Evil has come upon us, and bad omens.
I will speak out, however much he threaten.
Let us have freedom to speak frankly. Mourning
Has settled on the town, the light of the leaders
Dies out in darkness, while that confident hero,
Confident, but in flight,[15] attacks the Trojans
And frightens heaven with arms. To all these gifts
Promised and sent the Trojans, add, O king,
400   One more: let no one's violence dissuade you
From giving your daughter in a worthy marriage,
An everlasting covenant between us.
But if such terror holds our hearts, then let us
Beseech this prince, sue for his royal favor,
Let him give up his claim, for king and country.
Why, Turnus, fountain-head of all our troubles,
Consign us, wretches that we are, to danger

---

[15] Turnus had not intentionally fled; Juno had lured him away from
the battlefield by creating a phantom Aeneas. See X.716–74.

Open and often? In war there is no safety.
Turnus, we ask for peace, and, to confirm it,
The only proper pledge. You know I hate you,   410
Make no mistake in that regard. But still,
I, first of all, implore you, pity your people!
Put off that pride: give in, give up, and leave us!
We have seen enough of death and desolation.
If glory moves you, you with the heart of oak,
Or if the royal dowry is your passion,
Be bold, have confidence,—and face Aeneas!
So Turnus have his royal bride, no matter
If we, cheap souls, a herd unwept, unburied,
Lie strewn across the field. O son of Mars,   420
If son you really are, the challenger
Is calling: dare you look him in the face?"
   And Turnus' violence blazed out in fury,
A groan or a growl and savage words erupting:—
"A flow of talk is what you have, O Drances,
Always, when wars need men; and you come running
The first one there, whenever the senate gathers.
But this is not the time for words, that fly
From your big mouth in safety, in a meeting,
While the walls keep off the foe, and the dry trenches   430
Have not yet swum in blood. As usual,
Orator, thunder on! Convict me, Drances,
Of cowardice, you having slain so many
Tremendous heaps of Trojans, all the fields
Stacked with your trophies! Try your courage, Drances:
The enemy are not far to seek, our walls
Are circled with them. Coming? Why the coyness?
Will your idea of Mars be found forever
In windy tongue and flying feet? I, beaten?
Who says so? What foul liar calls me beaten,   440
Seeing the Tiber red with blood, Evander
Laid low with all his house, and the Arcadians
Stripped of their arms? Ask Pandarus and Bitias,[16]
The thousands I have sent to hell, cut off
Inside their walls, hedged by a ring of foemen.

[16] The slaying of these men by Turnus was described in IX.688–773.

In war there is no safety. Sing that song,
Madman, to your own cause and prince Aeneas!
Keep on, don't stop, confound confusion further
With panic fear, and praise those noble heroes
450 Of that twice-beaten race, despite the arms
Of King Latinus. Now the Myrmidons,
Or so we hear, are trembling, and their river
Runs backward in sheer fright, and Diomedes
Turns pale, and I suppose Achilles also![17]
Now he[18] pretends my threats, my anger, scare him—
A nice artistic piece of work!—he sharpens
Slander with apprehension. Listen to him!
Listen to me: I tell you, you will never
Lose such a life as yours by this right hand,
460 Quit worrying, keep that great and fighting spirit
Forever in that breast! And now, my father,
I turn to you and more important counsels.
If you have hope no longer in our arms,
If we are so forsaken, if we are lost,
Utterly, over one repulse, if fortune
Cannot retrace her steps, let us pray for peace,
Let us hold out helpless hands in supplication.
But still, if only some of our valor, something—
Happy the men who died before they saw it!
470 But if we still have any power, warriors
Standing unhurt, any Italian city,
Any ally at all, if any Trojans
Have ever died (their glory has been costly
As well as ours, and the storm has no more spared them),
Why do we fail like cowards on the edge
Of victory? Why do we shudder and tremble
Before the trumpet sounds? Many an evil
Has turned to good in time; and many a mortal

---

[17] The Myrmidons were the followers of Achilles, the greatest of the Greek war heroes. Turnus is sarcastically mocking an almost superstitious awe and fear of the Trojans, such as Diomede had expressed to the ambassadors.

[18] Drances. Turnus has shifted to the third person; in line 458 he again speaks to Drances.

Fate has despised and raised. Diomede, Arpi,
Refuse us help; so be it. There are others,   480
There is Messapus for one, Tolumnius
Whose luck is good, and all those other leaders
Sent by so many nations, and great glory
Will follow Latium's pride. We have Camilla
Of Volscian stock, leading her troop of horsemen,
Her warriors bright in bronze. If I am summoned
Alone to meet Aeneas, if I alone
Am obstinate about the common welfare,
If such is your decision, my hands have never
Found victory so shrinking or elusive   490
That I should fear the risk. Bring on your Trojan!
Let him surpass Achilles, and wear armor
Made by the hands of Vulcan! Second to no one
Of all my ancestors in pride and courage,
I, Turnus, vow this life to you, Latinus,
My king, my father. *The challenger is calling*—
Well, let him call, I hope he does. No Drances,
If heaven's wrath is here, will ever appease it,
No Drances take away my honor and glory."[19]
    So, in the midst of doubt, they brawled and quarreled,   500
And all the time Aeneas' line came forward.
A messenger rushed through the royal palace,
Through scenes of noise and uproar, through the city,
Filling the town with panic: *They are coming,*
He cries, *they are ready for battle, all the Trojans,*
All the Etruscans, rank on rank, from Tiber,
All over the plain! And the people's minds are troubled,
Their hearts are shaken, their passion and their anger
Pricked by no gentle spur. However frightened,
They call for arms, they make impatient gestures,   510
The young men shout, and the old ones moan and mutter;
The noise, from every side, goes up to heaven
Loud and discordant, the way jays rasp and chatter

---

[19] Turnus is saying that, if the Latins are hated by the gods and thus
are destined to fail, Drances will not be the gods' victim; if, on the other
hand, victorious glory is to be won, Drances is not to have any share in
it. He is to be insignificant, either way.

Or swans along Padusa's fishy river
Utter their raucous clamor over the pools.[20]
And Turnus, seizing on the moment, cries:—
"A fine time, citizens, to call a council,
To sit there praising peace. The enemy
Is up in arms against us!" That was all,
520   And he went rushing from the lofty palace.
"Volusus, arm the squadrons of the Volscians,
Lead the Rutulians forth! Messapus, Coras,
Deploy the horsemen over the plains![21] You others,
Some of you, guard the city gates and towers!
The rest, be ready to charge where I direct you!"
    So Turnus gave excited orders: quickly,
The rush to the walls was on, all over the city.
Latinus left the council, sorely troubled
In that sad hour, put off the plan he hoped for,
530   Blaming himself in that he had not welcomed,
More eagerly, his Trojan son Aeneas
For the welfare of the city. And his men
Were digging trenches, trundling stones, or setting
Stakes in the ground, and pitfalls; and the trumpet
Sounded for bloody war; and boys and mothers
Filled in the gaps along the walls. Amata,
The queen, with a great throng of matrons, rode
To Pallas' temple on the heights; beside her
The girl Lavinia, cause of all that evil,
540   Went with head bowed and downcast eyes. The women
Climbed on, and made the temple steam with incense,
And from the threshold chanted sorrowful prayers:—
"O mighty power in war, Tritonian virgin,[22]
Break off his spear, lay low the Trojan robber,
Stretch him in death before our lofty portals!"
    And Turnus, all impatience, hot for action,
Buckles his armor, the ruddy breastplate gleaming

[20] The Padusa, in northern Italy, was a branch of the river Po, near its mouth.
[21] This is the first mention of Volusus. For Messapus and his men, see the catalogue, VII.714–27. The twins Catillus and Coras, from Tibur (modern Tivoli, twenty miles east of Rome), are also mentioned there; see VII.695–99. See also lines 581–82 of the present book.
[22] Pallas Athena, or Minerva, was born near Lake Tritonis, in Africa.

Bright with bronze scales, the greaves on fire with gold,
The sword snapped to the baldric.[23] Still bareheaded,
A golden blaze, he runs down from the fortress,   550
Exulting in his spirit: he has the foe
By the throat already, in imagination.
You see that fire when a stallion breaks his tether,
Runs from the stable, free at last, a monarch
Of all the plain, and makes for the green pastures
Where mares are grazing, or splashes into the river
Out of sheer joy, and tosses his mane, and nickers,[24]
And the light plays across his neck and shoulders.
    To meet him came Camilla and her Volscians,[25]
And she reined in at the gate, dismounting quickly,   560
And all her band, at her example, followed,
Listening as she spoke:—"Turnus, if courage
Has any right to confidence, I promise,
I dare, to meet the horsemen of Aeneas,
I dare, alone, to face the Etruscan riders.
Let me try, first, the dangers of the battle;
You stay on guard as captain of the walls."
And Turnus, gazing at the warrior-maiden,
Replied:—"O glory of Italy, no words
Of mine can give you worthy thanks; your spirit   570
Surpasses all the rest of them. Share with me
The work we have to do. Faithless Aeneas,
So rumor says, and scouts confirm, is sending
His cavalry, light-armed, to scour the plains,
And he himself, crossing the mountain-ridges,
Comes down upon the city. I am planning
An ambush for him, where the forest narrows
To shadowy trails; I block both sides of the pass
With soldiery in arms. Do you, Camilla,
Take on the Etruscan horsemen, act as leader;   580
Messapus, a sharp fighter, will be with you,
And Latin squadrons and the troop from Tibur."
Messapus and the other captains listened

---

[23] Greaves were armor for the shins. A baldric was a sword belt suspended across the chest.
[24] Neighs.
[25] Camilla was introduced in the catalogue, VII.818–32.

To orders much like these, and they were heartened,
And Turnus left them, moving toward Aeneas.
   There is a valley, winding, curving, fit
For stratagems of warfare, a narrow gorge
Black with dense woods on either side; a trail
Winds through it, narrow and difficult: above it
590   There lies an unknown plain, a safe position
Whether you charge from right or left, or stand there
Heaving great boulders down the mountain-shoulders,
And Turnus knows this region well, finds cover,
Picks the terrain to suit him, waits and watches
In the dark menace of the woods.
                            And meantime,
High in the halls of heaven, Latona's daughter[26]
Was talking to a nymph of hers, a maiden
Of her devoted company, named Opis.
Diana's words were sorrowful:—"Camilla
600   Is going forth to cruel war, O maiden,
Our soldier, all in vain, and dearer to me
Than all the other girls; she has loved me long;
It is no impulsive whim that moves her spirit.
Perhaps you know the story—how her father,
Metabus, ruler of an ancient city,
Became a tyrant, and his people drove him
In hatred from Privernum,[27] and he fled
Through war and battles, taking as companion
To share his exile the little infant daughter,
610   Camilla, she was called, after her mother
Whose name was not so different, Casmilla.
So he was going on, toward ridge and woodland,
Long roads to loneliness, holding his daughter
Before him on his breast, and weapons flying
From every side against them, and the Volscians
Spreading the net of soldiers wide to catch them.
But Metabus went on, and came to a river
Out of its banks, the swollen Amasenus

[26] Latona was mother of Apollo and of Diana, the virgin goddess of
the hunt and the forest.
[27] This city, and the nearby river Amasenus (line 618), were in southern
Latium, about forty miles down the coast from Rome.

Foaming in flood from cloudburst. Could he swim it?
He thought so, but he checked himself; he feared   620
For the dear load he carried. He did some thinking,
And suddenly, or not quite all of a sudden,
He saw the only way. There was the spear
His stout hand bore: it was strong and heavy, knotted
Of seasoned oak, and he bound his daughter to it,
Gently, with bark of cork-wood all around her,
And carefully, to keep the missile's balance,
And let his right hand weigh its heft a little,
And then made prayer:—'O gracious woodland-dweller,
Diana, virgin daughter of Latona,   630
I consecrate my daughter to your service.
These are your darts she holds, the very first ones
She ever carried; she comes to you, a suppliant
Who flees her foe through pathways of the air.
Accept her, O dear goddess, I implore you,
Make her your own. Her father, I commit her,
Now, to the dubious winds.' The arm drew back,
The whirring spear shot forward, and the waters
Roared loud below, and over the rush of the river
Camilla, on the whistling spear, went flying,   640
And Metabus, as the great host came closer,
Dove into the flood, and safe across, a victor
And happy, pulled the spear and girl together
Out of the grassy turf, his votive offering
Made to Latona's daughter. No city ever
Received him to its walls or homes; he would not,
In his wild mood, give in to any city.
He lived with shepherds on the lonely mountains,
And there, where wild beasts lurked, in thorn and thicket
He raised his child; his hands would squeeze the udders   650
Of wild mares for their milk. When she could stand
And toddle a little, he armed her with a javelin,
A tiny pointed lance, and over her shoulder
Hung quiver and bow. There were no golden brooches
To bind her hair, no trailing gowns: her dress
Was black and orange tiger-skin. Her hand
Grew used to tossing childish darts, or whirling
The limber sling around her head; she learned

To hit her targets, crane or snowy swan.
660   And as she grew, many a Tuscan mother
Wanted her for this son, or that, but vainly:
Diana was her goddess, and she cherished,
Intact, an everlasting love—her weapons,
Her maidenhood, were all she knew and cared for.
I wish she had never been so possessed, so ardent
For soldiery like this, attacking Trojans
Instead of meeker game; she would have been
The one most dear of all my dear companions.
But now a bitter doom weighs down upon her.
670   Therefore, O nymph, glide down from heaven to Latium,
Where, under evil omens, men join battle.
Take these, my bow, my arrows; from my quiver
Draw the avenging shaft. His life is forfeit,
Trojan, Italian, whoever he is, whose wound
Profanes the sacred body of Camilla.
And when she has fallen, I will bring her home
By hollow cloud, both warrior and armor
Unspoiled, untaken, to her native country,
Home to her tomb, poor girl." And swift through air
690   Opis, on whirring wing, came down from heaven
In the dark whirlwind's center.
                                    And the Trojans
Were drawing near the walls, with Tuscan leaders
And all that host of cavalry, whose numbers
Filled squadron after squadron, and the horses
Snorted and reared and fought the bit and bridle,
Light-stepping sideways; far and wide the field
Bristled with iron harvest, and the plain
Burned with the arms raised high. And here against them
Come Messapus and Coras and his brother,
690   The Latins, moving fast, Camilla's squadron,
The hands drawn back already, and lances flying:
All fire and noise and heat and men and horses.
They ride, keep riding, and the distance closes
To spear-cast, and they halt, and a wild clamor
Breaks out, the charge is on, they spur the horses
Which need no spur, and from all sides they shower

The darts as thick as driving snow, the shadow
Darkens the sky. Tyrrhenus, wild Aconteus,[28]
Single each other out and come together
Head on, and the spears are broken, and men are thrown,   700
And the horses, smashing their great chests together,
Come down with a crash; Aconteus is hurled
Like a thunderbolt or something from an engine
Incredibly far off, and dies in the air.
And the lines waver, and the routed Latins
Let fall their shields behind them, head for the city,
With Trojans in pursuit: Asilas leads them.[29]
They near the walls, and the Latins turn, and, shouting,
Wheel to the charge, and the Trojans break and scatter
With reins let loose. You are looking at the ocean,   710
The way it comes, one wave, and then another,
Surging, receding, flooding, rushing shoreward
Over the cliffs in spray and foam or smoothing
The farthest sand with the shallow curve, withdrawing
Faster and faster, and undertow, slowly, slowly
Dragging the shingle back, and the surface gliding
Sleek from the visible beaches. Twice the Tuscans
Drove the Rutulians routed to the city;
Twice, driven back themselves, they slung behind them
The shields, reversed, quick-glancing over their shoulders.   720
But when, for the third time, they came together,
They stayed together, locked, all down the line,
And each man picked his man, and each man stayed there,
And the rough fight rose and thickened. Dying men
Groaned, and the blood was deep, and men and armor
And wounded horses and wounded men and bodies
Of men and horses were in it all together.
Orsilochus found Remulus a warrior
Too tough to take head on,[30] and flung his spear
At the head of the horse, instead, and left the iron   730

---

[28] Tyrrhenus is an Etruscan fighting for the Trojans; Aconteus is an Italian.

[29] The priest Asilas, from Pisa, was introduced in the catalogue of the Trojans' allies, X.212–15.

[30] Orsilochus is a Trojan, Remulus an Italian.

Under the ear, and the great beast, wounded, rearing,
Flailed the air with his forelegs, came down crashing,
And the stunned rider, thrown, rolled over and over.
Catillus killed Iollas, and another,
Herminius, giant in body, giant in arms,
Giant in spirit, a man who fought bare-headed,
Bare-shouldered, a fair-haired man, so huge in stature
He feared no wound. But through his shoulders driven
The quivering spear made way and bent him double,
740   Writhing in pain. Dark blood flows everywhere,
The sword deals death; men look to wounds for glory.
     In the thick of the fight Camilla rages, wearing
Her quiver like an Amazon, one breast
Exposed:[31] she showers javelins, she plies
The battle-axe; she never tires; her shoulder
Clangs with the golden bow, Diana's weapon.
If ever, turning back, she yields, the arrows
Are loosed from over her shoulder; even in flight
She makes attack. Around her, chosen comrades,
750   Larina, Tulla, and Tarpeia brandish
Axes of bronze. She chose them as her handmaids,
Good both in peace and war, Italian daughters,
Italy's pride, like Thracian[32] Amazons
Warring in colorful armor in the country
Where Thermodon river runs,[33] and women warriors
Hail fighting queens with battle-cries or clash
The crescent shields together.
                              First and last,
Camilla struck men down: who knows how many
She brought to earth in death? Clytius' son,
760   Euneus, faced her first, and her long spear
Pierced his unguarded breast. Rivers of blood
Poured from his mouth; he chewed red dust, and dying
Writhed on his wound. She stabbed the horse of Liris,
And the rider fell, and reached for the reins: Pagasus
Stretched out a hand to help him, to break his fall,

[31] The Amazons were women warriors from Pontus, a region of Asia
Minor south of the Black Sea. They fought for Troy in the Trojan war.
[32] Here the word means, simply, "northern."
[33] The river Thermodon was in Pontus, near the Black Sea.

And Camilla slew the pair of them together:
Amastrus next, Hippotas' son: far off,
Her spear caught up with four, Tereus, Chromis,
Harpalycus, Demophoön. For each dart
Sent flying from her hand, a Trojan fell.   770
Far off she saw the huntsman Ornytus,
Riding a native pony, in strange armor.
He wore a steer's hide over his wide shoulders,
A wolf's head for a helmet, with the jaws,
Wide-open, grinning above his head; he carried
A rustic kind of pike, and he was taller,
By a full head, than all the others, easy
Target for any dart. She cried above him:—
"What did you think, O Tuscan?—You were chasing
Beasts in the woods? The day has come when boasting   780
Like yours is answered by a woman's weapons,
But after all, you take to the shades of your fathers
No little cause for pride—Camilla killed you!"
And then she slew Orsilochus and Butes,
Two of the mightiest Trojans, stabbing Butes
With spear-point in the back, between the helmet
And breastplate, where the flesh shone white, and shield
Hung down from the left arm. Orsilochus
She fled from first, and, driven in a circle,
Became, in turn, pursuer; and, rising higher,   790
Brought down the battle-axe, again, again,
Through armor and through bone: his pleas for mercy
Availed him nothing; the wound he suffered spattered
His face with his warm brains. Next in her way
And stunned to halt by abject terror came
A son of Aunus, an expert at lying
Like all Ligurians.[34] He could not escape her,
And knew he could not, but he might outwit her,
Or so he hoped. "What's so courageous, woman,
Always on horseback? Forget the hope of fleeing,   800
Dismount; meet me on equal terms; try fighting
On foot for once. You will learn, I tell you, something,

[34] Liguria was the coastal region around modern Genoa, near what is
now the French border.

The disillusion of that windy glory."
She took the challenge, burned with angry temper,
Turned her horse over to another, savage
In equal arms, confronting him undaunted,
With naked sword. He leaped into the saddle,
Much pleased with his sly stratagem, drove the rowels
Deep in the flanks, took off. "O vain Ligurian,
810   Swollen with pride of heart, that slippery cunning
Will never get you home to father Aunus!"
So cried Camilla, and flashed like fire across
The horse's path, grabbed at the bridle, hauled him
To earth and shed his blood. A hawk in heaven
Is not more quick to seize a dove when, driving
From the dark rock toward lofty cloud, he fastens
The talons deep, and rips, and the feathers flutter,
All blood-stained, down the sky.
                                            On high Olympus
Jupiter watched the scene of battle, rousing
820   Tarchon the Etruscan with the spur of anger,[35]
And through the slaughter and the yielding columns
That warrior rode, calling each man by name,
Driving his ranks to battle with fierce outcry,
Rallying beaten men to fight:—"What terror,
O Tuscans, causes you such utter panic?
Will nothing ever hurt you? Does a woman
Chase you all over the field in this confusion?
Why do we carry swords? What silly weapons
Are these in our right hands? You are swift enough
830   For wrestling in the night time, or for dances
When the curved flute of Bacchus does the piping!
You have, it seems, one pleasure and one passion,
Waiting for feasts and goblets on full tables
When priests announce the sacrifice propitious
And the fat victim calls to the deep woodlands."[36]

---

[35] Tarchon was the leader of the Etruscan people that had expelled
Mezentius; along with Tarchon, they have since put themselves under
Aeneas' leadership.

[36] Bacchus was the god of wine, worshipped in orgiastic rites. Worshippers could not feast on a sacrificed animal until the priest examined it
and declared the sacrifice propitious, or favored by the gods.

So Tarchon had his say, and spurred his charger,
Himself not loath to die, fell like a whirlwind
On Venulus,[37] and swept him from the saddle,
And lifted him with his right hand, and held him
Before him as he rode, and all the Latins   840
Cheered with a noisy din that reached the heaven.[38]
The arms and man in front of him, over the plain
Rode Tarchon, swift as fire; broke off the point
Of Venulus' spear, and sought a place unguarded
Where he might thrust a deadly wound; the other
Struggled against him, kept the hand from the throat,
Matched violence with violence. An eagle,
Soaring to heaven, carries off a serpent
In just that manner, in the grip of talons,
And the wounded reptile writhes the looping coils   850
And rears the scales erect and keeps on hissing,
While the curved beak strikes at the struggling victim,
So, from the battle-line of the Etruscans,
Tarchon swept off his struggling prey in triumph,
An inspiration to his rallied people.
    Then Arruns, as the fates would have it, started
Stalking the fleet Camilla with the javelin,
Ahead of her in cunning. He took no chances,
Seeking the easiest way. When that wild maiden
Dashed fiercely into the battle, there he followed   860
Stealthily in her footsteps, or turned the reins
When she came back victorious. This way, that way,
Wary in each approach, he circled after,
The sure spear quivering as he poised and held it.
It happened Chloreus, Cybele's[39] priest, was shining
Far off in Phrygian armor, spurring a horse
Covered with leather, scales of brass and gold,
And the rider was a fire of foreign color,

[37] Venulus had headed the delegation to Diomedes described earlier
(lines 251–335).

[38] Other translators (supported by the Latin text) render this as, "A
great shout went up, and the Latins turned their eyes to watch," or words
to that effect. Humphries' rendering seems to be a slip of the pen; the
Latins have no reason to cheer Tarchon's feat.

[39] The "mother of the gods," a deity closely associated with Troy and
mentioned several times earlier in the poem.

Launching his Cretan darts: the bow was golden,
870   The helmet golden, and the cloak of saffron,
So stiff it had a metal sound, was fastened
With knots of yellow gold; some foreign needle
Had worked embroidery into hose and tunic.
Camilla picked him out from all the battle,
Either to take that spoil home to the temple,
Or flaunt the gold herself; she was a huntress
In blind pursuit, dazzled by spoil, a woman
Reckless for finery. In hiding, Arruns
Caught up his spear and prayed:—"Most high Apollo,
880   Soracte's warden, whose adorers feed
The pine-wood fire, and trustful tread the embers,[40]
Let me wipe out this shame. I seek no plunder,
No spoil, no trophy, of Camilla beaten;
I may perhaps find other ways to glory.
All I ask here is that this scourge may vanish
Under a wound I give; for this I am willing
To make return, however inglorious, home."
Half of his prayer was heard: Apollo granted
The downfall of Camilla; the returning
890   Safe home was not to be,—the south winds carried
That much to empty air. So the spear, whirring,
Spun from his hand; the sound turned all the Volscians
With anxious eyes and minds to watch their ruler.
She heard no stir in the air, no sound, no weapon
Along the sky, till the spear went to its lodging
In the bare breast and drank the maiden blood.
Her frightened comrades hurry, catch her falling,
And Arruns, frightened more than any other,
Half joy, half fear, makes off: no further daring
900   Is his, to trust the lance or face encounter.
As a wolf that kills a bullock or a shepherd
Before the darts can reach him, down the mountains
Goes plunging through the brush, the sign of guilt
His tail clapped under the belly, bent on flight,

---

[40] Soracte was a mountain just north of Rome. Offerings were made there to Apollo, by worshippers who walked through the embers of a pine-wood fire.

So Arruns sneaks to cover through the armies.
Dying, she pulls at the dart, but the point is fast,
Deep in the wound between the ribs; her eyes
Roll, cold in death; her color pales; her breath
Comes hard. She calls to Acca, her companion,
Most loved, most loyal:—"I have managed, Acca,   910
This far, but now—the bitter wound—I am done for,
There are shadows all around. Hurry to Turnus.
Take him this last direction, to relieve me
Here in the fight, defend the town, keep off—
Farewell!" The reins went slack, the earth received her
Yielding her body to its cold, resigning
The sagging head to death; and she let fall,
For the last time, her weapons, and the spirit
Went with a moan indignant to the shadows.[41]
And then indeed the golden stars were smitten   920
By a wild outcry; with Camilla fallen,
The fight takes on new fierceness: all the Trojans
Rush in, Etruscan leaders, all the squadrons
That came, once, from Evander.
                              High in the mountains
Opis, Diana's sentinel, unfrightened,
Had watched the battle, and seen, through all that fury,
Camilla slain in pitiful death. She sighed
And spoke with deep emotion:—"Cruel, cruel,
The punishment you pay, poor warrior-maiden,
For that attempt to battle down the Trojans!   930
It comes to nothing, all the lonely service
In woodland thicket, the worship of Diana,
The wearing of our arrows on the shoulder.
And even so, in the last hour of dying,
Your queen has not forsaken you, nor left you
Unhonored altogether; through the nations
This will be known, your death, and with it, surely,
The satisfaction of vengeance. He whose wound
Profaned your body will die as he deserves to."
Under the lofty mountain stood the tomb   940

[41] The words *the spirit . . . shadows* are repeated as the last words of
Book XII, concluding the poem.

Of an old king, Dercennus of Laurentum,
A mound of earth under a holm-oak's shadow.
Here first the lovely goddess, sweeping down
From heaven, paused, and from that height watched Arruns,
And saw him puffed with pride, exulting vainly,
And called:—"Why go so far away? Come nearer!
Come to the death you merit; for Camilla
Receive the due reward. Shall you die also
Under Diana's weapons?"[42] She drew an arrow
950   Swift from the quiver of gold, drew back the bow
Till the curved ends were meeting, and her hands
Were even, left at arrow-tip and right
Brushing her breast as she let loose the bow-string.
And as he heard the twang and the air whirring,
He felt the steel strike home. Gasping and moaning,
He lay there in the unknown dust; his comrades
Forgot, and left him where he lay, and Opis
Soared upward to Olympus.
                                        Camilla's squadron
Was first to flee, their leader lost; Atinas,[43]
960   Keen though he was, sped off; in reel and rout
Rutulians followed; captains and troops uncaptained,
Shattered and broken, turned and wheeled their horses
On a gallop toward the walls. No one can halt
The Trojans now, nor stand against the havoc;
They carry unstrung bows on nerveless shoulders,
And the horses drum in the rush in the dust of the plain.
A cloud of dust, black murk, rolls toward the walls,
And from the watch-towers mothers wail to heaven,
Beating their breasts, screaming in lamentation.
970   The first ones stumble through the gates; upon them
The enemy presses hard, and friend and foe
Are all confused together. Men are dying,
Gasping away their lives on their own threshold,
In sight of home and shelter, unprotected
Within their native walls. Some close the gates,
Dare not admit their wretched comrades, pleading,

---

[42] Opis means that Arruns is too contemptible to be really worth killing
with the goddess's arrows.
[43] A Latin warrior, not previously mentioned.

Nor take them to the town. And slaughter follows,
Most pitiful: the sword that guards the portals
Kills citizens who try to rush in blindly.
Their parents, weeping, see them shut from the city,   980
And some, who are driven back, go rolling headlong
Into the trenches, and others, dashing wildly
With loosened rein, crash into gates and portals
Locked tight against them. Along the walls the mothers
Try to be fighters (love of country taught them)
And, as they saw Camilla do, fling weapons
With trembling hands, or grasp at stakes or oak-poles
To do the work that steel should do, poor creatures,
Eager to die, before the walls, in the vanguard.
    Meanwhile, to Turnus in his forest ambush   990
The terrible news is borne: Acca reports it,
The Volscian ranks destroyed, Camilla fallen,
The enemy, deadly, massing thick, and sweeping
All things before them in triumphant warfare,
Fear at the very walls. And Turnus, raging—
(As Jupiter's relentless will commanded)
Forsook the ambush in the hills, abandoned
The rugged woodland, and scarcely had he done so,
Passing from sight to valley, when Aeneas
Entered the pass in safety, crossed the mountain,   1000
Came out of the dark woods. And both were striving
To reach the city, swiftly, in full column
And almost side by side: in a single moment
Aeneas saw the plain and the dust rising
And Turnus saw Aeneas, fierce for battle,
And heard the stamp and snorting of the horses.
There was almost time for fighting, but the Sun-god,
Colored in crimson, brought his weary horses
To bathe in the Western ocean; day was over,
Night coming on. They camped before the city.   ▣   1010

BOOK XII

◻

The
Final Combat

As Turnus saw the Latins failing, broken,
With Mars against them, and all eyes upon him
Awaiting the fulfillment of his promise,[1]
He burned with wrath, implacable, and lifted
His spirit high, as in the fields of Carthage
A lion, sorely wounded by the hunters,
Fights harder for the hurt, the happier for it,
And the mane rises on the neck and shoulders,
And the jaws break off the weapon, and the bloody mouth
Roars out defiance, even so in Turnus   10
The violent spirit raged. He spoke to the king
In angry words:—"Turnus won't keep them waiting;
No reason for these cowards to renounce
Their bargain. Start the holy ritual, father,
Arrange the terms. I go to meet the Trojan;
Let the Latins sit and watch it if they want to,
And this right arm will send him down to Hell,
The renegade from Asia. I alone
Answer the argument that calls us cowards,
I, with one single sword. Or we are beaten   20

---

[1] Turnus had emphatically declared his willingness to engage in single combat with Aeneas; see XI.486–97.

293

And he takes Lavinia home."
                                Latinus answered
With quiet in his heart:—"O youth, distinguished
Above them all in spirit, the more your courage
Rises to fierceness, the more I find it needful
To take slow counsel, to balance every hazard.
You have the kingdom of your father Daunus,
And many a captured town; and I, Latinus,
Lack neither gold nor spirit. In our country
There are other girls, unwed, and not ignoble.
30   Let me say this—I know it is not easy—
As frankly as I can, and listen to me:
It was not right for me to give my daughter
To any of her former native suitors,
And gods and men so prophesied. I loved you,
Turnus, and I gave in: we are related
By blood, I know, and when Amata sorrowed,
I broke off every bond, cancelled the promise,
Took up unholy arms.[2] From that day, Turnus,
You see what wars pursue me, and what dangers,
40   What sufferings you, above all men, submit to.
We have been beaten twice in a great battle,
And now we hold, just barely, in our city
The hopes of Italy. The streams of Tiber
Are warm with blood of ours, and the broad fields
White with our bones. In what direction
Do I keep turning, back and forth? What madness
Changes my purpose? If, with Turnus dead,
I stand prepared to join them to me as allies,
Why not, while he still lives, break off the conflict?
50   What will they say, all your Rutulian kinsmen,
All Italy, if I (may fortune keep
The word I say from coming true!) betray you
To death, the suitor of my only daughter?
Consider war's uncertainties, and pity

---

[2] An oracle had insisted that Latinus' daughter, Lavinia, must not marry
one of her own Latin people; see VII.48–99. Turnus was not only a Latin
but the nephew of Latinus' queen, Amata. He did wrong, he tells Turnus,
to go against the oracle by withdrawing the pledge given to Aeneas that
Lavinia should marry him.

Your aged father, far from us and grieving
In Ardea, his homeland." The king's appeal
Moved Turnus not at all; his temper worsened,
Was aggravated by the attempt at healing.
He managed, with an effort, to say something:—
"Most kindly father, the care you have for me   60
Lay down, for my sake; let me have permission
To trade death for renown. I too, dear father,
Toss no mean dart, swing no mean sword, and blood
Follows the wounds I give. His goddess-mother
Will not be there, this time, to hide him, running
To the folds of her gown and cloud and empty shadows."[3]
    But Queen Amata, sick and almost dying
From fear of the new battle-chance, was weeping;
He was the son she wanted; she would not let him
Risk that heroic life, and, clinging to him,   70
She made her plea:—"Turnus, our only hope,
Our only comfort in our sad old age,
The pride and honor of Latinus' kingdom
Rest in your keeping, and our sinking house
Depends on you to shore it up from ruin.
If tears of mine can move you, if my daughter
Merits the least devotion, I implore you,
I beg one favor: do not fight the Trojan!
Whatever danger waits you in that duel
Awaits me also, Turnus; I shall leave   80
The hateful light when you do, I shall never
Be such a captive as to see Aeneas
Come to my home as son-in-law." Lavinia
Listened and wept and blushed, her maiden features
Suffused with color, as the stain of crimson
Adds hue to Indian ivory, or lilies
Lose something of their whiteness, mixed with roses.
And Turnus, troubled enough, was troubled further
Watching the girl, and burned the more for battle,
And spoke, however briefly, to Amata:—   90

---

[3] The sneer refers, once more, to the incident, related in Homer's *Iliad*,
Book V, in which Aeneas while fighting at Troy was saved from Diomede
by his mother Venus.

"Do not, O mother, follow me with tears
Or any such omen as I go to battle.
Turnus can not delay his death." He turned
To Idmon, then, and told him:—"Be my herald:
Deliver to that Phrygian usurper[4]
These words from me—I know that he will hate them—
When dawn to-morrow, riding in the heaven
In crimson chariot, glows and reddens, let him
Hold back his Trojans, let their weapons and ours
Have rest, let us end the war, two of us only;
There let Lavinia be sought, her husband
The victor on that field!"
                          And he went home
To his own quarters, hurrying, demanding
His horses, given Pilumnus by Orithyia,
Whiter than snow, swifter than wind.[5] And he was happy
Looking at them, all spirit, as they nickered
Seeing their master. The drivers stood about them,
Grooming the manes, patting the chests. And Turnus
Fits to his shoulders the stiff coat of armor,
The gold, the bronze, and tests the readiness
Of sword and shield and the horns of the ruddy crest.[6]
Vulcan had made the sword for Daunus, metal
Glowing white-hot and plunged in Stygian water.
The spear stood leaning on a mighty pillar
In the great hall, a trophy won from Actor;[7]
He seized it, poised it, shook it, cried aloud:—
"Be with me now, good spear that never failed me!
The time has come. Let me lay low that body,
Let my tough hands rip off his coat of armor,

100

110

---

[4] Phrygia was the region that included Troy; *Phrygian* is still another sneer, directed at alleged Eastern decadence. Idmon does not appear elsewhere in the poem.

[5] Turnus was a descendant of the god Pilumnus. Orithyia was wife of Boreas, god of the north wind who, as such, was a symbol of swiftness.

[6] The horns were sockets holding the plumes that formed the crest of a helmet.

[7] Turnus has inherited the supernaturally tempered sword from his father Daunus and has taken the spear from Actor, a man not mentioned elsewhere in the poem. The Styx was a river in the Lower World.

Let me shove that eunuch's crimped and perfumed tresses   120
Deep in the dust!" So he was driven by fury,
Sparks leaping from his countenance, and fire
Flashing at every glance; he is like a bull
Bellowing before battle, charging tree-trunks
To get the anger into his horns, head lowered
As if to gore the winds, and pawing sand.
And in the other camp Aeneas, likewise,
Fierce in the arms his mother brought from Vulcan,
Sharpens his fighting spirit and rejoices
That the war's end is near through this agreement.   130
He comforts comrades, reassures Iulus,
Sad in his fear, tells them the fates, and orders
Definite answer brought to King Latinus
With proper terms of armistice.
                              And dawn
Had scarcely touched the mountain-tops with light
And the Sun-god's horses risen from the ocean,
When Trojans and Rutulians left the city
And came to the great plain, the field of combat,
Under the walls, and in the midst erected
The hearths and altars for their common gods.   140
Others, their temples bound with holy vervain,[8]
Veiled with the sacred robes, brought fire and water.
Through the full gates the Ausonian host came streaming,
And from the other side, Trojans, Etruscans,
Harnessed in steel, as if a battle called them,
With leaders flashing there, amid their thousands,
Brilliant in gold and purple, brave Asilas,
Mnestheus, Assaracus' high-souled descendant,
Messapus, tamer of horses, son of Neptune.[9]
Each, at a signal, found his post; the spears   150
Were fixed in the earth, and the shields rested on them.
Then came the mothers in their eagerness,
And the unarmed throng, and the weak old men, all crowding

[8] Sacred boughs.
[9] Assaracus, ancestor of Mnestheus, was a Trojan king and the great-grandfather of Aeneas. Asilas was one of the Etruscan leaders allied with the Trojans. Messapus was one of the Italian leaders allied with Turnus.

Towers and house-tops, or standing by the portals.
But Juno, from the summit now called Alban,[10]
Nameless in those days, lacking fame and glory,
Looked over the plain, the lines of Latin and Trojan,
The city of Latinus, and she turned,
A goddess to a goddess, to Juturna,
160   Sister of Turnus, guardian of still pools
And sounding rivers; Jupiter had given
This honor[11] to her, for the honor taken,
The lost virginity. Juno addressed her:—
"O glory of the rivers, dear Juturna,
You know you are the only one I have favored
Of all the Latin girls who have made their way
To great-souled Jove's ungrateful couch; I gave you,
Gladly, a place in Heaven; learn, Juturna,
A sorrow of yours; do not reproach me for it.
170   Where fortune seemed to grant it, and the Fates
Let things go well for Latium, I protected
Your brother and your city. Now I see him
Faced with unequal destiny. The day
Of doom and enemy violence draws near.
I cannot watch this battle and this treaty;
You, it may be, have in you greater daring,
Resourceful for your brother's sake. Go on;
That much is only decent. Happier fortunes
Will follow the unfortunate, if only—"
180   As she broke off, Juturna wept; her hand
Struck thrice, four times, her lovely breast. And Juno
Cried:—"This is not the time for tears, Juturna!
Hurry; and if there is some way to save him,
Snatch him from death; or stir up war, break off
The covenant: be daring—you are granted
Authority from Juno!" And she left her
Doubtful and suffering, with wounded spirit.
Meanwhile, the kings were riding forth, Latinus
Imposing in his four-horse car, his forehead
190   Gleaming with twelve gold rays of light, the symbol

---

[10] The mountain where, in the future, Aeneas' son Iulus was to found
the city of Alba Longa; see I.278–85.
[11] The honor of immortality as a water-nymph.

Of his ancestral Sun,[12] and Turnus coming
Behind a snow-white team, and Turnus' hand
Brandishing spears with two broad heads of steel.
And on this side, burning with starry shield
And arms from Heaven, came Aeneas, father
Of Rome to be, and from the camp Iulus,
The second hope of Roman greatness, followed.
In robes immaculate, the priest was waiting
Beside the blazing altars, swine and oxen
And sheep, unshorn, ready for sacrifice,   200
And the leaders faced the rising sun, and sprinkled
The salted meal, and marked the victims' foreheads
With knives that took the holy lock,[13] and poured
Libations on the altars, and Aeneas,
Drawing his sword, made prayer:—"Sun, be my witness,
And Earth be witness to me in my praying,
This Earth, for whom I have been able to bear
Such toil and suffering, Almighty Father,
Queen Juno, now, I pray, a kinder goddess,
Be witness, and Mars, renownèd god of battles,   210
Rivers and Fountains, too, I call, and Powers
Of lofty Heaven and deep blue ocean, witness:
If victory comes to Turnus, the Trojans, beaten,
Go to Evander's city, and Iulus
Will quit these lands forever, and hereafter
No son or follower of Aeneas ever
Will rise again in warfare, or with sword
Attack these kingdoms. But if Victory grants us,
As I expect, and may the gods confirm it,
To win the battle, I will not have Italians   220
Be subject to the Trojans; I crave no kingdom,
Not for myself: let both, unbeaten nations,
On equal terms enter eternal concord.
I will establish gods and ceremonial;
My sire, Latinus, keep his arms, his sceptre.
The Trojans will build walls for me; Lavinia

---

[12] Latinus was descended from Circe, whose father was the Sun. (The
family tree described in VII.42–47 is different, however.)
[13] The burning of a lock of hair was a gesture consecrating the victim
to the gods.

Shall give the city her name."
                                   And so Aeneas
Made solemn pledge, and after him Latinus,
Lifting his eyes to heaven, and outstretching
230   His right hand to the stars, confirmed the treaty:—
"By these same Powers I swear, Aeneas, by Earth,
Sea, Stars, Latona's offspring, two-faced Janus,
The power of the world below, and Pluto's altars;[14]
May the Almighty Father, who sanctions treaties
With lightning, hear my words: I touch the altars,
I call these fires and presences to witness:
No day shall break this peace, this pact, Italians,
However things befall; no force shall turn me
From this intention, not if the force of deluge
240   Confounded land and water, Heaven and Hell.
Even as this sceptre" (and he gestured with it)
"Shall never bloom with leaf in branch or shadow,
Once it has left its forest-trunk, its mother,
And lost to steel its foliage, a tree
No more, when once the artist's hand has edged it
With proper bronze, for Latin sires to carry."
So they affirmed the covenant, in sight
Of leaders and people, and duly, over the flame,
Made sacrifice of victims, and tore out
250   The entrails while the beasts yet lived, and loaded
The altars high with offerings.
                                   But more and more
Rutulian hearts were wavering; the fight
Began to seem unequal, and they stirred,
Shifted and doubted. And Turnus moved them strangely,
Coming on silent footstep to the altar,
Looking down humbly, with a meek devotion,
Cheeks drawn and pale. Juturna heard the whispers,
The muttered talk, and sensed the stir in the crowd,
And suddenly plunged into their midst, disguised

---

[14] Latona was the mother of Apollo and Diana, who represent here the
sun and moon. Janus, the double-faced god of gateways, was a symbol
of reciprocity. Pluto was the god of the Lower World.

As Camers, noble in birth and brave in arms, and son   260
Of a brave father.[15] She knew what she was doing,
Putting the fuel of rumor on the fire,
And crying:—"Are you not ashamed, Rutulians,
That one should be exposed for all this army?
In strength, in numbers, are we not their equal?
Here they all are, the Trojans, the Arcadians,
The Etruscans, all the lot of them: and we
Are almost twice as many; man to man,
Two against one! But no: we are willing to let him[16]
Rise to the skies on deathless praise; the gods   270
Receive him, by his own decision bound,
An offering at their altars, and we sit here
Sluggish as stone on ground, our country lost,
Ready to bow to any arrogant master."
They are moved; at least the young are, and a murmur
Runs through the ranks: the Latins and Laurentians
Are ripe for change. Rest from the war, and safety
Count less than arms. They want the treaty broken,
They pity Turnus. It's not fair, this bargain.
And now Juturna adds a greater warning,   280
A sign from heaven, and nothing could have stirred them
With more immediate impetus to folly.
For, flying through the sky, an eagle, orange
In the red light, was bearing down, pursuing
The birds along the shore, and they were noisy
In desperate flight, and the eagle struck, and the talons
Seized the conspicuous swan. And as the Italians
Looked up in fascination, all the birds,
Most wonderful to tell, wheeled, and their outcry
Clanged, and their wings were a dark cloud in heaven,   290
A cloud that drove their enemy before them,
Till, beaten down by force, by weight, the eagle
Faltered, let go the prey, which fell to the river
As the great bird flew far to the distant clouds.
This omen the Rutulians cheered with shouting,

[15] Camers was the wealthy king of Amyclae (on the Italian coast south
of Rome), the "city known for silence"; see X.634–36 and note.
[16] Turnus.

With hands that cry for action. And their augur,
Tolumnius,[17] roused them further:—"I have prayed
Often for this, and here it is! I own it,
I recognize the gods. With me as leader,
300   With me, I say, take arms, unhappy people,
Whom, like frail birds, the insolent marauder
Frightens in war, despoils your shores. He also
Will take to flight, far to the distant oceans.
Combine, come massing on, defend in battle
The king snatched from you!"[18]

                          He went rushing forward,
Let fly his spear: the whistling shaft of cornel
Sang its determined way through air, and with it
A mighty shout arose, formations broken,
Hearts hot for battle, as the spear went flying.
310   Nine handsome brothers, their mother a Tuscan woman,
Good wife to the Arcadian Gylippus,[19]
Stood in its path, and one of them, distinguished
In looks and gleaming armor, fell; the spear-point
Struck where the belt was buckled over the belly,
And went on through the ribs. The brothers, angry,
Grieving, drew swords, or picked up spears in frenzy,
Went blindly rushing in, and the Latin columns
Came charging at them; from their side the Trojans,
Men from Agylla,[20] brightly-armed Arcadians,
320   Poured in a rushing flood. One passion held them,—
Decide it with the sword! They strip the altars,
The sky is dark, it seems, with a storm of weapons,
The iron rain is a deluge. Bowls and hearth-fires
Are carried off; Latinus flees: the gods
Are beaten, the treaty ruined by corruption.

---

[17] The augur (prophet) Tolumnius had been praised by Turnus in XI.481–82 as a dependable ally.

[18] The "king" is Turnus, whom Tolumnius is comparing to the nearly-victimized "conspicuous swan" (line 287), Aeneas being the eagle, in the vision the people have just seen.

[19] Gylippus had migrated to Italy with king Evander, from Arcadia in Greece, and married an Italian (Tuscan) woman.

[20] Agylla was the city whose inhabitants had driven out the wicked king Mezentius and then allied themselves with the Trojans; see VIII.494 ff.

Other men rein their chariots, leap on horses,
Come with drawn swords.
                                Messapus, most eager
To break the truce, rides down a king, Aulestes,
Wearing the emblem of a Tuscan monarch.[21]
Staggering backward from that charge, and reeling,   330
He falls upon the altars, there behind him,
Comes down on head and shoulders. And like fire
Messapus flashes toward him, spear in hand,
And, from the horse, strikes heavily down; the spear
Is like a plunging beam. For all his pleading
Aulestes hears no more than this:—"He has it!
Here is a better victim for the altars!"
His limbs are warm as the Italians rob them.
Ebysus aims a blow at Corynaeus[22]
Who snatches up a firebrand from the altar   340
And thrusts it in his face, and his beard blazes
With a smell of fire. And Corynaeus follows,
Clutches the hair with the left hand, and grounds him
With knee-thrust; the relentless steel goes home.
And Podalirius, sword in hand, looms over
The shepherd Alsus,[23] rushing through the weapons
In the front line, but Alsus, arm drawn back,
Swings the axe forward, cleaving chin and forehead,
Drenching the armor with blood. An iron slumber
Seals Podalirius' eyes; they close forever   350
In everlasting night.
                                But good Aeneas,
Head bare, holds out his hand, unarmed, calls loudly
In hope to check his men:—"Where are you rushing?
What sudden brawl is rising? Control your anger!
The treaty is made, and all the terms agreed on,
The fight my right alone. Let me take over;
Lay down your fear: this hand will prove the treaty,
Making it sure. These rites owe Turnus to me."

[21] Aulestes was introduced in the catalogue of the Trojans' allies from Etruria, X.242–49.
[22] Ebysus was an Italian, Corynaeus a Trojan.
[23] Alsus was an Italian, Podalirius a Trojan.

And even as he cried, an arrow flew
360 Winging against him; no one knew the hand
That turned it loose with whirlwind force; if man
Or god, nobody knew; and no man boasted
Of having been the one to wound Aeneas.
    And Turnus saw him leave the field, and captains
And ranks confused, and burned with sudden spirit.
He is hopeful now; he calls for arms, for horses,
Leaps proudly into his chariot, plies the reins,
Drives fiercely, gives to death many brave heroes,
Rolls many, half alive, under the wheels,
370 Crushes the columns under his car, and showers
Spear after spear at men who try to flee him.
Even as Mars, along the icy Hebrus,[24]
In blood-red fury thunders with his shield
And rousing war gives rein to his wild horses
Faster than winds over the open plain
As Thrace groans under their gallop, and around him
Black Terror's forms are driven, and Rage, and Ambush,
Attendants on the god,—with equal frenzy
So Turnus rages through the midst of battle,
380 Lashing the steeds that steam with sweat, and killing
And riding down the slain; the swift hooves spatter
A bloody dew and the sand they pound is bloody.
He has given Sthenelus to death, and Pholus,
And Thamyrus, by spear or sword, close in,
Far off, no matter; Glaucus also, Lades,
Imbrasus' sons, from Lycia, where their father
Reared them and gave them either kind of armor,
For fighting hand to hand, on foot, or mounted
On chargers swift as wind.
                                        Elsewhere Eumedes
390 Comes riding to the battle, son of Dolon,
Named after Dolon's father, and in daring
True son of Dolon, who claimed Achilles' chariot
For spying on the Grecian camp, and went there
And Diomedes paid him for his daring

---

[24] The Hebrus was a river in Thrace (the region north of the Aegean
Sea), which was noted as warlike and therefore especially devoted to the
war-god Mars.

With somewhat different tokens, so that Dolon
No longer craved the horses of Achilles.[25]
And Turnus saw that son of his, Eumedes,
Far on the open plain, and overtook him
With the light javelin, through long emptiness,[26]
And stopped his horses, and leaped down, and landed   400
On a man fallen, half-alive, and stood there,
Foot on Eumedes' neck, twisted the sword
From Eumedes' right hand, and changed its silver
To red, deep in Eumedes' throat, and told him:—
"Lie down there, Trojan; measure off the acres
You sought in war! Any who dare attack me
Are paid rewards like these; they build their walls
On such foundations!" He flung the spear and brought him
Companions in his death, Asbytes, Chloreus,
Thersilochus and Sybaris and Dares   410
And finally Thymoetes, slain on horseback.[27]
As the north wind roars over the deep Aegean
Piling the combers[28] shoreward, and in heaven
Clouds flee the blast of the gale, so, before Turnus,
The columns yield, the lines give way, and his onrush
Bears him along, and the wind of his going tosses
The nodding plume. And Phegeus tried to stop him,[29]
Flinging himself before the car, and grabbing,
With his right hand, the bridle, twisting, wrenching
The foaming jaws, and while he rode the yoke   420
The spear-point found his side uncovered, piercing
The mail with grazing wound, but Phegeus managed
To keep the shield before him and for safety

[25] During the war at Troy, a Trojan named Dolon hoped, presumptuously, to gain Achilles' chariot and immortal horses for his efforts in spying on the Greeks, but he was discovered and killed by Diomedes; see Homer, *Iliad*, Book X.

[26] That is, from long distance.

[27] Chloreus was the warrior-priest whose ornate trappings had fatally attracted Camilla (XI.865–78); Dares was the battered boxer in the funeral games (V.363–468); Thymoetes was mentioned briefly in the siege episode (X.156).

[28] Breaking ocean-waves.

[29] Turnus had killed another man named Phegeus inside the Trojan camp; see IX.785.

Tried to keep coming forward—the drawn sword
Would be the best protection, but the axle
Caught him, the wheels went over him, and Turnus
Swept by and the scythe of Turnus' sword cut through him
Between the shield and helmet, and the body
Lay headless on the sand.
                        While Turnus, winning,
430   Slaughtered across the field of war, Achates,
With Mnestheus at his side, and young Iulus,
Brought back Aeneas to camp, bleeding and limping,
Using the spear as crutch, struggling, in anger,
To pull the barb from the wound; the shaft had broken.
The thing to do, he tells them over and over,
The quickest way would be to cut around it,
Let the sword do the probing, find the spear-point
No matter how deep it tries to hide, expose it,
Get it out of there, and send him back to battle.
440   And Iapyx came to help, the son of Iasus,
Dearest beyond all others to Apollo,
Who once had offered him his arts, his powers,
His augury, his lyre, the lore of arrows,
But Iapyx made another choice; his father,
It seemed, was dying, and he chose to save him
Through what Apollo had the power to offer,
Knowledge of simples and the arts of healing,
And so he chose the silent craft, inglorious.[30]
So there was Iapyx, trying to be helpful,
450   Aeneas, leaning on his spear, and cursing,
Indifferent to Iulus' tears, and others
Standing around, and anxious. The old doctor
Tucked up his robe, compounded potent herbs,
Applied them, fussed around, all to no purpose;
Tried to extract the dart by hand, and then by forceps,—
No luck at all: Apollo does not guide him,
And more and more across the plains the horror
Thickens, and evil nears. They see the sky

[30] Iapyx chose skill in medicine over other things Apollo was god of: prophecy, music, and bowmanship. *Simples* (line 447) is an archaic pharmaceutical term meaning medicines or medicinal plants.

Standing on dust; horsemen come on, and arrows
Are falling thick, and a mournful din arises   460
As fighting men go down, with Mars relentless.
    Then Venus, shaken with a mother's anguish
Over a suffering son, from Cretan Ida[31]
Plucked dittany, a plant with downy leaves
And crimson blossom: the wild goats know and use it
As cure for arrow-wounds. This herb the goddess
Brought down, her presence veiled in cloud, and
      steeped it
With secret healing in the river-water
Poured in the shining caldrons, and she added
Ambrosia's healing juice, and panacea,[32]   470
And agèd Iapyx washed the wound, unknowing
The virtues of that balm, and all the pain
Suddenly, and by magic, left the body;
The blood was staunched, deep in the wound; the arrow
Dropped from the flesh, at the least touch; the hero
Felt all his strength return. "Quick! Bring his weapons!"
Iapyx cries out, the first to fire their spirit
Against the foe, "Why are you standing there,
What are you waiting for? These things have happened
By more than mortal aid or master talent,   480
It is not my hand, Aeneas, that has saved you,
Some greater god is working here, to send you
To greater deeds." Aeneas, eager for battle,
Had the gold shin-guards on while he was talking,
Makes the spear flash, impatient, gets the armor
Buckled about the body, and the sword
Ready at the left side, and through the helmet
Stoops down to kiss Iulus:—"Learn, my son,
What I can show you, valor and real labor:
Learn about luck from others. Now my hand   490
Will be your shield in war, your guide to glory,
To great rewards. When you are grown, remember;

[31] There was a famous Mount Ida in Crete and another Mount Ida near
Troy.

[32] Ambrosia was the food of the gods; here the word refers to an ointment
or plant having supernatural powers. *Panacea,* probably another plant,
means "universal cure."

You will have models for your inspiration,
Your father Aeneas and your uncle Hector."[33]
   So from the gates he rushed, a mighty warrior
Wielding a mighty spear, and all the column
Came pouring forth; Mnestheus, Antheus, others,
Leave the forsaken camp. The dust is blinding
Over the plain, the tramp of armies marching
500   Makes the earth tremble, and from the opposite hillside
Turnus and the Ausonians saw them coming
And a cold chill ran through their bones; Juturna,
Quicker than all the Latins, heard the sound,
Knew it, and fled in terror. And Aeneas
Rushed his dark column over open country
As a cloud-burst sweeps to land across the ocean
And farmers know it, far away, and shudder
Fearful and sure of ruin to woods and cornfield,
And the winds fly on before the storm and herald
510   The roaring sound to the shore; so, like a cloud-burst,
Aeneas brings his armies on; they gather,
Each company, at his side. Thymbraeus' sword
Strikes down Osiris; Mnestheus slays Arcetius;
Achates Epulo, and Gyas Ufens.[34]
Tolumnius, that augur whose spear had broken
The armistice, lies low. A shout arises:
The Rutulians turn back in rout; the dust-clouds
Follow them over the field in flight. Aeneas
Disdains to kill retreating men, refuses
520   Attack on such as face him; it is Turnus
He watches for, hunts through the gloom of battle,
It is Turnus, Turnus only, whom he summons.
   And this Juturna knows, and in her panic
She flings Metiscus, charioteer of Turnus,
Out of the car, far from the reins and axle,
And takes his place, plying the supple reins,

---

[33] Hector, killed at Troy, was the greatest of the Trojan warriors. His
sister Creusa was Aeneas' Trojan wife.
[34] Gyas had commanded one of the racing ships in the funeral games,
V.114 ff.; Ufens was introduced in the catalogue of the Latins, VII.763–
67.

Calls with Metiscus' voice, assumes his armor.
As a dark swallow through a rich man's mansion
Flies winging through great halls, hunting for crumbs
For the young birds at home, and now chirps under   530
The empty courts, now over the quiet pool,
Even so, Juturna, by the horses carried,
Darts here and there, quarters the field,[35] and proudly
Makes a great show of Turnus, her cheering brother,
Yet never lets him close in fight or grapple,
Forever wheeling and turning. But Aeneas
Is dogged in pursuit and loud in challenge.
Whenever he sees that car, and runs to meet it,
Juturna shifts the course. What can he do?
Nothing, it seems, but boil in rage; one anger   540
Makes conflict in his heart against another.
Messapus comes against him; his left hand
Holds two tough lances, tipped with steel: advancing,
He levels one, well-aimed; Aeneas crouches
On one knee under the shield, but the spear, flying,
Picks off the crested plume from the top of the helmet.
Aeneas' anger swells; this treachery rankles.[36]
Messapus' chariot and steeds, withdrawing,
Are far away. He has made appeal to Jove
And the broken treaty's altars all too often,   550
And now he fights in earnest;[37] Mars beside him,
He rouses terrible carnage, giving anger
Free rein: he makes no choice of opposition.
     What singer or what god could tell the story
Of all these deaths? Both Turnus and Aeneas,
In turn, drive victims over all the plain.
Jupiter willed it so, that mighty nations,
Destined, in time, for everlasting friendship,
Should meet in that great struggle. A Rutulian,
Sucro, held off Aeneas for a little,   560

[35] Sweeps across in one direction and then in the other.
[36] To Aeneas it seems an act of treachery to be attacked by a warrior other than his chosen opponent, Turnus.
[37] Aeneas at last gives up the idea, embodied in the violated agreement, of settling matters through single combat with Turnus.

And died more quickly, with the sword-point driven
Through ribs' protecting framework. Turnus met
Amycus, and unsaddled him; his brother,
Diores, fought on foot,[38] and Turnus killed them,
The one by spear, the one by sword; his chariot
Bore off their severed heads, blood dripping from them.
Aeneas, in one charge, brought down three warriors,
Talos and Tanais and brave Cethegus,
And then one more, the sorrowful Onites,
570 Whose mother was Peridia; and Turnus
Killed brethren, Lycian born, and young Menoetes
Who hated war, in vain, and once loved fishing
In Lerna's rivers; his Arcadian dwelling
Had been a cottage, and his father planted
Land that he did not own.[39] Like fire through forest
When underbrush is dry, and laurel crackles,
Or like two mountain-torrents roaring seaward,
Each leaving devastation, so Aeneas
And Turnus swept the battle, anger surging,
580 Surging in those great hearts, swollen to bursting,
Not knowing how to yield, all strength devoted
To death and wounds.
                    There was a man, Murranus,
Whose pride of ancestry was loud and boastful,
Last of a line of Latin kings. Aeneas
Brought him to earth and laid him low; a stone,
A mighty whirling rock served as the weapon,
And under reins and under yoke the wheels
Rolled him along, and over him the horses
Trampled in earth the lord they had forgotten.
590 Hyllus rushed Turnus, and a javelin met him
Through the gold temple-band, and pierced the helmet
And lodged there, in the brain. A brave man, Cretheus,
Had no defense against the might of Turnus,
And no god saved Cupencus from Aeneas,

---

[38] This is presumably the same Diores who placed third in the foot-race during the funeral games; see V.281–357.
[39] The father was a tenant farmer. Lerna was a marshy lake near Arcadia, in Greece.

No shield of bronze delayed the speeding weapon.
Aeolus fell, stretched on the plains, a hero
Too powerful for all the Greek battalions,
Whom even Achilles, overthrower of Troy,
Could not bring down. He reached his goal of death
Here in Laurentum, a man whose home, Lyrnesus,   600
Lay at the foot of Ida, but his tomb
Was on Italian soil. So all the lines
Turned to the battle, Mnestheus, Serestus,
Messapus, tamer of horses, brave Asilas,
Etruscan columns and Evander's squadrons,
Latins and Trojans, all of them contending
With all their might, no rest, no pause, no slacking.
    And now his goddess-mother sent Aeneas
A change of purpose, to direct his column
More quickly toward the town, confuse the Latins   610
With sudden onslaught. He was tracking Turnus
Here, there, all up and down the columns, watching,
Shifting his gaze, and so he saw that city
Immune from that fierce warfare, calm and peaceful.
The vision of a greater fight comes to him:
He calls Sergestus,[40] Mnestheus, brave Serestus,
And takes position on a mound; the Trojans
Come massing toward him, shield and spear held ready.
And as he stands above them, he gives the orders:—
"Let there be no delay: great Jove is with us.   620
Let no man go more slackly, though this venture
Is new and unexpected. That city yonder,
The cause of war, the kingdom of Latinus,
Unless they own our mastery, acknowledge
Defeat, declare obedience, I will topple,
Level its smoking roof-tops to the ground.
Or should I wait until it suits prince Turnus
To face the duel with me, and, once beaten,
Consent to fight again? This[41] is the head,
O citizens, this the evil crown of warfare.   630

[40] Sergestus had commanded a ship in the race during the funeral games;
see V.114 ff.
[41] This city.

Hurry, bring firebrands, win from fire the treaty!"
His words inflame their zeal, and, all together,
They form a wedge; a great mass moves to the wall,
Ladders and sudden fire appear from nowhere;
The guards at the gate are butchered; steel is flying,
The sky is dark with arrows. Toward the city
Aeneas lifts his hand, rebukes Latinus,
Calling the gods to witness that his will
Was not for battle, it was forced upon him
640   By the Italians, double treaty-breakers,
His foes for now the second time.[42] The townsmen
Quarrel among themselves: "Open the town!"
Cry some, "Admit the Trojans!" and would drag
The king himself to the ramparts. Others hurry
With arms, man the defenses. When a shepherd
Trails bees to their hive in the cleft of a rock and fills it
With smarting smoke, there is fright and noise and fury
Within the waxen camp, and anger sharpened
With buzzing noises, and a black smell rises
650   With a blind sound, inside the rock, and rolling
Smoke lifts to empty air.
                    Now a new sorrow
Came to the weary Latins, shook the city
To its foundations, utterly. The queen
Had seen the Trojans coming and the walls
Under attack and fire along the gables
And no Rutulian column, nowhere Turnus
Coming to help. He had been killed, her hero,
She knew at last. Her mind was gone; she cried
Over and over:—"I am the guilty one,
660   I am the cause, the source of all these evils!"
And other wilder words. And then she tore
Her crimson robes, and slung a noose and fastened
The knot of an ugly death to the high rafter.
The women learned it first, and then Lavinia:
The wide hall rings with grief and lamentation;

[42] The Italians had first violated the treaty of alliance with the Trojans, including the plan for Aeneas to marry Lavinia (VII.263–85), then violated the single-combat treaty earlier in Book XII.

Nails scratch at lovely faces, beautiful hair
Is torn from the head. And Rumor spreads the story
All up and down the town, and poor Latinus,
Rending his garments, comes and stares,—wife gone,
And city falling, an old man's hoary hair   670
Greyer with bloody dust.
                         And meanwhile Turnus
Out on the plain pursues the stragglers, slower
And slower now, and less and less exultant
In his triumphant car. From the city comes
A wind that bears a cry confused with terror,
Half heard, but known,—confusion, darkness, sorrow,
An uproar in the town. He checks the horses,
Pauses and listens. And his sister prompts him:—
"This way, this way! The Trojans run, we follow
Where victory shows the path. Let others guard   680
The houses with their valor. The Italians
Fall in the fight before Aeneas. Let us
Send death to the Trojans, in our turn. You will not
Come off the worse, in numbers or in honor."
Turnus replies:—"O sister, I have known,
A long while since, that you were no Metiscus,
Since first you broke the treaty and joined the battle.
No use pretending you are not a goddess.
But who, from high Olympus, sent you down
To bear such labors? Was it to see your brother   690
In pitiful cruel death? What am I doing,
What chance will fortune grant me? I have seen
A man I loved more than the rest, Murranus,
A big man, slain by a big wound, go down.
Ufens is fallen, lucky or unlucky,
In that he never saw our shame;[43] the Trojans
Have won his body and arms. Our homes are burning,
The one thing lacking up to now,—and shall I
Endure this, not refute the words of Drances
With this right hand?[44] Shall I turn my back upon them?   700

[43] For the deaths of Murranus and Ufens, see lines 582–89, 514.
[44] See Drances' attack on Turnus, in XI.387–422, especially his jeers
in 396–98 and 420–22.

Is it so grim to die? Be kind, O shadows,[45]
Since the high gods have turned their favor from me.
A decent spirit, undisgraced, no coward,
I shall descend to you, never unworthy
Of all my ancient line."
                              He had hardly spoken
When a warrior, on foaming steed, came riding
Through all the enemy. His name was Saces,
And his face was badly wounded by an arrow.
He called the name of Turnus, and implored him:—
710   "We have no other hope; pity your people!
Aeneas is a lightning-bolt; he threatens
Italy's topmost towers; he will bring them down
In ruins; even now the brands[46] are flying
Along the roof-tops. They look to you, the Latins,
They look for you; and king Latinus mumbles
In doubt—who are his sons, who are his allies?[47]
The queen, who trusted you the most, has perished
By her own hand, has fled the light in terror.
Alone before the gates the brave Atinas
720   And Messapus hold the line. Around them, squadrons
Crowd close on either side, and the steel harvest
Bristles with pointed swords. And here is Turnus
Wheeling his car across a plain deserted."
    Bewildered by disaster's shifting image,
Turnus is silent, staring; shame and sadness
Boil up in that great heart, and grief and love
Driven by frenzy. He shakes off the shadows;
The light comes back to his mind. His eyes turn, blazing,
From the wheels of the car to the walls of that great city
730   Where the flame billowed upward, the roaring blast
Catching a tower, one he himself had fashioned
With jointed beams and rollers and high gangways.
"Fate is the winner now; keep out of my way,
My sister: now I follow god and fortune.

---

[45] The gods of the Lower World. They are contrasted with the "high gods" mentioned in the following line.
[46] Firebrands; flaming missiles.
[47] Latinus wonders whether the women among his people are to marry Trojans or Italians.

I am ready for Aeneas, ready to bear
Whatever is bitter in death. No longer, sister,
Shall I be shamed, and you behold me. Let me,
Before the final madness, be a madman!"
He bounded from the chariot, came rushing
Through spears, through enemies; his grieving sister 740
He left behind, forgotten. As a boulder
Torn from a mountain-top rolls headlong downward,
Impelled by wind, or washed by storm, or loosened
By time's erosion, and comes down the hillside
A mass possessed of evil, leaping and bounding,
And rolling with it men and trees and cattle,
So, through the broken columns, Turnus rushes
On to the city, where the blood goes deepest
Into the muddy ground, and the air whistles
With flying spears. He makes a sudden gesture, 750
Crying aloud:—"No more, no more, Rutulians!
Hold back your weapons, Latins! Whatever fortune
There may be here is mine. I am the one,
Not you, to make the treaty good, to settle
The issue with the sword. That will be better."
They all made way and gave him room.
                                         Aeneas,
Hearing the name of Turnus, leaves the city,
Forsakes the lofty walls; he has no patience
With any more delay, breaks off all projects,
Exults, a terrible thunderer in armor, 760
As huge as Athos, or as huge as Eryx,
Or even father Apennine, that mountain
Roaring above the oaks, and lifting high
His crown of shimmering trees and snowy crest.[48]
Now all men turned their eyes, Rutulians, Trojans,
Italians, those who held the lofty ramparts,
Those battering at the wall below; their shoulders
Were eased of armor now. And king Latinus
Could hardly, in amazement, trust his senses

[48] Athos and Eryx were mountains in, respectively, northern Greece and Sicily. The Apennines were the mountains forming the geographical backbone of Italy.

770 Seeing these two big men, born worlds apart,
Meeting to make decision with the sword.
The plain was cleared, and they came rushing forward,
Hurling, far off, their spears; the fight is on,
The bronze shields clang and ring. Earth gives a groan.
The swords strike hard and often; luck and courage
Are blent in one. And as on mighty Sila
Or on Taburnus' mountain,[49] when two bullocks
Charge into fight head-on, and trembling herdsmen
Fall back in fear, and the herd is dumb with terror,
780 And heifers, hardly lowing, stare and wonder
Which one will rule the woodland, which one the herd
Will follow meekly after, and all the time
They gore each other with savage horns, and shoulders
And necks and ribs run streams of blood, and bellowing
Fills all the woodland,—even so, Aeneas
And Daunus' son clash shield on shield; the clamor
Fills heaven. And Jupiter holds the scales in balance
With each man's destiny as weight and counter,
And one the heavier under the doom of death.
790   Confident, Turnus, rising to the sword
Full height, is a flash of light; he strikes. The Trojans,
The Latins, cry aloud and come up standing.
But the sword is treacherous; it is broken off
With the blow half spent: the fire of Turnus finds
No help except in flight. Swift as the wind
He goes, and stares at a broken blade, a hand
Unarmed. The story is that in that hurry,
That rush of his, to arms, when the steeds were harnessed,
He took Metiscus' sword, not the one Daunus
800 Had left him. For a while it served its purpose
While the Trojans ran away, but when it met
The armor Vulcan forged, the mortal blade
Split off, like brittle ice, with glittering splinters
Like ice on the yellow sand. So Turnus flies
Madly across the plain in devious circles:
The Trojans ring him round, and a swamp on one side,

[49] Sila was a mountain range and forest in southern Italy, Taburnus a mountain in central Italy.

High walls on the other.
                                   Aeneas, the pursuer,
Is none too swift: the arrow has left him hurt;
His knees give way, but he keeps on, keeps coming
After the panting enemy, as a hound,   810
Running a stag to bay, at the edge of the water
Or hedged by crimson plumes,[50] darts in, and barks,
And snaps his jaws, closes and grips, is shaken
Off from the flanks again, and once more closes,
And a great noise goes up the air; the waters
Resound, and the whole sky thunders with the clamor.
Turnus has time, even in flight, for calling
Loud to Rutulians, each by name, demanding,
In terrible rage, the sword, the sword, the good one,
The one he knows. Let anybody bring it,   820
Aeneas threatens, and death and doom await him,
And the town will be a ruin. Wounded, still
He presses on. They go in five great circles,
Around and back: no game, with silly prizes,
Are they playing now; the life and blood of Turnus
Go to the winner.
                            A wild olive-tree
Stood here, with bitter leaves, sacred to Faunus,[51]
Revered by rescued sailors, who used to offer
Ex-votos[52] to the native gods, their garments
In token of gratitude. For this the Trojans   830
Cared nothing, lopped the branches off to clear
The run of the field. Aeneas' spear had fastened
Deep in the trunk where the force of the cast had
        brought it,
Stuck in the grip of the root. Aeneas, stooping,
Yanks at the shaft; he cannot equal Turnus
In speed of foot, but the javelin is wingèd.
And Turnus, in a terrible moment of panic,

---

[50] In hunting, barriers made of colorful feathers were used to scare game animals and keep them inside the hunting precincts.

[51] Latinus' father, a rustic god.

[52] Offerings made in fulfillment of a vow or in acknowledgement of a prayer answered.

Cries:—"Faunus, pity me, and Earth, most kindly,
If ever I was reverent, as Aeneas
840 And those he leads have not been, hold the steel,
Do not let go!" He prayed, and he was answered.
Aeneas tugged and wrestled, pulled and hauled,
But the wood held on. And, while he strained, Juturna
Rushed forward, once again Metiscus' double,
With the good sword for her brother. Then Venus, angry
Over such wanton interference, enters
And the root yields. The warriors, towering high,
Each one renewed in spirit, one with sword,
One with the spear, both breathing hard, are ready
For what Mars has to send.
850   And Juno, gazing
From a golden cloud to earth, watching the duel,
Heard the all-powerful king of high Olympus:—
"What will the end be now, O wife? What else
Remains? You know, and you admit you know it,
Aeneas is heaven-destined, the native hero
Become a god,[53] raised by the fates, exalted.
What are you planning? with what hope lingering on
In the cold clouds? Was it proper that a mortal
Should wound a god?[54] that the sword, once lost, be given
860 Turnus again?—Juturna, of course, is nothing
Without your help—was it proper that the beaten
Increase in violence? Stop it now, I tell you;
Listen to my entreaties: I would not have you
Devoured by grief in silence; I would not have you
Bring me, again, anxiety and sorrow,
However sweet the voice. The end has come.
To harry the Trojans over land and ocean,
To light up war unspeakable, to defile
A home with grief, to mingle bridal and sorrow,—
870 All this you were permitted. Go no farther!
That is an absolute order." And Juno, downcast
In gaze, replied:—"Great Jove, I knew your pleasure:

[53] In the future, Aeneas will be deified and regarded as their own hero
by the natives of Italy.
[54] The "god" is Aeneas; the "mortal" is the anonymous person who
wounded Aeneas in lines 359–63.

And therefore, much against my will, left Turnus,
Left earth. Were it not so, you would not see me
Lonely upon my airy throne in heaven,
Enduring things both worthy and unworthy,
But I would be down there, by flame surrounded,
Fighting in the front ranks, and hauling Trojans
To battle with their enemies. Juturna
I urged, I own, to help her wretched brother,   880
And I approved, I own, her greater daring
For his life's sake, but I did not approve,
And this I swear by Styx, that river whose name
Binds all the gods to truth, her taking weapons,
Aiming the bow. I give up now, I leave
These battles, though I hate to. I ask one favor
For Latium, for the greatness of your people,
And this no law of fate forbids: when, later,
And be it so, they join in peace, and settle
Their laws, their treaties, in a blessèd marriage,   890
Do not command the Latins, native-born,
To change their language, to be known as Trojans,
To alter speech or garb; let them be Latium,
Let Alban kings endure through all the ages,[55]
Let Roman stock, strong in Italian valor,
Prevail: since Troy has fallen, let her name
Perish and be forgotten." Smiling on her,
The great creator answered:—"You are truly
True sister of Jove and child of Saturn, nursing
Such tides of anger in the heart![56] Forget it!   900
Abate the rise of passion. The wish is granted.
I yield, and more than that,—I share your purpose.
Ausonians[57] shall keep their old tradition,
Their fathers' speech and ways; their name shall be
Even as now it is. Their sacred laws,

[55] Latium was the region in west-central Italy where the action of the
second half of the poem has been taking place. The royal line of Alba
Longa, the city Iulus/Ascanius will found, had been described prophetically
by Anchises in VI.787–808.
[56] The Greek god Cronus, identified by the Romans with Saturn, was
notoriously violent, fiercely devouring almost all his children.
[57] Italians.

Their ritual, I shall add, and make all Latins
Men of a common tongue. A race shall rise
All-powerful, of mingled blood; you will see them
By virtue of devotion rise to glories
910   Not men nor gods have known, and no race ever
Will pay you equal honor."[58] And the goddess
Gave her assent, was happy, changed her purpose,
Left heaven and quit the cloud.
                  This done, the father
Formed yet another purpose, that Juturna
Should leave her fighting brother. There are, men say,
Twin fiends, or triple, sisters named the Furies,
Daughters of Night, with snaky coils, and pinions
Like those of wind. They are attendant spirits
Before the throne of Jove and whet the fears
920   Of sickly mortals, when the king of heaven
Contrives disease or dreadful death, or frightens
The guilty towns in war. Now he dispatches
One of the three to earth, to meet Juturna,
An omen visible; and so from heaven
She flew with whirlwind swiftness, like an arrow
Through cloud from bowstring, armed with gall or poison,
Loosed from a Parthian quiver,[59] cleaving shadows
Swifter than man may know, a shaft no power
Has power of healing over:—so Night's daughter
930   Came down to earth, and when she saw the Trojans
And Turnus' columns, she dwindled, all of a sudden,
To the shape of that small bird, which, in the night-time,
Shrills its late song, ill-omened, on the roof-tops
Or over tombs, insistent through the darkness.
And so the fiend, the little screech-owl, flying
At Turnus, over and over, shrilled in warning,
Beating the wings against the shield, and Turnus
Felt a strange torpor seize his limbs, and terror
Made his hair rise, and his voice could find no utterance.
940   But when, far off, Juturna knew the Fury

---

[58] Juno was one of the three deities worshipped in the great Roman
temple at the Capitol (the other two being Jupiter and Minerva).
[59] Parthia, in what is now Iran, was noted for skill in archery.

By whir of those dread wings, she tore her tresses,
Clawed at her face, and beat her breast, all anguish
Over her brother:—"What can a sister do
To help you now, poor Turnus? What remains
For me to bear? I have borne so much already.
What skill of mine can make the daylight longer
In your dark hour? Can I face such a portent?[60]
Now, now, I leave the battle-line forever.
Foul birds, I fear enough; haunt me no further,
I know that beat of the wings, that deadly whirring;   950
I recognize, too well, Jove's arrogant orders,
His payment for my maidenhood.[61] He gave me
Eternal life, but why? Why has he taken
The right of death away from me? I might have
Ended my anguish, surely, with my brother's,
Gone, at his side, among the fearful shadows,
But, no,—I am immortal. What is left me
Of any possible joy, without my brother?
What earth can open deep enough to take me,
A goddess, to the lowest shades?" The mantle,   960
Grey-colored, veiled her head, and the goddess, sighing,
Sank deep from sight to the greyness of the river.
    And on Aeneas presses: the flashing spear,
Brandished, is big as a tree; his anger cries:—
"Why put it off forever, Turnus, hang-dog?
We must fight with arms, not running. Take what shape
You will, gather your strength or craft; fly up
To the high stars, or bury yourself in earth!"
And Turnus shook his head and answered:—"Jove,
Being my enemy, scares me, and the gods,   970
Not your hot words, fierce fellow." And his vision,
Glancing about, beheld a mighty boulder,
A boundary-mark, in days of old, so huge
A dozen men in our degenerate era
Could hardly pry it loose from earth, but Turnus

---

[60] Bad omen. The appearance here of one of the Furies, agents of retribution and punishing fate, gives the ending of the poem an effect like that of Greek tragedy.

[61] See lines 159–63 and note.

Lifts it full height, hurls it full speed and, acting,
Seems not to recognize himself, in running,
Or moving, or lifting his hands, or letting the stone
Fly into space; he shakes at the knees, his blood
980   Runs chill in the veins, and the stone, through wide air going,
Falls short, falls spent. As in our dreams at night-time,
When sleep weighs down our eyes, we seem to be running,
Or trying to run, and cannot, and we falter,
Sick in our failure, and the tongue is thick
And the words we try to utter come to nothing,
No voice, no speech,—so Turnus finds the way
Blocked off, wherever he turns, however bravely.
All sorts of things go through his mind: he stares
At the Rutulians, at the town; he trembles,
990   Quails at the threat of the lance; he cannot see
Any way out, any way forward. Nothing.
The chariot is gone, and the charioteer,
Juturna or Metiscus, nowhere near him.
The spear, flung by Aeneas, comes with a whir
Louder than stone from any engine, louder
Than thunderbolt; like a black wind it flies,
Bringing destruction with it, through the shield-rim,
Its sevenfold strength, through armor, through the thigh.
Turnus is down, on hands and knees, huge Turnus
1000   Struck to the earth. Groaning, the stunned Rutulians
Rise to their feet, and the whole hill resounds,
The wooded heights give echo. A suppliant, beaten,
Humbled at last, his hands reach out, his voice
Is low in pleading:—"I have deserved it, surely,
And I do not beg off. Use the advantage.
But if a parent's grief has any power
To touch the spirit, I pray you, pity Daunus,
(I would Anchises), send him back my body.
You have won; I am beaten, and these hands go out
1010   In supplication: everyone has seen it.
No more. I have lost Lavinia. Let hatred
Proceed no further."
Fierce in his arms, with darting glance, Aeneas
Paused for a moment, and he might have weakened,
For the words had moved him, when, high on the shoulder,

He saw the belt of Pallas, slain by Turnus,
Saw Pallas on the ground, and Turnus wearing
That belt with the bright studs, of evil omen
Not only to Pallas now, a sad reminder,
A deadly provocation. Terrible   1020
In wrath, Aeneas cries:—"Clad in this treasure,
This trophy of a comrade, can you cherish
Hope that my hands would let you go? Now Pallas,
Pallas exacts his vengeance, and the blow
Is Pallas, making sacrifice!"[62] He struck
Before he finished speaking: the blade went deep
And Turnus' limbs were cold in death; the spirit
Went with a moan indignant to the shadows.

---

[62] Aeneas' killing of Turnus was foreshadowed in the passage (X.534–63) relating Turnus' killing of Pallas.

APPENDIX

□

Cast of Characters

In the fighting between the Greeks and Trojans around Troy, Virgil calls both sides by tribal names as well as national names, and sometimes uses patronymics: thus the Greeks are also called Achaeans, Argives, Danaans, Dolopes, Ithacans, Myrmidons, and so on; and the Trojans are called Dardanians, Ilians, Teucrians, Phrygians. I have used these terms much less than Virgil did, and tried, for the sake of avoiding confusion and clutter, to stick to the terms Greek and Trojan, wherever possible.

Likewise, in the wars between the Trojans and Latins in Italy, we find the enemies of Aeneas described as Italians, Latins, Rutulians, and Etruscans. But there were also some Etruscans on his side; these were led by Tarchon, the anti-Aeneas faction by Mezentius. His other principal allies were the Arcadians, whose king was Evander.

The principal Greek warriors were Agamemnon, Menelaus, Ulysses, Diomedes, and Ajax; the most conspicuous on the Trojan side Aeneas, Hector, and possibly Paris.

Of the gods and goddesses, Juno, in the *Aeneid,* is actively opposed to Aeneas, and Venus equally active on his behalf. Apollo gives the Trojans considerable help with counsel, especially in the course of their wanderings; Vulcan makes armor for Aeneas when he arrives in Italy, and Neptune helps put down a storm that all but wrecked the Trojan fleet. Jupiter maintains neutrality, in so far as the pressure applied by Venus and Juno will permit.

A list of the important characters in the narrative follows:—

Aenḗas, son of Anchises and Venus, leader of the Trojans, hero of the poem.

Amắta, wife of king Latinus, mother of Lavinia; favors Turnus, opposes Aeneas as suitor for her daughter.

Anchīses, son of Capys, father of Aeneas.

Andrómache, widow of Hector, subsequently wife of Helenus, settler, after the fall of Troy, at Buthrotum in Epirus.

Anna, sister of Dido, queen of Carthage.

Ascānius, or Īūlus, son of Aeneas and Creusa.

Camílla, daughter of Metabus and Casmilla, a Latin warrior-maid, ally of Turnus in the fight against Aeneas in Italy.

Creūsa, daughter of Priam, wife of Aeneas, mother of Ascanius, lost in the confusion following the last night of Troy.

Deīphobe, a Sibyl, priestess of Apollo and guide to Aeneas during his visit to the Lower World.

Dīdo, queen of Carthage.

Dīomede, or Dīomēdes, an important Greek warrior, founder, after the fall of Troy, of Arpi in Italy; declines to help the Latins in their warfare against Aeneas.

Drănçēs, an eloquent Latin orator, opposed to Turnus.

Eurýălus, son of Opheltes, a young Trojan athlete and warrior, boon companion of Nisus.

Evánder, king of Pallanteum, father of Pallas, ally of Aeneas in the fighting in Italy.

Hélĕnus, son of Priam, husband of Andromache, ruler of Buthrotum in Epirus, priest and prophet of Apollo.

Iliōnĕus, a Trojan, responsible spokesman for his people on missions to Dido and Latinus.

Īūlus, also known as Ascanius, son of Aeneas and Creusa.

Jutúrna, a nymph, sister of Turnus.

Latīnus, king of Latium, husband of Amata, father of Lavinia, favors Aeneas as his daughter's suitor.

Laúsus, a young Etruscan warrior, son of the exiled king Mezentius.

Lavínia, daughter of king Latinus and Amata, sought in marriage by both Turnus and Aeneas.

Mezéntius, an Etruscan king, exiled by his people for barbarity, despiser of the gods, ally of Turnus against the Trojans.

Neŏptŏlemus, or Pyrrhus, a son of Achilles, killer of King Priam, war-lord of Hector's widow Andromache.

Nīsus, a young Trojan athlete and warrior, son of Hyrtacus, boon companion of the younger Euryalus.

Palīnūrus, pilot of the fleet of Aeneas.

Pállas, son of king Evander, ally of Aeneas in the Latin wars, slain by Turnus.

Sínon, a Greek, principal agent in the scheme to bring the wooden horse inside the walls of Troy.

Tárchon, an Etruscan prince, ally of Aeneas against Turnus and Mezentius.

Túrnus, son of Daunus and the nymph Venilia, prince of the Rutulians, principal enemy of Aeneas in Italy.

Vĕnŭlus, an Italian leader, sent by the Latins on a fruitless mission for the help of Diomede.

Virgil's Meter

The Aeneid is written in a classical verse form called dactylic hexameter. This is a "quantitative" meter, depending on the duration of syllables, not, as in English, on the presence or absence of stress accents. The line is hexameter because it contains six feet (metrical units). Each foot is, theoretically, a dactyl, which consists of one long syllable followed by two short ones; in any foot, however, except the fifth one (and even there, in rare instances), a spondee (two long syllables) can serve instead of a dactyl, and the sixth foot always consists of two syllables. A word ending with a vowel or with *m* after a vowel is "elided," or slurred over, with a following word beginning with a vowel, so that the two syllables where the words come together are considered a single syllable.

In normal speech, however, Latin has stress accents just as English does. When Latin verse is read aloud, these

stresses are to be observed, along with the rhythms arising
from the quantity, or duration, of the syllables. The interplay
between the two sound systems, of stress accent and of quantitative scansion, produces highly interesting and varied patterns, especially in Virgil. One such pattern occurs in every
line, since in the last two feet the stressed-unstressed pattern
coincides with the long-short pattern. In other words, each
line plays these two kinds of rhythm against each other until
they come together in harmonious resolution—what in music
might be called a cadence—in the last two feet.

Here are the first seven lines of *The Aeneid*, with the slash
marks indicating the divisions into metrical feet, the marks
— and ˘ indicating, respectively, long and short syllables,
and the italics indicating normal stress accents in prose or
speech:

Ārmă vĭ/*rum*quĕ *cā*/no, Trŏ/iaē quī / *prī*mŭs ăb / ōris
Ītălĭ/am, *fā*/to prŏfŭ/gŭs, Lā/*vīn*iăquĕ / *vē*nĭt
lītŏră, / mūltum ĭl/le et tĕr/rīs iăc/tātŭs ĕt / ālto
vī sŭpĕ/rum, saē/vaē mĕmŏ/rem Īu/*nō*nĭs ŏb / īram,
mūltă quŏ/que et bĕl/lō păs/sūs, dŭm / *con*dĕrĕt / ūrbĕm,
īnfĕr/*ret*quĕ dĕ/ōs Lă*tĭ*/o, gĕnŭs / ūndĕ Lă/*tī*nŭm,
Ālbā/*nī*quĕ pă/trēs, āt/que āltaē / moēnĭă / *Rō*maē.

Memorable Lines from The Aeneid

Many people have considered the entire *Aeneid* worth mem-
orizing. (Dante, for one, claimed to know it by heart.) No
quotation, in isolation, means exactly what it means in the
context of the poem, but that fact has not stopped readers,
over the centuries, from singling out the following passages,
among others, as especially memorable. The appeal of certain
passages is their proverbial distillation of perennial insights.
Others are famous for their onomatopoeia or other sound-
effects. Still others have become a kind of shorthand, used
in passing, almost conversationally, as handy flourishes of
discourse. Some are magniloquent; some have an uncanny
brevity that is immensely suggestive.

Line numbers of the Latin quotations refer to the original

Latin text; line numbers of the English translations refer to Humphries' version.

Arma virumque cano, Troiae qui primus ab oris
Italiam, fato profugus, Laviniaque venit
litora, multum ille et terris iactatus et alto
vi superum, saevae memorem Iunonis ob iram. (I.1–4)

> Arms and the man I sing, the first who came,
> Compelled by fate, an exile out of Troy,
> To Italy and the Lavinian coast,
> Much buffeted on land and on the deep
> By violence of the gods, through that long rage,
> That lasting hate, of Juno's. (I.1–6)

Tantae molis erat Romanam condere gentem! (I.33)

> Such a struggle
> It was to found the race of Rome! (I.40–41)

o passi graviora, dabit deus his quoque finem. (I.199)

> we have been through worse,
> . . . . This, too, the god will end. (I.208–210)

forsan et haec olim meminisse iuvabit. (I.203)

> Some day, perhaps, remembering even this
> Will be a pleasure. (I.212–13)

Durate, et vosmet rebus servate secundis. (I.207)

> Endure, and keep yourself for better days. (I.217)

dux femina facti. (I.364)

> with a woman for a captain. (I.380)

et avertens rosea cervice refulsit,
ambrosiaeque comae divinum vertice odorem
spiravere; pedes vestis defluxit ad imos,
et vera incessu patuit dea. (I.402–05)

> And as she turned, her shoulders
> Shone with a radiant light; her hair shed fragrance,
> Her robes slipped to her feet, and the true goddess
> Walked in divinity. (I.423–26)

En Priamus! Sunt hic etiam sua praemia laudi,
sunt lacrimae rerum, et mentem mortalia tangunt. (I.461–62)

> There is Priam!
> Look! even here there are rewards for praise,
> There are tears for things, and what men suffer
>   touches
> The human heart. (I.481–84)

In freta dum fluvii current, dum montibus umbrae
lustrabunt convexa, polus dum sidera pascet,
semper honos nomenque tuum laudesque manebunt,
quae me cumque vocant terrae. (I.607–10)

> While rivers run to sea, while shadows move
> Over the mountains, while the stars burn on,
> Always, your praise, your honor, and your name,
> Whatever land I go to, will endure. (I.643–46)

non ignara mali, miseris succurrere disco. (I.630)

> Not ignorant of evil,
> I know one thing, at least,—to help the wretched.
>   (I.665–66)

Infandum, regina, iubes renovare dolorem,
Troianas ut opes et lamentabile regnum
eruerint Danai, quaeque ipse miserrima vidi,
et quorum pars magna fui. (II.3–6)

> A terrible grief, O Queen,
> You bid me live again, how Troy went down
> Before the Greeks, her wealth, her pitiful kingdom,
> Sorrowful things I saw myself, wherein
> I had my share and more. (II.2–6)

equo ne credite, Teucri.
Quidquid id est, timeo Danaos et dona ferentis. (II.48–49)

> Do not trust it, Trojans,
> Do not believe this horse. Whatever it may be,
> I fear the Greeks, even when bringing presents.
> (II.56–58)

crimine ab uno
disce omnis. (II.65–66)

> learn all
> Their crimes from one. (II.75–76)

tacitae per amica silentia lunae. (II.255)

> under the friendly silence
> Of a still moon. (II.279–80)

Fuimus Troes, fuit Ilium et ingens
gloria Teucrorum. (II.325–26)

> Trojans we have been, Troy has been, and glory
> Is ours no more. (II.353–54)

Una salus victis nullam sperare salutem. (II.354)

> One safety for the vanquished
> Is to have hope of none. (II.382–83)

dis aliter visum. (II.428)

> The gods thought otherwise. (II.453)

Polydorum obtruncat, et auro
vi potitur. Quid non mortalia pectora cogis,
auri sacra fames! (III.55–57)

> . . . Slew Polydorus, took the gold. There is
>   nothing
> To which men are not driven by that hunger.
>   (III.51–52)

monstrum horrendum, informe, ingens, cui lumen ademptum.
(III.658)

a shapeless monster,
Lumbering, clumping, blind in the dark.
(III.656–57)

Agnosco veteris vestigia flammae. (IV.23)

I recognize
The marks of an old fire. (IV.22–23)

tacitum vivit sub pectore vulnus. (IV.67)

the silent
Wound grows, deep in the heart. (IV.69–70)

nec me meminisse pigebit Elissae,
dum memor ipse mei, dum spiritus hos regit artus. (IV.335–36)

I will not
Regret remembering Dido, while I have
Breath in my body, or consciousness of spirit.
(IV.342–44)

Varium et mutabile semper
femina. (IV.569–70)

A shifty, fickle object
Is woman, always. (IV.601–02)

exoriare aliquis nostris ex ossibus ultor. (IV.625)

Rise from my bones, O great unknown avenger.
(IV.666)

possunt, quia posse videntur. (V.231)

They can because they think they can. (V.231)

te, Palinure, petens, tibi somnia tristia portans
insonti. (V.840–41)

Looking for Palinurus, bringing him,
A guiltless man, ill-omened dreams. (V.803–04)

nudus in ignota, Palinure, iacebis harena. (V.871)

O Palinurus, on an unknown shore,
You will be lying, naked. (V.837–38)

Tu ne cede malis, sed contra audentior ito
quam tua te fortuna sinet. (VI.95–96)

Do not yield to evil,
Attack, attack, more boldly even than fortune
Seems to permit. (VI.108–10)

facilis descensus Averno
(noctis atque dies patet atri ianua Ditis);
sed revocare gradum superasque evadere ad auras,
hoc opus, hic labor est. (VI.126–29)

By night, by day, the portals of dark Dis
Stand open: it is easy, the descending
Down to Avernus. But to climb again,
To trace the footsteps back to the air above,
There lies the task, the toil. (VI.144–48)

Procul o, procul este, profani. (VI.258)

Keep off, keep off, whatever is unholy. (VI.276)

Vestibulum ante ipsum primisque in faucibus Orci
Luctus et ultrices posuere cubilia Curae,
pallentesque habitant Morbi, tristisque Senectus,
et Metus, et malesuada Fames, ac turpis Egestas. (VI.273–76)

At the first threshold, on the jaws of Orcus,
Grief and avenging Cares have set their couches,
And pale Diseases dwell, and sad Old Age,
Fear, evil-counselling Hunger, wretched Need.
    (VI.291–94)

tendebantque manus ripae ulterioris amore. (VI.314)

> Their hands, in longing,
> Reach out for the farther shore. (VI.332–33)

Per sidera iuro,
per superos, et si qua fides tellure sub ima est,
invitus, regina, tuo de litore cessi. (VI.458–60)

> I swear by all the stars,
> By the world above, by everything held sacred
> Here under the earth, unwillingly, O queen,
> I left your kingdom. (VI.480–83)

Quisque suos patimur Manis. (VI.743)

> Each of us suffers
> His own peculiar ghost. (VI.772–73)

Excudent alii spirantia mollius aera
(credo equidem), vivos ducent de marmore vultus,
orabunt causas melius, caelique meatus
describent radio, et surgentia sidera dicent:
tu regere imperio populos, Romane, memento
(hae tibi erunt artes), pacisque imponere morem,
parcere subiectis, et debellare superbos. (VI.847–53)

> Others, no doubt, will better mould the bronze
> To the semblance of soft breathing, draw, from
>   marble,
> The living countenance; and others plead
> With greater eloquence, or learn to measure,
> Better than we, the pathways of the heaven,
> The risings of the stars: remember, Roman,
> To rule the people under law, to establish
> The way of peace, to battle down the haughty,
> To spare the meek. Our fine arts, these, forever.
>   (VI.888–96)

flectere si nequeo superos, Acheronta movebo. (VII.312)

> If I cannot
> Bend Heaven, I can raise Hell. (VII.328–29)

O mihi praeteritos referat si Iuppiter annos. (VIII.560)

> If Jupiter would only
> Bring me my lost years back. (VIII.574–75)

quadripedante putrem sonitu quatit ungula campum. (VIII.596)

> the echo of the gallop
> Comes clopping back through the ground where
> the dust is rising. (VIII.611–12)

Prisca fides facto, sed fama perennis. (IX.79)

> the story is old,
> Men have believed it long, its glory endless.
> (IX.78–79)

periisse semel satis est. (IX.140)

> Once to have perished
> . . . is enough. (IX.144–45)

dum domus Aeneae Capitoli immobile saxum
accolet, imperiumque pater Romanus habebit. (IX.448–49)

> While rock stands firm beneath the Capitol,
> While the imperial house maintains dominion.
> (IX.462–63)

audentis Fortuna iuvat. (X.284)

> luck helps men who dare. (X.323)

experto credite. (XI.283)

> Believe an expert,
> Take it from one who knows. (XI.320–21)

di me terrent et Iuppiter hostis. (XII.895)

> Jove,
> Being my enemy, scares me, and the gods.
> (XII.969–70)

ast illi solvuntur frigore membra,
vitaque cum gemitu fugit indignata sub umbras. (XII.951–52)

> And [his] limbs were cold in death; the spirit
> Went with a moan indignant to the shadows.
> (XII.1027–28)

BIBLIOGRAPHY

□

*Books marked with the symbol ** are line-by-line commentaries.*

Anderson, W. S. *The Art of the Aeneid,* 1969.
**Austin, R. G. *P. Vergili Maronis Aeneidos Liber Primus* [on Book I], 1971. *Liber Secundus* [on Book II], 1964. *Liber Quartus* [on Book IV], 1955; rev. ed. 1963. *Liber Sextus* [on Book VI], 1977.
Bailey, C. *Religion in Virgil,* 1935.
Bowra, C. M. *From Virgil to Milton,* 1945.
Camps, W. A. *An Introduction to Virgil's Aeneid,* 1969.
Commager, S., ed. *Virgil: A Collection of Critical Essays,* 1966.
**Conington, J., and H. Nettleship. *The Works of Vergil,* Vol. III, 1883.
**Conway, R. S. *P. Vergili Maronis Aeneidos Liber Primus* [on Book I], 1935.
Dudley, D. R., ed. *Virgil,* 1969. [Essays by several authors.]
**Fletcher, F. *Virgil, Aeneid, VI,* rev. ed., 1972.
**Fordyce, C. J. *P. Vergili Maronis Aeneidos Libri VII–VIII,* introduction by P. G. Walsh, 1977.
Fowler, W. W. *Aeneas at the Site of Rome* [on Book VIII], 1917.
————. *The Death of Turnus* [on Book XII], 1919.
————. *Virgil's Gathering of the Clans* [on Book VII], 1916.
**Gransden, K. W. *Virgil, Aeneid Book VIII,* 1976.
Highet, G. *The Speeches in Vergil's Aeneid,* 1972.
Knight, W. F. Jackson. *Roman Vergil,* rev. ed., 1966.
**Mackail, J. W. *The Aeneid of Virgil,* 1930. [Contains a long introduction.]
Newman, J. K. *Augustus and the New Poetry,* 1967.
Otis, Brooks. *Virgil: A Study in Civilized Poetry,* 1963.
**Page, T. E. *The Aeneid of Virgil,* 1894–1900.
**Pease, A. S. *Publi Vergili Maronis Aeneidos Liber Quartus* [on Book IV], 1935.
Pöschl, V. *The Art of Virgil: Image and Symbol in the Aeneid,* 1950; trans. G. Seligson, 1962.
Putnam, M. C. J. *The Poetry of the Aeneid,* 1965.
Quinn, K. *Virgil's "Aeneid": A Critical Description,* 1968.
**Sidgwick, A. *P. Vergili Maronis Opera,* Vol. II, 1890.

Syme, R. *The Roman Revolution,* 1939.
**Tilly, B. *P. Vergili Maronis Aeneidos Liber XII,* 1969.
**Williams, R. D. *P. Vergili Maronis Aeneidos Liber Tertius* [on Book III], 1962. *Liber Quintus* [on Book V], 1960.
**Williams, R. D. *The Aeneid of Virgil,* 1973.